Organized Business, Economic Change, and Democracy in Latin America

Organized Business, Economic Change, and Democracy in Latin America

Edited by
Francisco Durand and Eduardo Silva

North-South Center Press
UNIVERSITY OF MIAMI

The publisher of this book is the North-South Center Press at the University of Miami.

The mission of the North-South Center is to promote better relations and serve as a catalyst for change among the United States, Canada, and the nations of Latin America and the Caribbean by advancing knowledge and understanding of the major political, social, economic, and cultural issues affecting the nations and peoples of the Western Hemisphere.

All copyright inquiries should be addressed to the publisher: North-South Center Press, 1500 Monza Avenue, Coral Gables, Florida 33146-3027, U.S.A., phone 305-284-8912, fax 305-284-5089, or e-mail mmapes@nsc.msmail.miami.edu.

To order or to return books, contact Lynne Rienner Publishers, Inc., 1800 30th Street, Suite 314, Boulder, CO 80301-1026, 303-444-6684, fax 303-444-0824.

Cataloging-in-Publication Data on file in Library of Congress

Organized Business, Economic Change, and Democracy in Latin America / Francisco Durand and Eduardo Silva

p. cm.

Includes bibliographical references and index.

ISBN 1-57454-048-3 (alk. paper: pbk.)

Printed in the United States of America/TS

02 01 00 99 98   6 5 4 3 2 1

Contents

Preface

"Caminante, no hay camino. Se hace camino al andar."
(Wayfarer, there is no path. You forge the path as you go.)

— Antonio Machado

E ach chapter in this volume strikes a path through the contemporary history of a Latin American country. Along the way, rich detail and insightful views elucidate the role of organized business in that country's economy and politics. Although every case is unique, each chapter deals with the same unit of analysis: encompassing business associations in a context of accelerated change brought about by economic crisis, free market restructuring, and democratization.

Much time and effort have gone into the preparation of this book. The editors organized panels that took place at meetings of the American Political Science Association in Chicago in 1992 and the Latin American Studies Association in Los Angeles in 1993. Experts from several countries who are knowledgeable in the formation and institutional trajectory of encompassing business associations gathered. With a significant volume of country studies at hand, it became possible to develop a common analytical framework. The editors' participation in a congress organized by the Business and the State Section of the Latin American Social Science Research Council in Mexico City in 1994 provided an opportunity to test hypotheses and explain similarities and differences across cases.

The project was inspired by the existence of similar studies in Western Europe.[1] In Latin America, the last decade has brought with it a surge of case studies and analyses of organized business's relationships with governments. These studies focus on firm size and conglomeration within and across economic sectors, the dynamics of sectoral performance, and the political influence of sectoral and subsectoral trade associations. Yet, despite the growing political importance of encompassing associations in Latin America, no other study has investigated this important form of organized business from a comparative perspective. This volume attempts to fill that gap in the rapidly expanding field of business studies. We hope it contributes in significant measure to the knowledge of encompassing associations in the region and their impacts on a number of the policy and political battles of our time.

---

1. John P. Windmuller and Alan Gladstone, eds. 1984. *Employers' Associations and Industrial Relations* (Cambridge, U.K.: Clarendon Press-Oxford).

i

In editing *Organized Business, Economic Change, and Democracy in Latin America*, several colleagues have provided invaluable support and encouragement. Ben Ross Schneider helped with thoughtful and rigorous comments that forced us to produce a more articulate, analytically stronger version. Jeffrey Stark, director of research and studies of the North-South Center at the University of Miami, welcomed the project from its beginnings. The North-South Center Press's Kathleen Hamman, editorial director, guided the editing process, assisted by Mary D'León; Mary Mapes, publications director, designed the book's cover and graphics, assisted by consulting graphic artist Susan Kay Holler, who created the index. Graduate students at our home institutions, Michael Jordan and Susana Brugada at the University of Missouri at Saint Louis, and Sean Ward at the University of Texas at San Antonio, also contributed by sharing administrative tasks and collaborating in proofreading. Two chapters were translated from Spanish with the help of Ismael Silva-Fuenzalida.

The editors of the volume, whose names appear in alphabetical order, have worked side by side, taking turns to lead the project in a mutually supportive editorial partnership.

Francisco Durand
Eduardo Silva

CHAPTER ONE

Organized Business and Politics in Latin America

EDUARDO SILVA AND FRANCISCO DURAND

L atin American business and landowning elites historically have suffered from an unflattering characterization. Due to the region's late or dependent development, during the 1960s and 1970s even optimists of the region's development potential saw these elites as obstacles to modernization. Landowning elites were too tied to the traditions of an *hacienda* system inherited from colonial times and too dependent on labor repression. Economically weak industrialists were equally incapable of transforming the economy and society of Latin American nations.[1] State-led development and import-substitution industrialization (ISI) had failed to convert business elites into dynamic, modernizing agents of change (Canak 1984). At best, they were seen as the weakest partner of a triple alliance led by the state and transnational corporations (Evans 1979). The evaluation of business organizations was, if anything, even more negative. They tended to be poorly organized and were primarily reactive, meaning they strenuously defended parochial economic interests against government reforms when faced with competition from other economic sectors and in industrial relations.[2] In a further display of ineffectiveness, business organizations frequently were unsuccessful in blocking unwanted policies and political changes, even when they had ample access to the policy-making process. In short, the political behavior of Latin American business elites was characterized by ambivalence and accommodation rather than initiative and leadership (Strassman 1964, 172; Wils 1969).

Beginning in the late 1970s and gathering force into the 1990s, pressure for free market restructuring and democratization rekindled interest in the economic and political behavior of business and landowning elites. If the business climate of the 1950s to the 1970s had not generated dynamic entrepreneurs, how would they behave in a new historical period potentially more favorable to them? For, although the region was in the midst of a deep economic crisis, adjustment from ISI- to market-oriented economics conferred more responsibility over the public functions of investment and employment to the private sector. This gave policymakers an incentive to be more attentive to their policy preferences than when state investment was more prevalent (Lindblom 1977). Moreover, the defeat of the armed left, the decline of leftist political parties, and the weakening of organized labor further strengthened the hand of business elites (Sidicaro 1994, 17-18).

Latin American business elites responded to these challenges with a new political activism in a number of countries. They took forceful public positions on economic change, mobilized public opinion on their behalf, took direct action if necessary, and even declared their support for democracy. This was indeed a reversal from behavioral patterns in which Latin American business elites generally negotiated policy behind closed doors and had an elective affinity for military governments.

These changes in the political behavior of Latin American business elites raised a number of questions. Did the new policy advocacy signify that they were playing a more positive, proactive, and transformative economic role than they had in the past? What form of business-state relationship was most conducive to the exercise of a transformative role? Under what conditions did business groups support transitions to democracy, and what were its likely effects on the consolidation of democracy?

Of the comparative studies that addressed those questions, organized business generally was not the center of analysis. Most efforts focused on business as capital (and the structural constraints it placed on the state); business as sector (and the consequences of sectoral competition); and business as firm (the impact of size, structure, and conglomeration).[3] When mentioned, business organizations mostly were used in an ad hoc manner to give agency to the interests of economic sectors (Story 1978). Also, studies generally did not reevaluate the impact of organized business on the twin processes of democratic consolidation and economic restructuring in Latin America.

Despite these trends, some analysts did observe significant changes in the associational behavior of business and landowning elites. They noticed a resurgence of efforts to form or fortify encompassing business associations (umbrella organizations that aggregate sector-specific associations) (Garrido 1988). They also underscored the occasional strengthening or professionalization of sectoral peak associations (those that aggregate the firms of an economic sector, such as industry, commerce, agriculture, finance) (Estrada and Masi 1983; Schneider and Maxfield 1997), yet they did not systematically analyze the causes and effects of their findings.

This volume explores the causes and effects of these new trends in the associational life of Latin American entrepreneurs, with a special emphasis on the recent proliferation of the private sector's highest organizational form: the encompassing business association. All of the chapters in this book address a set of common questions: What conditions affected the formation and consolidation of encompassing business organizations in some cases and their dissolution or failure to emerge in others? What roles have they played in the economic policy-making process, particularly with respect to free market economic restructuring? The main point here was to assess their participation in the various stages of the policy process and evaluate whether encompassing associations are more effective supports for free market economic reforms than sectoral associations. And last, the authors grappled with the contributions of organized business for the process of redemocratization and democratic consolidation. In this chapter, we explore the comparative implications of the rich empirical material of the country chapters.

Several theoretically driven characteristics motivated the focus on encompassing business associations, features that postulate a constructive role for encompassing business associations in the twin processes of economic and political change. First, in theory, encompassing business organizations have a greater potential to make positive contributions to economic policymaking than sectoral associations or firms (Olson 1982). Because encompassing business associations aggregate sectoral and regional interests, they generate policy consensus among business elites with divergent points of view. Thus, encompassing organizations help overcome debilitating and developmentally counterproductive distributional struggles born of the selfish, narrow concerns of sectoral and regional associations. Moreover, because business organizations give public voice to the interests of capital and landowners, encompassing associations help generate and train business leaders able to articulate and defend general interests instead of sectoral interests (Useem 1984).

Second, despite the disapproving view of sectoral associations in theory and practice, they are not doomed to play a negative role in the policy process either. Ben Ross Schneider and Sylvia Maxfield (1997) have found that more professional and technically competent sectoral peak associations also ameliorate distributional conflicts. This feature is strengthened when their actions reinforce broad agreements over policy reached in the encompassing associations of which they are members (Silva 1996).

In the context of the profound economic and political changes that are sweeping Latin America, these potential qualities of encompassing business associations and professionalized sectoral organizations make them deserving of further study. These potential qualities endow them with the capacity to be effective support groups for market-oriented reforms. The associations' and organizations' emergence, consolidation, and institutional development have important consequences for the consolidation of democracy.

In democratic theory, the associational density of civil society constitutes a prerequisite for democratic consolidation and is a key indicator of the quality of democracy.[4] The representative organizations of social groups, in this case businesspeople, are said to act as more transparent, legitimate, and accountable transmission belts of societal demands to state institutions than particularistic (clientelistic) relations with individual business leaders (Nelson 1994b, 181). Encompassing business associations are also a prerequisite for building neocorporatist systems of interest intermediation between state and society — such as those in some European countries. In the view of many observers, establishing such systems is normatively desirable because they strengthen the participatory dimension of democracy in policymaking.

This volume sheds light on the extent to which the theoretical promise of higher levels of organizational development in the Latin American private sector is being realized. Although the book focuses on encompassing business associations, we recognize that this is only one of many ways that business elites exercise their influence in business-state relations (Offe and Wiesenthal 1980). Businesspeople also act through firms as well as sectoral associations. Firms defend their individual interests in private, closed-door, hidden negotiation with policymakers. Sectoral associations carry out their tasks more publicly but generally seek to protect the interests of their economic sector.

We concentrate on encompassing associations because they have the capacity to represent the collective interests of businesspeople as a whole; thus, in business-state relations, encompassing associations focus on issues that cut across sectors and firms. The effectiveness of encompassing associations, however, depends on their ability to coordinate with sectoral associations and powerful firms, particularly conglomerates. This means that, from time to time, analysis necessarily turns to conglomerates and sectoral organizations when examining intrabusiness consensus-building bargaining. We also analyze the effects of their actions in the absence of encompassing business associations.

In order to study these issues, this introductory chapter begins with an analysis of favorable and unfavorable conditions for the emergence and consolidation of encompassing business associations in Latin America. The second part of the chapter continues with an examination of the role of encompassing business associations and sectoral organizations in the policy process. This section explores the policy stances of organized business — with an emphasis on free market economic restructuring — and examines the stages of the policy process to which they have contributed the most. The third part looks into the question of organized business and democracy. It investigates the regime loyalties of businesspeople (their support for democracy, dictatorship, or intermediate types of government), and it examines the consequences of current patterns of business-state relations for the construction of neocorporatist or pluralist systems of interest intermediation in the consolidation of democracy.

ENCOMPASSING BUSINESS ASSOCIATIONS IN LATIN AMERICA: ORIGINS AND DEVELOPMENT

Encompassing business associations are umbrella organizations that have most of the major firms of a country as members. How the encompassing associations accomplish this goal varies. In some cases, membership in the encompassing association is limited to the major sectoral peak associations, usually those that aggregate industry, agriculture, cattle ranching, oil and mining, commerce, finance, and construction. In other cases, however, membership may also include regional organizations, subsectoral associations, individual large-scale firms, or associations of especially powerful companies. Some even embrace medium- and small-scale businesses. The heterogeneity of the business community — including the competitiveness of firms and sectors in the international economy — suggests significant collective action problems for the establishment of encompassing business associations (Martinelli 1994, 497). Moreover, most Latin American encompassing organizations have exhibited a fundamental difference from European ones. Instead of forming separate organizations to deal with economic issues (trade associations) and labor relations (employers' organizations), the two roles were integrated in one organization.[5] This further compounded the difficulties of holding the encompassing organizations together once they had been established.

The organization of encompassing business associations in Latin America began with a trickle in the first half of the twentieth century, gathered momentum in the 1950s and 1960s, and continued developing apace in the 1970s and 1980s (see Table 1). Not all of these efforts succeeded. In some cases, they either collapsed outright, or repeated attempts failed to take hold. In other cases, their trajectories were punctuated by periods of relative dormancy followed by spurts in which they consolidated and strengthened organizationally. Backsliding, however, was not uncommon. The encompassing business associations may not have disintegrated, but deep tensions generated by sectoral competition, disputes over leadership, ideological divisions, and attacks by the state rendered them inactive or ineffectual at times.

A general trend, nevertheless, gradually emerged. Over the past 30 years, business and landowning elites in countries with varying degrees of economic development increasingly found it necessary to form encompassing business organizations (Estrada and Masi 1983; Levaggi 1993). Today, more Latin American countries have encompassing business associations than ever before. What explains this organizational tendency? Why have encompassing business associations formed in some countries and not others? How does one understand their different trajectories, from barely functioning to well consolidated? These are the themes of this section.

This volume includes major countries, with the exceptions of Colombia and Venezuela, and many that have not received adequate treatment in the literature to date.[6] Happily for comparative analysis, the cases provide a full range of variation. In Chile and Peru, encompassing business associations formed and consolidated. In Mexico, Nicaragua, the Dominican Republic, and El Salvador, they emerged, acted, and declined but continued to exist. In Argentina and Brazil, significant encompassing business associations simply failed to emerge.

The Origins of Encompassing Business Associations

The growing comparative literature on business elites in Latin America recognizes the importance of business unity for the policy-making process. Two complementary yet separate strands have developed. One maintains that encompassing associations are the highest expression of business unity because of their consensus-building and development-enhancing qualities (Nelson 1994b; Haggard and Kaufman 1995; Schneider and Maxfield 1997, 21-25).[7] Most analysts in this camp, however, left unexplored the reasons for the formation of encompassing business associations. The second thread in the literature lauded the virtues of business unity without specifying how it is expressed institutionally and noted some favorable conditions for it. In a study of Bolivia, Ecuador, and Peru, Catherine M. Conaghan and James M. Malloy (1994) argued that collective threats were the primary catalysts of business unity. Ernest Bartell and Leigh A. Payne (1995, 267-271), in a more comprehensive work, arrived at similar conclusions. These authors defined threat mainly as the exclusion of business elites from policymaking during economic hard times in the authoritarian and populist regimes of the 1970s and 1980s. This situation fed perceptions of arbitrary state action and fear of the rapid, extreme, and negative economic policy changes that followed.

We concur that encompassing associations are the highest institutional expression of business unity and that threats to the private sector were important catalysts for generating business unity. The evidence from our country chapters strongly suggests that a severe threat to all business and land-owning sectors — that is, to their general interests — was a key factor in the emergence of encompassing business associations and their subsequent development in Latin America. In the absence of such threats, they failed to form.

We also address a number of unanswered questions raised by the recent literature. First, more careful and extensive specification of what constitutes a general threat is required. The current definition of threat is too narrow. It points to important factors, but these are not sufficient to explain the emergence and evolution of encompassing business associations in Latin America in historical perspective, that is, from the 1930s to the present. Second, the causal connection between those threats and the formation of encompassing business organizations in Latin America must be established. Third, the role of encompassing business associations in the policy process during free market economic reforms may be in need of some refinement. This section addresses the first two issues, and the following section deals with the third.

What literature might aid in the search for a more precise specification of the conditions conducive to the formation of encompassing business associations in Latin America? Studies about organized business in Europe offered important insights. John P. Windmuller and Alan Gladstone (1984, 1) argue that in Europe business organized to advance collective interests in relation to threats from three sources: competing business sectors, other social groups, and the state. The main issues at stake were generally the regulation of trade and competition as well as defense against unwanted social and labor legislation.[8]

In Europe, encompassing business associations formed and developed to face the combined threats of centralizing unions, the political left, and increasingly centralized governments that paid attention to the demands of those subordinate social and political forces (Windmuller and Gladstone 1984, 3; Berger 1981, 14-16; Coleman and Grant 1988; Martinelli 1994, 497).[9] The emergence of common problems and the need to face them through collective and associative action forced consensus building and organizational forms that allowed the private sector to speak with one voice (Katzenstein 1984, 62). After World War II, European governments found durable consensus building useful in the conduct of tripartite negotiations over economic, social, and labor policy (Schmitter and Streeck 1981; Katzenstein 1984, 1985; Streeck and Schmitter 1985). Under these circumstances, business elites felt that effective representation demanded centralization of business organization. Presenting a united front increased the bargaining power of the business community.

In an insightful paper, Philippe C. Schmitter and Wolfgang Streeck (1981) added that many European employer associations originated as the organizational expression of upper-class social movements. Strong conflicts with labor, especially when governments took labor's side, frequently induced the private sector to mobilize and organize outside established channels of political action in order to pressure the state (Tarrow 1994). In encompassing business associations born from such struggles, opposition to a common foe furnished the glue that held otherwise diverse private sector interests together. The demise of the threat brought internal tensions to the fore and threatened encompassing business associations born of such dynamics with disintegration.

The origins and consolidation of European encompassing business organizations were not all rooted in conflict (Schmitter and Streeck 1981; Katzenstein 1984 and 1985; Windmuller and Gladstone 1984). Because of their structural power — and because they are less influenced by party politics than labor unions and more easily linked to the state — businesspeople may not have to struggle outside the established policy-making channels to defend their interests regarding economic, social, and labor policy. Instead, governments invite emerging business sectoral and encompassing associations to the negotiating table with organized labor in the interests of social, economic, and political stability. Under these circumstances, governments value the durable consensus-building capacities of organized business, as was the case with some European countries both during World War II and in the postwar era. This recognition by the government of the freely formed organizations of civil society during the postwar period, a central condition of societal corporatism or neocorporatism, provided a powerful incentive to establish encompassing business organizations, again, especially in those cases with centralized political systems and labor organizations.

The conflictual sources of business association formation in Europe were by far the most relevant for Latin America. In this subsection, we explore how particular facts from European history help flesh out the "threat variable" and connect it to the formation of encompassing business associations in Latin America. The next subsection grapples with the implications for the consolidation of Latin American encompassing business associations of their movement-like origins. If Latin American encompassing associations were born to meet severe threats to business and landowning elites, what conditions permit the consolidation of encompassing business associations once the threat has faded? Toward the end of this chapter, the section on the prospects for neocorporatism examines the likelihood that encompassing business associations in some Latin American countries may be established through more cooperative means in the future.

With respect to the specification of severe threat as a key variable for the formation of encompassing business associations in Latin America, the literature on European business organization suggests that, in addition to arbitrary state action, we need to examine factors such as struggles against labor and centralizing governments that at times sided with labor's demands. These were powerful inducements to movement-like collective action by Latin American business elites, as were government policies to modernize national economies, especially when they forced established business and landowning elites to restructure their enterprises. In other words, the organizational development of antagonistic social groups and their linkages to a state more autonomous from the private sector were as important for explaining the emergence of encompassing business associations in Latin America as the more recent focus on exclusion from the policy process and arbitrary policy by states highly autonomous from all social groups.

How did centralizing unions, the political left, and centralizing governments that paid attention to their demands threaten the general interests of business and landowning elites and induce them to form encompassing business associations? At the broadest level, the chapters reveal that such threats were both political and economic, touching on a wide range of issues such as property rights, business's relationship to subordinate social groups, and the general economic model (the "business climate"). Political threats came from below or from above, depending on whether they emanated from subordinate, class-based groups or from the state. The main threats from below were mass movements, national rebellions, and widespread guerrilla movements that demanded radical social and labor reforms. Threats from the state accompanied those from below when governments engaged in widespread expropriation, attempted radical redistribution of the national wealth, or instituted widespread government controls. Economic threats, such as crises originating from hyperinflation, depression, or deep recession, also played a role, especially in the consolidation and unravelling of encompassing business associations.

General exclusion of the private sector from the policy-making process or a sharp breakdown in government-business relations was another form of severe threat that affected the formation and trajectory of encompassing business associations. This was the case under populist and socialist governments when they attempted to shift public policy radically in favor of the people, when they altered property rights, and when they increased the degree of state intervention in the economy, measures that often received wide support from the general public. By the same token, governments supportive of free market economics also frequently excluded businesspeople from the policy process through top-down policy initiatives designed to stabilize and restructure the economy. In the eyes of businesspeople, economic hard times — to which Latin America is no stranger — magnified these threats.

In all of these circumstances, influencing public opinion and policymakers (or having them removed) required the combined weight of the private sector. At critical junctures, there was little room for free riders or independent tactical moves by individual sectoral associations. Obtaining the support of other social and political groups in a highly volatile environment demanded proposals that represented the general interest of all business sectors. In this context, obstructionist efforts of individual firms or sectors were ignored and failed to attract wider societal support because they were perceived to be the struggle of narrow, selfish, and privileged interest groups. For some countries, external support for organization building accelerated the associational trends already set in motion by domestic forces.

How do these factors explain the formation of enduring encompassing business associations in five of the eight cases — Nicaragua, El Salvador, Mexico, Peru, and Chile? In all of these countries, business groups were confronted by a severe threat that affected the entire private sector. The key issues were civil war, strong redistributive economic and social policies, and extensive nationalization. These conditions engendered political uncertainty and significantly increased the risks of doing business. In all five cases, the threat was compounded by lack of access to the policy-making process or a sharp breakdown in business-government relations, in addition to widespread economic disorder. The precise nature of threat varied across cases, and often several elements either combined or appeared sequentially, reinforcing the tendency toward unity through the formation and consolidation of an encompassing association.

In her chapter, Rose Spalding shows how the patrimonial political system of the Anastasio Somoza dynasty in Nicaragua allowed only those few capitalists who were political allies of the Somozas to prosper. However, economic and social diversification led to the rise of new business elites that formed an encompassing organization in defense against discrimination under Somocismo. After the Somoza dynasty's downfall, an early breakdown of relations with the Sandinistas — whose redistributive policies and nationalizations severely threatened all large-scale business — prompted business elites to coordinate their public political action through their encompassing peak association for more than a decade.

Kenneth Johnson argues that El Salvador's encompassing business association formed in response to a breakdown in cozy business-state relations when a reformist government bent on social and economic reforms in the mid-1960s took power. The reforms included income and property taxes for the wealthy and minimum wage laws and a mandatory day of rest for rural labor. The political activation of popular classes and guerrilla movements in El Salvador threatened the entire economic and political system upon which all capitalists (modern and traditional) depended. The U.S. government, via the United States Agency for International Development (USAID), intervened directly to promote collective action among new business leaders by creating a business think tank. Its actions tilted the balance of forces in favor of a more forward-looking group of business leaders that challenged the obstructionist leadership of conservative landowners. The USAID-business alliance that emerged rejuvenated El Salvador's encompassing business association.

In the case of Mexico, Ricardo Tirado analyzes how that nation's encompassing business association emerged in response to the expansion of state enterprise, the resurgent populism of the Luis Echeverría administration, and a breakdown in the traditional system of business-state relations. In response to these problems, several business associations from the commercial and industrial sectors tried to achieve greater autonomy from the state by circumventing their corporatist ties to it. Then, in the midst of a deepening economic crisis, the nationalization of the banking system under José López-Portillo (a collective threat to private property rights) radicalized the encompassing association in the early 1980s. This event, in addition to their exclusion from the policy-making process, fostered a unity of purpose that otherwise might have been lacking in an organization that harbored such diversity.

Francisco Durand examines how the rise of neopopulist social democrats in Peru under the American Popular Revolutionary Alliance (Alianza Popular Revolucionaria Americana —APRA) under Alan García, widespread social and political violence by the Shining Path, and a deep, prolonged economic recession made business unity critical for the defense of private property. As in the case of Mexico, the nationalization of the banking industry under García in 1987 was the catalyst for unity among diverse business interests. The encompassing association became an effective shield against populist attacks on private property, as it provided its diverse membership with refuge and advice at a time when lack of access to the policy-making process and unpredictable policy decisions prevailed; these were issues that further compounded the need for unity.

Eduardo Silva argues that the electoral rise of the left and labor unionism from the 1930s to the early 1970s led to the formation and strengthening of an encompassing organization in Chile. By the end of 1972, during the government of the Unidad Popular, radical agrarian reform, extensive nationalization, and redistributive social policy unified sectoral organizations. During the military government's experimentation with radical free market economic reforms, the closed economic policy-making style and deep economic crisis of 1982-1983 severely threatened all business sectors with bankruptcy and the stability of the military government. This galvanized the revival of Chile's encompassing business peak organization, which had been dormant in the early years of the military dictatorship.

In Nicaragua, El Salvador, and Peru, the U.S. government, in the form of the USAID, helped to form or restructure encompassing business associations. These were the countries whose national rebellions of the 1980s, the last decade of the Cold War, were most threatening. USAID funded the creation of business think tanks that provided a nucleus for the formation and agglutination of a shared business outlook on common problems. The think tanks furnished leadership, information, analyses, and proposals that strengthened emerging encompassing associations. In Peru, USAID funding came at a critical moment, at the founding of the encompassing business association.

The Consolidation of Encompassing Business Associations

After the initial formation of encompassing business associations, what might account for their different trajectories? In Peru and Chile, they consolidated, remained strong and active in the policy arena, and performed important service functions for the business community. Conversely, they have weakened in Mexico, Nicaragua, and El Salvador. Having been subjected to debilitating internal divisions, those encompassing associations have become less effective in influencing the policy-making process, and they have lost membership or failed to attract new organizations. Still, they do exist and function after a fashion. In other words, after encompassing business associations were established, what influenced the shift from movement-induced unity to more enduring, institutionally based unity?

The cases suggest that four conditions are important for explaining these outcomes: internal organization, the type of government-business relationship, the level of intersectoral conflict, and leadership characteristics. In broader comparative perspective, the presence or absence of USAID involvement mentioned above does not appear to be a key factor for the degree of consolidation of encompassing business organizations. While in specific cases, such as El Salvador, USAID's retreat may have had some bearing, in Peru the encompassing association became stronger. Of course, continued threats from below and above, combined with problems in business-state relations, could maintain the unity of an encompassing business association. The issue here, however, is what contributes to such outcomes once the movement elements of business unity have waned. That is, what occurs once "normal" politics is restored?

Peru and Chile, the most remarkable cases of institutional consolidation, share a number of characteristics, though their historical trajectories differ. In terms of the internal organization of their encompassing associations, in both cases sectoral peak associations are the principal members; more specifically, it is the presidents or vice presidents (or both) of the sectoral associations who control the encompassing association's executive board. Moreover, the sectoral organizations represent primarily large- and medium-scale firms and exclude small-scale companies. These features impart a greater homogeneity to the encompassing association's leadership, which facilitates collective action. The Chilean and Peruvian encompassing associations have additional distinctive institutional mechanisms. To manage internal conflict, they have formed executive committees that deal only with issues that affect all members, and they rotate the presidency by sector. To resolve disputes between sectors, they have established a "one-organization, one-vote" rule, set quorums to bring issues on the agenda, and encouraged members to fight sectoral battles over policy on their own.

The professionalization of these organizations — that is, their ability to generate sophisticated economic studies and to use them in public policy debates — has been another important internal feature contributing to consolidation. It has allowed the encompassing business associations of Peru and Chile to take principled stands and offer concrete proposals for the policy debate. Thus, they have moved from reactive, defensive, political, and ideologically based opposition to more proactive, economically based opposition. This is crucial for eras in which public policy issues focus more on economic rather than political concerns, as is the case in the late 1990s. This shift has helped the encompassing business associations of Chile and Peru to remain attractive to their members.

These trends amply corroborate Alberto Martinelli's (1994, 495-496) arguments that proper organizational structure can help overcome the internal tensions of encompassing business associations rooted in competing economic sectors, regions, and firm size. When in place, such structures turn organizational complexity into a tool for business leaders to develop much needed autonomy from and authority over their members. Successfully managed, broad representation also helps to legitimize business leaders in the eyes of the state, making encompassing associations an effective vehicle for negotiation.

Nevertheless, developments in business-government relations also have played an important role in the consolidation of encompassing business associations in Chile and Peru. Toward the end of the military governments of Gen. Augusto Pinochet, Juan Alvarado Velasco, and Francisco Morales Bermúdez, and most importantly during the newly inaugurated democratic period, governments recognized them as significant interlocutors in the public policy process, especially where issues affecting the general interests of businesspeople and landowners were concerned. To be sure, this has been more the case in Chile than in Peru, where redemocratization opened opportunities to APRA's populism, but even in Peru, where policymakers tend to be more insular and governments have been more unstable, encompassing organizations get a hearing, and their views are partially incorporated into the ensuing policies. In addition, the relationship between state and business actors in these two cases tends to be based more on an exchange of positions rooted in rational-technical criteria rather than particularistic linkages. Again, this trend is stronger in Chile than in Peru, which still suffers from moderate degrees of particularism.

Another significant similarity between Chile and Peru is that intersectoral conflict has become more moderate. Deep divisions between agrarian and urban business (commerce, industry, finance) or intrabusiness conflict on key economic policy issues are less pronounced than elsewhere. Under these circumstances, the internal mechanisms for consensus building can handle remaining differences. Perhaps this has been the result of deep and complex processes of economic change begun in the 1960s and 1970s. In Chile, extensive land reform under Eduardo Frei and Salvador Allende, followed by far-reaching, free market economic and social reforms under Pinochet (privatization, deregulation, and trade liberalization) helped create a nucleus of strong conglomerates in favor of economic change and forced the modernization of traditional landowners and industrialists. The Peruvian government's reforms of the 1970s under Juan Velasco helped homogenize the private sector. The military government massively expropriated the landed oligarchy, and its policies paved the way for the emergence of a nucleus of new financial institution-centered conglomerates similar to those of Chile.

Key leadership and organizational characteristics of Chile's and Peru's encompassing business associations also contributed to their consolidation. Most important, leaders have been flexible and have developed an institutional culture of compromise. Thus, they have had the foresight to elect presidents of their organizations who possessed the right quality for dealing with the problem at hand. If the times required confrontation with government, combative presidents were elected. If internal consensus building was the main issue, business leaders capable of mediating interests and forging internal coalitions were sought. When crises subsided, more moderate directors who focused on economic issues came to the fore. Overall, leadership's capacity to shift from political confrontation with government to constructive negotiation and bargaining cannot be overemphasized. This flexibility and internal rules that complimented it facilitated trends toward professionalization and client service in the sectoral peak associations.[10] The Nicaraguan case with its difficulties stands in sharp contrast to Chile and Peru.

Encompassing business associations, while still in existence, have been less active of late in Mexico and El Salvador, and Nicaragua's has waned considerably. Systematic variance between these countries and Chile and Peru on the conditions discussed above — internal organization, the government-business relationship, level of intersectoral conflict, and leadership characteristics — is lacking. Nevertheless, in all of the cases where encompassing associations have weakened, differences in one or more of those factors are in evidence. These results strongly support the conclusion that those factors are indeed the relevant ones for explaining the transition from movement-generated encompassing business associations to more institutionally based unity.

In Mexico, the organizational heterogeneity of the encompassing business association's membership fueled debilitating internal conflicts over the retreat of the state from the economy and the opening of the nation to international trade. Mexico's encompassing association included chambers that represented medium- and small-scale businesses and large-scale firms oriented primarily toward domestic markets. And, while many of the member associations were sectorally based, others represented large-scale national firms or large-scale firms drawn mainly from a particular region. Thus, state corporatism (where the state compels the formation of functional organizations for interest representation, charters them, and regulates their internal management) was a mixed benefit for the encompassing business association. Although it was a "free" organization (not legally part of the corporatist system), governments exerted influence over its leadership, which, in turn, used the corporatist structure to control member organizations.

Organizational heterogeneity made consensus building more difficult. The most serious conflicts pitted organizations that represented large-scale firms against those that represented medium- and small-scale firms. Had the encompassing association been formed exclusively by sectoral organizations dominated by large-scale firms, these conflicts may not have been so significant; they might have been contained in the individual sectoral peak associations, as were the cases in Chile in the 1970s and Peru in the 1980s.

Government-business relations in Mexico also differed from those of Chile and Peru. This supports the hypothesis that a government's willingness to open space for the encompassing business association in the policy-making process once economic and social threats have receded contributes to their strengthening or decline. According to Tirado, the encompassing association was most active after the nationalization of the financial sector and during the Miguel de la Madrid administration, which consistently sought to mend fences with an aggrieved and increasingly politicized private sector. De la Madrid frequently included business elites in the policy process, inviting them to participate in tripartite negotiations over economic stabilization policy. The Salinas administration, however, displayed less interest in Mexico's encompassing business organization. Racked by internal conflict over the withdrawal of subsidies and reductions in trade barriers, the large-scale internationally competitive firms formed a separate ad hoc organization to deal with the North American Free Trade Agreement (NAFTA). This association worked closely with Carlos Salinas' administration in negotiations with the United States and Canada.

The main difficulty with the encompassing business associations in Nicaragua and El Salvador lay not so much in internal organization or business-government relations as had been the case in Mexico. More like Chile and Peru, their membership was based on sectoral organizations representing large- and medium-scale firms, thus, avoiding differences of interest over scale. They were also affiliated with think tanks capable of producing competent economic policy analysis. Moreover, and this was especially the case in Nicaragua after the Sandinistas lost control of the government, conservative governments invited them to participate in the policy process; however, unlike Chile and Peru, high levels of sectoral conflict over free market economic policies, especially opening to trade, significantly weakened the capacity of the encompassing business associations of El Salvador and Nicaragua to speak with a united voice. With this key function diminished, their capacity to act also suffered.

Perhaps more significant than intersectoral conflict, Nicaragua's encompassing business association also suffered from a leadership crisis. This condition was largely absent in the other cases where leadership rotated among sectors or was elected to fit the times. Spalding argues that the Nicaraguan encompassing association was in the firm grip of a leadership permeated by a culture of confrontation over political issues stemming from the revolution. Tooth-and-nail opposition to the Sandinistas and the legacy of their rule resulted in missed opportunities to participate constructively in the policy-making process at the invitation of conservative governments. Sectoral associations that did not belong to the encompassing organization and that were more linked to external commerce and foreign companies questioned the encompassing association's leadership and criticized its confrontational tactics. The leadership of the sectoral associations was more concerned with the issue of economic adjustment in the 1990s and the promotion of the growing new sectors of the economy to which they belonged. Because of these differences, the dynamic new Nicaraguan businesspeople preferred to keep their industry organizations independent of the encompassing association.

Failure to Build Enduring Encompassing Business Associations

The emergence of encompassing business organizations in Latin America, and their consolidation in a few cases, may be interpreted as a positive development from several standpoints. Those include support for private-interest government and the strengthening of key institutions for the development of societal corporatism (key for the containment of economic and social conflict in deeply divided yet democratic polities). Many analysts have argued these are crucial for the general fortification of systems of interest representation in Latin America and the consolidation of democracy. However, encompassing business organizations have not emerged in all countries, which belies the existence of a unilinear historical developmental path for business organization. In this volume, Brazil, Argentina, and the Dominican Republic are cases where encompassing associations failed to emerge, made only sporadic appearances, or declined sharply. Moreover, in the instances where they did form, they never managed to represent the private sector as a whole or to articulate a coordinated posture on common problems.

Two factors seem to account for these outcomes. First, corporatism and particularistic systems of business-state relations provided strong incentives for individual action. They permitted the state to establish an exclusive relationship with each sectoral or regional association and even with firms. Second, the absence of a severe threat to the fundamental interests of business (property, profits, and access to policymaking) was a permissive condition for the lack of collective action by business elites caught in these systems of interest intermediation.

In all three cases, sectoral organizations had access to the policy-making process through either strong corporatist (Brazil) and particularistic arrangements (Argentina and the Dominican Republic) or both. This access allowed each of them to press for redress of their grievances individually with success measured in partial policy change or special relief for the firms of key business leaders. As a result, it was difficult to overcome organizational traditions that exacerbated divisions among business groups, thus blocking their coordination. In Brazil, these divisions were mainly regional; in Argentina and the Dominican Republic, they took the form of sectoral clashes between agroexporters and industrialists.

The weakness of collective business action in Argentina, Brazil, and the Dominican Republic was also due to the lack of a serious collective threat to capitalists. This relative absence permitted corporatism and particularistic channels of access to the policy-making process to exercise their divisive roles. Clearly, there were challenges and difficulties, particularly in Argentina and the Dominican Republic, but these paled in comparison to events in Peru, Chile, Nicaragua, and, to only a slightly lesser extent, Mexico and El Salvador.[11] There was no widespread expropriation of leading firms or whole economic sectors, as was the case with banking in Mexico and Peru and even more extensively in Chile between 1971 and 1973. Business elites were not excluded from policymaking for long, as had been the case in Chile, Mexico, Nicaragua, and Peru. Neither were there escalating cycles of threat from social reform, exclusion from policymaking, or expropriation as had occurred in Chile, Mexico, Nicaragua, and Peru. When business elites were excluded from the policy-making process, military governments or dictatorships quickly restored access.

Nevertheless, and consistent with the hypothesis of the significance of the threat level to explain the rise of encompassing business organizations, when stiff challenges to the prerogatives of business elites occurred, efforts in that direction emerged. The results, however, were weak and impermanent rather than lasting because the level of threat was not high enough to overcome the divisive effect of restored corporatism or particularistic channels of access.

Kurt Weyland, in his chapter, shows how, in the absence of severe collective threats to business elites, Brazil's state corporatism and deeply rooted regional and sectoral divisions prevented the consolidation of an encompassing business association. Size and regional differences caused rivalries to develop around the powerful and highly individualistic São Paulo industrial organization, Federation of Industries of São Paulo (Federacão das Industrias do Estado de São Paulo — FIESP), and the rest of the country. Corporatism, in turn, has allowed special access for sectoral associations to policymakers. Clientelistic and patronage relationships have provided strong disincentives to collective action, especially when tied to successful negotiation or payoffs to key leaders. In other words, the myriad channels of access and obligations to political patrons have effectively isolated horizontal linkages between different business sectors.[12]

Carlos Acuña argues that Argentina lacks an encompassing business peak organization because the sectoral associations of large-scale economic interests in agriculture and industry are deeply antagonistic. Their access to the policy-making process in both civilian and military governments exacerbates their divisions. Not affected by the corporatist structures to which President Juan Perón subjected medium and small businesses, they each jealously use that access to defend their sectoral interests. By the same token, for the most part, Argentine capitalists and landowners have not faced severe collective threats to their existence from subordinate class-based groups or their political allies, who might have united them on a more permanent basis. They have not been subjected to extensive expropriation or long-lasting exclusion from the policy-making process. Significantly, when those subordinate groups confronted business elites with reformist challenges in Peronist governments, sectoral associations formed encompassing organizations. However, these dissolved once military governments put an end to those threats because renewed access to policymaking brought the deep divisions between town and country to the fore.[13]

Rosario Espinal shows that in the Dominican Republic a perceived collective threat — democratization — spurred the formation of an encompassing business organization. It was seen as a collective threat because of the very real electoral possibilities of a social democratic political party coming to power. A few years later, however, access to policymaking by individual sectoral associations in a deeply rooted particularistic style, initiated by Rafael Trujillo and continued by Joaquín Balaguer, and the policies that resulted under both social democratic and conservative political party rule blunted the extent of the perceived dangers. As a result, sectoral tensions during the formulation and implementation of neoliberal economic reforms significantly weakened the encompassing organization.[14]

These cases reveal yet another important facet of the problem of collective action among business elites. A comparison of Brazil and Mexico shows that corporatism in Latin America by itself is not a sufficient condition to account for the lack of encompassing peak associations. The presence or absence of a severe collective threat is also a necessary condition. Compared to Mexico, the disturbances of the 1960s in Brazil did not constitute a severe collective threat to large-scale business. João Goulart's populism firmly subordinated Marxist parties to far less ideologically committed political currents and essentially only spouted a rhetoric of benefits for the downtrodden. His reformist measures never reached the level of profound or extended challenges to the core interests of capitalists. There was no widespread expropriation of leading firms or whole economic sectors (such as banking in Mexico); nor were business elites excluded from policymaking for long (as occurred during the Echeverría administration and part of López Portillo's); neither were there escalating cycles of threat from reform, exclusion from policymaking, or expropriation, as had been the case in Mexico (as well as in Chile, Nicaragua, and Peru, for that matter). Moreover, in Brazil the military government quickly reestablished the status quo.

ORGANIZED BUSINESS, POLICY PROCESS, AND FREE MARKET ECONOMIC RESTRUCTURING IN LATIN AMERICA

If there has been a steady tendency toward the formation of encompassing business associations in Latin America, what impact has their presence or absence had on the policy process for free market economic restructuring? This question raises the ubiquitous issue of state autonomy versus social group explanations for policymaking. State-centered approaches credit the decisionmaker, the executive, and the bureaucracy with the capacity to introduce policy innovations; pressure groups are viewed as intervening variables. Society-centered explanations focus on the role of social classes and interest groups in policy change; they place less emphasis on public officials and institutional context (Grindle and Thomas 1991, 20-29).

Most studies — as does ours — approach the problem empirically. At which stage of the policy process do either state-centered or society-centered variables play a significant role? In recent studies of the policy-making process in Latin America, analysts have usually focused on either the policy initiation and formulation stages or the policy implementation stage. Practically all have concluded that business and organized business in particular played no significant role in the first two — where international and state actors predominate — but participated heavily in the latter. The evidence from this volume, as presented in the next two subsections, tends to confirm this pattern, with the partial exceptions of Chile and Mexico. Previous studies, however, have largely ignored the significance of the demand-raising and agenda-setting stages of the policy process, as well as the policy evaluation or feedback loop stages. This study finds that organized business and especially encompassing associations have played a meaningful but unnoticed role in those stages. We briefly summarize those arguments below.

With respect to their demand-raising and agenda-setting roles where encompassing organizations were present, an internal debate took place that gradually generated a consensus in favor of free trade. Once the correlation of forces shifted toward economic liberalization, demand for market-oriented reforms became stronger than in cases where encompassing associations were absent. These demands added the voice of business to an agenda for economic reform echoed by international institutions and state actors, and they also provided domestic sources of legitimation for that agenda. Thus, organized business gradually formed part of a support coalition for market-oriented reform, giving institutional expression to the policy demands of business groups before the economic reforms were initiated. Moreover, maintaining that coalition was especially important for the policy implementation stage and the prospect of consolidating reform.

In the cases without an encompassing business association, business leaders lacked a forum for exchanging ideas and crafting political agreements. This meant that those who opposed free trade were unable to assess realistically the strength of private-sector support for policy shifts. The absence of clarity over the changing balance of forces in the private sector fueled sectoral competition. Instead of accommodating to changing times, intersectoral struggle escalated.

As was the case with the demand-raising and agenda-setting stages of the policy process, the evaluation or feedback stage has also suffered from a relative lack of attention in extant studies. Once policies have been formulated and implementation has begun, proposals for change by those most affected by the reforms — emanating from organized business in this case — flourish. If the proposals are sweeping enough and if the authorities heed them, the act amounts to participation in policy formulation. Moreover, substantial revisions or improvements at the policy-evaluation stage can even amount to participation in policy initiation, especially when state actors resist such efforts. At that point, the added weight of specific proposals by the encompassing business association for policy adjustments can help to settle policy disputes in the state. In other words, breaking with economic orthodoxy without abandoning commitment to the market can be the equivalent of initiating new policies — and that is an area where organized business and encompassing associations in particular have been breaking new ground.

From Demand Raising to Policy Formulation

The general literature on economic reform consistently agrees that business interests and organized business in particular did not play a significant role in either the initiation or the formulation stages of the policy process.[15] For example, Robert H. Bates and Anne O. Krueger (1993) concluded that free market reforms resulted from changes in governments that brought in new elites that restructured political institutions. These political elites faced economic crises that, together with international economic actors, shaped the pro-reform policy agenda. By shifting policy-making away from representative institutions to economic institutions (central banks and ministries of finance), technocrats initiated and formulated policy reforms independently of organized social groups.

According to Bates and Krueger (1993), organized business was either too fragmented, quiescent, or ineffectual to affect the initiation or formulation of market-oriented reforms. In the first two instances, economic and political disorder made it extremely difficult for organized business to calculate where their interests lay. Thus, they were open to persuasion by political elites and technocrats. Yet, even in those instances when organized business was clear about its interests, a large gap existed between understanding them and organizing politically effective demands. In other words, Bates and Krueger argue that business leaders were unable or unwilling to act in support of favorable policies or in defense against unwanted reform.

Stephan Haggard and Robert R. Kaufman (1995) also conclude that the policy initiation and formulation stages of free market economic reforms were dominated by political elites and technocrats and maintain that it was better that way. State autonomy contributed to greater coherence in overall policy design and to the timing and sequencing of the reforms.

The evidence from this volume tends to confirm that organized business, by and large, has not played a key role in the initiation and formulation of policies for free market economic reform in Latin America. Yet, the data also strongly suggest that such conclusions cannot be stated as baldly as some authors do. First, in Chile and Mexico — cases where new governments sought to patch relations with a particularly militant and well-organized business community — encompassing and sectoral business associations were involved in policy formulation. Second, the punctuated development of the encompassing organizations of Chile and Mexico (periods of institutional development, followed by "dormancy," followed by greater proactiveness) has interesting implications for cases in which encompassing business associations have formed but have temporarily weakened or have yet to become actively involved in policy formulation. Even if "dormant," once encompassing associations are organized, their potential for more significant involvement in policy formulation increases with each economic and/or political crisis that engulfs the region.

Perhaps more important, at least in an immediate sense, the general literature on political and economic change has neglected the part played by encompassing business associations in the demand-raising and agenda-setting phases of the policy process. Studies more focused on business-state relations in political and economic reform, such as those by Conaghan and Malloy (1994) and Bartell and Payne (1995), picked up on this theme. They conclude that organized business in many Latin American countries articulated increasingly coherent demands for economic reform. Economic competition from state enterprise, insecurity over property rights and labor laws, and economic stagnation or crises generated an antistatist discourse centered on demands for privatization, security against nationalization, a general reduction of the role of the state in the economy via economic liberalization and deregulation, and more flexible labor relations. These demands contributed to agenda setting because they were formulated before governments undertook them. Policy stability was a complementary demand. Sudden, arbitrary changes in policy (very intense in Peru, for example) contributed to the distrust of the state by businesspeople (Durand 1994).

These were important insights that left several questions open for further research regarding the early stages of the policy process. Which of business's many organizational forms — sectoral, industry-wide, or encompassing associations and firms — contributed most to building a broad policy consensus in favor of economic reform? By what mechanism or process did consensus emerge, and what were the consequences of its lack? Did organized business's participation in demand raising and agenda setting have any significance for the construction of support coalitions for market-oriented economic change? What was the impact of their participation in such support coalitions for the implementation of reform?

This volume shows that in countries where encompassing business associations have existed, they have tended to provide more specific, early, broad, consistent private sector demands for free market economic reforms. Where associations were present, business groups articulated the antistatist, deregulatory, liberalization-oriented, and antilabor components of those reforms more forcefully than in their absence. This was the case in Chile, Nicaragua, Mexico, Peru, El Salvador, and the Dominican Republic. (However, because trade liberalization often proved to be a thorny and divisive issue, it was frequently avoided for as long as possible.) By contrast, in the absence of encompassing business associations, early, cohesive private sector support for economic liberalization was more ambivalent and fractured, and organized business provided conflicting signals to policymakers. This contributed to governments treading more carefully on the path of reform, as was the case in Brazil.

Why did encompassing business associations rather than other forms of "business-as-actor" — such as sectoral organizations or conglomerates — usually come to play this important support role for market-oriented reforms? The theoretical argument has been that because they aggregate sectoral and industry-based interests, encompassing associations mitigate divisive distributional politics based on the selfish, narrow interests of sectoral or industry-based associations. Forging a policy position in an encompassing business association requires consensus building, which forces the more narrowly based member organizations to repress their immediate interests in favor of more general economic issues (Olson 1982; Nelson 1994b; Maxfield and Schneider 1997). Their focus on issues held in common also means that encompassing business associations are functional for economic efficiency, growth, and development.[16]

Consensus building is not without its tensions and strife because more narrowly based organizations are forced to give up specific interests in favor of general interests. Encompassing organizations help resolve those tensions by facilitating intrabusiness coalition building. In the case of free market economic reforms, internationally competitive producers and landowners, import-export merchants, and the financial sectors of encompassing associations often have allied against protectionist industrialists and landowners. The fact that the leading firms in many of the sectoral associations belonged to only a few conglomerates also facilitated consensus building by blunting the sectoral association's propensity to defend narrow interests tooth and nail. The financial capacity and multisectoral structure of those conglomerates allowed them to adjust more rapidly to economic change and to take advantage of new business opportunities. They could divest themselves more easily of unprofitable firms and invest in the growth sectors of an open economy.

The chapters on countries with encompassing business associations confirm the theoretical expectations about their consensus-building role, especially as they apply to the demand-raising and agenda-setting stages of the policy process. Latin American businesses have perceived antistatist, free market economic reforms to be in their general interest, a posture that had its origins in the very threats to business that either forged or strengthened encompassing business associations. The private sector had united in the encompassing associations in response to common threats such as national rebellion, strong state competition, nationalization, overregulation, labor-friendly governments, distorted price systems that were the result of myriad subsidies, and the inability of those policies to overcome deepening economic crises. In response to these general threats of the private sector, encompassing associations articulated strong demands for free market economic reform and changes in labor relations.

This was the case of the encompassing business associations of Chile in the early 1970s and of Peru, Mexico, Nicaragua, El Salvador, and the Dominican Republic in the 1980s and 1990s. They articulated strong antistatist, deregulatory, proliberalization, antipopulist stances. Their pronouncements and the pressure they placed on governments contributed to a political climate favorable to the initiation of economic reforms when new, promarket-minded governments came into power. In some instances, most clearly in the case of Chile, they even helped to usher in the new government. In keeping with the movement origins of many of these encompassing associations, the commitment to promarket discourse was the most frail in the Dominican Republic, where the threat was weakest.

This point is in clear contrast to cases without encompassing business associations or where they failed to consolidate. In Brazil, the Dominican Republic, and Argentina before Carlos Menem, broad business support for economic liberalization was weaker. The antistate discourse, while present, had many shadings because industry and sectoral organizations individually sought to protect subsidies, access to credit, and preferential relationships with state enterprise. Classic Olsonian distributional politics on the part of organized business prevailed and contributed to the difficulties of reform-minded governments. Kurt Weyland shows that in Brazil, the São Paulo-based organization defended the protectionist industrial policies of the developmental state. The Rio de Janeiro-based organizations were more supportive of neoliberal reforms. In the fragmenting context of corporatist relations to the state, these divisions have meant that in Brazil the shift to market-oriented policies has taken longer because the debate was more intense and controversial.[17] Rosario Espinal demonstrates that in the context of particularistic relations with the state, strong sectoral clashes between agroexporters who support market reforms and industrialists who often oppose them have had much the same effect in the Dominican Republic. And Carlos Acuña argues that Argentina before Menem followed the same pattern with the same results.

Argentina under Menem, however, suggests that broad business support for market-oriented neoliberal reforms by business elites can arise in the absence of encompassing peak associations and in the context of strong sectoral clashes between agroexporters and industrialists. This weakens the robustness of the correlation between the presence or absence of an encompassing organization and initial demands for such policies. Acuña's chapter suggests this was a function of the strong movement component to sectoral association action against Peronist governments. Peronism had favored populist policies generating strong state competition with the private sector and had created business associations of medium- and small-scale producers tied to Peronism. This engendered enduring antistatist and antipopulist sentiments among well-established, large-scale business elites from the outset.

Before Menem, however, Argentina had been the victim of classic sectoral clashes between industry and export agriculture on trade and subsidy issues, clashes that influenced stop-and-go economic politics, especially in the 1960s, 1970s, and early 1980s (Smith 1989). Intersectoral conflict, according to Acuña, diminished due to internal factors. The decline in the economic importance of medium- and small-scale industrialists and Menem's political rejection of their organizations elevated industrialists linked to conglomerates that survived the past 20 years of policy swings. Large-scale businesses found that they could shift resources within their economic empires to accommodate economic reforms. This gave them leverage against their perennial foes — labor and medium- and small-scale manufacturers linked to the traditional wing of the Peronist party. These circumstances made it easier for them to shift from traditional opposition to new-found support for market reforms.

In sum, this study shows that Bates and Krueger's (1993) bald assertions that organized business either does not know its interests or cannot act effectively on behalf of these interests if it does know them require more nuance. At the height of conflictual periods, encompassing business associations can generate private sector consensus around common interests: in this case in favor of market-oriented reforms rather than against them. Whether encompassing associations act effectively on behalf of these interests is a thornier issue. If the criteria are the formulation and imposition of an economic reform model, the answer must be no; in fact, one would be hard-pressed to say this occurs anywhere. Nevertheless, the country chapters strongly suggest that encompassing business associations, more than any other form of business organization, played a significant role in raising and publicly articulating demands for market-oriented policies. Thus, encompassing business associations were active in defining national political agendas supportive of policy change. Of course, such postures first required a shift in the correlation of forces within the encompassing association away from protectionist sectors and in favor of the internationally competitive, financial, and nontradable sectors.

It is worth noting that in three cases (Mexico, Chile, and, to a lesser extent, Peru), encompassing business associations went beyond the support role and participated in policy formulation, albeit not in a central capacity. Mexico's association participated in tripartite socioeconomic pact-making that underpinned economic stabilization. Its spin-off organization also indirectly took part in the NAFTA negotiations. Chile's encompassing association supported and took part in the formulation of privatization, trade, and economic liberalization policies during the initial, short-lived period of gradual market reforms. In the subsequent policy period of radical reform, Chile's encompassing business association was, as Bates and Krueger (1993) assert, quiescent; however, spurred by the 1982-1983 economic crisis, it once again took a more proactive and participatory stance in the policy process. In Peru, once the correlation of forces moved in the direction of free trade at the end of the García administration, the encompassing association participated in the formulation of a package of legislative initiatives approved by President Alberto Fujimori. These cases illustrate the critical importance of encompassing business associations for the process of *concertación* — the crafting of political pacts among the state, business, and labor in transitions to democracy (Dos Santos 1987).

Moreover, quiescence on the part of encompassing business associations — defined by Bates and Krueger (1993) as the absence of opposition — did not mean that the dominant business groups under ISI, which depended on protected and regulated markets, failed to know their interests during a period of rapid change. Instead, the chapters by Silva and Durand suggest that quiescence often actually amounted to support for reform, based on the balance of forces in the encompassing association among sectoral organizations that "knew their interests," even if they were not involved in policy initiation or formulation.[18]

The key here is to understand that opponents of radical reform in the Chilean and Peruvian private sector could not mount a counteroffensive because they were isolated within the broader business community represented in the encompassing association. This occurred for two reasons. First, the largest Chilean and Peruvian conglomerates came under the control of directors who favored radical market reforms. They believed their conglomerates could adjust to a more internationally competitive profile. It was their influence in the private sector, rather than confusion over their interests, that led industrialist associations to endorse reform officially. Second, as the balance of forces shifted in favor of policy reforms, many sectoral organizations, such as the commercial, mining, financial, and, later, the construction sectors, backed the measures. This only left the agricultural sector and industry-specific organizations of the manufacturing sector (such as metal working and electrical manufactures) to protest the implementation of radical market reforms. Their isolation within the broader policy community was compounded by their inability to forge an intersectoral alliance. Under these circumstances, they could not be expected to turn the encompassing organization against reform.

The fact that organized business, whether in the form of sectoral or encompassing associations, was seldom, if ever, centrally involved in policy formulation did not mean that the private sector was absent from the process. Ben Ross Schneider and Sylvia Maxfield (1997) and Joan M. Nelson (1994b, 178) have recently reiterated the old truism that business elites often act directly through their myriad connections to policymakers quite independently of their organizations. Thus, although it is not the subject of this volume, business was involved in policy formulation in a number of our cases. For example, in Argentina (Smith 1989), Chile (Silva 1996), and Mexico (Maxfield 1990), the directors of leading conglomerates or large firms — or technocrats who were their close associates — were directly involved in policy initiation and formulation.

These clarifications notwithstanding, if new governments rarely included encompassing business associations in policy initiation and formulation, what was the effect of their drumbeat of early demands for market-oriented reforms? It was that many of those new regimes, often ushered in with enthusiastic support from the private sector, enjoyed significant, legitimating, and well-articulated support from business elites for the initiation of reforms. In other words, the demand-raising and agenda-setting role of encompassing associations turned organized business into allies of the state, technocratic, external, and business actors who were more active in policy initiation and formulation. As their allies, encompassing business associations gradually helped to generate a climate of acceptance and desirability for economic reforms through mass media, public fora, and meetings with policymakers at a time of uncertainty. Moreover, as will be seen, a number of studies underscore the significance of this role in the coalition for economic change, especially as it relates to the implementation and consolidation of free market reforms (Haggard and Kaufman 1995; Nelson 1994b; Pastor and Wise 1996).

The significance of the indirect support role of encompassing business associations in the initiation of free market reforms was underscored by what happened when their support dissipated. As previously seen, encompassing associations failed to consolidate in a number of cases. When that occurred, their capacity to build private sector consensus for such reforms also faltered. That was hardly surprising because the failure to consolidate was often due to intersectoral conflicts over the consequences of market reforms once their implementation had begun, as was the case in Mexico, the Dominican Republic, and Nicaragua. By contrast, in countries where encompassing associations consolidated, as was the case in Chile under Pinochet and Peru under Fujimori, broad support for free market reforms continued.

Nevertheless, more often than not, encompassing business associations failed to consolidate after the initiation of market reforms, and their support for the reforms waned. At first glance, these results seem to corroborate Bates and Krueger's (1993) thesis that business groups were not fully aware of their interests; however, this study shows that the lack of consolidation was closely related to fragilities of internal organization that weakened the consensus-building role of the encompassing association. These were the source of intrabusiness policy wrangling, not confusion over interests. For example, in Mexico, the organizational difficulty was that the encompassing association included sectoral organizations that, in addition to large-scale firms also represented medium- and small-scale industry as well as regional organizations. The demands for free market reforms by Mexico's encompassing association were contingent on the dominance of representatives of large-scale firms who had more capacity to adjust to economic change. Ultimately, the representatives of medium- and small-scale firms revolted, and broad private-sector support for free market reforms waned. In the Dominican Republic, rivalry between the two dominant, regionally based member associations was at least as important to the lack of consolidation as sectoral conflict, and leadership problems mixed with ideological rigidity contributed greatly to the difficulties of the Nicaraguan encompassing association.

Yet, with or without the endorsement of encompassing business associations, governments proceeded with market reforms once initiated. Political leaders in the state, technocrats, external actors, and selected businessmen who headed large conglomerates did not need their approval to forge ahead. What are the implications of this for the role of organized business in processes of market-oriented economic change? Does it mean they are irrelevant? We think not.

Policy Implementation and the Consolidation of Free Market Reforms

A number of recent studies on the politics of free market economic reforms have argued that significant participation by business groups in the policy process is limited to the implementation and evaluation stages. Those studies concluded that their role in those stages is key to the consolidation of market-oriented economic reform. Once initiated, the reform process requires interaction with business groups whose support is necessary to sustain it (Haggard and Kaufman 1995; Nelson 1994a, 1994b; Bates and Krueger 1993; Pastor and Wise 1996). Haggard and Kaufman (1995) articulated the logic best. Building on Charles Lindblom (1977) and other theorists of the structural power of capital (Przeworski and Wallerstein 1988), they hypothesized that state actors need support from key social groups, such as business, because their opposition may foil implementation. This is particularly true for market-oriented economic reforms in countries where the private sector must step in with investment and more crucial when the Latin American debt crisis of the 1980s left fiscally strapped governments more dependent on private capital for economic growth.

Involving entrepreneurs has two positive functions, according to Peter Evans (1995) and Schneider and Maxfield (1997). If communication channels to the executive branch are open, entrepreneurs can make observations on how to improve the policies so that the private sector may respond to them better. By the same token, participation in formulating investment-enhancing adjustments boosts private sector confidence in the state sector's commitment to workable reform. These improvements to the business climate then have positive effects on investment and growth in free and open markets.

For example, a comparative study of Peru, Venezuela, and Colombia shows that a constructive, stable climate of business-state relations can influence economic management and performance in a positive way by providing a framework within which to negotiate policy change (Thorp and Durand 1997). In Colombia, trust between state and economic leaders from firms and trade associations was established on the basis of informal, close, and permanent networking. This relationship generated a positive environment for investment even in the context of widespread violence. In contrast, a climate of distrust, uncertainty, and conflict between business elites and the government in pre-Fujimori Peru contributed to lower private investment and a more troubled process of policy change. When business confidence was restored under Fujimori, organized business played an active role in backing policy shifts. In Venezuela during the oil boom, the encompassing business association participated in negotiations over the allocation of burgeoning fiscal resources, which unfortunately also involved rent-seeking behavior. As Venezuela's oil-based model for economic development deteriorated, lack of communication between business leaders and the government contributed to political instability.

Most of these valuable studies, nevertheless, leave open the question of which type of business actor is best suited to participate in the implementation stage of the policy process. Bates and Krueger (1993) argue in favor of organized business in general. Schneider and Maxfield (1997), in the most systematic work on these issues, are more eclectic. It can be either businessmen who head leading conglomerates or organized business; however, if the task befalls organized business, they show a preference for encompassing associations because of their consensus-building and general-interest-promoting qualities. Joan M. Nelson (1994b, 181) and Rosemary Thorp and Francisco Durand (1997) agree on that point as well.

This general agreement regarding the proper place for the development-enhancing involvement of organized business in the policy process raises an interesting problem. Earlier studies had also concluded that the implementation stage was the principal locus of business action; yet, the evaluation of their performance was almost universally negative. For example, Schmitter (1971) argued that organized business in Brazil usually took a reactive, defensive stance to state-led economic policies. State actors defined agendas and formulated policy; business, organized or otherwise, then lobbied for changes congruent with its narrow economic interests. In short, business organizations and firms engaged in classic Olsonian distributive politics. Most studies conducted during the 1960s and 1970s reached similar conclusions. Under conditions of dependent or late development, an inchoate capitalist or business class in Latin America was too weak to be the main agent of socioeconomic transformation; hence, the state had to take the lead and deal accordingly with entrepreneurs and traditional landowners seeking exceptions to economic reform measures in the implementation stage of the policy process. In short, domestic business and landowning elites were perceived to be obstacles to progress; their intervention in the policy process often disarticulated or pulled the teeth from the state's industrial and social policy (Cardoso 1971; Cardoso and Falletto 1979; Véliz 1963; Anderson 1967).

This "checkered past" suggests that organized business must somehow alter the behavioral patterns that turned it into an "obstacle to progress," especially if it is to play the positive role in the implementation stage of the policy process assigned to it by contemporary studies. How much has organized business changed? Do encompassing business associations provide a locus for such a conversion?

The chapters by Silva and Durand on Chile and Peru, where encompassing business associations have consolidated the most, offer a hopeful sign. The consensus-building qualities of "encompassingness" generated an enduring, proactive policy stance. Proactiveness is the key here. In the past, sectoral and industry associations reacted defensively against policies in order to obstruct their implementation. The object was to retain as much of the status quo as possible. In contrast, in the 1980s and 1990s, Chile's and Peru's encompassing organizations offered proposals on how to adjust policies to ensure that the private sector responded to them in the way technocrats intended. The idea was to smooth out the adjustment process to avoid economic disruptions that might cause wild, destabilizing swings in growth. With these strategies and tactics, encompassing business associations and sectoral organizations working from general consensus made significant progress in introducing policy adjustments.

Several common qualities facilitated this change. First, the encompassing associations of Chile and Peru had similar processes for consensus building. The sectoral organizations developed a slate of concerns and proposed solutions. Meeting in the encompassing organization, sectoral association leaders discussed them. Those found to be of common interest were approved. Sectoral associations, as was the case in Chile, then tailored general policy positions to the sector's specificities. Second, sectoral associations were free to lobby on behalf of policies that affected them even if they were not in the common interest. Thus, the cohesiveness of the encompassing association was not threatened.

Professionalization was a third common trait that allowed encompassing business associations to take a more positive proactive role in the implementation and evaluation stages of free market reforms. Schneider and Maxfield (1997) singled this out as a crucial element in the development of organized business for overcoming Olsonian distributional politics. Chilean and Peruvian encompassing associations were linked closely with think tanks capable of sophisticated economic analysis, or they had their own economic analysis units. Their leaders approached technocrats with studies that showed why the proposed adjustments were necessary for the success of the government's policies, or they demonstrated that relieving business of some of the burdens of adjustment would not distort the thrust of economic reform.

Similar developments had taken place in Mexico and El Salvador, according to the evidence presented by authors Tirado and Johnson. Leaders of the member organizations met in the encompassing association to decide which issues were amenable to compromise, and individual organizations then tailored the general policy to their needs. However, these negotiations took place in less consolidated encompassing associations, especially in the case of Mexico. There, the heterogeneity of the member organizations meant that consensus often depended on which faction dominated; thus, it could be reversed if another faction came into power.

Although the encompassing associations of Mexico and El Salvador were not as consolidated as those in Chile and Peru, linkages to think tanks improved the technical quality of their policy postures, positions which, again, instead of being at odds with reform complemented it. The more proactive, proposal-oriented, technical, positive approach contributed to more collaborative rather than confrontational business-state relations in policy implementation than in the past.

The cases in this volume reveal great variety in the mechanisms and means for participation in the implementation stage of the policy process. Where encompassing organizations exist, their leadership tends to meet with top policymakers to discuss the large questions on the government's agenda, their implications for business sectors, and what business elites think ought to be done. These meetings, in most cases, are not institutionalized. There are no production boards or planning meetings with prescribed schedules and agendas for discussion, with set rights and responsibilities for the participants. Moreover, they may be initiated either by government officials or the private sector. The relationship is more ad hoc. Government officials may call them when they perceive a need for business support for major policy initiatives. Conversely, business leaders might decide that policymakers need some orientation in the proper design of a proposed reform. Of course, over time, such meetings set a tradition of informal, occasional consultation.

Following these meetings, sectoral organizations draft specific plans for the implementation of policy congruent with the consensus arrived at within the encompassing association and between it and government officials. The sectoral organizations then work out the details with the corresponding line ministries. The process is greatly facilitated when the sectoral peak associations possess well-developed technical departments. As Schneider and Maxfield (1997, 8-9) have pointed out, a high degree of professionalization inhibits the tendency of sectoral organizations to engage in distributive politics. Moreover, because professionalization is an indication of institutional strength, Thorp and Durand (1997) argue that it helps create a more stable climate of business-government relations.

In countries without encompassing organizations, key sectoral organizations also were active in the implementation stage of the policy process. The difference was that commitment to formulating positive adjustments to neoliberal reforms was not as uniform; they understandably tended to defend more narrow sectoral economic interests. This meant that opposition to sweeping reforms emerged more strongly. For example, Weyland's chapter shows that the presence of powerful key sectoral peak associations, such as FIESP in Brazil, strongly influenced policy in favor of the status quo, despite governments that wished to move more rapidly on market reforms. The case of FIESP also calls into question the assumption that the mere connection to a strong technical department guarantees that a sectoral organization will have the general interests of business at heart — defined as liberalized, open markets. FIESP is connected to such an institute, but it defines the general interest of business differently, although very eloquently and rationally. Meanwhile, Espinal's rendering of the Dominican Republic in the 1990s demonstrates that sectoral associations may simply press for less orthodox versions of the market reforms pushed by technocrats and the international community. They prefer a more gradual approach to the withdrawal of subsidies for various economic sectors and the dismantling of protective barriers.

The existence of rival encompassing business associations may also blunt the effect of organized business's participation in policy implementation. This occurs when one association favors market reforms and only demands minor adjustments but the other insists on challenging the content, timing, and sequencing of policy change. Under these conditions, competing policy initiatives tend to cancel each other out because the government finds it easy to ignore both.

The country chapters also show that where only well-developed key sectoral associations exist, the system of intermediation between them and policymakers is similar in form, although not in content, to cases with encompassing associations. The leadership of a sectoral organization may meet first with the president of the republic or with the top economic policymakers. Based on the results, the sectoral association then negotiates policy implementation with the line ministry. Conversely, on more circumscribed questions, the sectoral organization may appeal only to the line ministry. The content of what is discussed, however, is much more sector specific rather than a broader discussion of the impact of economic policy on all business sectors.

Where corporatist arrangements exist, such as in Brazil and partially in Argentina and Mexico, more formal institutional relations are established with line ministries and government financing institutions. This provides additional arenas for access with more codified rights and obligations between government and business. There are, however, drawbacks to such arrangements. The structure is more rigid, which implies a lack of innovation in problem solving. Furthermore, in Latin America, corporatism and its institutional compartmentalization also creates vested interests between bureaucrats and private interests. This makes defense of the status quo easier.

Acuña's chapter also shows what happens in the face of declining state corporatism coupled with substantial deindustrialization. In Argentina, the Menem government has rescinded preferential treatment for the association of medium- and small-scale business linked to government by corporatist mechanisms, preferring to deal with the traditional sectoral organizations dominated by large-scale interests. Menem's government has also taken a more probusiness attitude toward labor relations. Deindustrialization during the military governments of the 1970s and 1980s meant that the remaining large-scale businesses basically had adjusted to international competition. As a result of these trends, the industrialists and the export-oriented landowners' association both agreed on market-oriented reforms with openness to international competition. Muted intersectoral conflict is a new development in the Argentine political economy. These associations, along with the representatives of large conglomerates, support market-oriented reforms and negotiate their implementation with government officials.

In conclusion, organized business in many of our cases has shown a new proactiveness in demand raising, agenda setting, and, in particular, policy implementation and evaluation for market-oriented reforms. This was especially strong in cases where encompassing organizations emerged and either consolidated or held together reasonably well, particularly in Chile, Peru, El Salvador, and Mexico.

Where encompassing organizations failed to consolidate or never existed, organized business engaged more in old-time distributive politics, as was the case in the Dominican Republic and Brazil. Special circumstances conspired to turn Argentina under Menem into an exception to the rule. Nicaragua showed that an inflexible leadership bent on confrontational state-business relations could wreck potentially fruitful connections between an encompassing association and conservative governments. In the end, this significantly weakened the organizational, representational, and political efficacy of the encompassing organization.

Involvement in the policy implementation stage of the policy process was not automatic and reached various levels of institutionalization, from none (Peru) to relatively high (Chile). Nevertheless, in all cases, encompassing associations raised demands and struggled for inclusion in policy formulation and implementation, although during the most radical reform phases, only the Mexican association managed to participate in some policy formulation. However, as implementation proceeded in Mexico, Peru, Chile, El Salvador, and, for a while, in the Dominican Republic, the encompassing organizations pressured their governments to hear them and to negotiate implementation. They succeeded in forcing governments to reformulate policies in a direction more to their liking.

The cases of Mexico, Chile, and Peru also call into question Bates and Krueger's (1993) assertion that in countries with successful reforms, political elites and technocrats were primarily responsible for restructuring the relationship with business. They argue that organized business played a secondary and relatively passive part in the decision of state actors to include organized business at later stages of the policy process. Yet, the evidence regarding Mexico, Chile, and Peru in this volume reveals that political elites negotiated the inclusion of business elites only after encompassing organizations vociferously campaigned for it. At that point, policymakers realized that consolidation of the reforms required keeping business in the coalition, which the private sector had become a part of by virtue of the encompassing association's early demand raising — and that necessitated consulting with organized business on implementation.

Consultation in policy implementation can shade into policy evaluation and contribute to adjustments in economic reform packages. If sweeping enough and if initially opposed by the government, as was the case in Chile until 1983, those adjustments are tantamount to new policy, even though they are not departures from the fundamental principles of market economics. In other cases, such as Peru, the process reinforced the deepening of market-oriented economic restructuring. Throughout, as shown in the the cases of Chile, Peru, and Mexico, encompassing and sectoral associations acted as transmission belts, nodal points for the exchange of information between the state and the private sector (Schneider and Maxfield 1997, 8-9). Encompassing and sectoral associations aggregated data for distribution to government officials and controlled for distortion in the interest of effective policymaking. In turn, they passed on government information to their members for internal debate over policy responses.

ORGANIZED BUSINESS AND THE QUESTION OF DEMOCRACY IN LATIN AMERICA

The literature has long recognized that in market economies, business's support for a form of government — whether democratic, authoritarian, or intermediate forms — is vital for its stability. At its roots, business's power stems from its capacity to influence the public functions of employment and investment. The decisions of business elites, then, significantly affect economic stability, which, in turn, is central for the health of governments. If they find a particular form of government intolerable, they may exacerbate economic crises in order to bring down a government (Lindblom 1977; Przeworski and Wallerstein 1988). In the process, business organizations and other business leaders may join broader coalitions for political change (Haggard and Kaufman 1995); they may even take part in political mobilization.

Given the structural power of capitalists, observers have been interested in their democratic proclivities for some time. With ample evidence to back it, the early literature on business and democracy of the 1960s and 1970s concluded that socioeconomic elites were inherently antidemocratic. Economic modernization weakened established elites (landowners) and rendered new ones (industrialists) too feeble to defend their vital interests in democratic regimes dominated by coalitions of middle classes, labor groups, and center-left political parties (Moore 1966; O'Donnell 1973; Cardoso and Faletto 1979).

Beginning in the late 1970s and cresting in the 1980s, the tidal wave of democratization in Latin America called such conclusions into question. Since then, scholars have grappled with three issues. First, they observed that, with varying degrees of conviction, business turned against authoritarianism and supported democratization in Ecuador, Bolivia, Nicaragua, Panama, Peru, and Brazil. In other cases, once democracy was established, the private sector displayed little yearning for the restoration of authoritarianism, as was the case in Chile and Argentina. Given this turn of events, scholars again examined the conditions that influenced the regime loyalties of businesspeople, in particular those conducive to support for democracy. Second, as time wore on, the object of study shifted from transitions to democracy to concerns over the consolidation of democracy. This raised questions over the type of democracy socioeconomic elites were willing to tolerate. Third, as democratic governability became an issue, analysts began to examine the probabilities for neocorporatist systems of interest intermediation. We turn to these issues below with a special focus on the contributions of organized business.

The Regime Loyalties of Businesspeople

Recent literature on democratization agrees that businesspeople have no intrinsic allegiance to either authoritarianism or democracy. Their first loyalty is to the maintenance of a good business climate and stable rules of the economic game. This prompted Haggard and Kaufman (1995, 7-8) to argue that severe economic downturns created tensions in the authoritarian coalitions that business elites were a part of. As economic crisis set in, technocratic teams and economic policy changed, often frequently and drastically. Military leaders became more insular, and their actions often became unpredictable, even for economic elites well-connected to policy circles. Those circumstances frequently prompted business elites to join coalitions that supported democratization.

Conaghan (1988) and Conaghan and Malloy (1994) observed that a number of additional conditions affected the regime loyalties of business elites, especially inclusion in the policy-making process. Such inclusion gives them confidence that, in general, government policy will be beneficial to them: it provides a measure of stability and predictability. Authoritarian governments between 1964 and 1989 often failed to provide these conditions, which exacerbated business's frustration with hard economic times. In contrast, beginning in the 1970s, postauthoritarian democratic regimes, more in need of private investment, offered the possibility of the private sector's inclusion in the policy-making process, which is why, according to these authors, capitalists supported democratization in the Andean cases.

The chapters in this volume confirm these hypotheses. To varying degrees, business associations in Peru, Argentina, the Dominican Republic, El Salvador, and Nicaragua all turned against authoritarianism and supported democratization. The reasons were invariably intertwined with economic downturns, receding threats from below, and exclusion from economic policymaking at times when business leaders perceived economic policy to be detrimental to their interests. Similar trends were occurring in Brazil in the early 1980s (Cardoso 1986; Payne 1994).

In a few cases, such as Mexico, Chile, and, more recently, Peru, businesspeople were more ambivalent about democratization. This was mainly, but not exclusively, because of their inclusion in the policy-making process under authoritarianism. Tirado shows that business elites in Mexico did not necessarily support democratization, even though they helped strengthen the conservative opposition political party. Instead, they backed political liberalization and were content to leave it at that, once the Mexican executive restored their access and influence in policymaking. Durand's chapter demonstrates that in 1992, Peruvian business elites welcomed a return to limited authoritarian rule when threatened by a situation of generalized ungovernability. The support for authoritarian rule, however, was conditioned on a return to democratic rule. Durand thinks this was largely due to a pragmatic appreciation of negative international reactions to Fujimori's *autogolpe*. Silva, in this volume, and others elsewhere, have pointed out that Chilean capitalists wanted Pinochet to continue his authoritarian rule. Silva argues that this was mainly because their access and influence in the policy-making process under Pinochet had been reestablished between 1983 and 1985.

What role does organized business play in the process of democratization? The question is particularly relevant because many analysts have observed that, in addition to using business associations, business elites act politically in a variety of ways (Nelson 1994b; Maxfield and Schneider 1997; Haggard and Kaufman 1995). For example, firms carry out most of the private sector's politically significant economic actions, such as disinvestment. By the same token, heads of prominent companies and conglomerates may participate directly in the policy process without the involvement of organized business or concomitant with it. In this volume, this was clearest in Argentina's case. Espinal's constant references to personalism and clientelism strongly suggest similar connections in the Dominican Republic.

These observations notwithstanding, organized business has its own special role in processes of authoritarian maintenance and democratization. It is the premier form for carrying out the *public* role of business participation in the policy process. The solidarity pacts in Mexico were subscribed to by organized business; organized business participated in the peace negotiations in El Salvador; organized business promoted fair and free elections in the Dominican Republic; and organized business worked with economic ministries in both authoritarian and newly democratic Chile. Some theorists, such as Mario Dos Santos (1987), even argued that organized business could play a key role in stabilizing the emerging Latin American democracies. He believed that *concertación* could become a negotiating forum that paralleled the Congress. He no doubt hoped that the practice would contribute to building neocorporatist systems of interest governance, a subject that will be discussed in the next section. While some countries engaged in *concertación*, the attempts were usually short-lived and not institutionalized.

Organized business brings greater transparency to the private sector's participation in public policy debates and to the process of crafting bargains with the state and organized labor. First of all, and without wishing to idealize, they are part of a more *public* debate. As representative organizations, they have a need to publicize, justify, and demonstrate the effectiveness of their interventions in the policy process, thereby invigorating policy debates in democracy. Their declarations necessarily reflect an internal deliberative process of some sort, which is more than one perceives when firms act directly on their own behalf.

The cases in this volume amply support such observations. In El Salvador, the decline of traditional elites and the rise of competing economic sectors in the encompassing association clearly influenced business's turn from an antidemocratic to a more democratic public posture. Moreover, the leaders of organized business negotiated and signed the peace accords on behalf of the private sector. In newly democratic Chile, the leaders of the encompassing organization and sectoral organizations carried out the public negotiations between the private sector and ministers of state, the president of the republic, and the Congress. In Nicaragua, the public declarations by organized business revealed to all the struggle between old-guard authoritarians in the private sector and more progressive supporters of democracy. In the Dominican Republic, leaders of organized business appealed to the public and to their own following for support for democracy and for antistatist liberalizing economic policies. Argentine business leaders also began supporting democracy in the wake of extremely arbitrary and incompetent military governments, the initial electoral defeat of Peronism in 1983, and the reform of Peronism in 1988.

The public role of organized business contributes to a second function that is crucial for regime stability. Organized business has the capacity to mobilize political support for its cause among broader publics. By molding public opinion, its declarations shape national agendas and public discourse. Business's critique or praise can sway the foreign sector, middle classes, and even elements of the poorer classes to its side. Thus, public support by organized business confers legitimacy to a government's policies, which reinforces the regime's legitimacy. However, if business turns against a government, business associations, in extreme cases, can shake governments by organizing mobilization against it. This occurred in Chile under Salvador Allende, Peru under Alan García, Nicaragua under Daniel Ortega and, to a lesser extent, in Mexico under José López Portillo. There, organized business backed conservative political parties seeking to upset the Partido Revolucionario Institucional's hold over the Mexican state. Moreover, as Dietrich Rueschemeyer, Evelyne Stephens, and John D. Stephens (1992, 222-225) have observed, the private sector has less difficulty supporting democracy where business — and organized business — forge links with strong conservative political parties. This view is corroborated in this volume by the cases of Nicaragua, El Salvador, and postauthoritarian Chile.

Encompassing business organizations add value to these political functions during crises by stimulating debate over regime preferences among a wide spectrum of business leaders. These debates have significant consequences whether agreements are reached or not. Durand's chapter shows that Peruvian business leaders routinely discussed the "coup card." During García's administration, business leaders failed to agree on a course of action. This helped to avoid a coup against him. During Fujimori's administration, business's support for his coup was critical to its success, second only to the military's full backing. The encompassing association's insistence on a limited coup added to pressure on Fujimori to restore democracy in a prudent time frame. In Chile, business leaders frequently discussed political issues. Under authoritarian rule, the encompassing association organized a crusade to support Pinochet in the October 1988 plebiscite. Under democracy, business has campaigned vigorously against constitutional reforms that might weaken Chile's authoritarian enclaves. And, as previously mentioned, the Dominican Republic's encompassing organization deliberated over whether to support democratization, concluding that it should mobilize public opinion in favor of free and fair elections.

Despite the private sector's current support for democracy, Bartell and Payne (1995) note that such backing among business elites remains fragile. Both their strengths and weaknesses contribute to authoritarian temptation. If their associations are conflict ridden, or if they lack entrepreneurial ability and are economically weak, they might feel overly threatened by mass politics, especially where subordinate social groups are better organized politically. If the opposite holds true, business elites may use their privileged structural position in the economy and their organizational strength to limit the consolidation and deepening of democracy.

This last point was an issue of some concern to Rueschemeyer, Stephens, and Stephens (1992, 222-225) and Silva (1996). Indeed, a number of analysts have noted the tendency toward "democracy with adjectives" (Collier and Levitsky 1997). Many Latin American democracies either have authoritarian enclaves or unbalanced executive-legislative relations that concentrate power in the executive, shutting off civil society's access to technocrats and other government decisionmakers.[19]

The chapters in this volume attest to the unabashed public support of organized business for such limited or protected democracies in Chile and Peru. In El Salvador, Nicaragua, and the Dominican Republic, institutional constraints on "populists" and politicians with redistributive ideals are missing. But close relationships between organized business and well-developed, dominant, or governing conservative political parties offer them reassurance that their fundamental interests are safe from harm. The connection to conservative political parties also helps to tranquilize business elites in circumstances where they do not enjoy a significant role in policy formulation, situations where they are usually relegated to lobbying government during the policy-implementation stage. Despite business's lack of access, policy tends to be probusiness. If the economy is improving, at worst, sectoral conflict between associations occurs but not a general questioning of the political regime.

What about the regime loyalties of business elites in situations where strong conservative political parties are absent? This is a condition that Ruschemeyer, Stephens, and Stephens (1992, 222-225) have identified as unstable bases of business support for democracy. This, for example, was the case in Peru before the military government of 1968 and has been the perennial problem of Argentine upper classes (Durand 1994; Acuña in this volume). Under these circumstances, a good collaborative relationship in the policy process — together with political weakness of the forces that had once presented a threat from below — can also help to solidify support for democracy, as long as labor is relatively excluded or underrepresented, as is the case in Argentina.

In sum, for the moment, it seems that business elites have little to fear from democracy. The catalysts for antidemocratic mobilization by organized business are in abeyance. In some cases, democracies have formal institutional constraints on political forces that once constituted a threat from below. In others, conservative political parties or neopopulist leaders such as Menem and Fujimori dominate the political system and offer adequate protection for the key interests of business; even if economic policies and access to policymaking are not ideal in these cases, they only contribute to intrabusiness conflict, not to a turn against democracy. Where neither institutional constraints or conservative political parties exist to comfort business fears, weak political opponents and governing parties committed to market-oriented policies can assuage insecurities. The situation can be improved upon with greater participation in the policy process by business, preferably organized business.

This picture, and the discourse of organized business in general, corroborates concern by a number of analysts that support for democracy by socioeconomic elites is tentative. It seems contingent upon the presence of "democracy with adjectives," with its myriad obstructions to deepening democracy and the extension of democracy's egalitarian ideals. In the past, advancing on those fronts involved pressure for greater inclusion in the political system by middle classes, labor, peasants, and shantytown dwellers. In the future, they will have to act again. This does not have to be threatening to business elites; there is no reason why many issues cannot be part of the normal give-and-take of democratic politics, as long as extremes and polarization can be avoided and as long as business elites are included in the policy process and compromises can be reached.

Democracy, State Corporatism, Societal Corporatism, and Pluralism

Now that most Latin American countries have democratic political systems, the literature has focused on the conditions for democratic consolidation and governance. Consolidation usually involves overcoming the authoritarian enclaves of current democracies, limiting the executive branch's power, and improving the quality of societal participation in policymaking (Mainwaring 1995). Governance addresses improvements in the efficacy and efficiency of political institutions to craft and implement policy and the establishment of the rule of law (Linz 1978; Lowenthal and Domínguez 1996).

Societal corporatism or neocorporatism has long attracted scholars as an institutional vehicle for democratic consolidation and governance. Corporatism refers to a system of interest intermediation in which the government recognizes the associations of the functional groups of society as the legitimate representatives of social groups in the policy-making process (Schmitter 1974). In practice, corporatism involves negotiation and tripartite bargaining among state agencies, organized business, and organized labor, also referred to as *concertación*. Policies that affect general interests bring together ministers (or the presidency) and the encompassing organizations of business and labor or, in their absence, the relevant sectoral peak associations of business and industrywide unions. Because all of the most important affected interests are present, tripartite bargaining is expected to improve policy consensus and, therefore, policy implementation.

Although others have recognized the difference (Schmitter 1974; Stepan 1978), Peter J. Katzenstein (1985) coined the distinction between state and societal corporatism. In state corporatism, the government officially charters and frequently organizes the representative associations of social groups, as occurred in Brazil and Mexico and to a lesser extent in Argentina. Under these circumstances, social organizations usually become instruments of government control. This is particularly true in the case of labor but may apply more subtly to business interests as well. Because of this feature, analysts do not look to state corporatism as a tool for democratic consolidation and governance. Nevertheless, the evidence suggests that a state corporatist political system's degree of centralization has an effect on the formation of encompassing business associations. Highly centralized ones such as Mexico's encourage them because business groups need centralization to protect their interests. More decentralized political systems such as Brazil's have the opposite effect.

In contrast, many analysts have a normative preference for societal corporatism as an instrument for consolidating democracy and improving democratic governance. In this system of interest intermediation, the state recognizes specific organizations as the legitimate representatives of well-defined social groups, principally labor and the private sector, but it does not license, charter, or directly organize them or become involved in their internal governance. Instead, social organizations evolve according to their independent interactions. That dynamic determines the levels of aggregation of organized interests and their hierarchy, meaning which ones dominate. State actors then simply deal with them.

The normative preference for this system of interest intermediation stems from two closely related sources. First, the absence of state control of organized interests strengthens a crucial feature of democracy: a vibrant civil society. Second, the institutionalized tripartite negotiating system of societal corporatism provides a meaningful channel for the participation of civil society in public policy. Tripartite bargaining, in turn, enhances consensus building among class-based groups and the state, thus decreasing the likelihood of politically and economically debilitating polarization and increasing the chances for effective policy implementation. Streeck and Schmitter (1985) extended the idea even more. Because of the representative legitimacy of the organizations involved, private interest governance could alleviate much of the pressure on public policymaking, reduce tension between the private and the public sectors, and improve policy implementation. A strongly organized, vibrant civil society could regulate itself and monitor compliance with policy without the need for government intervention in many instances.

The interest in societal corporatism notwithstanding, we agree with Haggard and Kaufman's (1995) conclusions that, with a few partial exceptions (Chile, for example), the conditions for it are not ripe in Latin America. By extension, private-interest governance is even more of a dream. One might argue that the trend toward encompassingness in the private sector is an encouraging institutional development on the road to societal corporatism, but societal corporatism is predicated on strong, centralized organized labor as well. That institutional requirement is woefully underdeveloped and likely to remain so for a long time. Moreover, societal corporatism requires greater degrees of institutionalization of state-society relations. With the partial exception of Chile, this is not the pattern in the cases examined in this volume. Finally, even if we limited the concept to business-state relations, in the hope of including a stronger organized labor movement in the future, again only Chile seems a likely case for success at the moment. In other countries, either state corporatism (Mexico) still prevails, the encompassing associations are too weak (Dominican Republic, El Salvador), or governments are simply not interested (the cases already mentioned and Peru).[20]

The fate of *concertación* attempts among the state, the private sector, and labor over free market economic reforms in a number of cases, such as Mexico, Argentina, Brazil, and Peru, bears out these observations. In the mid-1980s, Dos Santos (1987) and others believed *concertación* might develop into societal corporatism, or something very much like it. But, in the end, *concertación* proved to be a short-lived, ad hoc arrangement. Once the economic policy pact had been approved, further negotiation (much less institutionalized bargaining mechanisms) was not forthcoming. In addition to this shortcoming, labor was placed in a thoroughly subordinate role to business interests. Perhaps Latin America, taking its cue from the United States, will follow a more pluralist rather than societal corporatist system of interest intermediation. Such seems to be the case already; competing organized interests are busy lobbying state actors and congressional leaders directly.

Organized business probably finds this arrangement to its advantage. Bartell and Payne (1995), Silva (1996), and the evidence from many of the chapters in this volume suggest that business elites have struggled for inclusion in the policy-making process, particularly within the state. Having achieved that goal and policies more conducive to a good business climate, they are reluctant, not to say opposed, to accept the participation of organized labor (whether urban or rural). After all, the demands of those groups are the very ones business and landowning groups have opposed since the 1920s. In short, business leaders prefer an exclusive relationship of close collaboration with the government. A pluralist rather than societal corporatist form of interest representation offers a better chance of providing that.

A more pluralist rather than societal corporatist system of interest intermediation also suits most political leaders. Many of Latin America's new democracies are characterized by strong centralization of authority, high insulation of policymakers, and wide discretionary powers of the executive branch. Political leaders have used their powers to push free market economic reform (Smith and Acuña 1994; Gamarra 1994; Conaghan and Malloy 1994). But, as a number of analysts have pointed out, they must also craft support coalitions (Haggard and Kaufman 1995; Nelson 1994b; Pastor and Wise 1996). Thus, slightly modifying the arguments of Smith and Acuña (1994), strong presidencies together with more pluralist systems of interest intermediation give political leaders a freer hand in the choice of allies than societal corporatism. The combination also facilitates the fragmentation and disruption of the opposition more than societal corporatism.

CONCLUSIONS

L atin American business elites (with notable delays in some instances) are shedding their historical image as a defensive, economically feeble, weakly organized, politically submissive or accommodating, and antidemocratic class. In many cases, they now appear to be more dynamic, entrepreneurial, forward-looking, and proactive in public policy debates. Moreover, Latin American businesspeople in many countries began to support the very things they had so vehemently rejected in the past: market reform and political democracy.

Several factors influenced these changes. More proactive policy stances were partially the result of the fact that decisionmakers had a stronger incentive to pay attention to their policy preferences because free market economic reforms made Latin American entrepreneurs more responsible for the public functions of investment and employment. The defeat of the left and the weakening of labor organizations further strengthened the hand of businesspeople. Highly visible and forceful proactive intervention in policy debates had another source as well. In several cases, the emergence and consolidation of encompassing associations forged a new generation of leaders capable of addressing a wide range of economic and political issues. More broadly, business leaders have begun to grapple with ideological issues by participating in the "battle of ideas." These conditions, especially the structural power of capital and the weakness of the left, affected business support for democracy. They gave business leaders privileged (and near exclusive) access to the policy-making process, a key demand of theirs, which significantly raised the instrumental value of polyarchy for business elites. By the same token, greater entrepreneurialism and support for free market reforms were influenced by an internal restructuring of the private sector. The crisis of ISI weakened business groups, traditionally dependent on state subsidies and protectionism, and strengthened the more internationally competitive business groups, whose members were traditional and nontraditional exporters and diversified conglomerates.

In the context of these general trends, how the twin processes of economic and political change affected the propensity of business elites to act collectively through employer associations, the use they have made of those organizations in the economic policy-making process, and the implications of those actions for the consolidation of democracy are the main subjects of this book. We focus on Latin American business associations because organized interests are a key indicator of the vibrancy of civil society, and a vibrant civil society is a necessary condition for a healthy democracy — both for the policy-making process and for its resilience and stability. Business associations are the public expression of private sector partici-pation in policy debates. As such, they are the primary vehicle for negotiating economic and social policy — as well as constitutional issues — with other social actors and the state.

We have a particular interest in analyzing the proliferation of the highest expression of business's organizational development: the encompassing business association. According to theory, the consensus building characteristics of this organizational form bestow it with greater potential to contribute to positive, proactive participation in the policy-making process than sectoral organizations. Because they are the highest expression of business unity, they are also necessary building blocks for the eventual establishment of societal corporatism, or, in its absence, of negotiating binding and, perhaps, enduring issue-specific pacts with government and labor. Given these characteristics, this introductory chapter evalu-ated the extent to which Latin American encompassing business associations lived up to their theoretical promise for economic policymaking and democratization. Comparison with cases in which encompassing business associations were lacking or very weak strengthened the robustness of our conclusions.

The recent proliferation of encompassing business associations also led us to inquire into the causes of their formation and consolidation or the lack thereof. We concluded, along with extant literature, that a general threat to the private sector was a powerful catalyst. Our contribution, we hope, lies in a more careful specification of what constitutes such threats. We noted that — as had occurred in Europe earlier — the centralization of government and labor movements was a powerful cause for the rise of encompassing business associations in the latter half of this century. This was especially true in countries where more centralized governments supported the demands of organized labor (or of the "popular" sectors). These findings were an important addition to earlier arguments about the nature of threat from below to the Latin American private sector's interests: that it stemmed from arbitrary and frequent policy change by authoritarian governments that excluded business elites from policymaking. In the absence of such severe threats, encompassing business associations either did not emerge or dissolved.

Significantly, state corporatism was not a cause of either the formation of encompassing business associations or of their absence. The centralization of government and the severity of the threat were. Thus, Mexico, with a highly centralized political system and a strong threat to the general interests of the private sector in the 1970s, generated an encompassing business association. Brazil, in contrast, has a much more decentralized form of government and, as we argue, presented a much lower threat to business. Of course, we fully recognize that state corporatism had significant consequences for the organizational form, strategies, and tactics of the Mexican encompassing business association. It has also affected the operation of Brazil's sectoral and regional business associations, which, in the absence of a severe threat, proved sufficient to discourage the formation of an encompassing association.

Since encompassing business associations originated in reaction to severe threats, their waning imperiled the private sector's organizational unity, as is the case with all social movements. What, then, allowed some encompassing organizations to consolidate when the threat declined while others weakened or dissolved? We found that differences in internal organization explained these outcomes. Encompassing associations whose membership consisted mainly of sectoral associations and that represented mostly large-scale firms were more likely to consolidate. Small executive committees with mechanisms for dispute resolution (for example, only addressing issues that affected the general interests of the private sector) also predominated in those cases. In contrast, encompassing associations that included small and medium-scale business sectors, regional or subsectoral organizations, individual firms as members, and that had large executive committees and admitted more particularistic concerns on their agendas weakened when the external threat waned.

A second set of questions focused on organized business's participation in the policy process — whether it was more proactive than in the past, the stages in which it participates, and the effects of encompassingness on private sector support for free market economic reforms. The evidence strongly suggests that important changes have taken place with respect to the past. First, organized business, in general, has become more proactive. In a number of countries, encompassing organizations and sectoral organizations have professionalized their operations and developed greater capacities for basing policy proposals on technical studies. Second, organized business has extended its historical participation in the policy process from the implementation stage to demand raising, agenda setting, evaluation, and even (in a few cases) to the formulation stage of the policy process. Third, more often than not, consolidated encompassing business associations supported free market economic reforms.[21] Where consolidation was weak, debates over economic reforms exacerbated internal conflicts and debilitated or destroyed the encompassing association. The more extensive, professionalized participation of organized business in the policy process and the policy posture of consolidated encompassing business associations imply that — as expressions of business unity — they are important members of support coalitions for neoliberal economic adjustment.

What of business elites and democracy? Our conclusions mirror the ambivalence of other volumes (Bartell and Payne 1995; Conaghan and Malloy 1994). On the positive side, disenchantment with authoritarian rule due to exclusion from the policy process and economic crisis, the decline of the left, and greater dependence of government on the private sector for investment and economic growth have contributed to a greater valuation of democracy by business leaders. Democratic governments are more inclined to address their demands and include them in the policy process, and they have little to fear from traditional political threats. With respect to democratic processes, organized business acts as a more transparent and legitimating transmission belt of the private sector's interests than clientelistic and particularistic linkages between business elites and the state.[22] Encompassing business associations add value to these functions by stimulating debates over regime preferences among a wide spectrum of business groups in times of crisis. They also contribute to democratic stability by negotiating binding pacts with government and organized labor during unsettled times.

Yet, the allegiance of Latin American business elites to democracy is contingent on issues that raise questions for the consolidation of democracy. For the most part, democratization produced tutelary or protected democracies in which participation in the policy-making process, such as it is, is mostly reserved for business leaders.[23] These political systems and their fragmented systems of state-society intermediation are functional for designing and implementing economic restructuring and for the maintenance of good business climates — which are also thought to be crucial conditions for political stability.[24] Thus, part of the challenge of extending and consolidating democracy lies in reforming authoritarian enclaves and in perfecting systems of intermediation between state and society in ways that do not threaten political order. Business leaders and their allies in conservative political parties, however, are reluctant to support such changes. They seek to protect their privileged and exclusive access to the policy-making process.[25] Combined with the current weakness of organized labor, this means that (the proliferation of encompassing business associations notwithstanding) the establishment of European-style societal corporatism remains a distant goal.[26]

In many ways, today's challenge is similar to that of earlier periods in this century: How to structure democratic institutions and broad societal participation in policymaking in ways that moderate the perception of threat to business elites.[27] Such a formula would be beneficial for democratic consolidation, political stability, and economic growth. A small step in the right direction might be for business elites to recognize the legitimacy of the claims of social groups other than capital — many are compatible with market economies. By the same token, business leaders might feel more at ease if those social actors acknowledged business associations' right to exist and to act politically. Perhaps the demise of revolutionary socialism will help.[28]

Table 1.
Encompassing Business Associations in Latin America

Country	Association	Year Formed
Argentina	Asociación del Trabajo (active until 1940s)	1918
	Confederación Económica Argentina, CGE (dissolved in '55, reactivated in '58, dissolved in '76, reactivated in '83)	1952
Bolivia	Confederación de Empresarios Privados de Bolivia	1962
Brazil	União Brasileira de Empresarios, UBE (active 3 years)	1986
Chile	Confederación de la Producción y el Comercio, CPC	1935
Colombia	Consejo Gremial Nacional	1992
Costa Rica	Unión Costaricense de Cámaras y Asociaciones de la Empresa Privada	1973
Dominican Republic	Confederación Patronal de la R. Dominicana, CPRD	1946
	Consejo Nacional de Hombres de Empresa, CNHE	1978
Ecuador	Consejo de Cámaras y Asociaciones de la Producción	1980
El Salvador	Asociación Nacional de la Empresa Privada, ANEP	1966
Guatemala	Comité de Asociaciones Agrícolas, Comerciales, Industriales y Financieras, CACIF	1957
Honduras	Consejo Hondureño de la Empresa Privada	1967
Jamaica	The Jamaica Employers Confederation	1958
Mexico	Consejo Coordinador Empresarial, CCE	1976
Nicaragua	Consejo Superior de la Empresa Privada, COSEP	1972
Panama	Consejo Nacional de la Empresa Privada, CONEP	1964
Paraguay	Federación de la Producción, la Industria y el Comercio, FEPRINCO	1951
Peru	Unión de Empresarios Privados del Perú, UEPP (dissolved in 1988)	1977
	Confederación de Empresarios Privados, CONFIEP	1984
Uruguay	Consejo Superior Empresarial, COSUPEM	1978
Venezuela	Federación Venezolana de Cámaras y Asociaciones de Comercio y Producción, FEDECAMARAS.	1944

Source: International Organization of Employers.

Notes

1. Several scholars from different schools of thought regard economic elites as economically weak, ideologically traditional, and politically undecided. For a discussion of modernization theory and industrialists, see Lipset and Solari (1967) and Wils (1969). The best source on landowners and the dilemmas of modernization is Graciarena (1967). For a Marxist perspective, see Frank (1969), Prieto (1983), and Cardoso (1971).

2. Sectoral competition was so intense that some scholars developed a theory of sectoral clashes to explain the behavior of Latin American business elites (Mamalakis 1969).

3. For a theoretical treatment of these distinctions, see Haggard, Maxfield, and Schneider (1997).

4. For a thorough treatment of democratic theory, see Held (1987).

5. The only exceptions are the Dominican Republic and Jamaica. In the former, the Confederación Patronal de la República Dominicana functions as an employer's association while a second encompassing organization represents economic interests. By contrast, Jamaica has only one encompassing association — the Jamaica Employers Confederation — but it is exclusively an employers association.

6. For Venezuela, see Martz and Myers (1977); Salgado (1987); and Thorp and Durand (1997). For Colombia, see Thorp (1991); and Thorp and Durand (1997).

7. In public policy debates, such unity can be measured in two ways: through accounts of internal disputes among the member organizations and through the correspondence of the public positions of the member organizations with those of the encompassing association.

8. Historically, in the early era of local markets, business organizations tended to form on a local or, at most, on a regional scale. As economies became national in scale, so did business associations through either mergers of local and regional organizations or directly (Windmuller and Gladstone 1984, 3). This stage was followed by the creation of encompassing business associations for representational and political purposes some 20 years after the establishment of national organizations (most commonly in the 1920s) (Windmuller and Gladstone 1984, 3; Berger 1981, 14-16; Coleman and Grant 1988). In short, business elites channeled their collective action through encompassing organizations for political reasons: when "the power to invest [was] no longer sufficient for [businesspeople] to realize their economic interests" (Martinelli 1994, 497). Consequently, the formation of encompassing business associations, together with how active they were, also was an indicator of the politicization of business elites.

9. In some cases, they were forced to deal with strong fascist governments that incorporated business as one of the "functional sectors" of corporatist political systems, as occurred in Spain, Italy, and Germany, and in France's Vichy government (Brady 1943; Sarti 1971; Guerin 1973).

10. Peru's CONFIEP (Confederación de Instituciones Empresariales Privadas — Peruvian Confederation of Business Institutions) adopted a popular aphorism that captures this strategy: "Lighting a candle too close to a Saint will burn him; but set it down too far away and the Saint will not be illuminated."

11. It is true that Argentine businesspeople faced the Montoneros, an urban guerrilla group adept at bank robbery and kidnapping; however, they never amounted to a severe political threat to collective interest, especially to property rights and market share.

12. For an early study of Brazil, see Schmitter (1971).

13. For a history of Argentina, see Smith (1989).

14. For a brief political history of the Dominican Republic, see Knippers Black (1993).

15. The possibility cannot be discounted that researchers may have overemphasized the point. Large-scale businesspeople have many private, closed-door contacts, meetings, and communications with policymakers, many of them intense. Thus, their role in the policy process may not be transparent to outside observers.

16. Schneider and Maxfield (1997) have amended Olson's formulation slightly. They argue that the professionalization of sectoral peak associations can have the same beneficial effects as encompassing organizations at lower organizational levels.

17. Schneider (1997-1998) elaborates these and other themes as well.

18. Silva (1996) argues that the directors and upper-level managers of key Chilean conglomerates knew their interests very well — both for and against radical economic restructuring. Moreover, those in favor participated directly in the policy-formulation process.

19. Many studies have commented on these conditions. See Conaghan and Malloy (1994); Smith and Acuña (1994); O'Donnell (1994); Loveman (1994); Nelson (1994b); Collier and Levitsky (1997); and Lowenthal and Domínguez (1996).

20. There is an additional danger in such a path. Once institutionalized systems of collaboration between the state and organized business are formed, odds are they will be difficult to change. Strong resistance from well-entrenched forces is to be expected.

21. In all of these cases, the encompassing business organization provided an institutional instrument for generating consensus, or basic agreement, over the direction of economic change and investment and the best means for generating an acceptable business climate for all of them. Under the umbrella provided by the encompassing organization, the leadership of the sectoral peak associations discussed such wide-ranging issues as fear of state interventionism, acceptance of a changing and irreversible balance of forces in favor of neoliberalism, and how to take advantage of a weakened labor opposition and a shrinking entrepreneurial state. In some cases, such as Chile, Mexico, and El Salvador, the leadership of the dominant sectors, or firms, may discipline members who defect from the established policy line.

22. On this point, also see Schneider and Maxfield (1997, 8-9).

23. For tutelary democracies in Latin America, see Loveman (1994).

24. For the concept of fragmented democracy and dual democracy, see Smith and Acuña (1994).

25. For similar points, see Bartell and Payne (1995).

26. Haggard and Kaufman (1995, 340-345) have also noted the problem with organized labor and its significance for constructing societal corporatism. Nelson (1994b) concurs, yet believes that intermediate stages, which she calls ad hoc bargaining and negotiation, are symbolic way stations.

27. Anderson (1967) had already remarked on the problem of the inclusion of new social groups in the political arena and the difficulties that that created for political order.

28. Nelson (1994b) has advanced similar arguments.

References

Anderson, Charles W. 1967. *Politics and Economic Change in Latin America: The Governing of Restless Nations*. New York: D. van Nostrand.

Baloyra-Herp Enrique A. 1995. "Elections, Civil War, and Transition in El Salvador, 1982-1994." In *Elections and Democracy in Central America, Revisited*, eds. Mitchell A. Seligson and John Booth. Durham, N.C.: University of North Carolina Press.

Bartell, Ernest, c.s.c., and Leigh A. Payne, eds. 1995. *Business and Democracy in Latin America*. Pittsburgh: University of Pittsburgh Press.

Bates, Robert H., and Anne O. Krueger. 1993. "Generalizations Arising from the Country Studies." In *Political and Economic Interactions in Economic Policy Reform: Evidence from Eight Countries*, eds. Robert H. Bates and Anne O. Krueger. Oxford: Blackwell.

Berger, Suzanne, ed. 1981. *Organizing Interests in Western Europe*. Cambridge: Cambridge University Press.

Booth, John A., and Thomas W. Walker. 1993. *Understanding Central America*. Boulder, Colo.: Westview Press.

Brady, Robert A. 1943. *Business as a System of Power*. Freeport: Books for Library Press.

Bravo Mena, Luis Felipe. 1987. "COPARMEX and Mexican Politics." In *The Government and Private Sector in Contemporary Mexico*, eds. Sylvia Maxfield and Ricardo Anzaldúa Montoya. San Diego: Center for U.S.-Mexico Studies.

Campero, Guillermo. *Los gremios empresariales en el período 1970-83: comportamiento sociopolítico y orientaciones ideológicas*. Santiago: Instituto Latinoamericano de Estudios Transnacionales.

Canak, William. 1984. "The Peripheral State Debate: State Capitalism and Bureaucratic-Authoritarianism in Latin America." *Latin American Research Review* 19 (1): 33-36.

Cardoso, Fernando Henrique. 1986. "Entrepreneurs and the Transition to Democracy in Brazil." In *Transitions from Authoritarian Rule: Comparative Perspectives*, eds. Guillermo O'Donnell, Philippe C. Schmitter, and Laurence Whitehead. Baltimore: The Johns Hopkins University Press.

Cardoso, Fernando Henrique. 1971. *Las ideologías de la burguesía industrial en sociedades dependientes: Argentina y Brasil*. Mexico: Siglo XXI.

Cardoso, Fernando Henrique, and Enzo Faletto. 1979. *Dependency and Development in Latin America*. Berkeley, Calif.: University of California Press.

Centro de Investigación Económica de América Latina-Fundación Adenauer. 1984. "El empresariado latinoamericano: algunos aspectos de su organización y pensamiento." Buenos Aires: CIEDLA.

Claudín, Fernando. 1975. *The Communist Movement: From Comintern to Cominform*. New York: Monthly Review Press.

Coleman, William, and Wyn Grant. 1988. "The Organizational Cohesion and Political Access of Business: A Study of Comprehensive Organizations." *European Journal of Political Research* 16 (5): 467-487.

Collier, David. 1979. *The New Authoritarianism in Latin America.* Princeton, N.J.: Princeton University Press.

Collier, David, and Steven Levitsky. 1997. "Democracy with Adjectives: Conceptual Innovation in Comparative Research." *World Politics* 49 (3): 430-451.

Conaghan, Catherine. 1988. *Restructuring Domination: Industrialists and the State in Ecuador.* Pittsburgh: University of Pittsburgh Press.

Conaghan, Catherine M., and Rosario Espinal. 1990. "Unlikely Transitions to Uncertain Regimes? Democracy without Compromise in the Dominican Republic and Ecuador." *Journal of Latin American Studies* 22 (3): 553-574.

Conaghan, Catherine M., and James M. Malloy. 1994. *Unsettling Statecraft: Democracy and Neoliberalism in the Central Andes.* Pittsburgh: Pittsburgh University Press.

Conaghan, Catherine M., James M. Malloy, and Luis A. Abuggatas. 1990. "Business and the 'Boys': The Politics of Neoliberalism in the Central Andes." *Latin American Research Review* 25 (2): 3-30.

Cook, María Lorena, Kevin J. Middlebrook, and Juan Molinar Horcasitas, eds. 1994. *The Politics of Economic Restructuring: State-Society Relations and Regime Change in Mexico.* San Diego: Center for U.S.-Mexico Studies.

de Soto, Hernando. 1989. *The Other Path.* New York: Harper and Row.

Dos Santos, Mario. 1987. *Concertación y democratización en América Latina.* Buenos Aires: Centro Latinoamericano de Ciencias Sociales.

Drake, Paul W., and Iván Jaksic, eds. 1995. *The Struggle for Democracy in Chile.* 2nd ed. Lincoln, Neb.: University of Nebraska Press.

Durand, Francisco. 1996. *Incertidumbre y soledad: reflexiones sobre los grandes empresarios de América Latina.* Lima: Fundación Ebert.

Durand, Francisco. 1994. *Business and Politics in Peru: The State and the National Bourgeoisie.* Boulder, Colo.: Westview Press.

Edwards, Sebastian, and Alejandra Cox-Edwards. 1987. *Monetarism and Liberalization: The Chilean Experiment.* Cambridge: Ballinger.

Eguizábal, Cristina. 1992. "Parties, Programs and Politics in El Salvador." In *Political Parties and Democracy in Central America,* eds. Louis W. Goodman, William M. LeoGrande, and Johanna Mendelson Forman. Boulder, Colo.: Westview Press.

Estrada, Francisco F., and Laura Masi. 1983. *El empresariado latinoamericano: algunos aspectos de su organización y pensamiento.* Buenos Aires: Centro Interdisciplinario sobre el Desarrollo Latinoamericano.

Evans, Peter. 1979. *Dependent Development: The Alliance of Multinational, State, and Local Capital in Brazil.* Princeton, N.J.: Princeton University Press.

Evans, Peter. 1992. "The State as Problem and Solution: Predation, Embedded Autonomy, and Structural Change." In *The Politics of Economic Adjustment,* eds. Stephan Haggard and Robert R. Kaufman. Princeton, N.J.: Princeton University Press.

Evans, Peter. 1995. *Embedded Autonomy.* Princeton, N.J.: Princeton University Press.

Foley, Michael W. 1996. "Laying the Groundwork: The Struggle for Civil Society in El Salvador." *Journal of Interamerican Studies and World Affairs* 38 (1): 67-104.

Frank, Andre G. 1969. *Lumpenbourgeoisie: Lumpen Development.* New York: Monthly Review Press.

Frieden, Jeffrey F. 1991. *Debt, Development, and Democracy: Modern Political Economy and Latin America, 1965-1985.* Princeton, N.J.: Princeton University Press.

Gamarra, Eduardo A. 1994. "Market-Oriented Economic Reforms and Democratization in Latin America: Challenges of the 1990s. In *Latin American Political Economy in the Age of Neoliberal Reform: Theoretical and Comparative Perspectives for the 1990s*, eds. William C. Smith, Carlos H. Acuña, and Eduardo A. Gamarra. Coral Gables, Fla.: North-South Center at the University of Miami.

Garrido, Celso, ed. 1988. *Empresarios y estado en América Latina*. Mexico: CIDE, Fundación Ebert, Instituto de Investigaciones Sociales de la UNAM, and Universidad Autónoma de Azcapotzalco.

Graciarena, Jorge. 1967. *Poder y clases sociales en el desarrollo latinoamericano*. Buenos Aires: Paidos.

Grindle, Merilee S., and John W. Thomas. 1991. *Public Choices and Policy Change: The Political Economy of Reform in Developing Countries*. Baltimore: The Johns Hopkins University Press.

Guerin, Daniel. 1973. *Fascism and Big Business*. New York: Monad Press.

Haggard, Stephan and Robert R. Kaufman. 1995. *The Political Economy of Democratic Transitions*. Princeton, N.J.: Princeton University Press.

Haggard, Stephan, Sylvia Maxfield, and Ben Ross Schneider. 1997. "Theories of Business and Business-State Relations." In *Business and the State in Developing Countries*, eds. Sylvia Maxfield and Ben Ross Schneider. Ithaca, N.Y.: Cornell University Press.

Handelman, Howard. 1997. *Mexican Politics: The Dynamics of Change*. New York: St. Martin's Press.

Harbron, John D. 1965. "The Dilemma of an Elite Group: The Industrialist in Latin America." In *Journal of Interamerican Studies and World Affairs* 19 (2): 43-62.

Held, David. 1987. *Models of Democracy*. Stanford, Calif.: Stanford University Press.

Higley, John, and Gunther Burton, eds. 1992. *Elites and Democratic Consolidation in Latin America and Southern Europe*. New York: Praeger.

Johnson, John J. 1958. *Political Change in Latin America: The Emergence of the Middle Sectors*. Stanford, Calif.: Stanford University Press.

Katzenstein, Peter J. 1984. *Corporatism and Change: Austria, Switzerland and the Politics of Industry*. Ithaca, N.Y.: Cornell University Press.

Katzenstein, Peter J. 1985. *Small States in World Markets: Industrial Policy in Europe*. Ithaca, N.Y.: Cornell University Press.

Knippers Black, Jan. 1993. "Democracy and Disillusionment in the Dominican Republic." In *Modern Caribbean Politics*, eds. Anthony Payne and Paul Sutton. Baltimore: The Johns Hopkins University Press.

Leff, Nathaniel. 1986. "Trust, Envy, and the Political Economy of Industrial Development: Economic Groups in Developing Countries." Cornell University-First Boston Working Paper Series, FB-86-38.

Levaggi, Virgilio. 1993. "The Role of Formal Business Organizations in Latin America." Paper presented to the Workshop on Market Reforms and Democracy in Latin America and the Caribbean, Center for International Private Enterprise, Washington, D.C., June.

Lindblom, Charles. 1977. *Politics and Markets*. New York: Basic Books.

Linz, Juan. 1978. *The Breakdown of Democratic Regimes: Crisis, Breakdown, and Reequilibration*. Baltimore: The John Hopkins University Press.

Lipset, Seymour Martin, and Aldo Solari, eds. 1967. *Elites in Latin America*. New York: Oxford University Press.

Loveman, Brian. 1994. *The Constitution of Tyranny: Regimes of Exception in Spanish America*. Pittsburgh: University of Pittsburgh Press.

Lowenthal, Abraham F., and Jorge I. Domínguez. 1996. "Introduction: Constructing Democratic Governance." In *Constructing Democratic Governance: South America in the 1990s*, eds. Jorge I. Domínguez and Abraham F. Lowenthal. Baltimore: The Johns Hopkins University Press.

Mainwaring, Scott. 1995. "Democracy in Brazil and the Southern Cone: Achievements and Problems." *Journal of Interamerican Studies and World Affairs* 37 (1): 113-179.

Mamalakis, Markos. 1969. "The Theory of Sectoral Clashes." *Latin American Research Review* 3 (Fall): 9-46.

Martinelli, Alberto. 1994. "Entrepreneurship and Management." In *The Handbook of Economic Sociology*, eds. Neil J. Smelser and Richard Swedberg. Princeton, N.J.: Princeton University Press.

Martz, John D., and David J. Myers, eds. 1977. *Venezuela: The Democratic Experience*. New York: Praeger.

Maxfield, Sylvia. 1990. *Governing Capital: International Finance and Mexican Politics*. Ithaca, N.Y.: Cornell University Press.

Maxfield, Sylvia, and Ricardo Anzaldúa, eds. 1987. *Government and Private Sector in Contemporary Mexico*. San Diego: Center for U.S.-Mexico Studies.

Maxfield, Sylvia, and Ben Ross Schneider, eds. 1997. *Business and the State in Developing Countries*. Ithaca, N.Y.: Cornell University Press.

Moore, Barrington, Jr. 1966. *The Social Origins of Dictatorship and Democracy: Lord and Peasant in the Making of the Modern World*. Boston: Beacon.

Nelson, Joan M. 1994a. "Overview: How Market Reforms and Democratic Consolidation Affect Each Other." In *Intricate Links: Democratization and Market Reforms in Latin America and Eastern Europe*, ed. Joan M. Nelson. New Brunswick, N.J.: Transaction Publishers.

Nelson, Joan M. 1994b. "Labor and Business Roles in Dual Transitions: Building Blocks or Stumbling Blocks?" In *Intricate Links: Democratization and Market Reforms in Latin America and Eastern Europe*, ed. Joan M. Nelson. New Brunswick, N.J.: Transaction Publishers.

O'Donnell, Guillermo. 1973. *Modernization and Bureaucratic-Authoritarianism: Studies in South American Politics*. Berkeley, Calif.: Institute of International Studies, University of California, Berkeley.

O'Donnell, Guillermo. 1994. "Delegative Democracy." *Journal of Democracy* 5 (1): 55-69.

Offe, Claus, and Helmut Wiesenthal. 1980. "The Two Logics of Collective Action. *Political Power and Social Theory* 1 (1): 67-115.

Olson, Mancur. 1982. *The Rise and Decline of Nations*. New Haven, Conn.: Yale University Press.

Pastor, Manuel, Jr., and Carol Wise. 1996. *The Politics of Free Trade in the Western Hemisphere*. North-South Agenda Paper 20 (August): 1-21.

Payne, Leigh A. 1994. *Brazilian Industrialists and Democratic Change*. Baltimore: The Johns Hopkins University Press.

Prieto, Alberto. 1983. *La burguesía latinoamericana contemporánea*. Havana: Casa de las Américas.

Przeworski, Adam, and Michael Wallerstein. 1988. "Structural Dependence of the State on Capital." *American Political Science Review* 82 (1): 11-29.

Rueschemeyer, Dietrich, Evelyne Huber Stephens, and John D. Stephens. 1992. *Capitalist Development and Democracy*. Chicago: University of Chicago Press.

Salgado, René. 1987. "Economic Pressure Groups and Policy Making in Venezuela: The Case of FEDECAMARAS Reconsidered." *Latin American Research Review* 22 (3): 91-105.

Sarti, Roland. 1971. *Fascism and the Industrial Leadership in Italy, 1919-1940*. Berkeley, Calif.: University of California Press.

Schattschneider, E.E. 1956. *The Semi Sovereign People*. New York: Holt, Rinehart and Winston.

Schmitter, Philippe C. 1971. *Interest Conflict and Political Change in Brazil*. Stanford, Calif.: Stanford University Press.

Schmitter, Philippe C. 1974. "Still the Century of Corporatism?" *The Review of Politics* 36 (1): 85-121.

Schmitter Philippe C., and Wolfgang Streeck. 1981. "The Organization of Business Interests: A Research Design to Study the Associative Action of Business in the Advanced Industrial Societies of Western Europe." Discussion paper IIM/LMP 81-13. Berlin: Wissenschaftzentrum.

Schneider, Ben Ross. 1997-1998. "Organized Business Politics in Democratic Brazil." *Journal of Interamerican Studies and World Affairs* 39 (4): 95-127.

Schneider, Ben Ross, and Sylvia Maxfield. 1997. "Business, the State, and Economic Performance in Developing Countries." In *Business and the State in Developing Countries*, eds. Sylvia Maxfield and Ben Ross Schneider. Ithaca, N.Y.: Cornell University Press.

Sidicaro, Ricardo. 1994. "Consideraciones sociológicas sobre la relación empresarios-estado en América Latina." In *Los empresarios ante la globalización*, ed. Ricardo Tirado. Mexico: UNAM and Instituto de Investigaciones Sociales.

Silva, Eduardo. 1996. "From Dictatorship to Democracy: The Business-State Nexus in Chile's Economic Transformation, 1975-1994." *Comparative Politics* 28 (3): 299-317.

Smith, William C. 1989. *Authoritarianism and the Crisis of the Argentine Political Economy*. Stanford, Calif.: Stanford University Press.

Smith, William C., and Carlos H. Acuña. 1994. "The Political Economy of Structural Adjustment: The Logic of Support and Opposition to Neoliberal Reform." In *Latin American Political Economy in the Age of Neoliberal Reform*, eds. William C. Smith, Carlos H. Acuña, and Eduardo Gamarra. Coral Gables, Fla.: North-South Center at the University of Miami.

Spalding, Rose J. 1994. *Capitalists and Revolution in Nicaragua: Opposition and Accommodation, 1979-1993*. Chapel Hill, N.C.: University of North Carolina Press.

Stepan, Alfred. 1978. *The State and Society: Peru in Comparative Perspective*. Princeton, N.J.: Princeton University Press.

Stolovich, Luis. 1994. *El poder económico en el MERCOSUR*. Montevideo: Centro Uruguay Independiente.

Story, Dale. 1978. "Industrialization and Political Change: The Political Role of Industrial Entrepreneurs in Five Latin American Countries." Ph.D. Dissertation, Indiana University.

Strassman, Paul W. 1964. "The Industrialist." In *Continuity and Change in Latin America*, ed. John J. Johnson. Stanford, Calif.: Stanford University Press.

Streeck, Wolfgang, and Philippe C. Schmitter, eds. 1985. *Private Interest Government: Beyond Market and State*. Beverly Hills, Calif.: Sage.

Tarrow, Sydney. 1994. *Power in Movement: Social Movements, Collective Action, and Politics*. Cambridge: Cambridge University Press.

Thorp, Rosemary. 1991. *Economic Management and Economic Development in Peru and Colombia*. Pittsburgh: University of Pittsburgh Press.

Thorp, Rosemary, and Francisco Durand. 1997. "A Historical View of Business-State Relations: Colombia, Peru, and Venezuela Compared." In *Business and the State in Developing Countries*, eds. Sylvia Maxfield and Francisco Durand. Ithaca, N.Y.: Cornell University Press.

Useem, Michael. 1984. *The Inner Circle: Large Corporations and the Rise of Business Political Activity in the U.S. and the U.K.* New York: Oxford University Press.

Windmuller, John P., and Alan Gladstone. 1984. *Employers Associations and Industrial Relations: A Comparative Study*. Cambridge, U.K.: Clarendon Press-Oxford.

Wils, Fritz. 1969. *Industrialists, Industrialization and the Nation-State in Peru*. Berkeley, Calif.: Institute of International Studies.

Véliz, Claudio. 1963. "La mesa de tres patas." *Desarrollo Económico* 3 (1-2): 241-247.

CHAPTER TWO

Political Struggle and Business Peak Associations: Theoretical Reflections on the Argentine Case

CARLOS H. ACUÑA

BUSINESS AND POLITICS: THEORETICAL COMMENTS

How are business associations organized? Why are business peak associations (BPAs) politically relevant? What do business peak associations tell us about the organization and importance of the bourgeoisie as a political actor? These are some of the enduring questions about organized business and politics addressed in this chapter.[1]

With respect to the first question, business associations have been classified into four types, depending on their "degree" of organization, as defined by the scope of sectors covered and inclusiveness of representation across firm type and region. Fourth-degree associations organize and represent the interests of all economic sectors (for example, agriculture, industry, commerce, banking, and others). Third-degree associations encompass only one such sector (for example, industry). First- and second-degree associations organize entrepreneurs by subsector, region, product type, and so on. Throughout the chain, lower degree associations provide the pool of members for higher degree associations.

The organizational patterns of business also depend on whether the associations emphasize their role as employers or as producers. An emphasis on "employer" functions often occurs when businesses are faced with organized and militant workers, active labor ministries, and courts or when wage levels and working conditions are determined by collective bargaining. Business organizations tend to stress the "producer" role when they are enmeshed in well-developed neocorporatist mechanisms of state-society relationships; these dictate the rules of action and the requirements necessary for becoming a "legitimate" participant in the policy-making process. Emphasis on the producer role also depends on tension between business groups with conflicting interests.

The types of struggles capitalists confront are also determinants of their organizational behavior. First, when businesspeople are involved in conflicts over specific narrow issues, such as the level of a particular benefit, they usually pursue their objectives within the existing legal and institutional structures. For example, they may seek to regulate competition or impose wage reductions. Second, in more severe conflicts, businesspeople may conclude that existing rules and regulations preclude the attainment of their goals. Under such circumstances, they will seek to change those rules by lobbying for reform of decrees and legislation, for instance, on price controls or collective bargaining agreements. The third and highest level of conflict is characterized by a situation in which capitalists may conclude that their objectives are impossible to achieve because the underlying distribution of power in the regime does not allow them to change unfavorable situations through established institutions. This leads capitalists to become involved in political struggles, as they seek to alter some aspect of the political regime itself. Strategies aimed at modifying legislation related to political participation and the decision-making process are typical of this level (for example, constitutional reforms or regime changes). Because each level of conflict involves a specific set of actors and particular forms of political struggle and conflict resolution, the extension of a conflict from one level to another implies the development of different alliance patterns, a different distribution of power, and a different way of using power resources.[2] It follows that the process of engaging in one level or another of conflict heavily influences the organizational structure and strategies of entrepreneurial associations.

According to Philippe Schmitter and Wolfgang Streeck (1981, 49-50), the organizational structure of business associations results from the interaction of two contradictory logics: the "logic of membership" and the "logic of influence." The logic of membership dictates that business associations are structured to offer their members incentives sufficiently attractive to obtain the support and resources they need to survive, grow, and fulfill the function of defending common interests. This feature of the logic of membership contains a central source of tension between individual and collective interests. For, rather than aggregating individual interests, the key function of a business association is to redefine them and to keep individuals from acting upon them for the sake of common interests. In contrast, the logic of influence involves the process by which business associations organize to define common interests and develop strategies vis-à-vis external actors. The purpose of associations is to influence the behavior of state authorities, rival business organizations, and unions and to protect themselves from such actors. An association's organizational form is the result of these "internal" and "external" tensions.

In sum, businesses may organize into employer or producer associations and at different levels of aggregation (first, second, third or sectoral, and fourth or encompassing). Which of these organizational forms develops and the political uses it employs depend on two factors: the type of conflict entrepreneurs face and the way in which the organization solves the conflict between the logics of "membership" and "influence."

Encompassing Business Peak Associations: When Are They Necessary?

Encompassing business peak associations are fourth-degree organizations. As such, they represent, aggregate, and organize business interests across the entire economy. Accordingly, encompassing peak associations can be thought of as the political organization of the capitalist class. This is reinforced by the fact that the logic of its members, or the "we" that is the object of their discourse and strategies, becomes a common point of reference for capitalists from all economic sectors as they engage in the logic of influence against non-capitalist social and political actors.

A number of theorists, however, argue that business associations are not very relevant for the analysis of politics and economics. Implicitly or explicitly, they maintain that capitalist collective action and, therefore, business organizations are unnecessary. Because the state defends the collective interests of capital, these theorists say capitalists do not need to organize or act collectively, and business organizations are politically irrelevant. One approach arrives at this conclusion after examining why conflict among individual firms in the marketplace does not sooner or later lead to falling profit rates, monopolistic practices, diminishing productivity, and, in the end, the crisis of the system as a whole. Their answer is that in market economies, governments must take actions to correct these ills or suffer the adverse consequences of socioeconomic and political upheaval.

A second viewpoint holds that the state is a class instrument, which in capitalism is in the hands of the bourgeoisie (Marx and Engels 1971, 136-137). Thus, capitalists do not need to organize to defend their collective interests. Proponents of this view argue that most capitalists are too busy struggling daily in the marketplace to engage in collective political action. Nevertheless, some — the producers of ideology — do concern themselves with state administration and "colonize" it. From within the state or in close alliance with policymakers they take measures to protect the collective interests of the bourgeoisie and to ensure the economic system's stability.

A third variant recognizes that interests different from and even opposed to those of capitalists may have access to government and may thereby gain control of the state. But even so, power is still in the hands of the bourgeoisie because it controls investment (Poulantzas 1978; Block 1977 and 1981; Offe and Wiesenthal 1980). Interests that diverge from those of business may gain access to the state through elections and the programmatic platforms of political parties. Capitalists, however, have a veto power over such actors because they control investment. They "approve" or "disapprove" of government policy by investing or withholding investment, hiring or firing workers, buying or selling public bonds, exporting or importing, and the like. Thus, measures contradicting bourgeois interests will be vetoed by capitalists via disinvestment and the threat of ensuing economic and social crisis. As a result, no matter who controls the state or what the preferences of the majority may be, any government that gives priority to the stability of the democratic political system ultimately must create the conditions for sociopolitical peace. For this, the government necessarily depends on investments, and so the government must, in turn, implement policies acceptable to the bourgeoisie. Also, no matter which political party controls the government, capitalists do not need to organize or develop collective strategies to defend their common interests. Those who advocate this third argument conclude that, thanks to the private sector's control of investment, the state must, in the end, defend the interests of capital.

Although these theoretical traditions elucidate the economic power of capitalists, empirically, states in capitalist systems do not always cater to the interests of capitalists. Consequently, the private sector does have an incentive to engage in collective action in defense of its interests. Understanding the emergence and significance of encompassing business peak associations requires that the relationship between business and politics not be reduced to the structural power of capital. Only by avoiding such reductionism can we begin to uncover the conditions under which the state achieves substantial autonomy from the bourgeoisie. And only then is it possible to recognize that explanations for the development of encompassing peak associations can be found in the political-institutional realm, particularly with reference to 1) the presence or absence of neo-corporatist structures, 2) the threat posed by the state as a political actor, and 3) the menace of strong labor associations and/or of confronting sectors of the bourgeoisie.

Autonomy of the State from Business

When does business control over investment prove ineffective in vetoing public policy that is inimical to the private sector's perceived interests? First, economic conditions may nullify the threat of disinvestment. Recessions, for example, are already producing disinvestment. If the state introduces reflationary economic policies and labor policies not welcomed by the bourgeoisie, capitalists are likely to find that the conditions for effective opposition have decreased markedly because the sociopolitical costs of economic downturn have already occurred and are a matter of serious public concern (Skocpol 1980, 164-169).

Second, the extent of public investment and the state's role in the distribution of resources via industrial policy and other measures magnifies or attenuates the potential impact of disinvestment by capitalists. For example, states that are heavily dependent on the capitalist agricultural sector for foreign currency, such as Argentina, are in a relatively weak position when compared to states that control the production or extraction and marketing of their major exports. Thus, in disinvesting, the pampa (from the prairie farm area) bourgeoisie places the Argentine state under greater dependency to a particular domestic capitalist group than is the case in, say, Chile or Venezuela. The likelihood that the state may derive resources from a productive "enclave" (as in the case of the extraction and marketing during important historical periods of tin in Bolivia, copper in Chile, and oil in Venezuela and Ecuador) redefines the terms of the relative influence of the state and capital. In sum, the veto power of disinvestment will decrease when, as was the case in Chile during the 1960s, the state controls over 70 percent of gross investment.[3]

Third, political-institutional penalties against disinvestment or low investment rates may render such strategies too costly for capitalists. Anything from taxes on potential revenues to threats of controls and even expropriation may serve to dissuade capitalists from disinvesting by redefining the structure of costs and benefits, with an emphasis on the former. Conversely, by underscoring the benefit side of the equation, tax exonerations or subsidies boost investment. The adoption and implementation of such measures imply the existence of government institutions capable of assessing and controlling the microeconomic behavior of capitalists. Whether such capability and political will exist depends on national and international political conditions and state-bureaucratic reforms. This means that it is impossible to infer the feasibility and/or effectiveness of such devices from the purely structural conditions of capitalism.

Fourth, the degree and pattern of contradictions among capitalists also condition the impact of disinvestment strategies. State policies that are inimical to one sector of capital may not affect another. As a result, continued or accelerated investment in one sector may counteract or cancel out disinvestment in another. By nullifying the socioeconomic consequences proper to disinvestment, disgruntled business groups find themselves deprived of a powerful political instrument.

These factors show that the degree of control exercised by capitalists over state policies can vary greatly as a function of historical contingencies; therefore, it is not valid to assume that the bourgeoisie does not "need" to organize as a collective actor in order to achieve some of its common interests. Such observations, of course, do not negate the key role of entrepreneurial control over investment in processes of capitalist accumulation and the reproduction of social relations. Neither do they deny the political consequences of the privileged position that capitalists enjoy, thanks to their structural power.

Explaining the Emergence of Encompassing Business Peak Associations

A key determinant of a high degree of aggregation in organized business, particularly for the emergence of encompassing peak associations, is the presence of neo-corporatist arrangements for state decisionmaking. Neocorporatism is characterized by a high level of organization and aggregation of functional interests that are autonomous from the state (Schmitter 1974; Schmitter and Lembrugh 1979). From an organizational point of view, neocorporatism is distinct from other systems of interest representation. As in pluralist systems, individuals are free to form and structure associations according to their own designs. However, interest associations also take on corporatist characteristics, including concentration, centralization, and internal mediation of interests; state-acknowledged or awarded monopoly of representation; professionalization; and relative independence from the individual interests of the members of the association.

This political-organizational system developed primarily in Europe after World War II, where states actively participated in the generation and distribution of societal resources. In the policy process, these states — commonly called "welfare states" because they take on social responsibilities — integrate business and labor representatives into tripartite bargaining institutions. The incentive for business organization is clear: in addition to specific bargaining functions with labor and the state at the first-, second-, and third-degree association levels, fourth-degree associations now have the opportunity to represent business interests as a whole in the formulation of monetary policy, trade liberalization, labor relations, health and social security, and other policy areas.

A second historical factor that influences the emergence and organizational characteristics of encompassing business peak associations is the existence of strong states that effectively have threatened the interests of the bourgeoisie. By "strong," we mean states that have achieved a significant measure of autonomy from business interests and pressures. In such cases, if the political regime, whether authoritarian or democratic, curtails business participation in public decisionmaking, fourth-degree business associations take on many of the functions of a political party. This is especially likely in the absence of a political party capable of efficiently representing business interests in the political system; it is also likely in the absence of neo-corporatist institutional arrangements that would assure business participation in public policymaking despite electorally weak right-wing political parties.

The organizational structure of business associations that originated in response to threats by the state and to the exclusion of business from policy has much in common with the structure of social movements. Instead of focusing on organizational density and bureaucratic rationality, both emphasize identity, inclusion versus exclusion from the group, and mobilization against outsiders. In contrast, business associations under neocorporatism emphasize long-term goals to be achieved by coordination, interdependence, and mediation between individual and collective interests (Alberti, Goldberg, and Acuña 1984, 117).

In fact, the basic features of "movement-like" organizations are 1) hegemonic and concentrated leadership, 2) exclusionary authoritarian decision-making practices in which minorities have no participation in the decision-making process, and 3) the persistence of unresolved conflicts of interest. When the latter can no longer be ignored, the association usually splinters as a result of the inflexibility and rivalries among those in the leadership. As in every organization with a homogeneous dominant sector that ignores internal differences, mechanisms for the administration, negotiation, and redefinition of contradictory interests are almost nonexistent, and diversity appears as a threat to unity, which would explain the absence of minority participation.

Organizational structures of this type act as pressure groups and are generally not very efficient in bargaining, when, by definition, some interests must be sacrificed for others with higher priorities. In movement-like associations, organizational dynamics and unity largely depend on the leadership's ability to "show" members that "authoritarian" external actors set the conditions for the associations' failures and successes. For this reason, "selective benefits" play a secondary role in this type of business organization.[4]

Movement-like business associations provide one way of resolving the organizational dilemma generated by the contradictory pressures of the logic "of membership" and the logic "of influence." They offer an acceptable degree of efficiency — the maintenance of unity and some policy successes — in threatening environments. However, they are weak and inefficient once the threat declines. Unity, political strategies, and organizational structure are also affected by changes in the association's relationship to other actors and policy reforms.

A third factor that accounts for the historical emergence of encompassing business peak associations is the presence of strong, active labor organizations that escape the retaining walls of neo-corporatist systems of interest intermediation. Labor's radical demands threaten profit rates and/or private property rights. For example, encompassing business peak associations that emerged toward the turn of the century were mainly movement-like employers' associations that limited their demands for state intervention to the repression of labor organizations.

A fourth factor that influences the emergence and actions of encompassing business peak associations is threats from competing encompassing associations. As will be seen in the Argentine case, intrabusiness struggles can lead to significant political conflict between competing capitalist groups. In order to advance their interests, these business groups (which often stand in a relationship of domination and subordination to each other in the structure of production) organize alternative umbrella associations. The umbrella organizations may also clash over the definition of their relationship to the state and to labor.

BUSINESS AND POLITICS IN ARGENTINA

Political Causes for the Organizational Patterns and Behavior of Business Associations in Argentina: Business and the State, 1955-1983

Argentine politics were persistently unstable between 1955 and the restoration of democracy in 1983, due to the defensive behavior of the country's main sociopolitical actors. During this period, actors who achieved success and gained benefits were soon neutralized by the veto of others. Instability spiraled as the cycles of success and failure grew shorter and the "neutralization" of benefits and transfers of power became more violent. Social and political actors pursued strategies of short-term action and the defense of narrow sectoral interests for the most part. As a consequence, strategies based on common interests, which had to be anchored in mid- to long-term objectives, were inherently uncertain and risky. Caught in the logic of the prisoner's dilemma, Argentine social actors adopted a highly rational behavior at the individual-sectoral level, which frustrated collective interests. With each iteration of the game, political tension and the violation of individual and social rights became more acute.

In this context, to think of the Argentine sociopolitical process as a pendulum swinging between democracy and authoritarianism and between civilian and military governments is simplistic. Obviously, there was a pattern in which democracy was associated with attempts to broaden participation, while authoritarianism attempted to exclude the majority. However, when we speak of instability, the emphasis is on the fact that *each* government, civilian and military alike, attempted policies that were very different from its predecessor. Moreover, in each issue area (role of the state, export policies, capital/labor relationship, industrialization, and the relationship between domestic and foreign markets), there was great policy diversity not only between civilian and military governments but also within them. Hence, the degree of instability and uncertainty was not merely related to changes in the political regime but to any administrative change, even if it was just at the ministerial level.

Because of the instability and the risks implicit in changes of government, each time the political parties or the armed forces came to power, they tried to redefine institutions and the rules of the political game "once and for all," thereby systematically reproducing and heightening instability. This increased the potential costs for political actors if displaced from government; as a result, the magnitude of the changes they attempted when in power also increased. In this context, negotiation and go-slow methods became dangerously "inefficient," which prompted the presidency to become the center of all policies and decisions, while Congress and the judiciary became mere "ballast" to be endured by the executive.

After four decades of successive, frustrated attempts to recast the nation, Argentine institutions were devastated. Each new attempt implied a redefinition of the role of the state and its organizational logic. The dynamics of instability molded a state that had great difficulty bringing together the remnants of reiterated, contradictory reforms that were frustrated soon after they began to be implemented. The result was a lack of coordination between ministries, which led to the "feudalization" of the state, meaning that ministries and key agencies ceased to function as cogs of the same wheel in the pursuit of common objectives and priorities. Instead, they behaved as separate entities bent on achieving their own urgent, disconnected, opposed, and even contradictory purposes.

Due to the instability of the party system and of the rules that governed participation in policymaking and conflict resolution, the business sector cultivated its independence from political parties. Unlike the fate of organized labor, strategic independence from political parties permitted some business groups to avoid costs and obtain benefits during the long periods of repression or proscription of the party of their sympathy. Raising demands and exerting pressure directly on the executive branch permitted these business groups to articulate their organizational logic in terms of the only relatively stable institutional power available. By not taking the Congress or the judiciary very seriously, such representatives of business interests could avoid the protracted, self-defeating task of becoming entangled in institutional channels of doubtful capacity for conflict resolution, whose instability affected not only operational criteria but also the institutions' own continuity. By ignoring the rules of the market, the business sector avoided the costs of unexpected regulatory changes. This praetorian-like behavior of social actors was efficient for the realization of short-term interests, with the drawback that it undermined those gains in the medium term.

By dealing directly with the executive branch, Argentine business associations made influencing state policy to win benefits and avoid costs their highest priority — even to the point of supporting military coups. This behavior made business more efficient at defending profit rates than at producing technological advancement or expansion into risky export ventures. Given this focus, business association leaders did not concern themselves with redefining the interests of their members or, having brought them into the organization, representing them collectively. Instead, they measured institutional success by their capacity to impose their will on other actors — mainly, competing business associations and organized labor — via their influence over state policy. This political-institutional context ensured that Argentine business associations developed movement-like organizational and behavioral characteristics.

Structural Causes for Argentine Organizational Heterogeneity and Intrabusiness Contradictions,1930s-1980s

Since the 1930s, organized business in Argentina has exhibited a high degree of intra- and intersectoral heterogeneity. Although other Latin American countries share this characteristic, the Argentine case is unique in a number of ways, especially in industry and agriculture. This uniqueness was caused by the process of import-substitution industrialization (ISI), the differential role of the state in production and consumption, and recurrent crises in the balance of payments and economic growth.

To begin with, the industrial sector is more heterogeneous organizationally than the agricultural sector. Import-substitution policies of the 1930s heavily influenced this pattern, when Argentina's industrial structure became increasingly diversified in regional and productive terms and a complex network of relationships among its different branches and sectors began to take shape. This process prompted industrial groups to develop more segregated organizational forms. Associations were meant to protect industrial groups not only against the labor movement, the state, and capitalist groups in other economic sectors (such as services or agriculture), but also against other organized groups with forward or backward linkages in the same industrial activity. The existence of the Argentine Industrial Union (Unión Industrial Argentina — UIA), which was closely associated with industrialists in and represented the more economically powerful industrial bourgeoisie, was not enough. Business chambers and associations proliferated and represented more specific interests, both in terms of type of production and of regions. Many also remained members of the UIA, while others sought alternative organizations to represent their interests, as was the case of provincial industrialists who, in the 1950s, organized the General Confederation of Industry (Confederación General de la Industria — CGI). Compared with the agricultural sector, the industrial sector's lack of a hegemonic group reinforced permanent intraindustrial conflict.

For the industrial sector, another significant factor in its greater organizational heterogeneity was that the state played a much larger role in industry as producer and consumer of goods than it played in the agricultural sector. This had two effects: First, heavier state intervention affected the logic of the market that industrial companies contended with (prices, concentration in the supply of critical inputs or in the demand of the goods produced). Second, because the state itself was a producer, it was a member of the associations. Yet, the state was also at the receiving end of the demands made by associations. Both factors made organizational strategizing far more complicated in the industrial than in the agricultural sector.

Associational heterogeneity and intersectoral conflict were also caused by recurrent crises in the balance of payments and economic growth. These crises defined the relationship between urban (industrialists and working class) and rural actors. The deterioration of terms of trade, which became severe in the early 1950s, accelerated the cycles of recurring economic instability.[5] The logic underlying the cycles of expansion and recession was rooted in the fact that export products — cereals and meats — were wage goods. This meant that wage increases generated greater domestic demand for export products, which negatively affected export balances and foreign currency revenues. However, wage increases also expanded demand for manufactured goods, which, in turn, influenced the growth of the manufacturing sector and the import of industrial inputs. As a result, balance of payment deficits occurred due to the negative effects of wage increases on foreign currency revenues, expenditures, and reserves.

Deficits generated during the expansive phase of the cycle were eased by reducing industrial imports and increasing agricultural exports. In other words, reducing the deficit in the balance of payments required curbing industrial activity and domestic demand for foodstuffs, namely, less production and falling real wages. This initiated the recessive phase of the cycle. Once the deficit was brought under control, the actors who suffered the cost of adjustment (industrialists and workers) pressured the state to recoup resources transferred to the agricultural bourgeoisie. When the state responded to the workers' and industrialists' pressure, the expansive phase of the cycle began, as wages and industrial activity increased. Thus, in addition to fixing real wages and the rate of exchange to transfer of resources between capital and labor sectors, manipulation of those variables performed the same task among propertied classes.

The role of wages and the rate of exchange in the transfer of resources among members of the private sector had a number of effects. It created common interests between the domestic bourgeoisie and labor and generated contradictory interests between those two groups and the exporting agricultural bourgeoisie of the pampa.[6] Moreover, these cycles privileged the *haute* industrial bourgeoisie composed of oligopolistic groups of domestic and, especially, foreign capital.[7] The most concentrated sectors of the industrial bourgeoisie benefited more than the domestic bourgeoisie from increases in aggregate demand during the expansive phase of the cycle and sustained fewer costs during the recessive phase. This occurred because these sectors had better access to national and international financing, which further accentuated the oligopolistic process to the benefit of large-scale industry.

Through these cycles, bargaining or pressure on the state to contain labor demands was a major determinant of the organization and behavior of most business associations. However, in a semi-closed economy such as Argentina's, conflicts among capitalist groups were equally important. Labor conflicts were more or less "resolved" by business as a whole, whether by supporting repression against workers and their organizations or by controlling the outcome of labor conflicts over wages and profits via nominal wage increases and the transfer of this "cost" to prices.[8] Transferring costs to consumers was also a mechanism to administer the contradictions among industrialists and between the industrial sector and the agricultural-ranching export sector, both based on differences of interest over exchange rates, export taxes, tariff barriers, and the like. For example, authoritarian governments, which defended the interests of business as "employers" by repressing workers and their organizations, simultaneously imposed measures that led to significant resource transfers among the same business sectors as "producers" (via taxation, increase or reduction of export taxes, tariff barriers, and even price controls). Under these circumstances, it should surprise no one that the state became business's central object of political action and that price increases were the result of capital-labor conflicts and significant intrabusiness strife.

In the context of ISI, business associations linked to the industrial sector demanded that the state reduce tariffs on imported inputs and keep or raise tariff barriers to protect their finished products. Because of their forward and backward linkages, the pressure to buy cheap imported inputs and sell finished products at high prices generated a permanent tension among industrialists. In this struggle, losers were typically those sectors that were less organized or less efficient in participating in the policy-making process. Moreover, the contradictions among capital-intensive and labor-intensive groups and among groups that were more or less dependent on the domestic market, state loans, or local economies, led to conflicts, such as those between the UIA and the CGI. Because successful pressure exerted today might be neutralized tomorrow by counterpressures from labor, agriculture, or any other industrial group, the resulting industrial panorama from the 1950s to the 1980s was one of permanent struggle.

In conclusion, the structural characteristics of the Argentine economy had several effects on business behavior. First, they produced particularly acute intrabusiness conflict, and dealing with it achieved an even higher priority than labor relations (although a full understanding of intrabusiness conflict must be linked to the struggle against organized workers and the state). Second, business associations defended their interests via political rather than economic action. When faced with a problem, they attempted to influence state economic and labor policy (which sometimes meant supporting military governments) instead of adjusting production and marketing strategies. Third, these characteristics encouraged inflationary strategies at the company and associational levels. At the company level, inflation neutralized the costs of intrabusiness conflict by raising consumer prices.[9] By the same token, business associations reduced tension in labor relations by accepting labor's wage demands and then transferring the cost to consumers.

ENCOMPASSING BUSINESS PEAK ASSOCIATIONS IN ARGENTINA, 1900s TO THE PRESENT

Political Causes for the First Encompassing Peak Associations in Argentina: From Labor Threat to Corporatist Incentives, 1900s-1955

Unlike sectoral associations, such as the UIA (1886-1946, 1955 to the present), encompassing peak associations have not been a permanent actor in Argentina. Moreover, Argentine history shows that when encompassing business peak associations periodically emerged, it was for reasons rooted in the unique forces that shaped different periods of political struggle.

From 1860 to 1930, Argentina's major political actors did not question the country's agricultural-exporting economic model. As a result, only first-, second-, and third-degree associations were founded. They defended sectoral interests within the limits of the framework imposed by the hegemonic, exporting rural bourgeoisie.

However, labor demands and actions intensified toward the end of the First World War, particularly after 1918 when the "threat from labor" spawned the emergence of Argentina's first two encompassing business peak associations. The first one, the Labor Association (Asociación del Trabajo), was founded in 1918 to organize collective action against labor, and its bylaws included the creation of an employers' defense fund. The Labor Association combated labor unions and pressured government to control and repress labor demands.[10] Although it was not formally dissolved until the early 1940s, its virulence and close ties with extreme right paramilitary groups such as the Patriotic League (Liga Patriótica) cost it the sympathy of the private sector as a whole long before then. The second encompassing peak association of the period, the Argentine Trade, Industry, and Production Confederation (Confederación Argentina del Comercio, de la Industria y de la Producción — CACIP), was also created to curb labor demands. Unlike the Labor Association, the CACIP participated in congressional debates over the rights of labor.[11] Also in contrast to the Labor Association, as the state reestablished social peace, the CACIP evolved, becoming more concerned with the defense of domestic markets. The CACIP remained active through the early 1930s.

Beginning in the mid-1940s, a second wave of Argentine encompassing business peak associations had its origins in the emergence of neocorporatism. After Juan Perón was elected president in 1946, he supported the creation of neo-corporatist structures of organization and participation in policymaking for workers and capitalists. Certain business groups availed themselves of this opportunity and began a series of experiments: the Argentine Production, Industry, and Trade Association (Asociación Argentina de la Producción, la Industria y el Comercio — AAPIC, 1946-1949); the Argentine Economic Confederation (Confederación Económica Argentina — CEA, 1949); and the Argentine Production, Industry, and Trade Confederation (Confederación Argentina de la Producción, la Industria y el Comercio — CAPIC, 1950-1952). These organizations, however, never matured into full-fledged institutions. Only the Argentine General Economic Confederation (Confederación General Económica Argentina — CGE), organized in 1952, became a stable institution, that is, until the Peronist government was overthrown in 1955 and the CGE was outlawed.

Although the emergence of these associations clearly was linked to the neo-corporatist strategy of Peronism, their creation also responded to deepening conflicts within the business sector. Thus, the Peronist government supported the CGE and dissolved the UIA for backing its opponents in the presidential elections, but the subsequent military government restored the UIA in 1955 and disbanded both the CGE and its third-degree member confederations. As will be seen in the next section, after a military coup ended Perón's rule in 1955, the importance of threats from labor and neo-corporatist incentives as causes of efforts to create encompassing peak associations declined. Instead, between 1955 and 1983 (a period marked by alternating military and civilian governments), the organization, disruption, and dissolution of encompassing business peak associations generally was caused by intrabusiness conflicts.

Encompassing Peak Associations as a Consequence of Intrabusiness Conflict, 1955-1983

Between 1955 and 1983, the emergence and dissolution of fourth-degree business associations was closely linked to the struggle between business associations that represented large-scale business and those that represented small and medium business interests connected to the internal market and provinces. The latter, for example, organized the CGE. Meanwhile, the first-, second-, and third-degree organizations associated with large-scale national and multinational capital (Argentine Rural Corporation [Sociedad Rural Argentina — SRA], Argentine Industrial Union [Unión Industrial Argentina — UIA], Argentine Chamber of Commerce [Cámara Argentina de Comercio — CAC], and so forth) twice organized fourth-degree associations. These were the Coordinating Action for Free Business Institutions (Acción Coordinadora de las Instituciones Empresarias Libres — ACIEL, 1958-1973) and the Permanent Assembly of Business Unions (Asamblea Permanente de Entidades Gremiales Empresarias — APEGE, 1975-1976). In both cases their main purpose was to counter the political presence of the CGE.

There was also a close relationship between politics and intrabusiness conflict. Despite its formal stance as an apolitical and nonpartisan organization, the CGE was closely linked to Peronism and by the 1950s to certain sectors of the Radical Party. Its experiences under military rule leave no doubt that it fared better under civilian governments. Following the coup that overthrew Perón in 1955, the new military government dissolved the CGE, alleging that it was "totalitarian" in nature. The CGE was revived during Arturo Frondizi's government (1958) as part of the Frondizi-Perón political pact, and it was dissolved again after the 1976 military coup, only to be newly organized under the current democratic regime (1984).

Because of the CGE's focus on political action instead of economic adjustment to advance its interests, its successes coincided with the upward stage of the economic cycle, and its widening power depended on a political opening that permitted the institutionalization of its alliance with working-class sectors. Ideologically, the CGE stressed the need for 1) strong state involvement in the economy, 2) the elaboration of socioeconomic policy in concert with the state and labor, and 3) reducing the presence of multinational capital in "strategic" areas. Multinational businesses could become members of CGE or its affiliated associations but could not be elected to executive positions.

The encompassing peak associations of large-scale business opposed the CGE politically. Both ACIEL and APEGE adopted conservative/free market ideological stances, arguing for 1) a reduction in the role of the state in the economy and society; 2) greater development through free market forces rather than by negotiation among "corporations"; from their point of view, the latter could only result in the inefficient allocation of resources due to their politicization; and 3) multinational capital as central to the development process. Given the electoral alignments of the era, the political power of forces sympathetic to ACIEL and APEGE under civilian rule was inverse to that of the CGE. As a result, between 1955 and 1973, the organizations that represented large-scale national and international capital opted, whenever possible, for authoritarian governments, which provided them with political and ideological support and important government posts to fill (Niosi 1974).

Sharp differences also existed with respect to the need for a single encompassing peak association that would represent both the medium- and small-scale sector of domestic market-oriented capital and the large-scale national and international capital sector. The CGE was in favor of a single association. Within its own domain, the CGE created a structure wherein the encompassing association exercised some authority over its lower ranking members. Further, the CGE consistently backed the creation of an Economic and Social Council to institutionalize and stabilize the participation of capital and labor in government decisionmaking.

In contrast, the ACIEL and the APEGE never agreed on the need for a single encompassing peak association to unify the sector's demands and proposals. For the most part, they only coordinated the actions of highly independent third-degree associations affiliated with them in their struggle against organized labor, principally the General Workers' Peak Association (Central Geral dos Trabalhadores — CGT) labor federation, and against the organized domestic bourgeoisie (under the CGE). The members of the ACIEL and the APEGE also regarded their associations as transitory in nature. They believed that only free market forces could optimize the allocation of resources and that encompassing peak associations — and, to some extent, even sectoral organizations — only distorted those dynamics. However, in order to abolish these associative practices, at best considered as a necessary evil, it was first essential to neutralize even more distorting factors, such as the CGE and the strength of organized labor, which distrusted the power of free markets.

To say the least, the relationship among the CGE, the ACIEL, and the APEGE and their respective associations (for example, the CGI and UIA) was conflictual. Each denounced the other's interests as "illegitimate."[12] They were trapped in a web of contending political and social alliances.[13]

The criteria upon which these contending industrial associations drew to assert their claims of representativeness were also different. Participation in the ACIEL and its third-degree organizations was based on the size of personnel, payroll, ownership of capital goods, and contribution to gross domestic product (and in the case of third-degree organizations, to the gross sectoral product) of affiliated firms. By contrast, the CGE and its members emphasized the number of producers and regional associations covered by the organization. Thus, until 1973, the UIA claimed that it covered between 85 percent and 95 percent of industrial employment, machines, and product, while the CGE affirmed that it represented 40 regional federations and 2,100 first-degree associations. Ironically, in the midst of this battle of figures, the UIA estimated that its member associations employed 1.2 million workers,[14] while the CGE claimed it represented 1 million businesspeople (La Nación 1973). Although it is important to keep in mind that double affiliation may have caused distortions in estimating representativeness, the estimates in this case obviously included a strong political component.

The articulation of structural and political variables generated a great deal of tension as well as many conflicts and divisions *within* and *between* encompassing peak associations. For example, among third-degree organizations within the ACIEL, continuing tensions between the UIA, the SRA, and the CAC led to the

UIA's disaffiliation and to the ACIEL's dissolution in 1972. When the CGE controlled the Ministry of Economy (1973-1974), the UIA joined CGE and merged with the CGI in a new third-degree association, the Argentine Industrial Confederation (Confederación Industrial Argentina — CINA), which was, in turn, dissolved by the military after the coup in 1976, together with the CGE and all of its member organizations. After four years of military rule, the UIA's comeback as an autonomous actor in 1980 recreated the usual cycles of collaboration and confrontation with other third-degree organizations, such as the SRA and the CAC. The CGE's third-degree associations also experienced conflicts and fractures. In fact, differences in the CGE over agricultural policy (implemented when the CGE was in control of the Ministry of Economy) led the Argentine Agrarian Federation (Federación Agraria Argentina — FAA) to break with the CGE in 1975.

There was a constant struggle among the UIA's second-degree organizations (representing industrial subsectors) over their different stances vis-à-vis the international market or with respect to their forward and backward linkages. At times, open conflict flared over their representation in the management and control of the association, to the point that some, such as the Association of Industrial Metalurgists (Asociación de Industriales Metalúrgicos — ADIMRA), left the association in 1972.

Controversies have also plagued first-degree organizations. Divisions between large and medium-small producers (for example, between the Argentine Construction Chamber (Cámara Argentina de la Construcción) and the Argentine Construction Union (Unión Argentina de la Construcción)) and between national and multinational capital (for example, the Argentine Bank Association (Asociación de Bancos Argentinos) versus the Association of Banks of the Argentine Republic (Asociación de Bancos de la República Argentina)) became a common pattern in some of the economy's most important sectors.

These patterns suggest two additional conclusions with respect to the organizational dynamics of Argentine capitalists and intre-business conflicts. First, intre-business contradictions and conflicts affected the *entire* spectrum of business organizations, from the first to the fourth degree, and generated a pattern of permanent tensions horizontally (between economic sectors and branches) and vertically (within the same branch, between forward and backward linked producers). Second, the intensity, dynamics, and resolution of intrabusiness conflicts became dependent on the resolution of national political struggles. These brought business associations potential benefits of the first magnitude, such as the direct control of the Ministry of Economy, as well as the risk of devastating costs, such as their intervention or dissolution by the state.

Business, Democracy, and Understanding the Absence of Encompassing Business Peak Associations in Argentina, 1983 to Present[15]

In the 1940s, political action by business associations was no novelty in Argentina. Business associations had actively participated in national governments, supported or opposed their policies, and collaborated in coups d'état (for example, the overthrow of Hipólito Yrigoyen in 1930). With the rise of Peronism and its overwhelming electoral majority, democracy became a high-risk political regime for "conservative" business associations that represented the interests of the haute bourgeoisie. Thus, as of the 1950s, they developed defensive (and frequently conspiratorial) stances toward democracy, frequently supporting military regimes because the latter were, until recently, the only ones that secured their vital interests.

However, the experience of the last dictatorship (1976-1983) changed the political significance of military authoritarianism for this sector of capitalists, leading to a revision of their view of democracy. The experience of the most powerful groups of the bourgeoisie with the previous military government induced them to rethink the costs and benefits of authoritarianism. Capitalists were systematically excluded from the design and implementation of technocratic economic policies that resulted in costs that, at times, were even higher than those incurred in democracy. For example, although the UIA was reinstated after the coup of 1976 (while the CGE was dissolved), it had to endure military intervention in its internal affairs during the harsh period when the military's economic plan devastated the industrial sector (1976-1980). With absolute concentration of political power, military bonapartism ceased to be predictable, and the armed forces became a risky actor, even for business associations linked to the haute bourgeoisie.

Furthermore, from the 1940s to 1983, democracy had meant the electoral victory of Peronist forces with the inevitable sequel of political benefits for both labor and the business associations representing small and medium-sized firms (the CGE). During this period, democracy also meant the implementation of strategies aimed at strengthening the socioeconomic role of the state. Furthermore, and independently from short-term measures, Peronist government policies openly confronted the pampa landed bourgeoisie (via taxes and nationalization of foreign trade), multinational capital (via the nationalization of public utility companies), financial capital (via the nationalization of bank deposits and credit operations), and capitalists as a class (via the institutionalization of a long list of labor rights and reiterated attempts to increase both real and relative wages).

To make matters worse, the proscription of Peronism (after the 1955 coup) led to civilian governments headed by the Radical Party. This party tended either to continue implementing policies aimed at strengthening the role of the state and at displacing multinational capital or to negotiate with or absorb Peronist organizations instead of dissolving them. This was the case of the developmentalist faction of the Radical Party in 1958, when it obtained the electoral support of Peronism in exchange for the legalization of the CGT and the CGE.

For the more economically powerful business sectors associated with conservative organizations, until 1983 democracy implied a very real threat for several reasons:

1. It reduced their influence over the state and allowed labor and the CGE to make greater inroads.
2. Large-scale industry suffered from the dwindling importance of the market as the key resource allocation mechanism.
3. Sectoral and encompassing peak associations such as the UIA and the ACIEL faced the risk of dissolution.

4. Civilian governments persisted in challenging the vital interests of the bourgeoisie.

These conditions, however, no longer held after redemocratization and the victory of the Radical Party in 1983. This event started to redefine the meaning of democracy for the haute bourgeoisie's business organizations. Between 1983 and the inauguration of the Austral Plan in June 1985, democracy offered four major advantages to business interests: First, the "iron law" that postulated Peronist electoral victories in open elections no longer held. Second, business associations no longer ran the risk of being dissolved or displaced by political maneuvering. Third, the government recognized the political hegemony of the UIA over its old CGE-CGI adversary (whose rebirth in 1984 had only shown that, after its dissolution under the military government, it was not capable of transcending a purely formal role and that it no longer had any significant political weight). Fourth, the government took an anti-corporatist stance and was willing to curb labor power and demands.

After June 1985, despite the chaotic socioeconomic policies of the Austral and Primavera plans, the Radical Party's administration proved receptive to capitalist participation in the decision-making process. It also implemented strategies to resolve the crisis affecting the "old" model of accumulation. These strategies, such as the opening of the economy, privatization, and confrontation with unions, favored important business interests and were no longer the monopoly of the traditional right-wing parties or the armed forces.

The 1989 presidential election, won by Peronist Carlos Menem in a context of hyperinflation, fiscal bankruptcy of the state, and deep social crisis initially caused some uneasiness about the value of democracy in the private sector. Although the election confirmed that Peronism had lost its majority party status, it also showed that — given the fragmentation of the other political forces — it remained capable of victory. However, the unexpected appointment of a representative of one of the more powerful Argentinean, oligopolistic, multinational groups (Miguel Roig of the Bunge and Born conglomerate) as minister of economy left no doubt about the orientation of the socioeconomic policies of Menem's administration. This shift in the Peronist party and its subsequent actions calmed business sectors' fears, as did the Menem administration's steady implementation of neoliberal economic policies even after Bunge and Born's policy failure and its eventual removal from office. Faced with a resurgence of hyperinflation between December 1989 and March 1990, the government responded by deepening market deregulation, opening the economy, accelerating privatizations, trimming government budgets, making labor markets more flexible, and curbing strikes. Since then, big business has systematically supported what Menem's Economy Minister Domingo Cavallo described as "changing everything that Perón did after the Second World War" (*La Nación* 1992, 13), including the constitutional reform of 1994 that allowed Menem's reelection in 1995.

These shifts suggest that the pattern of political struggle typical of Argentina since the inception of Peronism and its first administration (1946-1955) has changed dramatically. Both the situation described so far and the medium- to long-term effects of the policies implemented have convinced the private sector that democracy in Argentina is more functional and less risky for its interests than authoritarianism. Because a military government in Argentina is not feasible without the support of the more powerful economic groups and organizations, democracy is safe, even in the face of a deterioration of the economy, sharper social strife, and mounting tensions within the armed forces. The business sector's wager on the stability of the democratic regime is a long-term bet, and so are its effects.

The opening of the economy and privatization have released the state from traditional pressures demanding the transfer of resources. Most of the remaining transfers now either tend to be defined in terms of supply and demand or are trapped in the quagmire of intrabusiness contradictions. By the same token, the threat from the CGE and CGI to the hegemonic associations of the haute bourgeoisie has disappeared, and the contradictions between forward and backward linkages are redefined by the liberalization of the economy. Moreover, the "threat" from organized labor has also declined (due to the weakened structure of labor organizations). By the same token, labor code reforms are dismantling the traditional logic of bargaining and the relationship between capital and labor. These new developments caused a decline in the sources that had generated so much conflict between the fourth-degree associations of large-scale business and small and medium-scale business.

The current absence of politically relevant encompassing business peak associations is quite understandable. It is an indicator that the most powerful sectors of the bourgeoisie have imposed their hegemony over the state, labor, and small to medium-sized business groups, which, from the 1940s to the 1970s, attempted to build a neo-corporatist economic and social model under the aegis of domestic capital. Without a threat from labor, the state, small and medium-sized business groups, or neo-corporatist institutions, encompassing business peak associations are unnecessary.

CONCLUSIONS

This chapter began by raising a number of general theoretical arguments about the relationship between business peak associations and politics. Opening reflections contended that understanding the patterns of business associations and their political significance requires an analysis of whether businesses form employer or producer associations, the organization's degree of interest aggregation (first, second, third, fourth, or encompassing), the level or realm of conflict in which these actors are immersed, and the way in which the organization manages to articulate the conflicting logics of "membership" and "influence."

A second line of argumentation addressed theoretical debates regarding the need for business associations. Although theoretical traditions that stress the structural power of capital to influence policymaking offer useful elements to understand the power of capitalists as agents of accumulation, they, nevertheless, run up against the empirical fact that states in capitalist systems do not always cater to the interests of capitalists. Consequently, entrepreneurs do have an incentive to engage in collective action in defense of their interests. In order to understand the emergence and importance of encompassing business peak associations, we must move beyond reducing the explanation of the politics of business to the structural power of capital. Only then can we begin to uncover the conditions under which the state achieves substantial autonomy from the veto power of the bourgeoisie and control of its policies. And only then is it possible to recognize that explanations for the development of encompassing peak associations lie in the political-institutional realm. This conclusion does not negate the key role of entrepreneurial control over investment in the capitalist process of accumulation and reproduction of social relations. Neither does it deny the ensuing privileged position of capitalist interests or its political importance. Rather, it shows that the degree of control exercised by capitalists over state policies can vary greatly as a function of historical contingencies; therefore, it is not valid to assume that the bourgeoisie does not "need" to organize as a collective actor in order to achieve some of its common interests.

As explanations for the development of encompassing peak associations lie in the political-institutional realm, one must analyze the specific historical factors that have caused their emergence. These include the existence of neo-corporatist structures, the threat posed by the state as a political actor, and the menace of strong labor associations. Nor can one forget to explore the significance of competing business organizations.

Applied to Argentina, this framework for analysis led to several conclusions. First, Argentina's highly unstable politico-institutional context determined organizational and behavioral patterns in which business associations gave priority to influencing the state — to the point of supporting military coups — in order to obtain benefits and avoid costs. This strategy proved more efficient in defending profit rates than in generating technological renewal or helping businesspeople to embark on the risky adventure of exports. Consequently, associations gauged their institutional efficiency not by their capacity to redefine the interests of their members but by their capacity to impose the association's interests on the other actors via their influence over government policy. This meant that Argentine business associations took on movement-like characteristics.

Second, the structural characteristics of the Argentine economy also affected business organization and behavior. To begin with, a particularly acute intrabusiness conflict became a more salient issue for business associations than labor relations, although these cannot be forgotten. Moreover, business associations gave a higher priority to political advocacy over economic action in the defense of interests. Rather than redefine its production and marketing strategies, business preferred to influence the state's labor and economic policies — to the extent of supporting military government if necessary. This behavior encouraged both companies and business associations to promote inflationary strategies. In order to neutralize the costs of intre-business interest conflicts, firms raised consumer prices. Business associations alleviated tensions between capital and labor by accepting wage demands and transferring the cost to consumers.

Third, the structural characteristics of the Argentine economy and the nature of political struggle, particularly after 1955, fed intrabusiness conflict along the *entire* spectrum of business organizations, from the first to the fourth degree. This generated a pattern of permanent tensions horizontally (between economic sectors and branches) and vertically (within the same branch, between forward- and backward-linked producers). Moreover, the intensity, dynamics, and resolution of intrabusiness conflicts became dependent on the resolution of national political struggles. These dynamics brought business peak associations potential benefits of the first magnitude, such as the direct control of the Ministry of Economy, as well as potentially devastating costs, such as their intervention or dissolution by the state.

In conclusion, the emergence and decline of encompassing business peak associations from 1900 to the present had different causes over various periods of Argentine political history. From the 1900s to the 1940s, they were an answer to threats from labor. From the 1940s to 1955, encompassing business peak associations were the result of neo-corporatist incentives and of increasing state autonomy in shaping social actors. During the period from 1955 to the 1970s, intrabusiness contradictions were the dominant cause for the organization and political behavior of encompassing business peak associations. Finally, from the 1980s to date and as a result of the promarket political and structural changes prompted by the profound social and fiscal crisis suffered by Argentine society in the last 15 years, the autonomy and strength of the state has been dramatically reduced, labor weakened, and intrabusiness tensions diminished by the emergence of a clear hegemony on the part of the most powerful sectors of the bourgeoisie. The weakened Argentine state, the declining power of labor, and intrabusiness harmony are all conditions that render the formation of an encompassing peak association unnecessary. This is why, as of 1998, Argentina has none.

Notes

1. The terms "entrepreneurs," "businesspeople," and "capitalists," as well as "business" and "bourgeoisie" are used as functional equivalents.

2. For example, party contacts are more useful in the second and third levels than in the first, and the support of a 51-percent majority of congressional representatives may be sufficient to modify a law (at the second level of conflict) but insufficient to modify a rule that demands a two-thirds majority (at the third level of conflict).

3. In 1969, the Chilean state contributed 75 percent of gross investment (50 percent direct and 25 percent indirect).

4. "Selective benefits" are benefits that are only for members of the organization and that act as incentives for affiliation and permanence (health coverage, market information, economic analysis, personalized advisorship, financing formalities, and the like).

5. This synthesis draws from O'Donnell (1976).

6. Here, reference is made to the capitalist sector predominantly associated with domestic markets and mainly composed of provincial local capital in small and medium-sized labor-intensive firms. Organizationally, this sector is linked to the CGE and the CGI (O'Donnell 1978).

7. Capital-intensive foreign firms are affiliated with the UIA.

8. Such calls for government action are typical of the urban bourgeoisie, industrial conglomerates, and the pampa-exporting bourgeoisie.

9. If intrabusiness conflict were a more salient issue than the wage/profit confrontation, this conclusion would imply that, contrary to common belief, the former had a greater impact on inflation in Argentina than the latter.

10. The discussion of the period prior to the 1950s summarizes several passages from Dardo Cúneo (1967).

11. Luis E. Zuberbrühler, CAICIP's president in 1923, was also vice president of the Patriotic League (Liga Patriótica).

12. The CGE lambasted the UIA for the strong presence of multinational corporations, and the UIA scorned the CGE for its relatively minor contribution to GDP.

13. The CGE was generally more open to associating with organizations representing large-scale business than vice versa (Cúneo 1967; Freels 1979).

14. *Clarín* (1972) as cited in Roudil (1985).

15. This section draws substantially from Acuña (1994) and Acuña (1995).

References

Acuña, Carlos H. 1994. "Politics and Economics in the Argentina of the Nineties." In *Democracy, Markets, and Structural Reform in Latin America: Argentina, Bolivia, Brazil, Chile, and Mexico*, eds. William, C. Smith, Carlos Acuña, and Eduardo Gamarra. Coral Gables, Fla.: North-South Center Press at the University of Miami.

Acuña, Carlos H. 1995. "Entrepreneurial Interests, Dictatorship and Democracy in Present Argentina (or Why the Bourgeoisie Abandons Authoritarian Strategies and Opts for Democratic Stability)." In *Business and Democracy in Latin America*, eds. Ernst Bartell and Leigh Payne. Pittsburgh: University of Pittsburgh Press.

Alberti, Giorgio, L. Golbert, and Carlos Acuña. 1984. "Intereses industriales y gobernabilidad democrática." *Boletín Techint*.

Block, Fred. 1977. "The Ruling Class Does Not Rule: Notes on the Marxist Theory of the State." *Socialist Review* (May-June).

Block, Fred. 1981. "Beyond Relative Autonomy: State Managers as Historical Subjects." *New Political Sciences* 7 (Fall).

Confederación General Económica (CGE). 1973. *La Nación*, May 9.

Cúneo, Dardo. 1967. *Comportamiento y crisis de la clase empresaria*. Buenos Aires: Pleamar.

Freels, John W., Jr. 1979. *El sector industrial en la política nacional*. Buenos Aires: Eudeba.

Marx, Karl, and Friedrich Engels. [c1947] 1971. *The German Ideology*. New York: International Publishers.

Nación, La. 1992. February 11, 13.

Niosi, Jorge. 1974. *Los empresarios y el estado argentino, 1955-1969*. Buenos Aires: Siglo XXI.

O'Donnell, Guillermo. 1976. "Estado y alianzas en Argentina, 1956-1976." *Desarrollo Económico* 16:64 (January-March).

O'Donnell, Guillermo. 1978. "Notas para el estudio de la burguesía local, con especial referencia a su vinculación con el capital transnacional y al aparato estatal." *Estudios Cedes* 12.

Offe, Claus, and Helmut Wiesenthal. 1980. "Two Logics of Collective Action: Theoretical Notes on Social Class and Organizational Form." *Political Power and Social Theory* 1 (1).

Poulantzas, Nicos. 1978. *Political Power and Social Classes*. London: Verso.

Roudil, Héctor. 1985. "El comportamiento del empresariado argentino en la etapa previa al período 1973/1976." *Justicial Social* 1.

Schmitter, Philippe. 1974. "Still the Century of Corporatism?" *Review of Politics* 36 (1): 85-131.

Schmitter, Philippe, and Gerhard Lembrugh, eds. 1979. *Trends Toward Corporatist Intermediation*. London: Sage.

Schmitter, Philippe, and Wolfgang Streek. 1981. "The Organization of Business Interests." Discussion Paper. Berlin: International Institute of Management.

Skocpol, Theda. 1980. "Political Response to Capitalist Crisis: Neo-Marxist Theories of the State and the Case of the New Deal." *Politics and Society* 10 (2): 155-201.

CHAPTER THREE

The Fragmentation of Business in Brazil

KURT WEYLAND

INTRODUCTION

As this volume and Ernest Bartell and Leigh Payne (1995) show, several Latin American countries experienced a political awakening and organizational strengthening of private business in the 1980s and early 1990s. Encompassing business peak organizations have formed anew, as in Peru (Francisco Durand's chapter), or have gained in political prominence, as in Chile, Mexico, and Venezuela (Eduardo Silva's and Ricardo Tirado's chapters; Hernández 1991; Becker 1990). These encompassing peak associations aggregate the major sectors of business, have represented entrepreneurs' common interests, and have, on occasion, advanced comprehensive development projects for their countries (CONFIEP 1989; CPC 1994). The associations have sought to limit inter-sectoral conflicts that otherwise might weaken the private sector politically. As in Western Europe (Coleman and Grant 1988), organizational unification in Latin America has enhanced the political influence of business.

Brazil's private sector, however, has lacked an encompassing peak association. Despite efforts to create one, fragmentation has continued to prevail as existing sectoral and regional associations have jealously guarded their autonomy and as new organizations have sprung up (Boschi and Diniz 1978; Diniz and Boschi 1989; Payne 1994). Why has Brazilian business been unable or unwilling to unify? How has the absence of an encompassing peak association affected the political influence of business? This chapter focuses on the former question but also considers the latter.

These questions are of great relevance to Brazilian democracy in the age of market-oriented reform. Both the transition from authoritarian rule and the crisis of state-led, import-substituting development have weakened the state, which used to make major decisions on the country's future with considerable autonomy. The decline of state power has led to a dispersal of authority and a lack of direction. Business is one of the prime candidates to help fill this void. The private sector is

---

An earlier version of this paper was translated into Portuguese and published as "A fragmentação do setor empresarial no Brasil," in *Digesto Econômico*, Año LIII, No. 386, September/October 1997.

expected to be the engine of growth in the emerging market-oriented development model. Together with other societal segments, business could also hold the country's "political class" more accountable and force it to improve its low performance, as measured by persistent fiscal problems, recurrent political crises, and rampant corruption.

In order to attain sustained influence and help redefine Brazil's development model, business needs to coordinate its own activities. If different associations would stop acting at cross-purposes, the private sector could gain a more important role under democracy. According to Mancur Olson (1982, 47-53), an encompassing peak association could direct the demands of business toward common, overarching goals and limit the pursuit of narrow, sectoral interests, making business less narrowly self-seeking in its demand making and more willing to take the interests of other segments of society into account. For these reasons, organizational unification is crucial for giving the private sector a more influential and constructive role in public-policy debates and decisionmaking. The issue of unification is thus important both for Brazilian business and for the country.

Why, then, has an encompassing business peak association been absent in Brazil? The next section of this chapter points to the large size and internal heterogeneity of the country's private sector, the obstacles posed by the existing fragmented pattern of business organization, and the absence of a strong threat from the state or labor that might otherwise induce business to unify. The remaining sections substantiate this explanation through an overview of the organizational history of Brazilian business and an analysis of several failed efforts to form an encompassing peak association.

The chapter's third section traces the consolidation of business fragmentation to the state-corporatist system of interest representation created under the authoritarian rule of Getúlio Vargas (1930-1945) and to the disaggregative impact of massive state interventionism beginning in the 1950s. The disunity of Brazil's private sector was reinforced under the country's military regime (1964-1985), which restricted broad-based demand making and gave entrepreneurs close, particularistic access to decisionmakers, a practice that discouraged the pursuit of common interests.

The fourth and fifth sections examine the role of business in the civilian regime after 1985, which has been marked by entrepreneurs' greater political activism. Businesspeople and their associations have demanded input on a broader range of issues and have tried to develop comprehensive projects for the country. Nevertheless, several attempts at forming an effective encompassing peak association have failed. Constant rivalry among existing organizations and the absence of a clear threat that would motivate business to seek defensive unity have contributed greatly to these failures.

The sixth section shows how the absence of associational unity has limited business influence. Although the private sector has seen its basic interests guaranteed under democracy, it has been unable to exert sustained, constructive influence on public policymaking or to assume a leading role in the redefinition of Brazil's development strategy.

FACTORS INFLUENCING BUSINESS FRAGMENTATION IN BRAZIL

W hy have Brazilian business leaders not followed the example of their counterparts in other Latin American countries who have successfully created encompassing peak associations? One possible reason might be the large size and internal heterogeneity of the country's private sector, which makes it difficult to define and pursue common interests. Cleavages among industry, commerce, and finance are pronounced in Brazil and have led to tensions, despite the existence of powerful *grupos* that span several sectors.[1] These sectoral differences are reinforced by regional tensions stemming from the concentration of economic power in the state of São Paulo. Yet, in Mexico, large size and internal heterogeneity did not stop its business sector from creating an important and influential encompassing peak association, the Business Coordination Council (Consejo Coordinador Empresarial — CCE). Thus, the socioeconomic structure of Brazil's private sector may have hindered its unification, but it cannot be considered decisive in the country's failure to create an encompassing organization.

Instead, in Brazil, the crucial impediments to private sector unification have been political and organizational. First, the compartmentalized state corporatist structure, developed in the 1940s, has historically fragmented the business community. The existing organization of a business community conditions its reorganization. The higher the level of fragmentation, the less likely is organizational unification.[2] President Getúlio Vargas (1930-1945) imposed state corporatism on Brazil, coaxing business into narrow organizations, defined along sectoral and subsectoral lines, which were controlled by the government and led by individuals with a vested interest in maintaining their autonomy. Leaders' power over resources and their capacity to speak for their members made it possible for them to refuse to submit to another leader's authority for the sake of strengthening the influence of the overall business community through the formation of an encompassing peak organization.

Second, since the 1940s, state interventionism has induced businesspeople to forge particularistic links with state officials in order to gain access to the policy-making arena and, especially, to decision implementation. Strong state intervention made Brazilian business dependent on bureaucratic discretion and forced it to lobby for special favors. As a result, powerful entrepreneurs have long enjoyed close ties to and even friendships with public officials (Leff 1968, chapter 7; Cardoso 1975, 181-184, 206-209; Boschi 1979, 163-179), which they can exploit to advance and protect the specific interests of their individual firms without forming a united front with the rest of their class or sector. Thus, good informal access to public decisionmakers in the context of a fragmented business sector has helped to impede the formation of a private sector peak organization.

Third, in most countries, encompassing peak organizations emerged (at least partially) for defensive purposes; yet in Brazil, the absence of a powerful threat to private sector interests from the state, organized labor, or other popular sector groups has removed that crucial incentive for unification.[3] As the introduction to this volume stresses, the chapters by Carlos Acuña, Francisco Durand, Rose Spalding, and Ricardo Tirado show, and the experiences of social-democratic countries in Europe confirm, the strongest impulse for the creation of an encompassing business association is the perception of a substantial threat to private sector interests. In Sweden, for instance, the emergence of a powerful and initially militant labor movement induced employers to unite in order to defend the established order. In Mexico, President Luís Echeverría's (1970-1976) revival of radical rhetoric and his effort to reassert state autonomy from business prompted the formation of the CCE (Tirado's chapter). Thus, when facing a strong, militant labor movement, mobilized popular sectors, or a highly autonomous state that could infringe upon capitalist interests, the private sector tends to unify for purposes of defense. Facing danger, the incentive to suspend rivalries among different sectors and firms and form a strong peak association rises considerably. In order not to hang separately, businesspeople decide to hang together.

In contrast to other Latin American countries, no substantial threat to business interests has arisen in Brazil. Even the incipient mass mobilization of the early 1960s was defeated so rapidly and decisively with the military coup of 1964 that it had no lasting impact on business organization. The democratic transition of the mid-1980s has not given rise to a powerful, militant labor movement, unleashed mass mobilization, or boosted state autonomy. The organizational divisions within the labor movement, the pervasive clientelism enveloping many of the poor, and the bureaucratic politics undermining the unity of the state — that is, political-organizational factors — help account for the absence of deep threats to business.

The labor movement has been weakened by rivalries between a gradually advancing radical labor association, the Central Workers' Union (Central Única de Trabalhadores — CUT), and slowly retreating, more moderate groupings, the General Workers' Peak Association (Central Geral dos Trabalhadores — CGT) and the Union Force (Força Sindical — FS). This debilitating division has helped to prevent unions from challenging business frontally. Except for a temporary campaign in favor of agrarian reform (1985-1987),[4] mass mobilization among vast sectors of the poor has remained sporadic, primarily because of the pervasive clientelism that links poor people to better-off patrons. Additionally, the organizational weakness of Brazilian parties has enfeebled the democratic governments, and internecine infighting among public agencies, a result of weak central coordination, has often paralyzed state action (Weyland 1996a, chapters 3, 5). Because political-organizational factors have undermined the unity of the state, it has never acquired a degree of autonomy that entrepreneurs would perceive as dangerous to their interests. The formal and informal access of narrow business groupings to public officials and agencies has provided an additional guarantee against threats from the state. Since for all these reasons the private sector has not felt deeply threatened, it has not made any serious efforts to unify. The tensions and rivalries among business sectors and their established organizations have prevailed and kept Brazilian business divided.

THE HISTORY OF BUSINESS FRAGMENTATION

Organizational fragmentation has plagued Brazil's private sector for decades. Brazilian business has never had an encompassing organization that could advance its collective interests as a class (Guimarães 1977; Diniz 1989). Instead, many associations divided along sectoral and regional lines have co-existed. In the absence of substantial threats to business, two factors account for this long history of disunity: the state-corporatist system of interest representation created under the authoritarian regime of Getúlio Vargas (1930-1945) and massive government intervention in the economy, practiced frequently since the early 1950s.

Vargas' state corporatism organized the private sector along the lines of its main segments. It created separate National Confederations of Industry (Confederação Nacional da Indústria — CNI), Commerce (Confederação Nacional do Comércio — CNC), Agriculture (Confederação Nacional da Agricultura — CNA), and so forth,[5] without an encompassing peak association to connect them. The confederations themselves comprised numerous sectoral associations, reaching, for instance, from the metal-working industry to hat-making firms. All these sectoral groupings had the same voting power in internal decisionmaking, regardless of their tremendously different economic weight. The resulting distortion in interest representation has often impelled the stronger sectors to go their independent ways and bypass the confederations.

Regional differences have reinforced disunity in the private sector. The geographical imbalance of economic development, especially the concentration of industry in Brazil's southeastern corner, has led to tensions inside business organizations. For instance, the powerful Federation of Industries of São Paulo state (Federação das Indústrias do Estado de São Paulo — FIESP) is officially just one of more than 20 state federations under the CNI. Because most of the federations from the poor Northeast and North are economically and politically negligible, this formal equality does not reflect FIESP's enormous weight. Seeing its "modern" orientation inadequately represented through CNI, FIESP has always had strong direct connections to the government, state, and Congress. This has weakened the authority of CNI and its claim to speak for industry as a whole. Thus, Brazil's rigid corporatist framework has had a disaggregative effect on business organization.[6]

Since the 1960s, businesspeople have formed numerous interest organizations outside the state-corporatist framework, such as the Brazilian Association for the Development of Basic Industries (Associação Brasileiro para o Desenvolvimento das Indústrias de Base — ABDIB), the National Association of Motor Vehicle Manufacturers (Associação Nacional de Fabricantes de Veículos Automotores — ANFAVEA), and the Brazilian Federation of Bank Associations (Federação Brasileira de Associações de Bancos — FEBRABAN). The sectoral scope of most of these associations (Diniz and Boschi 1979) has increased the organizational fragmentation of Brazilian business rather than furthering its unification.

The second factor impeding the unification of business, especially of these noncorporatist associations, has been heavy state intervention in the economy, which has characterized Brazilian development since the early 1950s.[7] An array of licenses and permits, innumerable subsidies and tax incentives, and interconnections with para-state enterprises have meant that the operation and profitability of private enterprises have hinged on discretionary rulings by state officials. Since state interventionism has not been universalistic, but sector- or even firm-specific, this has created strong incentives for businesspeople to advance their own interests independently or together with a small number of other firms in their sector. Large-

scale state interventionism, therefore, has perpetuated the disaggregation of entrepreneurial demand making and the fragmentation of business organization.

In the absence of a substantial threat from below, these two main reasons —
state corporatism and massive state interventionism — explain why Brazil's private
sector has been organizationally fragmented for a long time. For lack of unity,
business has not elaborated and proposed comprehensive projects but has merely
reacted to state initiatives and made innumerable particularistic demands (Cardoso
1970, 1972; Leff 1968; Schmitter 1971). Entrepreneurs have cared less about
general rules than about exceptions from these rules for themselves. Most collective
demand making has been restricted to a sectoral scope.

Military rule helped maintain the organizational fragmentation of the private
sector. The authoritarian regime (1964-1985) strengthened state corporatism while
concentrating power in the executive branch and undermining the political role of
parties, elections, and Congress. It instituted bifrontal corporatism (O'Donnell
1977), which severely limited broad-based interest representation. This provided an
unfavorable environment for the formation of a private sector peak association.
Important businesspeople and sectors could, however, obtain access to government
officials and bureaucrats in order to advance their specific interests — hardly an
inducement for unity.

State agencies regularly consulted with sectoral business associations, giving
them considerable access to policymaking. For example, under President Ernesto
Geisel (1974-1979), who tried forcefully to concentrate decisionmaking in his own
hands, the Finance Ministry often submitted its projects to business associations and
requested their suggestions (interviews Freire 1990, Lima 1990). This associational
channel guaranteed the business community that the state would respect its basic
interests and consider its specific demands, but it did not provide business with a
high level of influence in decisionmaking. The policy initiative clearly lay with the
government. Given its organizational fragmentation, business only maintained a
reactive rather than proactive position.

To enhance their influence, businesspeople established personal links to state
officials. Informal connections were useful for articulating the many particularistic
interests that private firms had in an economy with a high degree of state intervention. These "bureaucratic rings" (Cardoso 1975, 181-4; 206-9; Boschi 1979, 163-
79) became a particularly attractive mode of interest representation, and they proved
effective in providing important businesspeople with special favors. Owners of
small and medium-sized firms were excluded from this mode of interest articulation
because only the owners or managers of big firms had enough clout and resources
to enter into bureaucratic rings. The big firms focused their attention on their own
particularistic interests, not on the collective interests of their sector or even their
class. Bureaucratic rings thus had a disaggregative effect on private sector demand
making, undermining the influence of business as a "class."

Within this fragmented framework, businesspeople continued to make narrow demands. Rather than designing comprehensive projects for the country, they
advanced a large number of specific, sectoral proposals (see, for example, CNI
1970). Even on the rare occasion when some entrepreneurs supported broad
demands, as in the campaign against expanding state interventionism ("statization")

in the mid-1970s, other actors, especially sectors of the media, were leading the charge (Cruz 1984). Again, in general, businesspeople reacted to state actions rather than taking the initiative.

Given the disaggregation of its demand making, business was unable and unwilling to direct Brazil's development process, instead leaving this task to the state. The private sector derived enormous benefits and had a say in the implementation of Brazil's growth strategy, but its basic outline was determined by the state. The state was in command, not business (Schmitter 1971, 361-65; Vianna 1987). Thus, organizational fragmentation helped to keep the private sector in a subordinate position vis-à-vis the state.

ENTREPRENEURS' POLITICAL ACTIVISM UNDER DEMOCRACY

How did Brazilian business respond to the installation of civilian rule in 1985?[8] Did it become more active in politics? Did business close ranks and begin to speak with a strong single voice? Did it, in this way, enhance its political influence? These important questions are addressed in this and the next two sections. This section discusses the increased political activism of Brazilian business. The next two sections analyze the failure of attempts at organizational unification and assess the private sector's political influence.

Since the early 1980s, Brazilian business has indeed increased its political activism and come to make demands on an ever wider range of issues. The private sector has not, however, been able to agree on a coherent development project for the country. The advent of civilian rule guaranteed the full autonomy of private sector organizations from government control. By allowing workers and the poor to advance their interests freely, the regime transition also intensified the political concerns of businesspeople and led them to increase their activism. In recent years, they have spoken out on a wider gamut of issues. While the private sector has continued to focus its attention on economic topics, it has also displayed a new interest in general political questions, such as the electoral system, presidential decree powers, and judicial reform.[9]

As one of its main goals, business has tried to use democracy for its own benefit, demanding protection against the state and increased participation in policymaking. For example, in his 1985 suggestions for a new constitution, FIESP's president proposed a neo-corporatist "social and economic council" (Vidigal Filho 1985; CNI 1987, 47). In this way, business leaders have tried to gain direct influence on the definition of economic policy. They have also advocated a strengthening of the legislative branch and the judiciary in order to counterbalance the preponderant power of the executive (CNI 1987, 21-39).

Not only has the private sector broadened the range of its demands, but, more importantly, businesspeople have begun to think about the basic outline of Brazilian development in a long-term perspective. For decades, they left this issue to the government and focused only on their immediate economic interests. Now, the length and depth of the economic crisis of the 1980s and early 1990s has prompted a broad debate about reorientation of Brazil's growth model. Private sector attacks on state intervention have grown more fierce (although business leaders have continued to lobby behind closed doors for special governmental favors for their own firms).

In order to design a vision of their own for Brazil's economic future, in 1989, leaders from São Paulo industry founded the Institute for Industrial Development Studies (Instituto de Estudos para o Desenvolvimento Industrial — IEDI). In contrast to established business associations that pressed short-term issues, IEDI has set itself the task to design a long-term development strategy (interview Cunha 1992; IEDI 1990a, 1992a). While this effort has produced interesting proposals, including, for instance, one on education (IEDI 1992b), President Fernando Collor de Mello's (1990-1992) decision to reduce trade barriers put IEDI on the defensive. Strong concern about the ability of many industrial sectors to withstand the onslaught of foreign competition (interview Arruda 1992) induced IEDI to demand immediate relief (IEDI 1990a, 2-3; 1990b, 2). In turn, government officials and even entrepreneurs dismissed IEDI as merely a lobbying group for import-substituting industries that feared being weaned off extensive state support. As short-term interests seemed to take precedence over IEDI's self-proclaimed concern for long-term issues and as prominent IEDI members were drawn into rivalries inside FIESP, the organization slid into an identity crisis (Schneider 1997-1998, 108-109). Thus, it has remained difficult for entrepreneurs to design a comprehensive development project even for a sector such as industry — not to speak of the whole economy.

In sum, the private sector has intensified its political activism in Brazil's new democracy. Although it has not succeeded in designing a coherent development strategy for the country, it has made demands that go beyond questions of immediate economic interest and include political-institutional changes. Has business managed to translate this increasing — albeit unfocused — activism into effective influence on public policy? For this purpose, the organizational unification of the private sector would be of crucial help.

EFFORTS AT ORGANIZATIONAL UNIFICATION

How has the advent of civilian rule affected the organization of Brazilian business? Has Brazil's private sector formed an effective peak association and started to speak with a single voice? Entrepreneurs have made several efforts to create encompassing organizations, but they have not been at all successful. Only in debates on the country's Constitution, both during the Constituent Assembly of 1987-1988 and the assembly for Constitutional Revision of 1993-1994, did more encompassing business groupings play a significant role. But as soon as these assemblies completed (1988) or abandoned (1994) their tasks, these broad groupings dissolved or disappeared from public view.

As mentioned in section two, the main reasons for this failure to form a private sector peak organization were threefold: First, the large size and internal heterogeneity of Brazilian business has made it exceedingly difficult to define common interests and pursue them in a unified fashion. Second, established business associations have insisted on their autonomy and refused to submit to the authority of an encompassing organization (interviews Amato 1992; Bornhausen 1992; Rio

Branco 1989). Third, the absence of a profound threat to business interests from the lower classes or the state has eliminated the main incentive that could overcome these impediments and prompt organizational unification (interviews Amato 1992; Coelho 1992).

Certainly, entrepreneurs and their associations have formed a number of encompassing organizations and coordinating bodies. Most of these organizations have spoken out on general political issues, rather than articulating the economic interests of their members; some have simply been vehicles of ambitious individuals.[10] Thus, they have not affected business interest representation at its core. In particular, none has gained predominance inside the private sector, not to speak of managing to unify it. The large number of these new groupings has reflected the internal heterogeneity of Brazilian business and the rivalries among its associations, rather than mitigating these problems.

Until the 1990s, only two encompassing associations, the Brazilian Business Union (União Brasileira de Empresários — UBE) and the Informal Forum (Fórum Informal — FI), had acquired some political importance, but tension between them limited their influence. The corporatist confederations and some important sectoral associations, for instance, the Organization of Auto Parts Producers, created UBE in 1986 in order to coordinate their lobbying and enhance their influence in the upcoming constituent assembly. Fearing that leftist forces, supported by popular mobilization, would dominate the constitutional deliberations, the most powerful elements of Brazilian business, in a rare decision, joined forces in order to combat potential threats to their interests more effectively.

The center-left did, in fact, strongly influence the elaboration of the first constitutional draft. The private sector abhorred some of its provisions, such as the prohibition against dismissing workers who had held their jobs for more than 10 years. Business rejected this and other proposed norms as undue interference in its autonomy and as impediments to economic efficiency. In order to block these provisions, business lobbied the assembly delegates actively. UBE coordinated these activities, which — among other pressures — contributed to the formation of a center-right alliance in the Constituent Assembly. This *Centrão* ("Big Center") split the main government party, the center-left Party of the Brazilian Democratic Movement (Partido do Movimento Democrático Brasileiro — PMDB), achieved a majority in the assembly, and watered down many of the original constitutional proposals. The Centrão, however, was never cohesively organized, and it soon disintegrated from its internal tensions. Its success, therefore, remained limited, and the new Constitution contained a number of rules that offended important sectors of business. For instance, article 192, paragraph 3, limits real interest rates to 12 percent per year, a restriction that banks strenuously oppose. Article 171 grants domestic capital special privileges that foreign business and transnationalized sectors of Brazilian business abhor.

Like the Centrão, UBE suffered from internal divisions that impaired its effectiveness. Some important constitutional issues, such as the rules for the operation of foreign capital, pitted transnationally oriented segments of business against protectionist, inward-looking sectors. More importantly, UBE restricted its activities to the Constituent Assembly and went into hibernation in late 1988 with the promulgation of the new charter (interview Coelho 1992). It never directed the interest articulation of business in other arenas, especially in the dense and crucially important relations between entrepreneurs and the governmental bureaucracy (interview Bornhausen 1992). UBE did not advance beyond the definition of a common business position on general constitutional principles, which was much easier to forge than an agreement on specific policy. Thus, UBE did not coordinate the different modes of private sector interest representation, and it never tried to turn into an effective peak association. Indeed, it did not have its own bureaucratic apparatus and always remained a temporary, ad-hoc creation (interview Coelho 1992).

A rival organization limited UBE's capacity to represent the private sector as a whole. In 1987, the São Paulo business community created its own coordinating body, the Fórum Informal (FI), because it did not see its interests adequately represented in the corporatist confederations sponsoring UBE. Drawing on the clout of its member organizations, particularly FIESP, FI has confronted the government on several occasions with the unified position of Brazil's strongest business community.[11] Contrary to UBE, which confined itself to influencing the constitutional debates, FI has used the close links between its member associations and the state bureaucracy to block harmful policy changes, such as increases in taxation.

The FI has, however, not been able to ensure internal unity among its member organizations (interviews Rio Branco 1989; Solimeo 1992; Szajman 1992). More importantly, as a state-level body, it cannot speak for all of Brazilian business. Its unifying capacity is inevitably limited. The formation of the FI exacerbated the disunity of Brazilian business. A powerful regional-level coordinating body with direct links to the federal government limits the capacity of any national organization, such as UBE, to give business a single voice. Through the FI, São Paulo business has strengthened its capacity to speak for itself, independent of — even against — the rest of Brazilian business.

Indeed, the very creation of the FI was an effort by FIESP, which wanted to preserve its autonomy and influence, to prevent UBE and the corporatist confederations sponsoring it from establishing their leadership inside the business community.[12] FIESP had initially supported, if not suggested, the formation of UBE. But when it became clear that the corporatist confederations — not the economically more powerful FIESP — would play the leading role in UBE, FIESP organized the FI to preserve its "space" against the coordinating efforts of UBE. While some national organizations spearheaded a drive for organizational unification, others, such as FIESP, defended their own autonomy. By founding competing coordinating mechanisms, they limited the role and undermined the influence of the new coordinating body and counteracted its rationale. Thus, strong rivalries among established associations prevented Brazil's private sector from creating an effective peak association in the 1980s.

During the government of Fernando Collor de Mello (1990-1992), organizational unification of the private sector did not advance. In his first year in office, Collor hoped to reduce the influence of established business organizations, especially FIESP. He sometimes used deliberate divide-and-rule tactics for this purpose. For example, he privileged a new, loose movement of small and medium-sized firms (Pensamento Nacional das Bases Empresariais —PNBE) as interlocutor to weaken FIESP (interview Butori 1992). Collor's market-oriented policies, which had a differential sectoral impact, aggravated interest divergences inside the private sector, making it more difficult for entrepreneurs to agree on common interests. Since business as a class did not face any major threat, it felt no urgency to form an encompassing organization.

Only in 1993, with the upcoming constitutional revision, did efforts to unify the private sector gather steam again. Leading entrepreneurs saw the reduced requirements for changing the constitution as a golden opportunity to take advantage of the move of public opinion to the right in order to roll back the advance of the center-left's agenda in the 1988 Constitution (Solimeo 1994; interview Cidade 1995). In this way, they hoped to remove the threat that certain of the new rules posed to private sector interests. The threat was exacerbated by the apparently likely victory of the socialist Workers' Party (Partido dos Trabalhadores — PT) in the upcoming 1994 presidential elections. An altered constitution could restrain an eventual PT government and thus minimize the danger that it could hurt business. Once again, anticipated risks — and opportunities, in this case — prompted efforts to unify the private sector.

A small group of leading entrepreneurs headed by Jorge Gerdau Johannpeter promoted the elaboration of a consensual minimum agenda for the constitutional revision (interviews Reis 1994; Cidade 1995). They achieved considerable success for two reasons: First, only very general principles — not specific policies — were at issue. Second, the "neoliberal" wave of the early 1990s had discredited the nationalist and state-interventionist currents of opinion that had divided the private sector in 1987 and 1988. This informal group convinced most business associations to accept a core agenda of constitutional revisions that included the removal of state monopolies of utilities and mineral wealth, the elimination of restrictions on foreign capital, the reduction of governmental regulation, the shrinking of the social security system, and the lowering of the tax burden (CNI 1993; *Propostas* 1993). Coordinated by this informal grouping called "Entrepreneurial Action" (Ação Empresarial), many business associations lobbied actively for these common goals (Secretaria Técnica 1993, 1994; interview Cidade 1995).

These efforts at coordination had only limited success, however. Some divergences among business associations remained, especially on taxation (*Propostas* 1993, 20-21, 31-33; Szajman 1994; interviews Solimeo 1995; Rio Branco 1995). Furthermore, the exceptionally high level of consensus within the private sector was brought about by an informal grouping of entrepreneurs (interview Reis 1994; Cidade 1995). Because this effort at forging unity was focused on a special occasion and did not aim at the formation of a permanent peak association, established business associations felt less threatened than they had by UBE, which was initially intended to be a lasting peak organization (interviews Bornhausen 1992; Cidade 1995; Rio Branco 1995). The lesser organizational ambitions of the Entrepreneurial Action may have been a precondition for its greater success in unifying the business lobby. This trade-off between effectiveness and permanence underscores the difficulties of forming an encompassing private sector organization in Brazil.

Moreover, the Entrepreneurial Action had only a limited impact on public decisionmaking. In order not to arouse hostility in public opinion, it initially acted discreetly. Only when it noticed that politicians were reluctant to make unpopular changes in the Constitution before the upcoming elections of late 1994, did it act more forcefully (interview Reis 1994). Yet despite the entrepreneurs' efforts, even conservative parliamentarians who were close to business preferred seeking votes in their home districts to debating constitutional changes in the capital. The constitutional revision, fiercely opposed by the left, was undermined by this lack of commitment from rightist and centrist politicians, who failed to guarantee the necessary quorum.

Since taking office in January 1995, President Fernando Henrique Cardoso has renewed the effort to amend the Constitution and thus promote market-oriented restructuring. Entrepreneurial Action has provided strong support while accepting the leading role of the government, which pursues less ambitious goals than the private sector (*Reformas Constitucionais* 1995; CNI 1995; interviews Rio Branco 1995; Solimeo 1995). Moreover, Entrepreneurial Action has merely coordinated the activities of existing business associations and not assumed a public role of its own. While some private sector representatives hope that this body will, in the medium run, turn into a business peak association, others, especially spokesmen for FIESP, are skeptical.[13] In fact, any legal effort to regulate and implement the constitutional amendments achieved by the Cardoso government will affect different business sectors in different ways and is therefore likely to intensify interest divergences among business sectors, thus threatening the fragile generic consensus achieved at this moment.

Thus, under the new democracy, Brazil's private sector has not significantly advanced its organizational unity. Given the absence of a severe threat to the capitalist class, the divergence of interests among business sectors and the organizational tensions among existing associations have prevented an encompassing peak organization from forming. The self-limitation of the most recent effort shows that entrepreneurs have recognized the enormous difficulty of creating an encompassing business organization in Brazil.

Rather than achieving internal unity, Brazilian business has seen its fragmentation increase. Above all, small and medium-sized firms have mobilized and formed new associations and movements (Nylen 1993). The main impulse has stemmed from democratization, which has raised the importance of numbers as a power capability (Anderson 1967, 90-91) and has enhanced the role of Congress as a decision-making arena. Owners of small and medium-sized firms, who are the majority among businesspeople, have protested against the predominance of big business in the country's major associations. They have tried to assert their own interests more forcefully and have skillfully used the new opportunities that democracy has opened up.

Since 1987, when small and medium-sized firms from São Paulo formed the PNBE, its leaders have attacked the "oligarchy" of big business in FIESP and criticized its close connections to the state, which they see as an impediment to the forceful pursuit of private sector interests. Rejecting the staunch conservatism of many FIESP officials, they have advocated a more flexible position vis-à-vis organized labor and displayed a reformist attitude in politics (PNBE 1989; interview Kapaz 1989). By creating an opposition inside FIESP, the most powerful business association in Brazil, the PNBE has increased the fragmentation of the private sector. While FIESP counterattacked and managed to divide the PNBE in 1992 (interviews Butori 1992; Couri 1992), the increased organizational diversity of business has persisted. Thus, rather than prompting the organizational unification of business, the democratic transition has made this goal more difficult to achieve.

THE DISPERSION OF BUSINESS INFLUENCE

In line with the general argument advanced in the introduction to this volume, the organizational fragmentation of Brazilian business has dispersed the political access and limited the influence on public policymaking of the private sector. Through narrow links to state agencies and officials, entrepreneurs have continued to obtain special favors, but they have failed to push for overarching goals. Unable to design a comprehensive project with broad appeal or make demands in a unified fashion, business associations have often acted at cross-purposes from each other. Rivalries among them and the absence of an encompassing peak organization have dispersed business power. Certainly, basic capitalist interests have not been endangered, and important firms have succeeded in obtaining many particularistic favors. But the private sector has had limited influence on broad policy decisions, especially the reorientation of Brazil's development strategy. While it has managed to slow down governmental proposals, it has not successfully advanced its own project. The main beneficiaries of the private sector's limited clout have not been labor and other lower classes, which have suffered from similar organizational fragmentation, but state agencies and Brazil's irresponsible "political class," who have enjoyed great latitude in decisionmaking and have frequently been able to use their unaccountable power for personal enrichment.

Businesspeople have continued to enjoy ample, dispersed access to the state. While the autocratic style of President Collor and the scandal over his corruption restricted informal connections somewhat, formal access improved in 1991 with the creation of "sectoral chambers." Through these bodies designed for meso-corporatist negotiations with the government and labor, entrepreneurs have managed to win special favors, such as sector-specific tax rebates (MEFP 1992; MICT 1994; interview Butori 1992). This modernization of Brazil's fragmented corporatist system has helped to perpetuate the tendency of businesspeople to define their goals narrowly and neglect collective action for overarching class interests. Continued dispersed access has reinforced the private sector's organizational fragmentation, which, in turn, has limited entrepreneurs' political influence.

The divisions inside the private sector have aggravated the difficulties that business has faced in responding to two new challenges, namely, the political requirements of democracy and Brazil's severe economic problems. The regime change has strengthened Congress, yet many business sectors have found it difficult to develop an efficacious lobby in the parliamentary arena, where demands must be articulated in a politically attractive, broadly appealing way. Nowadays, even "shock" programs designed to stabilize the economy, although still elaborated by a small number of public technocrats, have to pass through the filter of Congress, which takes electoral considerations into account. Deftly packaging self-interested demands by linking them to the needs of other societal sectors would, therefore, enhance entrepreneurs' clout. A peak association, whose encompassing scope induces it to focus on overarching interests, tends to tackle this task with considerable skill, as the "battle for ideas" launched by Chile's Confederación de la Producción y del Comercio in the late 1980s suggests.[14]

By contrast, the sectoral organizations prevailing in Brazil, such as FIESP, have had limited success in adapting to the new requirements of democracy. Under military rule, the political influence of entrepreneurs depended almost exclusively on their economic weight, their technical capacity,[15] and their direct contacts with top decisionmakers, usually maintained behind closed doors. Under democracy, a wider range of power capabilities count, particularly control over votes, and new avenues of interest representation have opened up. In order to be optimally effective, entrepreneurs now have to address political appeals to a larger audience. As business association representatives stress, the elaboration of a new discourse has not proved easy,[16] and the level of their political influence and the effectiveness of their demand making have suffered as a consequence.

The isolation of big business became glaringly obvious in November 1989, when Fernando Collor scornfully rejected FIESP's public endorsement of his presidential candidacy (Weyland 1993, 9). Collor enhanced his popularity by attacking this bastion of Brazil's elite as retrograde and selfish, which showed how much FIESP was out of touch with public opinion. The same problem is indirectly revealed in entrepreneurs' constant complaint that for electoral reasons they are often betrayed by politicians whose campaigns they have supported (interviews Coelho 1992; Cunha 1992; Ferreira 1995; Rio Branco 1989, 1995; Szajman 1992; Velloso 1995). This suggests that businesspeople have not successfully linked their own interests to the desires and demands of large numbers of voters, with the consequence that they have suffered important defeats in Congress.

Being vulnerable to "mobilization of bias" (Schattschneider 1975) from the government or other political forces has indeed lowered business influence on public policy. For instance, the private sector's long-standing demand to lower social security and health insurance taxes (IEDI 1991, 5-6; FIESP 1993, 7), which raise the cost of labor and thus arguably restrict employment, has never been met (Weyland 1996b). To the contrary, the government has invoked the presumed social purpose of these taxes to justify augmenting them further (SRF 1994, 36-41) but has then diverted the proceeds to other purposes. As another example, the financial sector, which has been especially inept at building support in society, was unable to block a constitutional provision in 1988 and enabling legislation in early 1995 to limit real interest rates to 12 percent per year. Banks unsuccessfully rejected this limit, given the risks of investing in Brazil, not to mention of the governmental manipulation of official inflation rates, which can affect the computation of real interest rates.[17] Finally, when FIESP denounced privileges introduced by Congress into the government's proposal for administrative reform, parliamentarians deflected this criticism and maintained their own privileges by attacking FIESP's lack of concern for income distribution (*Folha de São Paulo* 1997). Indeed, in May 1996, Congress voted down a constitutional amendment supported by business on the same day that almost 3,000 industrialists held an unprecedented demonstration in Brasília to push for constitutional reforms (Schneider 1997-1998, 113).

Due to entrepreneurs' difficulty in addressing broader sociopolitical concerns and their organizational fragmentation, they have not made a substantial contribution to the redefinition of Brazil's development strategy,[18] the second problem mentioned above. Rather than providing a strong impulse for market-oriented change, the private sector has mainly reacted to reforms initiated by the government.[19] Different business associations have often advanced divergent proposals.[20] Due to this lack of coordination, their pressures have often neutralized each other. This has contributed to the paralysis that has characterized policymaking in Brazil's new democracy on several occasions, especially in 1988-1989 and 1992-1993. As only the government was able to overcome this paralysis, it has remained the chief protagonist of policy change in Brazil. The private sector has had, at best, veto power.

Because disagreements among different business associations have weakened the influence of the private sector, seemingly powerful business groups have suffered bitter defeats on important issues. For instance, during the constitutional debates of 1987-1988, FIESP, the mouthpiece of big business with its transnational links, opposed governmental privileges for domestic capital, which many associations of small and medium-sized firms demanded. Since the latter sectors were better able to appeal to nationalist sectors of Brazil's society and state, FIESP lost this hotly contested battle (Diniz and Boschi 1989, 126-128; Dreifuss 1989, 219-226).

Divisions within the private sector also hindered attempts to find a negotiated solution to Brazil's economic crisis. Several times in the late 1980s, São Paulo business, led by FIESP, promoted a "social pact" among the private sector, labor, and the state. Other business associations, however, were often lukewarm. They feared FIESP's predominance and could not afford an accommodation with trade unions as easily as could the Paulista entrepreneurs, who were able to use their market power to transfer the cost to consumers (interview Fernandes 1990; Diniz 1991, 355-356). In addition to active opposition from radical sectors of organized labor and passive resistance by some state officials who defended their decision-making latitude, these divergences inside the private sector undermined the negotiations for a social pact. Business efforts to lead Brazil out of its economic crisis therefore failed.

Similarly, important business associations pursued for a long time such a wide variety of tax reform proposals that unified pressure for any one project proved impossible. In the early 1990s, the reduction of trade barriers by the Collor administration and the resulting intensification of foreign competition made it impossible for firms to transfer taxes to consumers via higher prices, as they had commonly done before. Several business associations therefore designed exceptionally far-reaching projects for tax reform. But these projects differed widely. Some proposed to raise the income tax, others to abolish it and augment indirect taxes; the most radical project wanted to scrap the whole tax structure and substitute it with a single levy on financial transactions (FCESP 1992; FIESP 1993; IEDI 1991; PNBE 1992; Rezende 1992; interview Fernandes 1992). This enormous divergence inside the private sector helped impede the adoption of any proposal. While business has since achieved a higher level of consensus on tax reform, important differences still persist (*Propostas* 1993, 20-21, 31-33; Szajman 1994 vs. CNI 1994, 16; interviews Reis 1994; Solimeo 1995).

Given the incapacity of Brazil's fragmented private sector to elaborate constructive and consensual policy proposals and its prevailing focus on particularistic interests, the government has led the reorientation of Brazil's development model. All major stabilization programs have been designed by public officials with minimal input from entrepreneurs.[21] A small group of experts working in strict seclusion designed President Collor's first economic plan. Business was overtly denied consultation and participation (interviews Amato 1992; Solimeo 1992; Temporal 1992).[22] And although the 1994 Plano Real was implemented after greater consultation with the private sector, it was still designed by state officials and experts.

Similarly, Brazil's move toward market-oriented restructuring has drawn its momentum from state action. The Collor government provided the biggest impulse in its first year in office, when it was most distant from business. Since then, important changes that have been implemented, such as the opening of Brazil's economy to foreign competition, have been opposed by some powerful sectors of business but with little success (IEDI 1990b; Bornhausen 1991, 11, 14, 16; interviews Arruda 1992; Collor 1995; Mello 1995; Moreira 1992, 1995). Reforms demanded by business, particularly a reduction in the tax burden and a "flexibilization" of labor laws (CNI 1994, 22-23), have not been enacted. In the renewed push for market-oriented reform under President Cardoso, who took office in January 1995, the government has once again assumed the leading role (interviews Cidade 1995; Velloso 1995). Thus, the initiation and progress of economic restructuring have owed much more to (shifting) governmental goals and capabilities than to pressure from the private sector.

Indeed, sectoral and regional business associations have systematically taken divergent stances on crucial parts of the market-oriented reform agenda, serving only to neutralize each other's demands and proposals. In addition to the case of tax reform, controversies over the opening of the economy to foreign competition are notably divisive. Thus, on policy issues that are central to Brazil's future, business has been divided and has had little capacity for initiative and limited veto power. Overall, the old "division of labor" in politics — the state initiates, and business reacts — has persisted. One major reason has been the organizational fragmentation of the private sector. Internal disunity, that is, the predominance of sectoral associations and the absence of a peak association, has weakened business politically. Brazil's entrepreneurs have remained divided and unable to design a consensual and viable policy strategy. Their major groupings have not forged a cross-sectoral alliance, as their counterparts in Chile did in the mid-1980s (Silva 1993, 549-555). The dispersed access of entrepreneurs to the state — an effect as well as a cause of their persistent organizational fragmentation — has helped to impede a proactive stance in policymaking and confined the private sector to a reactive posture.

Certainly, in many countries neoliberal reform has been initiated by top government officials without much consultation with the private sector (for example, Waterbury 1992, 191-193). But this is not always the case. In Chile, business associations coordinated by their encompassing organization, the Confederation of Production and Commerce (Confederación de la Producción y del Comercio — CPC), had considerable influence on the reequilibration of the market model after the deep crisis of 1982-1983 (Silva 1993; chapter in this volume). Mexican business, led by the Consejo Coordinador Empresarial, participated directly in the negotiation of the heterodox Pact for Economic Solidarity in 1987, which was decisive in reducing inflation (Kaufman, Bazdresch, and Heredia 1994, 377-380, 387-388, 391, 398-399; Tirado's chapter). In Peru, the business peak association National Confederation of Private Business Organizations (Confederación Nacional de Instituciones Empresariales Privadas — CONFIEP) "lent" experts to the Ministry of Economy so that they could participate directly in the elaboration of President Alberto Fujimori's structural adjustment measures.[23] Thus, where business has an effective encompassing peak organization, it can participate in the design and enactment of neoliberal reform. Given its great economic weight, Brazil's private sector would be a prime candidate for such an influential role, but the absence of a peak association poses obstacles that have so far proved insurmountable.

CONCLUSION

For a long time, Brazil's private sector has suffered from deep organizational fragmentation. The legacies of state corporatism and the disaggregative effect of massive government intervention in the economy account for this history of division. The transition to democracy induced entrepreneurs to increase their political activism and extend their demand making to an ever wider range of issues, but they have not been able to create a peak association that could effectively coordinate their political activities. Given the absence of organizational unity, business has had limited influence on public policy. Particularly, its power to initiate policy reforms has been limited, and even its veto power has suffered from its internal divisions.

In explaining the dispersion of business influence in Brazil's new democracy, this chapter has emphasized organizational factors. The lack of an encompassing peak association restricts the influence that Brazil's business community can exert through its uncoordinated demand making. As comparison with other cases in Latin America suggests, an encompassing organization could translate political activism more successfully into effective influence (see chapters by Durand, Silva, and Tirado in this book). A wide-ranging investigation of business associations in advanced industrial countries (Coleman and Grant 1988) confirms that the organizational unity of the private sector strongly conditions its political power. Together with my analysis of the contrasting Brazilian case, these studies show that organizational structure significantly affects the political influence of business.

What, then, accounts for the absence of an effective encompassing business peak association in Brazil? This chapter has pointed to socioeconomic, political, and organizational factors. First, the vast size and internal heterogeneity of the country's private sector have hindered organizational unification by making it difficult for entrepreneurs to define common interests and pursue them through unified collective action. However, given that Mexico's similarly large and heterogeneous private sector has formed an effective peak association, these socioeconomic factors are not decisive.

Organizational and political factors, namely, the existing fragmented pattern of business organization and the absence of severe threats to private sector interests, have also played a crucial role. The long-standing fragmentation of business organization and the entrenched associational and personal links between entrepreneurs and the state have aggravated collective action problems and helped prevent formation of an encompassing peak association. Sectoral and regional organizations have jealously defended their autonomy, and their leaders have viewed efforts at unification as attempts to undermine their own power. The organizational fragmentation of Brazil's private sector has thus had a self-perpetuating effect.

In addition, strong threats to business, which could have induced it to shelve internal differences and close ranks, have not emerged because fragmentation has also weakened the potential enemies of the private sector. Labor has been divided among rival peak associations; the more radical currents organized in CUT have, therefore, not been able to pose a powerful challenge to business. The poor masses have been particularly dispersed in organizational terms, often due to Brazil's pervasive clientelism; they have been capable of no more than fleeting mobilization. The state, finally, has suffered from rampant bureaucratic politics, which has paralyzed it and limited its autonomy from the private sector. Business groupings have also maintained multiple (though dispersed) channels to the state, which have allowed them to block serious threats to their interests. Since entrepreneurs have not faced any profound danger, they have not deemed it necessary to resort to broadly encompassing collective action.

Thus, organizational factors help explain the absence of a profound threat to business interests in Brazil, which, by impeding the formation of an encompassing private sector peak association, weakens business politically. Organizational factors therefore appear as critically important parameters of political life. The findings of this case study thus support the renewed emphasis in political science on organizational variables (March and Olsen 1989; Steinmo, Thelen, and Longstreth 1992).

Notes

1. The term "economic groups" refers to conglomerates, which are networks of firms generally controlled by a flagship or holding company. As a result, overlapping directorships are one of their principal characteristics. Some conglomerates vertically integrate different stages of their industry, but the most powerful ones diversify into several economic sectors, such as finance, consumer durables, agribusiness, communications, and commerce. The more diversified it is, the more flexibility a conglomerate has to have to adjust to changing economic conditions. For a more detailed definition, see Nathaniel Leff (1986).

2. This argument is more generally applicable, for example, to parties of the Latin American left. Where the left tried to unify existing parties, as in Peru (United Left or Izquierda Unida — IU) or Mexico (Party of the Democratic Revolution or Partido de la Revolución Democrática — PRD), success has been precarious and temporary. Only where the left has created a new party organization virtually from scratch, such as Brazil's Workers' Party (Partido dos Trabalhadores — PT), has unity been maintained.

3. Since threat is a matter of perception, it is difficult to measure. There is an important theoretical justification for emphasizing the threat factor, however. The threat argument draws on strong loss aversion that psychological experiments consistently find among people (Payne, Bettman, and Johnson 1992, 96, 122). Political scientists have started to invoke loss aversion to explain decisionmakers' much stronger concern with protecting their "assets" from losses than with making further gains (for example, Stein and Pauly 1993; Weyland 1998).

4. In 1989, Luís Inácio Lula da Silva of the socialist Workers' Party (PT) almost won the presidency, but established elites planned to deal with this threat through institutional engineering, specifically by introducing a parliamentary system to curtail severely presidential powers and boost the influence of Congress, where centrist and rightist parties predominated. This "solution" was imposed when President Jânio Quadros abruptly quit in August 1961, leaving "radical" Vice President João Goulart as his successor.

5. For the Brazilian case, see Schmitter 1971, chapters 8 and 9; on state corporatism in general, Schmitter 1974, 102-105.

6. On the continuing vitality of the corporatist framework, see Boschi 1990.

7. The following argument draws heavily on Schneider 1992, chapter 6.

8. For excellent analyses of the role of business during the transition process, see Cardoso 1986 and Cruz 1984.

9. FIESP/CIESP 1987; Ferreira Filho 1997a, 1997b. With these series, FIESP has organized and published round-tables and talks by well-known social scientists and intellectuals about general political issues.

10. For an early overview, see Dreifuss 1989, 49-69.

11. For example, a manifesto from ' was instrumental in blocking the tax reform proposed by Finance Minister Luiz Carlos Bresser Pereira in December 1987; this defeat induced the minister to step down (interview Bresser 1989).

12. Confidential author interview with an important FIESP official, São Paulo, December 1989.

13. Confidential author interviews in Brasília and São Paulo, June 1995.

14. Feliú 1988; CPC 1990; Silva's chapter in this volume. For a similar case, see CONFIEP 1989 and Durand's chapter in this volume.

15. Business had to advance its interests in a way that the "technocrats" of the authoritarian regime found convincing.

16. Interviews Cunha 1992; Rio Branco 1989; Solimeo 1989; see also Bornhausen 1991, 27-28; or a more positive assessment of these efforts: interviews Fernandes 1992 and Cidade 1995.

17. Only concerted pressure by the government — not business — managed to block the 1995 bill, which the Senate had already passed, in the Chamber of Deputies.

18. Diniz (1991, 351-357, 364, 371-372) advances a similar argument.

19. This point is confirmed by the new in-depth analyses by Kingstone (1994) and McQuerry (1995).

20. See, for instance, the differences between CACB 1989; Diniz 1989; and FIESP 1990.

21. For details of the Cruzado Plan, see Sardenberg 1987; Diniz 1988, 36-38; for President Collor's initial "shock plan," see interviews with Eris 1992 and Kandir 1992.

22. The frustration of businesspeople with the exclusionary policy-making style of the Collor government is reflected in the blunt discussion reported in Bornhausen 1991, 11, 13, 23, 27.

23. Tello 1995; confidential author interview with a top business leader, Lima, February 1995.

References

Amato, Mário. 1992. Author interview with President, Federação das Indústrias do Estado de São Paulo (FIESP). São Paulo, June 9.

Anderson, Charles W. 1967. *Politics and Economic Change in Latin America.* New York: Van Nostrand Reinhold.

Arruda, Mauro Fernando. 1992. Author interview with General Superintendent, Instituto de Estudos para o Desenvolvimento Industrial (IEDI). São Paulo, May 21.

Bartell, Ernest, and Leigh Payne, eds. 1995. *Business and Democracy in Latin America.* Pittsburgh: University of Pittsburgh Press.

Becker, David. 1990. "Business Associations in Latin America." *Comparative Political Studies* 23 (1): 114-138.

Bornhausen, Roberto Konder. 1991. "Reflexões sobre o Brasil." *Cadernos do IRS*, no. 18. São Paulo: FIESP/CIESP.

Bornhausen, Roberto Konder. 1992. Author interview with former President, Federação Brasileira de Associações de Bancos. São Paulo, June 9.

Boschi, Renato. 1979. *Elites industriais e democracia.* Rio de Janeiro: Graal.

Boschi, Renato. 1990. "Interesses empresariais e democracia." Paper presented at the second National Meeting of Industrial Leaders of the Confederação Nacional da Indústria, Rio de Janeiro, January 26-27.

Boschi, Renato, and Eli Diniz. 1978. *Empresariado nacional e estado no Brasil.* Rio de Janeiro: Forense Universitária.

Bresser Pereira, Luiz Carlos. 1989. Author interview with former Finance Minister (1987). São Paulo, November 10.

Butori, Paulo Roberto. 1992. Author interview with former Coordinator, Pensamento Nacional das Bases Empresariais (PNBE). São Paulo, June 12.

CACB (Confederação das Associações Comerciais do Brasil). 1989. *Rumo ao terceiro milênio.* Rio de Janeiro: Expressão e Cultura.

Cardoso, Fernando Henrique. 1970. "Hegemonía burguesa e independencia económica." In *Brasil: Hoy*, 2nd ed., ed. Celso Furtado. Mexico: Siglo Veintiuno.

Cardoso, Fernando Henrique. 1972. *Empresário industrial e desenvolvimento econômico no Brasil*, 2nd ed. São Paulo: DIFEL.

Cardoso, Fernando Henrique. 1975. *Autoritarismo e democratização*, 3rd ed. Rio de Janeiro: Paz e Terra.

Cardoso, Fernando Henrique. 1986. "Entrepreneurs and the Transition Process." In *Transitions from Authoritarian Rule. Comparative Perspectives*, eds. Guillermo O'Donnell, Philippe Schmitter, and Laurence Whitehead. Baltimore: Johns Hopkins University Press.

Cidade, Carlos Alberto Macedo. 1995. Author interview with Coordinator for Legislative Affairs, Confederação Nacional da Indústria. Brasilia, June 14.

CNI (Confederação Nacional da Indústria). 1970. *Convenção Nacional da Indústria. Tema: Política tributária e desenvolvimento econômico. Documento 1.* Rio de Janeiro: CNI.

CNI. 1987. *Proposições para uma nova constituição.* Rio de Janeiro: CNI.

CNI. 1993. *Seminário sobre revisão constitucional.* Rio de Janeiro: CNI.

CNI. 1994. *Rumo ao crescimento.* Rio de Janeiro: CNI.

CNI. 1995. *Custo Brasil.* Rio de Janeiro: CNI.

Coelho, José Washington. 1992. Author interview with Director of the Economic Department, Confederação Nacional do Comércio. Rio de Janeiro, May 14.

Coleman, William, and Wyn Grant. 1988. "The Organizational Cohesion and Political Access of Business." *European Journal of Political Research* 16 (5): 467-487.

Collor de Mello, Fernando. 1995. Author interview with former President of Brazil. Brasília, June 9.

CONFIEP (Confederación Nacional de Instituciones Empresariales Privadas). 1989. *CONFIEP propone: Una visión para el cambio.* Lima: CONFIEP.

Couri, Joseph. 1992. Author interview with President, Sindicato da Micro e Pequena Indústria do Estado de São Paulo. São Paulo, June 5.

CPC (Confederación de la Producción y del Comercio). 1990. *Cuenta de la presidencia de Don Manuel Feliú Justiniano.* Santiago: CPC.

CPC. 1994. *Modernización del estado.* Santiago: Universidad Nacional Andrés Bello.

Cruz, Sebastião Velasco. 1984. "Empresários e o regime no Brasil." Ph.D. Dissertation. Universidade de São Paulo, São Paulo, Brazil.

Cunha, Paulo Guilherme Aguiar. 1992. Author interview with Director and President, Instituto de Estudos para o Desenvolvimento Industrial (IEDI). São Paulo, June 11.

Diniz, Abílio, ed. 1989. *Reforma econômica para o Brasil.* São Paulo: Nobel and Grupo Pão de Açúcar.

Diniz, Eli. 1988. "Empresários, sindicatos e conflito distributivo no Brasil da Nova República." *Cadernos de Conjuntura,* no. 15. Rio de Janeiro: IUPERJ.

Diniz, Eli. 1989. "The Post-1930 Industrial Elite." In *Modern Brazil,* eds. Michael Conniff and Frank McCann. Lincoln, Neb.: University of Nebraska Press.

Diniz, Eli. 1991. "Empresariado e projeto neoliberal na América Latina." *Dados* 34 (3): 349-377.

Diniz, Eli, and Renato Boschi. 1979. "Autonomia e dependência na representação de interesses empresariais." *Dados* 22: 25-48.

Diniz, Eli, and Renato Boschi. 1989. "Empresários e Constituinte." In *Continuidade e mudança no Brasil da Nova República,* eds. Aspásia Camargo and Eli Diniz. São Paulo: Vértice.

Dreifuss, René. 1989. *O jogo da direita na Nova República.* Petrópolis: Vozes.

Eris, Ibrahim. 1992. Author interview with former President, Banco Central (1990-1991). São Paulo, May 27.

FCESP (Federação do Comércio do Estado de São Paulo). 1992. Reforma constitucional tributária (emendas constitucionais). São Paulo: FCESP.

Feliú, Manuel. 1988. *La empresa de la libertad.* Santiago: Zig-Zag.

Fernandes, José Augusto Coelho. 1990. Author interview with Director of the Economic Department, Confederação Nacional da Indústria. Rio de Janeiro, February 19.

Fernandes, José Augusto Coelho. 1992. Author interview with Executive Secretary, Confederação Nacional da Indústria. Rio de Janeiro, July 29.

Ferreira, Roberto Nogueira. 1995. Author interview with lobbyist for the Confederação Nacional do Comércio. Brasília, June 19.

Ferreira Filho, Manoel Gonçalves. 1997. Medidas Provisórias no Sistema Constitucional Brasileiro. São Paulo: FIESP/CIESP. Conselho Superior de Orientação Política e Social. Instituto Roberto Simonsen.

Ferreira Filho, Manoel Gonçalves. 1997. *A Reforma do Judiciário.* São Paulo: FIESP/CIESP. Conselho Superior de Orientaçao Política e Social. Instituto Roberto Simonsen.

FIESP (Federação das Indústrias do Estado de São Paulo). 1990. *Livre para crescer.* São Paulo: FIESP.

FIESP. 1993. "Uma proposta de reforma tributária e de seguridade social." *Conjuntura Social* 4 (1): 5-20.

FIESP and CIESP (Centro das Indústrias do Estado de São Paulo). 1987. "O voto distrital na perspectiva de uma nova constituição." *Cadernos do IRS*, no. 1. São Paulo: FIESP/CIESP.

Folha de São Paulo. 1997. "Relator estuda estender superteto." April 12: 1.

Freire, José Carlos Soares. 1990. Author interview with former Secretary-General, Finance Ministry (1974-79). Rio de Janeiro, February 12.

Guimarães, César. 1977. "Empresariado, tipos de capitalismo e ordem política." In *Estado e capitalismo no Brasil*, ed. Carlos E. Martins. São Paulo: HUCITEC-CEBRAP.

Hernández Rodríguez, Rogelio. 1991. "Los problemas de representación en los organismos empresariales." *Foro Internacional* 31 (3): 446-471.

IEDI (Instituto de Estudos para o Desenvolvimento Industrial). 1990. *Mudar para competir.* São Paulo: IEDI.

IEDI. 1990. *A necessidade de um projeto de desenvolvimento.* Carta N° 1 (October). São Paulo: IEDI.

IEDI. 1991. *Carga fiscal, competitividade industrial e potencial de crescimento econômico.* São Paulo: IEDI.

IEDI. 1992a. *Modernização competitiva, democracia e justiça social.* São Paulo: IEDI.

IEDI. 1992b. *A nova relação entre competitividade e educação.* São Paulo: IEDI.

Kandir, Antônio. 1992. Author interview with former Secretary for Economic Policy, Economy Ministry (1990-1991). São Paulo, June 8.

Kapaz, Emerson. 1989. Author interview with Coordinator, Pensamento Nacional das Bases Empresariais (PNBE). São Paulo, December 20.

Kaufman, Robert, Carlos Bazdresch, and Blanca Heredia. 1994. "Mexico: Radical Reform in a Dominant Party System." In *Voting for Reform*, eds. Stephan Haggard and Steven Webb. Oxford: Oxford University Press.

Kingstone, Peter. 1994. *Shaping Business Interests: The Politics of Neoliberalism in Brazil, 1985-1992.* Ph.D. dissertation, University of California-Berkeley.

Leff, Nathaniel. 1968. *Economic Policy-Making and Development in Brazil, 1947-1964.* New York: John Wiley.

Leff, Nathaniel. 1986. "Trust, Envy, and the Political Economy of Industrial Development: Economic Groups in Developing Countries." Cornell University-First Boston Working Paper Series, FB-86-38.

Lima, Antônio Milão Rodrigues. 1990. Author interview with former Assistant Secretary of Federal Revenue, Finance Ministry (1974-1977). Rio de Janeiro, February 9.

March, James, and Johan Olsen. 1989. *Rediscovering Institutions*. New York: Free Press.

McQuerry, Elizabeth. 1995. *Economic Liberalization in Brazil: Business Responses and Changing Patterns of Behavior*. Ph.D. Dissertation, University of Texas at Austin.

MEFP (Ministério da Economia, Fazenda e Planejamento), Secretaria Nacional de Economia (SNE). 1992. *Câmaras setoriais. Relatório de situação*. Brasília: MEFP, SNE.

Mello, Zélia Cardoso de. 1995. Author interview with former Economy Minister (1990-1991). Rio de Janeiro, July 7.

MICT (Ministério da Indústria, do Comércio e do Turismo), Secretaria de Política Industrial (SPI). 1994. *Relatório de andamento das câmaras setoriais*. Brasília: MICT, SPI.

Moreira, Marcílio Marques. 1992. Author interview with Economy Minister. Brasília, July 9.

Moreira, Marcílio Marques. 1995. Author interview with former Economy Minister (1991-1992). Rio de Janeiro, July 7.

Nylen, William. 1993. *Small Business Owners Fight Back: Non-Elite Capital Activism in 'Democratizing Brazil' (1978-1990)*. Ph.D. Dissertation, Columbia University, New York.

O'Donnell, Guillermo. 1977. "Corporatism and the Question of the State." In *Authoritarianism and Corporatism in Latin America*, ed. James Malloy. Pittsburgh: University of Pittsburgh Press.

Olson, Mancur. 1971. *The Logic of Collective Action*. Cambridge, Mass.: Harvard University Press.

Olson, Mancur. 1982. *The Rise and Decline of Nations*. New Haven, Conn.: Yale University Press.

Payne, John, James Bettman, and Eric Johnson. 1992. "Behavioral Decision Research." *Annual Review of Psychology* 43: 87-131.

Payne, Leigh. 1994. *Brazilian Industrialists and Democratic Change*. Baltimore: Johns Hopkins University Press.

PNBE (Pensamento Nacional das Bases Empresariais). 1989. *Relatório de atividades do PNBE*. São Paulo: PNBE.

PNBE. 1992. Proposta do PNBE sobre reforma tributária. São Paulo: PNBE.

Propostas de revisão constitucional. 1993. n.p.

Reformas constitucionais. Setor empresarial. 1995. Brasília, February 9.

Reis, José Guilherme Almeida dos. 1994. Author interview with Assistant Director of the Economic Department, Confederação Nacional da Indústria. Rio de Janeiro, October 31.

Rezende da Silva, Fernando. 1992. *Papel e custo do estado*. n.p. Comissão Empresarial de Competitividade.

Rio Branco, José Mário Paranhos do. 1989. Author interview in Legal Department, Federação das Indústrias do Estado de São Paulo. São Paulo, December 20.

Rio Branco, José Mário Paranhos do. 1995. Author interview with Political Action Coordinator, Federação das Indústrias do Estado de São Paulo. São Paulo, July 4.

Sardenberg, Carlos Alberto. 1987. *Aventura e agonia*. São Paulo: Companhia das Letras.

Schattschneider, Elmer. 1975. *The Semi-Sovereign People*. Hinsdale, Ill.: Dryden.

Schmitter, Philippe. 1971. *Interest Conflict and Political Change in Brazil*. Stanford, Calif.: Stanford University Press.

Schmitter, Philippe. 1974. "Still the Century of Corporatism?" In *The New Corporatism*, eds. Fredrick Pike and Thomas Stritch. Notre Dame, Ind.: University of Notre Dame Press.

Schneider, Ben Ross. 1992. "The Rise and Collapse of the Developmental State in Brazil and Mexico." Unpublished manuscript, Princeton University, Princeton, New Jersey.

Schneider, Ben Ross. 1997-1998. "Organized Business Politics in Democratic Brazil." *Journal of Interamerican Studies and World Affairs* 39 (4): 95-127.

Secretaria Técnica. 1993. *Revisão constitucional*. Brasília (November).

Secretaria Técnica. 1994. *Revisão constitucional. Reunião do Comitê Executivo*. Brasília (March).

Silva, Eduardo. 1993. "Capitalist Coalitions, the State, and Neoliberal Economic Restructuring: Chile, 1973-88." *World Politics* 45 (4): 526-59.

Solimeo, Marcel Domingos. 1989, 1992, and 1995. Author interviews with Director, Instituto de Economia "Gastão Vidigal," Associação Comercial de São Paulo. São Paulo, November 30, May 29, and June 26.

Solimeo, Marcel Domingos. 1994. "Revisão constitucional." *Digesto econômico. Associação Comercial de São Paulo* 50 (2): 20-26.

SRF (Secretaria da Receita Federal). COGET (Coordenação-Geral de Estudos Econômico-Tributários). 1994. *Um perfil da administração tributária Brasileira*. Brasília: SRF.

Stein, Janice Gross, and Louis Pauly, eds. 1993. *Choosing to Co-Operate. How States Avoid Loss*. Baltimore: Johns Hopkins University Press.

Steinmo, Sven, Kathleen Thelen, and Frank Longstreth, eds. 1992. *Structuring Politics*. Cambridge: Cambridge University Press.

Szajman, Abram. 1992. Author interview with President, Federação do Comércio do Estado de São Paulo (FCESP). São Paulo, June 2.

Szajman, Abram. 1994. "Contra o truque do IVV, a transparência do IVA." *Folha de São Paulo*, March 15: 2-2.

Tello, Arturo. 1995. Author interview with former manager, Confederación Nacional de Instituciones Empresariales Privadas. Lima: February 7.

Temporal, Amaury. 1992. Author interview with former President, Confederação das Associações Comerciais do Brasil (CACB). Rio de Janeiro, July 20.

Velloso, Antônio Augusto dos Reis. 1995. Author interview with Superintendent, Confederação Nacional das Instituições Financeiras. Brasília, June 19.

Vianna, Maria Teixeira Werneck. 1987. *A administração do "milagre."* Petrópolis: Vozes.

Vidigal Filho, Luis Eulálio de Bueno. 1985. *Contribuição para a futura constituição Brasileira*. São Paulo: FIESP.

Waterbury, John. 1992. "The Heart of the Matter?" In *The Politics of Economic Adjustment*, eds. Stephan Haggard and Robert Kaufman. Princeton, N.J.: Princeton University Press.

Weyland, Kurt. 1993. "The Rise and Fall of President Collor and Its Impact on Brazilian Democracy." *Journal of Interamerican Studies and World Affairs* 35 (1): 1-37.

Weyland, Kurt. 1996. *Democracy Without Equity. Failures of Reform in Brazil*. Pittsburgh: University of Pittsburgh Press.

Weyland, Kurt. 1996. "How Much Political Power do Economic Forces Have? Conflicts Over Social Insurance Reform in Brazil." *Journal of Public Policy* 16 (1): 59-84.

Weyland, Kurt. 1998. "Swallowing the Bitter Pill: Sources of Popular Support for Neoliberal Reform in Latin America." *Comparative Political Studies* 31:5 (October).

CHAPTER FOUR

Business and Politics in the Dominican Republic

ROSARIO ESPINAL

In the second half of the twentieth century, the Dominican business class experienced major changes in its organizational form, its relationship to the state, and its political role in Dominican society. These changes were the results of conditions internal to business (endogenous factors) and of major political and economic changes (exogenous factors) that arose after the end of Rafael Leonidas Trujillo's dictatorship in 1961. The most important endogenous factors were the increasing economic diversification and modernization of business. The most important exogenous factors were the democratic openings, first in the early 1960s and again in the late 1970s, and changes in economic conditions and incentives for business. These changes included economic growth, business expansion, and income concentration in the late 1960s and early 1970s; government attempts to redistribute income in the late 1970s; economic austerity through the mid-1980s; economic dislocations due to excessive government spending in the late 1980s; and mild efforts to open the economy in the 1990s.

In its attempts to adjust to these changing conditions, the Dominican business class vacillated between increasing unity and fragmentation. During the Trujillo dictatorship (1930-1961), Dominican business comprised a very small group with little autonomous power. Facing democratic transition, first in the early 1960s and again in the late 1970s, it united and was active in response to political uncertainty and the perception of acute threat. During the authoritarian administration of Joaquín Balaguer in the late 1960s and early 1970s, business marginalized itself as a political actor. Then, in the early 1980s and again in the early 1990s, it fragmented under friction over economic policy that arose between the business community and government or among business groups themselves.

In 1978, the uncertainties of the democratic transition posed new challenges for the business class, and it responded with increasing organization and activism. Business elites felt threatened by the rise of the Dominican Revolutionary Party (Partido Revolucionario Dominicano — PRD). Because industrialists had benefited from Balaguer's system of business incentives, they opposed the PRD government's (1978-1982) attempt to redistribute income and subsidize agriculture. In order to confront the government, the leaders of the National Council of Businessmen (Consejo Nacional de Hombres de Empresa — CNHE) sought to incorporate different sectors of business into its organization. Between 1979 and

1981, when it emerged as a true encompassing peak business association, the CNHE brought together many newly formed business associations.

In the context of the democratic transition of the late 1970s, the increasing organization and activism of the business class was a defining characteristic of a new politics. Yet, the organizational growth of business groups did not proceed peacefully, and major tensions ensued at different times and for different reasons. In the early 1980s, confrontations between regional and national associations of industrialists were severe. They fought over who had received the greatest benefits from Law 299 of Industrial Incentives and Protection, instituted in 1968: Large-scale industrialists in the city of Santo Domingo argued that the law had benefited business throughout the country, while regional industrialists, mostly in the city of Santiago, argued that the benefits had been concentrated in Santo Domingo. By the late 1980s, the major conflicts within the CNHE had shifted to confrontations between industrialists representing large and medium-sized industries, based in Santo Domingo City. The latter group felt threatened by the antisubsidy mood that was sweeping the country — especially with respect to protection from imports — but large-scale industrialists were willing to settle for lower levels of protection than they could bear. Conflicts also ensued in the early 1990s between import-substitution industrialists and importers — the former wanted to remain protected; the latter asked for a more open economy.

This chapter shows that the critical political junctures that emerged between the early 1960s and early 1990s produced varying organizational responses on the part of the business class. During the first transition in the early 1960s, the business elite began its process of organization. Under the authoritarian period that followed, business associations remained weak and politically inactive. During the political opening of the late 1970s, business organizations consolidated. Yet, during the economic difficulties of the early 1980s and early 1990s, these groups failed to remain united. In this regard, the Dominican case supports some basic arguments of this book, in that: 1) peak business associations form and develop in response to deep social, economic, and political changes; 2) they are more likely to form and unify when there is marked political instability and unusual levels of social and political violence; and 3) deep economic downturns or transformations contribute to business fragmentation by generating friction that, at times, is difficult to overcome.

This chapter's discussion of the process of organizational development of the Dominican business class from the 1940s to the 1990s encompasses issues pertaining to economic policy, the relationship between business and government, and the process of internal organization of business groups. It shows that endogenous and exogenous factors influenced the formation and development of the CNHE. Since its founding in 1963, political uncertainty would periodically increase the motivation to promote the growth of the CNHE, while internal dissent and conflicts over economic policy would divide the organization. In addition, it is worth underscoring that the Dominican business class organized and managed this and other associations free from state control, under both authoritarian and democratic rule.

By examining these arguments, this chapter on the Dominican case addresses the three questions posed by Francisco Durand and Eduardo Silva in the introduction to this volume: How did the twin processes of economic and political change affect the propensity of the business class to act collectively through their associations? How did business utilize its organizations to influence economic policymaking? And how did business actions affect the process of democratization?

BUSINESS UNDER AUTHORITARIAN RULE

Business under Trujillo

During the Trujillo dictatorship, the business class was small, economically vulnerable, and politically weak. It did not constitute itself as a political actor, and it was difficult to distinguish members of the "private" business class — those without close ties to the regime — from members of the "private-public" business class — those whose economic wealth derived primarily from the regime. President Trujillo, his family, and their collaborators controlled many of the country's economic resources, allowing for only limited market competition. To understand how this situation arose, it is important to assess the economic situation of the Dominican Republic when Trujillo took power and Trujillo's own centralized method of ruling.

In 1930, the Dominican economy experienced major difficulties due to a collapse in export prices and payments due on foreign loans. Soon after taking office, Trujillo announced an "Emergency Plan" to deal with budgetary and balance-of-payment problems. The government reached a moratorium on the foreign debt, paying only interest. Public expenditures were controlled, and public employees saw their salaries reduced by 10 percent while others lost their jobs. Tariffs were enacted to promote local production, and a tax policy was implemented to increase public revenue.

In the early 1940s, the United States ended its control of Dominican Customs, in place since the beginning of the century. Following the U.S. withdrawal, the Trujillo government established a national currency (the Dominican peso) and a national banking system (the Central Bank and the Reserve Bank of the Dominican Republic). With the foreign trade surplus in the 1940s, Trujillo also initiated import-substitution industrialization. From 1940 to 1960, investments in industries other than sugar (which was largely foreign owned) increased from 19 to 43 percent (Gómez 1979, 146); the number of industrial plants increased from 1,815 to 2,411, and the number of workers employed in industry increased from 10,224 to 24,718 (Moya Pons 1992, 375). Almost half of these industries were located in Santo Domingo and Santiago, the country's two largest cities.

The economic expansion of the post-war period served primarily to enlarge Trujillo's wealth. By the end of the dictatorship in 1961, the fortune of the Trujillo family was estimated at about US$800 million. It controlled about 80 percent of all industrial production and employed about 45 percent of the labor force in family enterprises and another 15 percent in government jobs (Cassá 1980; Moya Pons 1982).

The extent of the economic power exercised by Trujillo is aptly described by Jesús de Galíndez (1973, 187):

> Trujillo is the first businessman of the Dominican Republic ... his businesses have benefited the general economy by establishing factories or enterprises in the Dominican economy that represent improvement over earlier foreign monopolies. Nevertheless, each of these businesses has brought personal profit to Trujillo, and their success was often obtained through monopolies imposed from above, thanks to his hold on power.

The weakness of the business class contributed to Trujillo's growing power in the 1940s. This was the result of a long-term economic decline in the country beginning in the late nineteenth century, the prominence of foreign capital in the sugar-export sector, and the U.S. occupation of 1916 to 1924 that diminished the capacity of the local elite to rule the country.

In the context of a monopolized economy and politics, business organizations did not develop as a mechanism of class representation. The few that existed, including the Official Chamber of Commerce, Agriculture, and Industry of Santo Domingo (Cámara Oficial de Comercio, Agricultura e Industria de Santo Domingo — COCAI-SD) and the Employers' Confederation of the Dominican Republic (Confederación Patronal de la República Dominicana — CPRD), had a life of their own as long as they confined their activities to technical-business matters. In addition, these organizations were expected (as was the rest of the population) to praise the dictator and show support for him. On the occasion of Trujillo's Peace Fair in 1955, the front page of the December 1955 issue of *Revista Patronal*, the official magazine of the CPRD read: "Peace and Progress Are the Symbols and Reality of the Trujillo Era."

Trujillo's authoritarianism had exhibited limited traces of corporatism. Although he wanted praise and support, his strategy was one of demobilization and disorganization of political actors, business included. In this regard, the authoritarian experience of the Dominican Republic in the 1940s differed from that of other countries in Latin America that had populist regimes. This difference had consequences for the development of business organization and business-government relations in the post-Trujillo period.

BUSINESS AFTER THE FALL OF TRUJILLO

After the fall of Trujillo, the business class began to organize independently from the government. Increased organization was typical of all sectors of Dominican society in the early 1960s, generating new political parties, religious organizations, trade unions, and business associations. Indeed, some of the most important business associations still in existence today emerged in the early 1960s. The Industrialists' Association of the Dominican Republic (Asociación de Industriales de la República Dominicana — AIRD) was formed in early 1962 to protect the interests of industrialists and promote industrial development. It was conceived as a national organization, but it represented primarily the interests of the industrial elite of Santo Domingo. The Association of Merchants and Industrialists of

Santiago (Asociación de Comerciantes e Industriales de Santiago — ACIS) also was formed in early 1962 to protect the interests of industrialists and merchants of the northern region of the country. The CNHE was formed in early 1963 as an encompassing peak business association to unite the business class in the midst of the rapid socioeconomic and political change sweeping the Dominican Republic.

When the CNHE was formed, Juan Bosch had just taken office after winning the first democratic elections held in decades. Bosch's populist discourse was not appealing to business nor was the level of social mobilization in the country. The CNHE quickly incorporated the four main existing business organizations: the Chamber of Commerce, the Employers' Confederation, the Industrialists' Association of the Dominican Republic, and the Dominican Landowners' Association (Asociación Dominicana de Hacendados y Agricultores), but it showed little interest in regionally based associations, such as ACIS (Espinal 1985).

In the early 1960s, business focused on three main issues: 1) the fate of Trujillo's enterprises, 2) the challenge posed by a growing labor movement, and 3) the incentives to be granted to business under the new political conditions. The fate of Trujillo's enterprises was quickly resolved, even before the democratic elections of 1962, but not in favor of private business. In November 1961, Joaquín Balaguer, then president of the country, placed Trujillo's firms and properties under government control. To manage this massive transfer of productive assets to the state, Balaguer created the Office of General Administration, Control, and Recuperation of Properties on December 9, 1961 (Decree 7395). By 1962, the Dominican state had become the largest entrepreneur in the country.

Several reasons contributed to this outcome. Balaguer believed in the positive role of government in promoting economic development, the government needed to secure a clientelistic base of support through employment and contracts, the politically weak business class had limited resources and experience with which to acquire and run these enterprises, and the mobilized masses felt strongly that what had belonged to Trujillo should be transferred to the Dominican people. Yet regardless of the motives, by controlling Trujillo's assets, the Dominican state gained access to massive resources in agriculture, industry (including sugar, the country's main agro-industry at the time), and services.

With respect to the growing labor activism, business adopted a reactionary position. In 1962, both the newly formed AIRD and the existing CPRD opposed workers' increasing mobilization and demands. A letter to the Council of State, sent on May 17, 1962, claimed, "As a result of the sudden transition from an oppressive tyranny to an atmosphere of liberty that we currently enjoy, workers have gone too far in raising demands and engaging in labor action without consideration of legal constraints. This practice has a negative impact on business and the economy, and generates worries and chaos in the nation" (CPRD 1962, 5). In a press communiqué on May 19, 1962, AIRD also stated its concern, "The Industrialists' Association of the Dominican Republic, hoping to contribute to the social, moral, and economic recovery of the nation has observed with concern the increase in illegal labor action, which constitutes a serious problem for the normal development of the process of economic recovery" (AIRD 1962, 12).

The inauguration of Juan Bosch as president in February 1963 only contributed to worsen the tensions between government and business, which felt threatened by Bosch's populist discourse. Bosch appealed to the impoverished masses and spoke pejoratively about the rich, for whom he coined the term "*tutumpotes*." The government had failed to provide the legal framework of incentives that business expected, and businesspeople felt unprotected. AIRD formally complained in an April 1963 letter to President Bosch, asking him to submit a bill of Industrial Protection and Promotion to Congress. Bosch replied that before such a bill could be introduced, the legislature had to approve a new constitution and produce industrial legislation that would not be detrimental to small and medium-sized industries (Moya Pons 1992, 99-101).

The uncertainty continued. By mid-September, business had organized a general strike in opposition to the government, and on September 25, 1963, Bosch was overthrown. Interestingly, on that same day newspapers reported that Bosch had just introduced the Bill of Industrial Incentives and Protection in Congress. Although business alone did not bring down the Bosch government, it played a key role in the opposition to the PRD administration.

Following the overthrow of Bosch, the failure to produce a stable government continued to plague Dominican politics into the mid-1960s. Business became increasingly identified with the de facto government headed by Donald Reid Cabral, a prominent conservative businessman. On October 8, 1963, the government passed Law 4 of Industrial Protection and Incentives, spelling out a set of incentives benefiting the import-substitution industrialists. Who would benefit from these incentives, however, remained a source of controversy; new industrialists challenged the privileges of the traditional industrial elite that had formed during the Trujillo dictatorship.[1]

In spite of their pro-business stance, or perhaps because of it, the transitional governments from 1963 to 1965 failed to stabilize Dominican politics. Tensions escalated and popular discontent mounted, leading to a short civil war in 1965 and the subsequent U.S. intervention. The main characteristic of organizational activity by the business class during this turbulent period was its emergence as a political actor in response to threats by the state, a perceived exclusion from the allocation of incentives and benefits, and the growing activism of labor and other popular organizations.

BUSINESS UNDER BALAGUER

The 12-year presidency of Joaquín Balaguer (1966-1978) represented a golden age for business. The partnership between business and government was evident from the outset. Balaguer placed businessmen on his corporatist boards, either as representatives of business organizations or individual citizens, in what evolved into a complex web of patronage between the president and business. Balaguer himself would make special concessions to businessmen in the so-called *acuerdos de recámara*.[2] The government delivered economic growth, business incentives, and political stability, which enabled Balaguer to keep the support of much of the business class during his long presidency.

In the 1970s, many business associations formed; however, within the authoritarian and clientelistic framework of the Balaguer regime, they did not develop into powerful organizations. Instead, they remained isolated from one another, politically passive, and did not play an active role in the growing opposition to Balaguer in the mid- and late 1970s. Business leaders, however, did take an active part in the Balaguer administration, which regularly consulted with them and even placed them on the government boards dealing with economic, social, and cultural issues. Most important, their personal connections with the government were essential to their ability to access state resources such as contracts and tax exemptions.

Wage austerity, industrial incentives, and investments in public works were the pillars of Balaguer's economic program. Law 1 of Austerity of 1966 and Law 299 of Industrial Protection and Incentives of 1968 provided the legal framework for Balaguer's program, and Law 153 of Tourism Development, Law 171 of Financial Incentives of 1971, and Law 481 of Incentive to the Construction Industry of 1973 reinforced it. These incentives to private business were coupled with a massive public works program largely controlled by the presidency (the percentage of the national budget controlled by the presidency increased from 7.3 percent in 1966 to 50.2 percent in 1974) (Espinal 1986, 77).

To gather the support of business in what otherwise was a very exclusionary government, in 1966 Balaguer formed the National Commission for Development (Comisión Nacional para el Desarrollo — CND) to serve as his advisory council. According to Decree 775 of 1966, the Commission would have 19 members: 2 representatives from business organizations, 9 businessmen chosen by the president, and 8 representatives from government agencies. Decree 1941 of 1967 expanded it to 49 members: 2 representatives from business associations, 25 businessmen chosen by the president, and 22 representatives from government agencies. The CND's composition and the method of selecting business representatives illustrate the personalization and centralization of power that characterized the Balaguer regime. Business representation on the CND was not an expression of class strength or unity. It served, instead, to meet Balaguer's need for support from the business community, for which he exchanged special privileges. In this context, the particularistic interests of businessmen prevailed over a sense of class unity and organization.

Representation on the Board of Industrial Development, which Law 299 had empowered to grant industrial incentives, relied more than the CND on associational affiliation. The board included members from AIRD, the Chamber of Commerce, CNHE, and ACIS. Yet, Santo Domingo-based industrialists from AIRD dominated the Board and made decisions that favored its members. As a result, regional tensions appeared in 1971. Industrialists from Santiago complained that Law 299 had favored industrial investments in Santo Domingo over the rest of the country. The tensions continued throughout the 1970s with little success for the regionalists (Espinal 1985; Moya Pons 1992). Not only were they outnumbered on the board, but they also lacked institutional links within the business organizational structure that were needed to pressure the CNHE to represent their interests.

In the late 1970s, it was evident that the CNHE had failed to incorporate some of the old regional business associations, as well as many of the newly formed ones. During the first 10 years of its existence from 1963 to 1974, the CNHE consisted only of its four original members: the Industrialists' Association of the Dominican Republic; the Employers' Confederation; the Chamber of Commerce, Agriculture and Industry; and the Dominican Farmers' Association. Yet, when 102 associations formed between 1972 and 1980, this highly monopolized and unrepresentative structure was challenged (Espinal 1986, 80).

Cleavages within business and confrontations between business groups and the government gained significance in the mid-1970s. In 1974, the president of the CND resigned in opposition to the implementation of agrarian reform. In this context, the CND began to lose its effectiveness as a supportive mechanism for Balaguer's public policies. The Board of Industrial Development came under attack by government officials, who criticized the excessive protection extended to industrialists, and by regional business groups, who felt excluded from the benefits granted by Law 299. To address the growing discontent over his economic policies, Balaguer convened informal meetings with leaders from major business associations.

These meetings revealed a change in the relationship between business and government. *El Industrial*, the magazine of AIRD, described them as follows:

> A large group of representatives of the Industrialists' Association of the Dominican Republic held . . . a fruitful meeting with the Honorable President of the Republic. This meeting of executives had significant characteristics. The main one is that none of the guests expressed personal problems to the President. All the issues were presented in a proper and precise manner and reflected the concern of businesspeople with the state and health of the economy. Very remarkable was the fact that both parties avoided praising the other or mutual flattery (AIRD 1967, 3).

This suggested that changes in style in the relationship between President Balaguer and business were under way — moving from a personalistic and subordinate relationship to a more institutionalized and class-based approach. Businesspeople were also conveying their willingness and capacity to play a more active and responsible role in the nation's affairs. José del Carmen Ariza, a prominent AIRD member, affirmed this sentiment:

> I want to thank you, Mr. President, on behalf of those of us who have the honor of being your guests, for providing us with this opportunity to make a contribution in the solution of national problems given the experience we have acquired in the course of national development. . . . The Dominican businessman of today is not the mere merchant of the past. He has changed as a result of the dramatic socioeconomic changes . . . and has become conscious of his strengths and weaknesses, and he now has the necessary ability to rely on the former to achieve the common good (1976).

In brief, until the mid-1970s, the business class followed the government's design for development. Business leaders relied heavily on personalistic and clientelistic strategies to achieve their goals. They were influential in government as individuals but did not foster the growth of their organizations. With a government disinterested in corporatist arrangements, low levels of social unrest, and limited internal dissent, the business class had little incentive to promote powerful encompassing peak associations.

In the mid-1970s, however, the situation changed dramatically. Similar to the experience of other Latin American countries discussed in this book, the Dominican Republic experienced growing economic difficulties, the crisis of import-substitution industrialization, and increasing business diversification. These problems, coupled with signs of democratization, led business to seek more political power. Two factors are central to the transformation that occurred within business and in the relationship between business and government in the late 1970s. First, economic expansion and modernization in the early 1970s led to the growing organizational strength of business, as manifested by the formation of many new associations, and, second, the beginning of an economic downturn limited the capacity of government to provide significant subsidies to business, particularly to import-substitution industrialists.

BUSINESS UNDER DEMOCRATIC RULE

Business in the Transition to Democracy

In spite of its increasing economic diversification and growing organizational strength, the role of business in the 1978 election and the subsequent electoral crisis was ambivalent at best. Because business lacked consensus on the desirability of a PRD government, it was difficult for business associations to assert a unified position in favor of democracy. This was clearly the case when business was slow in responding to the threat of an electoral fraud after close collaborators of Balaguer attempted to rig the election as it became evident that the opposition PRD would win (Espinal 1986; Faxas 1995).

Business split in its support of political candidates and parties in the 1978 elections. An important segment of the Santo Domingo business elite, import-substitution industrialists, large importers, and construction contractors, supported Balaguer. These were the groups that had benefited from the patronage system and the system of economic incentives instituted during his presidency. Merchants and smaller producers, in both Santo Domingo and the interior, supported the opposition PRD in the hope of gaining access to the economic incentives that had been monopolized by a small business elite.

Aware of its long-standing conflicts with and mistrust of the major business associations, the PRD nominated Antonio Guzmán, a farmer with large holdings and a moderate candidate, to run for president. The party adopted a moderate platform, eliminating items such as the nationalization of private companies. It also sought international support from moderate social democrats in Europe and Latin America. In spite of these efforts to de-radicalize its platform, the PRD's emphasis on incentives to the agricultural sector and agribusiness over import-substitution industrialization troubled the powerful business groups influential within the CNHE, especially the highly protected industrialists of Santo Domingo. The fate of Law 299 was of particular concern since it had been under attack by economists and regional industrialists and the PRD had stated in its party platform that the law would be revised (Programa de Gobierno del PRD 1978, 56).

The PRD's proposed labor policy also worried business. The party platform included modification of the labor code to incorporate basic union rights, as granted by the Dominican Constitution; the creation of labor courts to provide speedier trials of labor-related cases; job security for labor activists; and revision and periodic adjustment of the minimum wage. In the years that followed the PRD victory, these issues caused major disputes between business and government.

The installation of a government that the traditional business elite did not trust and the growing labor unrest that followed the inauguration of the PRD government quickly led business leaders to promote class unity. The business elite of Santo Domingo encouraged the CNHE to enlarge its membership, and the organization asked many business associations to join it, become involved in politics, and protect their interests. As a result, the democratic transition of 1978 clearly favored higher levels of organization of business and the consolidation of the CNHE as a peak business association.

Between 1978 and 1982, the CNHE played a key role in uniting the Dominican business class. Its membership grew from four associations in 1974, to 11 in 1978, to 40 in 1982 (Espinal 1986, 80). The CNHE also spent a considerable amount of time and energy opposing the government, which ultimately generated intrabusiness conflicts. During the second PRD administration, headed by Jorge Blanco (1982-1986), the CNHE continued to provide unified leadership for business, but in a context of reduced tensions with the government. Yet, intrabusiness tensions reemerged in the late 1980s, when it became evident that industrial protection was dwindling and market-oriented reforms were likely.

Business Organizations and Opposition Politics during the PRD Governments

Economic difficulties in the late 1970s and the transition to democracy in 1978 were major contributors to the growing organizational and political activism of the business class. Business complained loudly about the alleged statist and leftist posture of PRD government officials, the increasing labor activism in the country, and inadequate allocation of economic incentives.

To understand the initial conflicts between business and the PRD government, one must take into account that key business groups regarded the PRD as a leftist-radical party. Shortly after the PRD took office, the CNHE announced its commitment to participate in the political process and the formulation of public policies. This activism represented a major shift in strategy, given the political passivity of the business community under Balaguer. At the opening of the legislative session in February 1979, the CNHE, led by pro-*balagueristas,* forcefully announced its decision to participate in politics. In a press communiqué, published in the daily newspaper *Listín Diario,* the CNHE (1979) stated that a fundamental principle of a democratic system was free enterprise, all things related to the organization of the economy deserved careful examination, and businessmen were committed to expressing their views, as circumstances required.

Much tension arose over what business perceived to be an exaggerated expansion of the role of the state in the economy. In line with the PRD's social democratic platform, soon after its inauguration, the Guzmán government sought to redistribute income by increasing the purchasing power of consumers through higher wages and the creation of new public jobs. In 1979, the government raised the minimum wage by about 30 percent (this was a PRD campaign promise), and by 1980, about 60,000 new public jobs had been created. As a result, current government expenditures rose from 58.3 percent of the total central government budget in 1977 to 68.9 percent in 1981 (Espinal 1987a, 206). This was of great concern to the private sector, which was accustomed to the Balaguer administration's preference for large public capital investments over current expenditures.

Price controls aimed at reducing inflation and the government's monopoly over the distribution of basic consumer goods, such as rice and sugar, also troubled business. Top CNHE leaders viewed these measures as a government assault on the market and the private sector. CNHE President Luis A. Ginebra Hernández led business opposition to the government, and between mid-1980 and mid-1981, he delivered six major speeches to business associations throughout the country. At a special "Dinner for Business Unity" in June 1980, which President Guzmán attended, Ginebra Hernández (1980, 10-11) complained about the radicalism of government officials who discredited businessmen and were guiding the national economy to chaos.

In a speech delivered in January 1981 to the American Chamber of Commerce in Santiago, Ginebra Hernández criticized the government's price control policy:

> Profitable prices for peanut growers are a good incentive for them. But what do you think of the proposal made by a government official to increase the price of peanuts but without transferring the increase to consumers. We ask: Who is going to pay for the increase? Who is going to pay high prices for peanuts to sell cheap oil? Should it be charged to the legitimate profit made by industrialists? Our answer is: Increase the price of peanuts and increase the price of oil according to the cost of the raw materials. Those who can afford the price of peanut oil will buy it — or we should export it — and those who cannot afford it should use another type of oil. . . . One should remember that state subsidies have to be paid either by increasing taxes, reducing public capital investment, or simply by printing more money, all of which will damage the economy even further (1981, 30).

Business also felt alienated from the decision-making process and threatened by newly empowered government officials. The CNHE complained strongly of its exclusion. At the Dinner for Business Unity, Ginebra Hernández (1980, 11) also declared, "It is important to indicate that the business sector is deeply concerned with the economic problems facing the nation. The government has analyzed them and proposed measures without consulting the private sector or requesting our participation. Nonetheless, we also are analyzing these problems and policies and will state our position at the appropriate time."

The conflicts over the government's position toward labor added to the disputes over economic policy. Labor activism during the PRD administration helped to disrupt the pattern of working-class subordination that had prevailed under Balaguer. The reduction in the use of coercion as a mechanism to regulate social relations, a natural outcome of the democratic transition, led to rising expectations on the part of workers, who increasingly demanded collective bargaining. To counteract this, business asked the government to act more decisively in its regulation of labor relations. Business also sought to influence congressional debates on modification of labor laws, and it took repressive measures in the workplace, including the dismissal of labor activists. A month after the inauguration of the PRD government, the AIRD and CPRD published a press communiqué, "The latest events linked to the demands of labor organizations, which have been supported by some trade confederations, have created a state of chaos, worsened by labor agitation that may lead to an economic recession of unpredictable consequences. . . . It is the responsibility of the government to guarantee the enforcement of the Law as it applies to workers and business" (CPRD 1978).

Similarly, the Industrialists' Association of the Northern Region (Asociación de Industriales de la Región Norte — AIRN) was extremely concerned with the strength of the labor movement and the pressures it put on employers, which had been escalating and spreading nationwide since the inauguration of the new government. According to the AIRN (1978), demands for wage increases were particularly detrimental at a time when the country was experiencing an economic downturn, caused by higher oil prices and a sharp drop in sugar prices. Taking a critical position toward union activism, the AIRN claimed that in the Dominican Republic, where 40 percent of the labor force was underemployed and a large percentage was unemployed, unionized workers belonged to a privileged class whose demands did not favor the underemployed or the unemployed.

In September 1978, a month after the inauguration of the PRD government, President Guzmán called a meeting with business to discuss labor issues. According to business reports, he asked businessmen to allow the formation of unions with the promise that the government would urge labor leaders to limit their demands in order to facilitate the economic recovery. Yet neither business nor labor came to the negotiating table, and tensions mounted.

The allocation of economic incentives was the other major conflict between business and government and within the business community itself. Law 299 was at the heart of the debate. Large-scale industrialists wanted reassurance that they would continue to receive the benefits provided by the law. Smaller-scale industrialists wanted access to those benefits. In the face of a mounting public deficit, the government, in turn, was under pressure to reduce subsidies overall.

Among business groups, the major public confrontation over Law 299 took place in 1980 between Santiago-based ACIS, on one side, and the Santo Domingo-based AIRD and the Association of Industrial Enterprises of Herrera (Asociación de Empresas Industriales de Herrera — AEIH), on the other. ACIS represented regional small and medium-sized industrialists; AIRD, the interests of the largest and best established industrialists; and AEIH, many of the newer, medium-sized, import-substitution industrialists of Santo Domingo.

In January 1980, ACIS (1980a) issued a press communiqué criticizing Law 299 for promoting uneven industrial development in the country and the Board of Industrial Development for not allocating incentives fairly. AIRD and AEIH (1980) reacted immediately by emphasizing that the law was beneficial to industrialization and economic development throughout the Dominican Republic. ACIS (1980b) responded with another communiqué that reaffirmed its criticisms in a harsher tone. Its proposal stressed the need for decentralization of the industrialization process, more incentives for investment outside the city of Santo Domingo, and the democratization of the Board through the incorporation of representatives from a wider array of business groups. This intrabusiness confrontation was unprecedented and reflected the level of political opening in the country.

In the midst of this conflict, the CNHE was in the process of broadening its membership, and it approached ACIS. In 1981, the CNHE promoted a series of meetings to strengthen relations with business associations in the northern region of the country. The agreements reached included a plan for more active participation and better representation of regional business associations within the CNHE; a concession allowing business associations to choose their representatives to the CNHE; a commitment to improving communication between the CNHE and the local and regional associations; and a program of financial lending to small business associations to make possible their incorporation into the CNHE (Revista de la Cámara Oficial de Comercio, Agricultura e Industria de Santiago 1981). Seven days after reaching this agreement, ACIS requested and immediately received membership in the CNHE (ACIS internal documents).

As the CNHE made progress in unifying the country's business associations, CNHE members sympathetic to the PRD began to criticize the perceived anti-PRD stance of the organization's leadership. PRD supporters chafed at the fact that well-known *balagueristas* led the CNHE and its drive for expansion in the late 1970s and early 1980s in response to the threat that the PRD posed to traditional business elites. Associations, such as ACIS and AEIH, hoped to benefit from the political opening brought about by the PRD government. By 1982, the CNHE had to moderate its anti-PRD rhetoric and actions or face the disaffection of its members. As AEIH President César Nicolás Penson (author interview 1983) explained, "Had the CNHE not changed its aggressive position toward the PRD government in 1982, the AEIH would have left the CNHE." This threat of disunity led the CNHE to move away from partisan politics.

AEIH and other new business associations also hoped to improve their access to power vis-à-vis the powerful traditional business groups that had controlled the CNHE and the AIRD since the early 1960s. The AEIH president summed up the situation in this way:

> In the 1960s . . . a traditional group of business associations and a traditional group of businessmen — the "sons of" — dominated and the scope of action was too narrow for the rest. During those years, it was also believed that businesses had to be big to be important. Then, when we — the "boys of Herrera" as we were called — appeared, we began to demand things that the old and established associations did not want to provide. We created new associations to promote our interests and emphasized that only by working together could we obtain benefits. There was a period, called by some "the golden age," when a few had access to power while the smaller entrepreneurs like us found the doors closed and could not solve our problems very easily. However, after the PRD came to power that changed. Now we have access to power, not to solve our individual problems, but to contribute with the institutionalization of the country (Penson 1983).

Intrabusiness conflicts resulting from the politicization of the CNHE and its anti-PRD rhetoric were also acknowledged by the newly elected CNHE president, Hugh Brache, in his inaugural speech:

> There is no doubt that many CNHE members had the impression that the organization had a political party orientation. This was due more than anything else to the former president's emotional intensity. CNHE members openly and cordially discussed this situation, and we reached the conclusion that business-men have the right to have their own political views and preferences, but that the policies of the CNHE should not be party oriented (1982).

The CNHE's past president, Luis Ginebra Hernández (1982), also acknowl-edged in a speech delivered at the end of his presidency that conflicts arising from the overlapping roles of business and party leader could be avoided in the future if CNHE presidents would take a vacation from political party activities while leading the organization.

CNHE Executive Director Francisco Castillo (1983) noted that, by 1982, the CNHE had moved from a "position of confrontation" with the PRD government to a "position of *concertación*." Brache set the new mood in a speech delivered in February 1983 at the now annual Dinner for Business Unity:

> We have to become aware of our responsibilities as businessmen and as citizens in a democracy facing an economic crisis.... Frequently, we say that in order to reactivate the economy and create jobs, the government should provide a favorable environment of confidence. This is certainly vital, but we should ask what our contribution should be as citizens and businessmen. A favorable environment is not the result only of government laws and decrees. Confidence is difficult when, in an almost threatening manner, we impose demands on the government when it does not have the resources to satisfy those demands.

Three factors contributed to the pacification of business-government rela-tions by 1982. One was that business groups supportive of the PRD pressured the aggressive CNHE leadership. Additionally, business began to fear the conse-quences of further political instability in the country. As the CNHE's Executive Director Castillo (1983) put it, "CNHE members understood that if the organization did not moderate the attacks on the government, the political situation could explode and deteriorate." Finally, by 1982, as part of the negotiations with the International Monetary Fund (IMF), the PRD government had changed its economic policy to give priority to fiscal austerity and price liberalization. With the 1982 election of Salvador Jorge Blanco, who had the support of key business sectors linked to the Santiago elite, and a new leadership in the CNHE, the relationship between business and the PRD government improved considerably. Throughout the mid-1980s, the CNHE was able truly to represent Dominican business, without major internal clashes.

In brief, business unity and representation were enhanced by the growth of the CNHE, which expanded from four associations in 1974 to 40 in 1982, and by the agreements to improve member participation in the decision-making process. The enlarged membership also helped to moderate CNHE opposition toward the PRD government, as newer business groups pressured the traditional *balaguerista* business elite to adopt a more conciliatory posture. The more moderate stance was visible by 1983, following the election of a new CNHE leadership, the election of a new PRD government in 1982, and the shift in economic policy toward greater fiscal austerity and more liberalized price and exchange policies. The Jorge Blanco administration (1982-1986) enjoyed a relatively peaceful relationship with business, while it implemented austerity measures endorsed by business that triggered social protest in 1984. Popular discontent with the PRD helped Balaguer win the election in 1986.

Business under Balaguer Again

Tensions between business and government grew in the late 1980s, and conflicts among business groups led to the division of the CNHE in 1991. In an attempt to preserve his state-led developmentalist program of economic recovery and urban renewal initiated in late 1986, Balaguer imposed sacrifices on the business sector that exceeded its willingness for compromise. Business groups were increasingly discontented with the government's economic policies; yet they were having difficulties reaching unified positions, and Balaguer was aware of this weakness. Exporters, hotel operators, and large importers sought a more competitive and open economy. Import-substitution industrialists, for their part, favored subsidies and protection. These different objectives led to intrabusiness conflicts that resulted in confrontations within the CNHE, first between large and medium-scale industrialists and later between industrialists and importers.

Balaguer's return to the presidency in 1986, based on business's previous experience, augured a positive relationship for business and government. But the reality was different this time. Most powerful business groups opposed Balaguer's state-led program of economic growth. Although his heavy investment in public works brought about an impressive 8 percent rate of economic growth, inflation jumped from 6.5 percent in 1986 to 100.7 in 1990 (*CEPAL News* 1995). In addition, the growing foreign debt put pressure on the currency exchange market. Balaguer blamed business for the repeated devaluations of the peso, and in 1987 and 1988, the Dominican government, as did other Latin American governments during this period, took drastic measures to control its exchange rate.

In a resolution on June 17, 1987, the Monetary Board enforced a policy of exchange controls, requiring exporters, exchange houses, and commercial banks to trade all U.S. dollars at the Central Bank. The Bank, in turn, would provide dollars to importers who, in order to import, were required to show evidence of government authorization to use foreign currency. This policy overturned Jorge Blanco's free exchange system instituted in January 1985, in the wake of an IMF standby agreement. Some business groups promptly opposed the new "System of Exchange Controls." The President of the National Association of Importers, Andrés Dauhajre (1987), expressed business's opposition to the new system in a speech delivered to the American Chamber of Commerce.

As discontent mounted, Balaguer met with business leaders, many of whom favored a free and unified exchange system. Exporters disliked exchanging their dollars at the Central Bank at a government-fixed rate. Importers disliked the bureaucratic rigidity of the Central Bank in the allocation of dollars. Commercial banks, for their part, hoped to benefit financially from the free exchange of foreign currency.

On November 13, 1987, the Monetary Board approved a new policy of a "unified exchange rate with segmented markets." This system unified the exchange rate but restricted the use and trade of foreign currency. In spite of this new measure, the devaluation of the Dominican peso continued. In June 1988, the Board, in an unprecedented move, closed all exchange houses and required commercial banks to trade all foreign currency at the Central Bank. As a result, the exchange rate stabilized for the rest of 1988. The question remained as to how long the new stipulations would last, given that powerful business groups, prominent Dominican economists, and international agencies strongly opposed them (Espinal 1990).

The following year saw growing discontent with the government's economic policies. The "Tripartite Dialogue" among business, labor, and government, with the mediation of the Catholic Church, began in 1988 but broke down in early 1989. The government was not a committed participant, and labor complained about the government's unwillingness to comply with the agreements reached, including a wage increase and the extension of medical benefits to workers' family members. Threatened by a growing popular movement, business and church leaders hoped to convince Balaguer of the need to negotiate, but nothing was achieved. In June 1989, the newly formed National Confederation of Popular Organizations (Confederación de Organizaciones Populares — CNOP) organized a general strike. At first, business, church, and labor leaders opposed the CNOP's call to strike, but the government's inability to negotiate with business, workers, and popular organizations, as well as the rapid deterioration in the standard of living of middle- and lower-income groups, advanced it. While most sectors of society mistrusted the CNOP, they used the strike, held on June 19 and 20, 1989, to show their discontent with the government's policies and the state of the economy. Even businesspeople, hoping the strike would scare the government and lead to policy changes, complied by not opening their establishments.

The next year began with major controversies between business and the government over economic policies. A key issue in 1990 was once again the exchange rate. The Dominican Association of Exporters (Asociación Dominicana de Exportadores — ADOEXPO) and the Dominican Association of Free Trade Zones (Asociación Dominicana de Zonas Francas — ADOZONAS) asked for the liberalization of the currency exchange market. Balaguer claimed that this measure would benefit only the wealthy, and he showed little willingness to change the course of economic policy. Facing a shortage of foreign exchange, Balaguer issued a decree on June 15, 1990, ordering the cancellation of all incentives and exemptions to firms that failed to trade their earnings in foreign currency at the Central Bank.

After his disputed reelection in May 1990, Balaguer recognized that his confrontation with business was at a turning point. In the midst of popular discontent and mobilization, he needed its support to begin a new term in office. Thus, on July 19, 1990, after four years of refusing to negotiate with the IMF, Balaguer announced that economic adjustments were overdue. On August 6, inspired by the Mexican experience with pact-making, the Dominican government and business leaders signed the "Pact of Economic Solidarity" (1990), which contemplated price increases in gasoline, cooking gas, flour, and sugar; an increase of 30 percent in the minimum wage of public employees; wage bargaining in the private sector; and a freer exchange market. In early 1991, the government began negotiations with the IMF to refinance the country's debt.

The adoption of an economic adjustment program in 1991 brought peace to the relationship between business and government. The rate of inflation dropped from 50 percent in 1990 to 4 percent in 1992 (Gutiérrez 1997, 343). The revenues from a gasoline surcharge tax allowed Balaguer to balance the central government budget while maintaining his massive public works program. The liberalization of the exchange market was welcomed by many business groups, and the exchange rate remained fairly stable between 1991 and 1994 as a result of debt refinancing, booming tourism, and remittances by Dominicans abroad.

Yet, in the early 1990s, intrasectoral and regional conflicts over subsidies, liberalization, wage levels, and exchange policies made it increasingly difficult for the CNHE to represent the entire business class. As a result, specialized business associations gained prominence in the defense of their interests, among them, the Dominican Association of Free Trade Zones, the National Association of Importers, the Dominican Association of Exporters, and the Association of Commercial Banks.

The CNHE experienced its most severe internal crisis in October and November 1991, when importers announced that they were leaving the organization because they believed it was controlled by a small group of industrialists who were seeking to preserve their own protections rather than modernize the business sector to make it more competitive. The efforts to form a new peak business organization, led by the National Association of Importers, began in late 1991. On January 9, 1992, 16 business organizations formed the National Union of Businessmen (Unión Nacional de Empresarios — UNE). Andrés Dauhajre, a leading importer and outspoken business leader, was appointed UNE president.

The CNHE continued to represent the protectionist interests of industrialists, and those committed to gradualism and moderation in economic reforms remained in control of the CHNE Executive Board. UNE, on the contrary, advocated sweeping neoliberal economic reforms, including significantly lower tariffs, and it stiffly criticized the efforts made by the CNHE and other associations to preserve protectionism.[3]

Yet, in the early 1990s, the CNHE became deeply involved in pressure politics in its efforts to force the Balaguer government to hold fair elections in 1994, make political reforms, modernize the state, and respect the rule of law. The controversies and irregularities surrounding the 1994 electoral results led to further involvement of business in the political process. In 1995, the CNHE changed its name to National Council of Private Enterprises (Consejo Nacional de la Empresa Privada — CONEP), and in November, it hosted a major business convention (Gran Convención Empresarial) to discuss how to modernize and democratize the Dominican state and to determine the role that the private sector should play in achieving this objective. Approximately 56 business associations participated in the convention, which led to the publication of an *Agenda Empresarial para el Desarrollo Integrado* (CONEP 1995). The convention sent a clear message to the government that business endorsed democratic reforms and would play a role in promoting them. CONEP also became actively involved in the civic Action for Democracy Group (Grupo de Acción por la Democracia — GAD), which was formed by business, labor, churches, and universities to promote a fair election in 1996 and to pressure the Balaguer government and political parties to comply with the "Pact for Democracy," signed in 1994 in the midst of the controversies surrounding the reelection of Balaguer.[4]

While political conflicts prevailed over economic issues between 1994 and 1996, the tensions between neoliberal reformers (UNE) and gradualists (CONEP) continued. CONEP was more powerful than UNE because it had more members and represented very powerful business groups linked to industries and banking, but UNE was not alone in promoting a neoliberal agenda. Indeed, for several years, the Economy and Development Foundation (Fundación Economía y Desarrollo), led by Andrés Dauhjare, Jr., had been the major force behind this project. The foundation had an aggressive strategy in support of free-market reforms, which it promoted through television programs and newspaper columns, and it continuously antagonized major industrialists who opposed sweeping market reforms.

Because the Balaguer government of 1994 to 1996 was viewed as a transitional government, no major economic reforms were expected, nor did they occur.[5] The disagreements between CONEP and UNE reemerged more clearly in late 1996, when the newly elected president, Leonel Fernández of the Dominican Liberation Party (Partido de la Liberación Dominicana — PLD), submitted a set of economic reforms to Congress along with the national budget. One of the major reforms was the lowering of tariffs over three years, between 1997 and 1999. In the context of this legislative proposal, neither the CONEP nor the UNE were capable of representing the interests of all major business groups. UNE endorsed the government proposal enthusiastically and hoped for quick approval. CONEP praised the government initiative for moving in the right direction, but it claimed that the lowering of tariffs would occur too rapidly to allow business to adjust and remain competitive. CONEP asked the government to separate the approval of the national budget, which had a short deadline, from the package of economic reforms, which, according to them, required lengthier deliberations.

In the end, industrialists' opposition to the economic reform plan stopped the enactment of the bill. The PLD, in turn, had a minority congressional representation, and the political opposition was unlikely to approve a major economic reform package that powerful business groups opposed and that eventually could benefit the president. Since President Fernández refused to separate the economic reforms from the national budget and Congress refused to evaluate them together, neither was ultimately approved. President Fernández opted to govern in 1997 under the stipulations of the 1996 budget. With a divided government and congressional and municipal elections scheduled for May 1998, the discussion of controversial economic reforms was removed from the government's economic agenda in 1997.

CONCLUSION

The different historical periods discussed in this chapter provide the background to understand changes in business organization and political strategies in the Dominican Republic. Each period is characterized by a combination of socioeconomic and political factors that helped to shape the relationship between business and government, intrabusiness relations, and the relationship between business and other social groups.

The analysis of the Dominican case supports the initial premise of this book, as stated by Durand and Silva in the introduction: Business elites organize in reaction to deep social, political, and economic changes. For the Dominican Republic, as for other Latin American countries discussed in this volume, these changes have been the arrival of political democracy and market-oriented economic reforms. Both have affected the propensity of business to act collectively through its newly formed or expanded business associations.

As the Dominican case illustrates, the business class has used its organizations for many purposes: to oppose authoritarian governments, as in the case of Balaguer in the late 1970s (even though the opposition was mild); to confront a democratically elected administration it did not trust, as in the case of the PRD government between 1978 and 1982; to push for further democratic reforms when the government's exclusionary politics left business with limited access to the decision-making process, as happened under the Balaguer administration in the late 1980s and early 1990s; and to promote or oppose economic restructuring, as the events surrounding the deliberations over the 1996 economic reform package illustrate.

The Dominican case also shows that business is more likely to oppose the government (whether authoritarian or democratic) when it feels excluded from access to particularlistic gains or from the decision-making process, and when the government implements economic policies it dislikes. It is this combination of factors that increases the likelihood of political action and unity by business, as happened in the Dominican Republic in the late 1970s under the first PRD administration and in the late 1980s under Balaguer. Threatened by the PRD's radical past, business discourse focused in the late 1970s on supporting private property and opposing state interference. In the late 1980s, however, business discourse focused on promoting democracy and institutional modernization since Balaguer had used exclusionary techniques to keep business at bay.

By the late 1980s, business united in its support for democracy, but the CNHE failed to build a consensus on economic reforms. Industrialists fought to keep protections alive, while importers and exporters fought for a more open and less regulated economy. With industrialists dominating the CNHE, a group of disaffected businesspeople left the CNHE in 1992 to form UNE. Deep-seated tensions remained in the area of economic policy between "gradualists," represented by the CNHE (renamed CONEP in 1995), and "free-marketers," represented by UNE.

This division undermined CONEP's authority to speak in the name of the business class, but the emergence and consolidation of both encompassing peak business associations forged a new generation of Dominican business leaders who actively engaged in a "battle of ideas," as Durand and Silva say in the introduction to this volume. While this battle of ideas was at times detrimental to business unity, it helped business become a vital force in Dominican politics and increased its visibility as a political actor.

Notably, Dominican business has been able to engage in open conflicts over economic policy because it has not felt severely threatened, either by the government or by popular sectors since the early 1980s. The government has been slow in promoting major economic reforms, while popular organizations have declined in significance and in their ability to mobilize the population. In business's internal battles, both sides have had their share of victories and defeats. Gradualists have succeeded in slowing the process of economic restructuring (which Dominican administrations have not fought hard for in the first place). Free-marketers, in contrast, have expanded their basis of ideological support and have benefited from international pressures on the Dominican government in favor of pro-market reforms. A consequence of this relative stalemate is that, while both the PRD and the Balaguer administrations implemented adjustment programs, neither carried out a major plan of economic restructuring. In this regard, the Dominican case differs significantly from those Latin American countries that implemented sweeping market-oriented reforms.

The introduction to this volume argues that a fragmented business community makes it harder to implement market-oriented economic reforms. While there is truth to this statement, the Dominican experience in 1996 indicates that the lack of determination on the part of the government to implement those reforms has contributed to business division. Unable to generate consensus over economic reforms within their own ranks, business organizations have limited their actions to supporting or opposing specific government policy initiatives, many of which reflect the government's desperate attempts to manage economic difficulties. The result is the lack of long-term economic planning, either by government or business, which generates unstable investment environments.

Notes

1. Frank Moya Pons (1992) argues that Law 4 promoted some democratization of incentives, which collided with the interests of the entrenched industrialist class that dominated the AIRD.

2. Several businessmen made this comment to Francisco Durand in interviews he conducted in 1997.

3. UNE used its regular column in the newspaper *El Siglo* to criticize protectionism. Two titles of articles published in 1992 reflect their offensive: "Reseña de una cruzada proteccionista: el caso de los aceites comestibles" and "Etiquetas proteccionistas para eliminar la competencia."

4. The Pact for Democracy was signed on August 10, 1994, to solve the crisis that ensued after the electoral fraud of May 1994. The Pact was signed by President Balaguer, representatives of the main parties, representatives from civic organizations, church leaders, and a mediator from the Organization of American States. It incorporated major constitutional changes, including the holding of new presidential elections in 1996. Because Balaguer's commitment to hold elections in 1996 was in question, Dominican civil society organized to pressure the government. The Action for Democracy Group was one of the most powerful, incorporating business, labor, and churches.

5. Because the 1994 election of Balaguer was found to be unfair, the major political parties in the country agreed to reduce his presidential term to two years and hold presidential elections again in 1996.

References

Ariza, José del Carmen. 1976. *Listín Diario*, July 1.

ACIS (Asociación de Comerciantes e Industriales de Santiago). Internal documents.

ACIS. 1980a. *Listín Diario*, January 16.

ACIS. 1980b. *Listín Diario*, January 18.

ACIS. 1980c. *Listín Diario*, January 23.

AIRD (Asociación de Industrias de la República Dominicana). 1962. *Revista Patronal* (April- May).

AIRD. 1967. *El Industrial* (September issue).

AIRD and CPRD (Confederación Patronal de la República Dominicana). 1978. *Listín Diario*, September 16.

AIRD and AEIH (Asociación de Empresas Industriales de Herrera). 1980. *Listín Diario*, January 18.

AIRN (Asociación de Industriales de la Región Norte). 1978. *El Industrial* (September issue).

Asociación Dominicana de Exportadores (ADOEXPO) and Asociación Dominicana de Zonas Francas (ADOZONAS). 1990. *El Siglo*. March 31.

Brache, Hugh. 1982. *El Nuevo Diario*, November 9.

Brache, Hugh. 1983. Speech manuscript (CNHE Documents).

Cassá, Roberto. 1980. *Historia social y económica de la República Dominicana*, Vol. 2. Santo Domingo: Editora Alfa y Omega.

Castillo, Francisco. 1983. Author interview with the Executive Director of the CNHE.

CEPAL [Comisión Económica para América Latina] *News*. 1995. 15 (2).

CNHE (Consejo Nacional de Hombres de Empresa). 1979. *Listín Diario*, February 26.

CNHE. 1980. *CNHE-Discursos*. Santo Domingo: CNHE.

CONEP (Consejo Nacional de la Empresa Privada). 1995. *Agenda empresarial para el desarrollo integrado*. Santo Domingo: Editora Corripio.

CPRD (Confederación Patronal de la República Dominicana). 1962. *Revista Patronal* (April-May).

Dauhajre, Andrés. 1987. *Listín Diario*, September 19.

Espinal, Rosario. 1985. "Classes, Power and Political Change in the Dominican Republic." Ph.D. Dissertation, Washington University, St. Louis, Missouri.

Espinal, Rosario. 1986. "An Interpretation of the Democratic Transition in the Dominican Republic." In *The Central American Impasse*, eds. Giuseppe DiPalma and Laurence Whitehead. London: Croom Helm.

Espinal, Rosario. 1987a. "Labor, Politics and Industrialization in the Dominican Republic." *Economic and Industrial Democracy* 8 (2).

Espinal, Rosario. 1987b. *Autoritarismo y democracia en la Política Dominicana*. San José, Costa Rica: CAPEL/IIDH; and Santo Domingo: Editorial Argumentos, 1994.

Espinal, Rosario. 1990. "The Dominican Republic." In *Latin American and Contemporary Caribbean Record* 7 (1987-1988). New York: Holmes and Meier Publishers.

Espinal, Rosario. 1995. "Economic Restructuring, Social Protest, and Democratization in the Dominican Republic." *Latin American Perspectives* 22 (3).

Faxas, Laura. 1995. "El empresariado dominicano: ¿de clase dominante autoritaria a clase dirigente democrática?" *Estudios Sociales* 28 (100): 63-102.

Galíndez, Jesús de. 1973. *La era de Trujillo*. Tucson: University of Arizona Press.

Ginebra Hernández, Luis A. 1980. *CNHE-Discursos*. Santo Domingo: CNHE.

Ginebra Hernández, Luis A. 1981. "Discurso en la Cámara Americana de Comercio en Santiago." Unpublished manuscript. Santo Domingo: CNHE Documents.

Ginebra Hernández, Luis A. 1982. Speech manuscript. Santo Domingo: CNHE Documents.

Ginebra Hernández, Luis A. 1990. "República Dominicana 1990: la cuestión económica y social." Santo Domingo: CNHE Document.

Gómez, Luis. 1979. *Relaciones de producción dominantes en la sociedad dominicana*. Santo Domingo: Editora Alfa y Omega.

Gutiérrez, Adolfo Martí. 1997. *Instrumental para el estudio de la economía dominicana*. Santo Domingo: Editora Buho.

Moya Pons, Frank. 1982. "El Impacto de la industrialización en la sociedad dominicana en el siglo XX." In *La política económica en la República Dominicana*, ed. Asociación Nacional de Jóvenes Empresarios. Santo Domingo: Editora La Palabra.

Moya Pons, Frank. 1992. *Empresarios en conflicto*. Santo Domingo: Fondo para el Avance de las Ciencias Sociales.

"Pacto de solidaridad económica. 1990." *El Siglo*, August 7.

Penson, César Nicolás. 1983. Author interview with the President of the Asociación de Empresarios de Herrera.

"Programa de Gobierno del PRD (1978-82)." 1978. *Revista Ahora*. No. 762.

Revista de la Cámara Oficial de Comercio, Agricultura e Industria de Santiago. 1981. September-October.

CHAPTER FIVE

Between Revolution and Democracy: Business Associations and Political Change in El Salvador[1]

KENNETH L. JOHNSON

In 1980, El Salvador stood at the threshold of violent revolution; in 1992, it stood at the threshold of peace and democracy. During the 12 years that measure the distance between the two, the country's business associations underwent important changes. Essentially, they successfully left behind their traditional role as defenders of the authoritarian ancien régime to accommodate democratic practices. To explain the changes in the political behavior of business associations, this chapter traces four phases of their development. During the first phase, from the late 1920s through the 1960s, the major sectoral and peak associations formed. The second phase, from the late 1960s through the 1970s, was characterized by the growing politicization of business associations as their interests became increasingly threatened by proposed government reforms. During the third phase, from 1979 until 1992, business associations faced multiple revolutionary challenges to their survival. At this critical juncture, these associations underwent key changes in organization, membership, and relative degree of political influence. The fourth phase began in 1990 with negotiations leading to the peace agreement that ended the civil war. Within this process of democratization, business associations have had to adjust to a more pluralistic, competitive political environment.

PHASE 1: FORMATION OF BUSINESS ASSOCIATIONS, 1920s-1960s

During the late 1920s, coffee growers in western El Salvador created the country's first business association. They sought to provide a system of private credit and marketing for area coffee growers and also to coordinate the provision of seasonal laborers. In this latter task, the association created a rural police force to enforce vagrancy laws and force people without jobs to work on coffee plantations. Thus, from the outset, business associations enjoyed a high degree of autonomy from the central government and a close relationship with rural security forces. Not until President Maximiliano Hernández Martínez asserted tighter control over the National Guard (rural police), the National Police, and the army in the early 1930s, did coffee elites have to depend upon the national government to ensure that their economic interests were protected.

In response to the development of an increasingly centralized state under Martinez' dictatorship of the 1930s, regional associations of landowners, ranchers, and coffee growers created the first national-level associations, the Salvadoran Association of Coffee Growers (Asociación Salvadoreña de Café — ASCAFE — or, more commonly, the Cafetalera), and the Association of Ranchers (Ganadería). But the Cafetalera and the Ganadería had also formed in response to scarce credit in the context of an economic depression, increasing rural unrest among landless peasants pushed out by competitive exclusion, and pressure for land redistribution by increasingly organized and militant peasant groups.

The Cafetalera wielded enormous influence over the government and was the country's most powerful business association for almost 30 years. It was established at a time when only five millers controlled over 50 percent of coffee production, and its members had primary control over credit and investment In fact, the Cafetalera was so powerful at the time that it formed a kind of "second state," an unseen government of coffee barons who controlled important economic decisions, as presidents came and went (Anderson 1971, 10). For example, in 1932, the Cafetalera convinced Martínez to devalue the currency in order to increase coffee exports; in 1934, the ranchers' association and the Cafetalera succeeded in getting the Martínez regime to establish a government credit house in which they controlled a majority of shares; and in 1942, the Compañía Salvadoreña de Café was created, giving the coffee elites control over the national marketing of coffee (Dunkerley 1988, 98). From the 1930s until the early 1960s, members of the Cafetalera also were regularly rewarded with ministerial portfolios, such as Treasury, Agriculture, and the Central Bank.

During the 1940s, millers who were also coffee growers and landowners created the Association of Coffee Processors and Exporters (Asociación de Beneficiadores y Exportadores de Café — ABECAFE). By the 1970s, ABECAFE represented the 42 largest processors in the country, controlling 60 percent of all coffee processing and 80 percent of all coffee exports. Many landowners and growers belonging to the Cafetalera also belonged to ABECAFE. Although these two associations included the wealthiest and most economically powerful sectors of Salvadoran society, they did not maintain a high public profile on political issues. Instead, they relied on their control over ministerial portfolios as well as informal, personal connections to government and military officials in order to influence policy. These associations were not prominent in a social sense, nor did they provide professional services for their members.

The Martínez dictatorship ended in 1944, only to be replaced by the institutionalized rule of the military high command. The junior officers who took over created a controlled electoral system under which retired officers were assured election to the presidency. This system of indirect military rule lasted until the 1980s. Throughout this period, successive administrations increased the government's role in economic planning, promoting a two-pronged modernization strategy: diversifying agriculture to limit dependence on coffee exports and promoting the development of industry. The latter involved extensively increasing the regulation and even ownership of certain sectors, such as transportation, telecommunications, ports, energy, and tourism. These changes had two effects on the formation of business elites. First, economic diversification increased the number and types of business associations, and second, this increased pluralism would later spur the creation of a peak association.

One of the most important associations formed during this period was the Chamber of Commerce and Industry (Cámara de Comercio e Industria), which represented a large number of diverse firms and became the principal voice of the Salvadoran elite. Chief among its members were exporters, manufacturers, bankers, and investors who were benefiting from the industrial growth connected to an expanding agro-industrial export sector (food processing, bottling, textiles, and so forth). Despite this diverse membership, the leadership of the Chamber was dominated by traditional agrarian interests — especially coffee and cotton producers. But, unlike the earlier regional and sectoral associations, the Chamber focused on professional development and support services for individual firms, and it lobbied the government on specific issues related to the sectoral interests of its members. It had a seat on the military government's economic planning board as well as on numerous commissions and agencies. However, the more important avenue of political influence was the informal personal connections that the Chamber created among the nation's economic and government elites (Campbell 1968).

In 1993, the Association of Salvadoran Industrialists (Asociación Salvadoreña de Industriales — ASI) was created to represent manufacturing and retail firms owned and managed by members of the agro-industrial elite and the industrial bourgeoisie. The emphasis the government placed on regional integration in the early 1960s gave the ASI a fairly high profile early in its formation. Salvadoran industrialists benefited from favorable government subsidies and a protectionist import tariff structure that gave them a competitive edge among Central American manufacturing and retail firms. ASI took the lead in supporting the development of the Central American Common Market (CACM) during the 1960s. However, the industrial bourgeoisie had to bargain for influence in government with the more powerful and established Chamber of Commerce and Industry. Because the Chamber was dominated by agrarian interests, the bourgeoisie sought to build allies among middle-class professionals, technocrats, and intellectuals represented by the political parties, such as the military's National Conciliation Party (Partido de Conciliación National — PCN), the Christian Democratic Party (and its factions), and others. Thus, ASI was more amenable to economic reform proposals emanating from the government and generally supported its role in economic planning. Indeed, because of the convergence of interests between military planners and ASI members, the organization's leaders were selected to head the ministries of Planning and Economy during the late 1960s and early 1970s. Until the 1969 Soccer War with Honduras sealed the fate of an already moribund integration effort and damaged the economic prospects of many of its members, ASI provided an institutional counterweight to the more conservative Chamber.

By the early 1960s, there were a total of 14 sectoral associations, testifying to the growth of Salvadoran business communities. During this period, government intervention in the economy also increased, creating a number of conflicts with business. Business leaders were particularly alarmed by the social and economic reforms of President Julio Adalberto Rivera (1962-1967), who raised taxes on property and the wealthy and also passed a minimum wage and a mandatory rest day for rural workers. In response to these developments, in 1966 the leaders of most of the country's business associations agreed to form El Salvador's first peak association, the National Association of Private Enterprise (Asociación Nacional de la Empresa Privada — ANEP) (White 1971, 119-20). With a membership that quickly grew to between 25 and 30 associations in the 1970s, ANEP became a key player in the political upheavals of the late 1970s and 1980s. It united business elites in defense of their strategic interests (sanctity of private property, minimal taxes and duties, and so on) and against efforts by successive governments to initiate reforms that might preserve stability by lessening the exploitative relationship between the private sector and the lower classes. Like the Chamber, ANEP had a privileged position compared to most associations, with official representation in government agencies, on planning commissions, and within the Central Bank. Indeed, ANEP proved powerful enough to acquire an informal veto over the military's selection of presidential candidates during the late 1970s.

Agrarian elites dominated the leadership of ANEP and, to a lesser extent, the Chamber. They used this power to ensure that their interests took precedence over those of the agro-industrial and the industrial bourgeoisie. The associational interests of the agrarian elites centered on excluding restrictions on land and capital accumulation in the agrarian sector; maintaining a seasonal pool of low-wage labor, which meant opposing efforts to organize rural workers; and favoring undervalued exchange rates to make their exports competitive. These goals became increasingly untenable and brought the business associations into open conflict with successive government administrations.

PHASE 2: THE POLITICIZATION OF BUSINESS ASSOCIATIONS, 1967-1979

During the 1960s and 1970s, business associations found themselves increasingly at odds with military planners. President Rivera's social and economic reforms were the result of multiple pressures: increased organizing among the lower and rural classes; the growth of political competition from a reformist Christian Democratic Party; pressure from international agencies and incentives offered by the Alliance for Progress and even from junior members within the officer corps. In response to Rivera's tax measures and growing government intervention in the agrarian sector, ANEP and the Chamber mounted a public relations campaign to pressure the government "not to penalize the most efficient producers" in the country. Despite the business associations' aggressive publicity campaigns, the government had few revenue alternatives apart from agro-export, simply because this sector dominated the entire economy (Bulmer-Thomas 1987, 122 and 182; Coto, Carcamo, and Recinos 1990, 74-76; Goitia 1989, 295-96).

The growth of economic and social programs expanded the government's economic bureaucracy. Key to the military technocrats' efforts to modernize the economy was the creation of a "super ministry," the Ministry of Planning and Coordination of Economic and Social Development (Ministerio de Planificación y Coordinación del Desarrollo Económico y Social — MIPLAN) in 1971. MIPLAN was responsible for strategic planning and was designed to help ensure that economic growth led to social development and stability. With its five-year plans, MIPLAN set the parameters of economic bargaining among the government, business elites, and others (Gordon 1977, 19). Although both the Chamber and ANEP had formal representation on MIPLAN planning councils, the agrarian elites still regarded MIPLAN as a double threat. First, it challenged business associations' decision-making monopoly on economic matters. Second, it increased the government's institutional autonomy to pursue economic and social objectives that violated the interests of the agrarian elites. It is revealing that on the eve of the creation of MIPLAN, ANEP denounced the economic technocrats of the government as *"cepalistas contaminadas por el virus del socialismo, del intervencionismo estatal"* ("minions of CEPAL, contaminated by the virus of socialism and state interventionism")[2] (López V. 1976, 11). CEPAL is the Spanish acronym for the Comisión Económica para América Latina y el Caribe (U.N. Economic Commission for Latin America and the Caribbean — ECLAC).

The creation of MIPLAN was symptomatic of a more profound change taking place in the relationship between business elites and the state. The two-pronged modernization strategy of the military governments had produced fissures within the economic bureaucracy itself, between those ministries and agencies dominated by and serving the interests of the agrarian elites and those ministries dominated by the military technocrats and their allies among the industrial and manufacturing interests (see Table 1). By the late 1970s, these intra-state conflicts would make the government increasingly vulnerable to challenges from excluded groups, paving the way for a crisis of revolutionary proportions.

The issue of land reform drove the military and the business elites into increasingly open conflict with each other. President Fidel Sánchez Hernández (1967-1972) signed an irrigation and drainage law that gave the government limited power to expropriate land. Building on their defensive responses to Rivera's reforms, business groups reacted to President Hernández's assaults on their traditional economic prerogatives by forming a party, the Independent United Democratic Front (Frente Unido Democrático Independiente — FUDI), to challenge the military's political monopoly. The conservative leadership of the Chamber, ANEP, and the agrarian associations threw their support behind FUDI, forcing the military's official party to scuttle plans for agrarian reform temporarily. The loss of business support also forced the military to resort to flagrant fraud to win the election. In 1976, new President Arturo Molina (1972-1977) initiated a timid land reform program administered by the newly created Salvadoran Institute of Agrarian Transformation (Instituto Salvadoreño de Transformación Agraria — ISTA). A progressive oligarch, Enrique Alvarez, was put in charge of transferring some 60,000 hectares of land, belonging to 250 landowners, to about 12,000 peasants.

The Cafetalera, ANEP, and the Chamber again mounted a highly aggressive public relations campaign against the government and its "communist-inspired" policies. In addition, coffee growers and ranchers formed a new association, Eastern Agrarian Front (Frente Agrario de Oriente — FARO) to fight the land reform. FARO sought to intimidate peasants and ISTA workers from participating in land transfers (Gordon 1977, 19; López V. 1976, 16-22; Zamora 1976).

The leaders of ANEP and FARO also used their personal contacts with conservative members of the military high command to influence the nomination of the 1977 presidential candidate. They succeeded in getting General Humberto Romero, President Molina's hard-line minister of defense and former chief of the National Guard and intelligence operations, nominated as the official party's candidate. ANEP leaders promised to fund Romero's campaign fully to ensure his victory if he would agree to rid the government of reformers and reimpose order in the countryside. Under President Romero (1977-1979), the antireformist interests of ANEP's leadership became the sole political focus of the state, which launched a national security campaign against communist subversion (Castro-Morán 1987, 253-54). Political polarization, violence, and mass mobilization soon followed, pushing El Salvador to the brink of revolution.

Table 1.
Bifurcation of El Salvador's Economic Bureaucracy, 1979

*Ministries and agencies controlled by business associations:
Ministry of the Economy
Ministry of the Treasury
Ministry of Foreign Trade
Central Reserve Bank
Coffee Marketing Board
**Ministries and agencies colonized or controlled by the military:
Ministry of Agriculture
Ministry of Planning (MIPLAN)
Ministry of Labor and Social Welfare
Institute of Agrarian Transformation (ISTA)
Institute of Rural Colonization (ICR)
Institute of Industrial Promotion (INSOFOP)
Institute of Basic Grains Regulation (IRA)
Institute of Social Security (ISSS)
Institute of Urban Housing
National Administration of Telecommunications (ANTEL)
Executive Commission of Rio Lempa Hydroelectic Facility (CEL)
Executive Commission of the Autonomous Port Authority (CEPA)

* "Controlled" indicates that a leader of a business association would be appointed to lead a ministry; the ministry primarily defended business interests.
** "Colonized" indicates that military leaders (retired) held leadership positions; these ministries defended national security interests of the government.
Source: Compiled by the author.

PHASE 3: BUSINESS ASSOCIATIONS AND REVOLUTION, 1979-1992

A coup d'état overthrew President Romero on October 15, 1979, initiating a violent and protracted civil war that lasted until a peace accord was signed in 1992. During this phase, business associations underwent a complex process of change in response to multiple threats to their survival. The first and perhaps most obvious was the threat "from below" posed by the armed insurrection of the Farabundo Martí National Liberation Front (Frente Farabundo Martí de Liberación Nacional — FMLN) and affiliated mass organizations and labor unions that sought to restructure economic relations radically. Moreover, the tactics employed throughout the insurgency, such as the FMLN's kidnappings and ransoming of wealthy members of the elite, the destruction of business property and public infrastructure, sponsorship of land invasions, and the general climate of insecurity, all had direct negative consequences for business. Added to this, elites needed to look no farther than neighboring Nicaragua for an example of what an FMLN victory might bring to El Salvador: the economic and political marginalization of private enterprise. Many Salvadoran business leaders were convinced that the Sandinistas had succeeded in taking power mainly because of the acquiescence of the Nicaraguan bourgeoisie (Inforpress 1988, 5-6).

A second threat, one "from above," was posed by the reformist civilian-military junta that governed the country from October 1979 until June 1982. Not only were the traditional business associations shut out of government decisionmaking during much of this period, but they were also subjected to a set of reforms that threatened to destroy their economic base. In March 1980, the junta, nominally led by Christian Democrat José Napoleón Duarte, pushed through three reforms: 1) a three-phase land reform, designed to break up the largest estates and create an agrarian cooperative sector; 2) the nationalization of the banking and credit sector; and 3) the nationalization of the coffee and sugar-export marketing sector. Some of the key goals of the reforms included economically emasculating the agrarian-financial fraction of the business elite, distributing the economic resources of the country more equitably, and increasing the autonomy of the state with respect to the economic elites.[3]

The third threat to business came "from without," in the form of a U.S.-sponsored series of elections in the midst of the civil war: in 1982, for a Constituent Assembly; in 1984, for president; and in 1985, for the national legislature, departmental assemblies, and municipal councils. These elections effectively shifted the business elites' institutional nexus of power from business associations to a political party of the right created in late 1981, the Nationalist Republican Alliance (Alianza Republicana Nacionalista — ARENA), which brought together an array of conservative hard-liners from the armed forces and business associations (Dunkerley 1988, 404).

A fourth threat also emerged from U.S. economic intervention, in the form of structural adjustment and neoliberal policies imposed after 1985 by the U.S. Agency for International Development (USAID) (Cuenca 1992; Rosa and Segovia 1989; Rosa and Suay 1986). The United States helped to sponsor the creation of a neoliberal think-tank in 1983, the Salvadoran Foundation for Economic and Social Development (Fundación Salvadoreña de Desarrollo Económico y Social — FUSADES), in order to cultivate support within the business community for neoliberal policies. From 1983 to 1986, FUSADES effectively replaced the traditional business associations, such as the Chamber and ANEP, in acting as the voice of business.

In the context of these four threats, business associations embarked on a path of change marked by two distinct stages. The first, from 1979 through 1984, involved the fragmentation, weakening, and political marginalization of traditional business associations. The second stage, beginning in 1985, consisted of their recomposition, modernization, and political re-emergence. In this latter stage, FUSADES played a pivotal role.

Fragmentation and Political Marginalization

The guerrilla threat, the structural reforms pursued by the military-PDC junta, and the U.S.-sponsored elections served to accentuate the sectoral and political divisions among business groups, thus weakening business associations' ability to play an influential role during this crisis period. Two major groups competed for control over the associations during the first half of the 1980s: "hard-liners," who vigorously opposed the reforms, and "soft-liners," those more willing to accept and accommodate change.

The hard-liners, composed primarily of those large landowners and growers most directly affected by the rural-based insurgency and the land and economic reforms promulgated in 1980, dominated the leadership of the Cafetalera, the Ganadería, ANEP, and the Chamber at the beginning of the decade. The leaders of the Cafetalera and the ranchers' association regarded Duarte as a communist who, along with the FMLN, was seeking to destroy the country and the entrepreneurs who had built it (Paige 1993, 32; Inforpress 1988, 9). Indeed, after 1981, Duarte barred ANEP and the Chamber from sitting on government planning boards and councils, and he refused to consult with them, even informally. From the perspective of the agrarian elites, the reforms involved a high-stakes, zero-sum game. Shut out of government, the hard-line leaders of these associations had little to lose by engaging in a high-profile confrontation with the government (Paige 1993, 30-36).

Although many members of the Chamber were not directly affected by the three reforms, they followed ANEP's lead in pursuing a confrontational strategy of opposition because they had a stake in restoring business associations' traditional prerogatives with respect to economic decisionmaking. In addition, the Chamber was also interested in maximizing the cohesion of its members by highlighting the double threat to the collective interests of the private sector posed by the FMLN and the reforms. Finally, ANEP leaders strongly pressured the leadership of the Chamber to go along with its strategy (Ramírez A. 1985, 176-77).

These groups used every means to oppose the reform process. In an effort to protect their assets, large businesses began moving their money to banks abroad, particularly to the United States. During 1980-1981, capital flight reached epidemic proportions in anticipation of the reforms and in the context of growing political instability during 1980-1981 (Instituto de Investigaciones 1982, 529, table 14). Many landowners who sought personal and financial security through self-exile in Guatemala, Miami, or elsewhere used their contacts and money to finance paramilitary "death squads." These organizations used threats and violence to intimidate and eliminate supporters of the insurgency as well as supporters of the government's reforms, labeling both as "subversives." Some landowners who faced expropriation even slaughtered their cattle, sold off farm equipment, or simply destroyed their property in order to prevent the government-owned cooperatives from benefiting from these assets. And of course, many hard-liners remained to fight the Duarte government through legal challenges and vociferous public campaigns (Montgomery 1995, 132-36).

Because their economic bases as well as membership were reduced as a consequence of the guerrilla threat and the reforms, the associations representing ranchers, cotton growers, and coffee producers pooled their remaining political capital to form the Productive Alliance (Alianza Productiva — AP). Barred from access to institutionalized channels and with little room for bargaining, the AP resorted to highly public and confrontational strategies in its attempt to prevent the implementation of the government's reforms (Montgomery 1985, 142-43).

Not all business associations in El Salvador followed the lead of ANEP and the Chamber in opposing the government through the use of intimidation and public confrontation. Obscured by the vociferous oppositional actions of the hard-liners were the apolitical tactics of the soft-liners — the agro-industrial elites, manufacturers, and retailers, whose most important institutional representatives were ASI, ABECAFE, the Association of Sugar Processors, and the Bankers' Association. The soft-liners accepted and supported the government's call for economic and political change, even while they joined the hard-liners in criticizing the method of reform (nationalization) and their exclusion from government decisionmaking. But the soft-liners believed that the confrontational tactics of the hard-liners were counterproductive and served only to hurt the longer-term interests of all business elites (Ramírez A. 1985, 176-182).

The members of ABECAFE provided only lukewarm support for the confrontational strategy of the Cafetalera, ANEP, and the AP. Although many coffee exporters were put out of business by the nationalization of coffee exports through the creation of the National Institute of Coffee (Instituto Nacional de Café — INCAFE), many coffee processors and exporters actually benefited from the favorable prices INCAFE paid to processors. Moreover, processors could pass on any increased costs to growers, by paying them less. The growers of the Cafetalera, rather than the processors of ABECAFE, were most vulnerable to costs and inefficiencies incurred by INCAFE (López 1986, 393-400). The soft-liners of ABECAFE pursued a dual strategy, combining public opposition with quiet collaboration with Duarte, even serving on INCAFE and the coffee advisory committee during the years when the Duarte administration excluded the Cafetalera and ANEP (Paige 1993, 32).

The Bankers Association also encouraged cooperation, enabling bank owners to fare better in the face of reforms than their nondiversified landowning counterparts (Ramírez A. 1985, 178). For financial and credit institutions, the liquidity of major assets enabled stockholders to take preemptive and protective measures. In the face of a deepening crisis during 1978-1980, the major stockholders of the banks were able to convert many of their assets to foreign holdings, thus ensuring that the banks would be largely decapitalized by the time the government nationalized them. Moreover, at the time of nationalization, many stockholders received compensation that exceeded the declared value of their remaining assets (Instituto de Investigaciones 1982, 529). The importance of maintaining financial stability combined with the technical nature of the banking nationalization made it crucial for the government to obtain the cooperation of the bank managers and major stockholders in order to execute the reform successfully.

The industrialists and retailers represented by ASI were not directly targeted by the reforms; in fact, government policy remained highly protective of local and regional industry during the crisis period of 1980-1984. President Duarte and his economic ministers consulted regularly with ASI representatives, seeking technical advice and keeping the channels of communication open. The industrialists and retailers were less willing to confront the government publicly because, in addition to perceiving less threat, they did not share the traditional social and political prerogatives of the landowning elites who dominated the Chamber, ANEP, and the Cafetalera. The industrial bourgeoisie belonged to a generation that had acquired its wealth through the state-sponsored process of export diversification and industrialization of the 1950s and 1960s; thus, it was more dependent on the state and less opposed to state intervention and structural change. Indeed, ASI's willingness to engage the government of Duarte constructively hurt its status within ANEP (Ramírez A. 1985, 181).

The soft-liners of the Chamber, ABECAFE, and ASI thus pursued a two-prong strategy in dealing with the government and its reform program. Due partly to strong pressure from ANEP (dominated by hard-line agrarian elites) and partly to their shared distaste for the uncertainty generated by the reform process, the soft-liners combined unified public defense of free enterprise and criticism of government intervention (with the Chamber and ASI mostly toeing ANEP's public line) with private efforts by individual associations to obtain the best deal possible with government officials.

FUSADES and the Modernization of Business Associations, 1986-1988

In 1983, as mentioned under Phase 3, a group of about 100 soft-liners, with considerable financial and political support from USAID, founded FUSADES. FUSADES was created as a non-sectoral think-tank that would provide technical analyses and economic data for business associations and firms and also advocate neoliberal policy alternatives for the government.[4]

For a number of reasons, the creation of FUSADES was a significant turning point for the fortunes of El Salvador's business associations. It permitted the soft-liners to develop a measure of institutional autonomy from the hard-liners, who controlled ANEP and were leading public opposition to reforms undertaken during the contentious period of 1982-1984. Through FUSADES, soft-liners could get beyond confrontational politics to establish a more positive and stable relationship with the newly liberalizing regime, helping business to gain regularized access to government economic policymaking. Second, FUSADES also provided an institutional bridge to USAID economic planners and managers. In FUSADES, certain interests of the U.S. government and of the soft-liners converged. Both parties wished to promote private sector development, especially in nontraditional export sectors; develop and articulate neoliberal policy alternatives to the statist policies of the Christian Democratic Party (Partido Demócrata Cristiano —PDC) government; and give the business elite an institutional stake in the democratization process.[5]

Third, the technical and financial resources of FUSADES and USAID lowered the cost of reform to those willing to diversify into non-traditional exports. FUSADES' programs and projects clearly showed a sectoral bias oriented toward strengthening El Salvador's small and medium-sized manufacturing and commercial businesses, especially in nontraditional export sectors and retail manufacturing, such as aquaculture, tropical flowers, melons, frozen foods, and light assembly (*maquila*) manufacturing operations. FUSADES' programs offered few direct benefits to El Salvador's traditional coffee, cotton, sugar, and ranching sectors. FUSADES also gave the agro-industrial elites and the bourgeoisie more access to and influence over government policy, even while the Christian Democrats were in office during 1984-1988.[6]

The *técnicos*[7] of FUSADES argued that excessive state intervention in the economy led to inefficiency, corruption, and extreme politicization of economic decisionmaking. Antistatism, privatization, deregulation, and liberalization became the banners of a new economic model based on markets and macro-economic growth to replace the failed statist and redistributive policies of the Christian Democrats (Table 2 compares the two models). [8]

Table 2.
Models of Development, PDC versus FUSADES

	PDC (Statist)	FUSADES (Neoliberal)
Model	import substitution	export promotion
Principle	protectionism	comparative advantage
Strategy	strengthening domestic markets	strengthening foreign markets
Policies	overvalued exchange rates	realistic exchange rates
	low interest rates	high interest rates
	high tariffs	free trade
	minimum wages	market wages
Role of State	leading, directive	subsidiary, facilitative

Source: Adapted from FUSADES 1985, 6.

Table 3.
Principal Macroeconomic Indicators, 1984-1988

Indicator	1984	1985	1986	1987	1988
% GDP*	2.3	2.0	0.6	2.6	1.6
GDP/per capita	1.0	0.7	-1.0	0.8	-0.3
% unemployment	32.9	32.2	23.8	23.0	n.a.
Inflation	11.7	22.3	31.9	24.9	19.8
Real wages	1.6	-15.9	-14.2	-18.3	n.a
Fiscal deficit (% GDP)	54.8	58.8	63.4	69.7	n.a

Sources: Pelupessy 1990, 271; Rosa and Segovia 1989, 234, table 1; and Fundación Salvadoreña
de Desarrollo Económico y Social 1989, 4.
*1962 constant prices   n.a.=not available.

Since most Salvadoran business elites perceived themselves to be unfairly excluded from economic policymaking by the PDC and military bureaucrats and since public opinion increasingly viewed the PDC as corrupt and inefficient in managing the economy, the antistatist perspective of FUSADES had growing political resonance, especially among business sectors and professionals. For hard-liners and soft-liners alike, privatization and deregulation became code words for getting rid of the hated INCAFE and its sugar counterpart, the National Sugar Institute (Instituto Nacional de Azúcar — INAZUCAR), and returning the nation-alized banks to private hands. The emphasis on trade liberalization and regional and nontraditional exports also helped bring small and medium-sized manufacturers and retailers into the neoliberal coalition (Marín 1989, 30-32).

Despite this convergence of interests, some leaders of ANEP and the Cafetalera were critical and publicly suspicious of FUSADES. Cafetalera leaders, already angry over U.S. support for the PDC reforms, tended to regard FUSADES as yet another effort by the U.S. government to increase its control over the Salvadoran economy at their expense. Some viewed FUSADES' emphasis on nontraditional exports as a threat to the coffee sector's leading economic role. A leader of ANEP scoffed at the idea that El Salvador's economy could recuperate by selling melons. He argued that coffee would remain the backbone of the economy for the foreseeable future, and, therefore, it was the coffee economy that required support. But within five years of its formation, the relationship between FUSADES and the hard-line major business associations began to thaw.[9]

In the mid-1980s, FUSADES was grooming a new generation of leaders for the traditional business associations. By the end of the decade, several leaders of ANEP, ASI, and the Chamber had served stints in FUSADES, usually on one of its operating committees. A comparison of the executive committees of FUSADES and the major business associations in the late 1980s and early 1990s reveals a considerable overlap. For example, ANEP officers and board members such as Roberto Vilanova, Victor Steiner, Hector Vidal, Roberto Murray Meza, and Jorge Zablah all served on various FUSADES committees or commissions. Even more pronounced is the degree of overlap between ASI and FUSADES. Nine out of the 13 members of ASI's 1990-1991 board of directors served in FUSADES. From the Chamber of Commerce and Industry, executive officers Armando Calderón Sol, Salvador Siman, Ricardo Hill, Carlos Andino, and Mario Andino also worked in FUSADES during the years when much of the business elite was shut out of the Duarte administration.[10]

FUSADES also enabled business associations to focus more on professional development and less on political confrontation. Throughout the Duarte administration, FUSADES published a steady stream of technical analyses and policy alternatives to administration policies, and it also sponsored numerous conferences, seminars, and roundtables to educate and promote debate on business conditions and government policy among broad sectors of society. By increasing the institutional capacity of business leaders to engage in data acquisition and analysis, FUSADES strengthened their ability to engage in constructive criticism and dialogue with the government. This was in marked contrast with the personal attacks and highly politicized charges against the government emanating from the traditional business associations, especially ANEP during the 1979-1984 period. Moreover, FUSADES had a key asset that the traditional business associations dominated by hard-liners lacked: professional and political credibility and respect among its opponents. FUSADES provided a means by which the "victim" or "siege mentality" of many in the business community could be transformed into constructive dialogue and the development of viable alternatives.

Finally, through its Private Sector Association Strengthening Program (Programa de Fortalecimiento Social — FORTAS), FUSADES provided some direct benefits to members of ANEP, ASI, the Chamber, and many other traditional business associations in the form of technical services, management training, and financial support. FORTAS has enabled these business associations to regain a measure of professional credibility.[11]

By 1986-1987, soft-liners were in control of the Chamber and ANEP. They had more pragmatic goals, were paying increased attention to providing professional services to the wider business community, and had converged their political posture with that of ASI and ABECAFE. The multiple threats had begun to recede: El Salvador's civil war was at a stalemate, the reform program of the PDC was emasculated, and the conservative business party, ARENA, was positioning itself for a victory at the polls in 1988 and 1989.

In January 1987, Duarte's austerity packages provided an opportunity for the business associations to assert their leadership among broad sectors of society in opposition to the PDC government. In the largest and most coordinated attack on government since Molina had proposed agrarian reform in 1976, ANEP and the Chamber denounced the austerity measures in the media, challenged their constitutionality in the Supreme Court, supported a legislative boycott by ARENA and PCN deputies, and sponsored a national work stoppage.[12] The only business association that did not join in the work stoppage was the National Council of Salvadoran Employers (Consejo Nacional de Empleadores Salvadoreños — CONAES), an organization with close ties to FUSADES whose leadership had personal differences with the leadership of the Chamber. The work stoppage, supported by most major unions and mass organizations, succeeded in shutting down an estimated 75 to 80 percent of businesses in San Salvador and 50 to 70 percent in other cities and towns. For the first time during the decade, the traditional associations, ANEP and the Chamber, were acting as the "voice" of society's economic interests, in the name of protecting individual freedom and private property from a corrupt and out-of-touch government (Gaspar 1989, 20-31). In contrast to past efforts to mobilize public opinion against a government program, the Chamber attacked the government primarily on economic, rather than political or personal, grounds. Instead of simplistically referring to the government or the president as "communist" or "anti-business," the Chamber published a stream of economic analyses to show why the measures would be injurious not only to business but to society as a whole (Gaspar 1990, 149-50).

These tactics worked. To placate the private sector, Duarte increased the representation of business associations on the governing board of INCAFE and allowed them more deductions in the tax reform. Although the hard-liners in control of the Cafetalera denounced Duarte's attempts at compromise, the more moderate leadership of ABECAFE and ANEP were conciliatory, suggesting that Duarte's efforts were a "good first step" ("Crónica del mes" 1987, 122). However, the basic strategy of the business associations, particularly the Chamber and ANEP, was to continue to engage in unrelenting criticism of Duarte's statist policies.[13] Duarte made overtures to the more reform-minded FUSADES by visiting its facilities in 1987.

With the continuing inability of the PDC to reactivate the economy or halt the civil war, ARENA swept the 1988 legislative and 1989 presidential elections. When ARENA took control, the influence of FUSADES and USAID on economic policy was already evident. Whereas the PDC administration had vacillated and resisted implementing stabilization and structural adjustment policies, the incoming ARENA administration brought coherence and unity of purpose to the program propounded by FUSADES. A comparison of ARENA's economic proposals during the campaign and those advocated by FUSADES shows them to be virtually identical.[14] Indeed, Alfredo Cristiani's economic team consisted largely of "FUSADES boys."[15]

PHASE 4: BUSINESS ASSOCIATIONS AND DEMOCRATIZATION, 1992-PRESENT

The peace accord signed January 16, 1992, in Chapúltepec, Mexico, not only brought peace to El Salvador for the first time in 12 years but also brought the country closer to democracy. By significantly improving the military, electoral, and judicial institutions, the peace accords succeeded where armed insurrection did not in terms of promoting revolutionary changes in the country's political structures. Some redistributive reforms were also mandated by the accords, including land-transfer and poverty-alleviation programs in the former combat zones (Spence and Vickers 1992; Spence, Vickers, and Dye 1995; Stahler-Sholk 1994).

The peace process consisted of two stages: the *negotiating phase* (1989-1992) and the *implementation phase*, which continues despite the departure of the United

Nations Salvadoran Observers (Observadores de Naciones Unidos en El Salvador — ONUSAL) at the end of October 1995.

Negotiating the Peace Accords

The behavior of El Salvador's business associations during the negotiation process was moderate and generally supportive of the need to bargain with the armed opposition and to reintegrate them into Salvadoran society. ANEP and the Chamber played only an indirect role during the negotiations, serving primarily as pressure groups in trying to prevent the Cristiani negotiating team from granting too many economic concessions, particularly in the areas of land and labor reform. Both associations supported the need for institutional changes, particularly in the military and the judiciary, key institutions implicated in past human rights abuses (Acevado 1991, 46-47). Leaders of the major business associations also supported electoral reforms that permitted the inclusion of leftist parties in the 1991 legislative elections. As one ASI leader explained, there was no reason to fear electoral competition from the left, as without guns, he believed, the FMLN would have few means to compel a following among Salvadorans.[16] Indeed, although the more moderate business leaders supported the peace negotiations, their interests were largely limited to ending the war and demilitarizing society in order to normalize business rather than as a prelude to further democratization and structural change.

With new national leadership less tied to the old power structure in which the military had provided the institutional link between land ownership and a coercive labor system, the soft-liners' emergence as leaders of business associations was a key development in reducing opposition to the compromises over institutional reforms integral to the peace process. For example, business associations supported the restructuring and reduction in size and role of the military and security forces. As an executive in the Chamber of Commerce proclaimed, "The military was responsible for getting this country into this mess and now we [ARENA] have finally gotten us out. We are not about to let it happen again."[17] It was clear that many business leaders felt as much concern for weakening the political role of the military as they did for ending the armed threat posed by the FMLN. The peace process promised to place the political advantage back with business. Even the Cafetalera, which had recently undergone a change to more moderate leadership in 1989, scaled down its attacks on Cristiani's efforts to reach an agreement.

The exclusion of hard-liners from leadership positions within the major business associations during the negotiations led some of them to resort to the same kinds of tactics employed when they were excluded from government decisionmaking during the attempted land reform of 1976 and the structural reform process of 1980-1982. Shadow organizations, such as Cruzada Pro-Paz y Trabajo, Frente Feminina, Frente de Unidad Nacional, and Frente Anti-Comunista Salvadoreña, sponsored demonstrations against the government and also took out full-page ads denouncing Cristiani's willingness to compromise with subversives. In addition, the conservative daily, *El Diario de Hoy,* served as a constant source of editorializing against the peace process. These organizations also issued dire warnings of a coup if the administration went too far in seeking retribution against past human rights abuses

(Acevado 1991). These familiar public and confrontational tactics by the extreme right demonstrated its relative lack of influence through normal institutional channels, such as the business associations and the ARENA party.

Implementation of the Peace Accords

During the more than three-year implementation phase of the peace accords, the attitude and behavior of the business associations stiffened, with opposition and resistance becoming more typical than compromise and compliance. The harsh criticism that the extreme right leveled at the ONUSAL mission, the human rights ombudsman, and even the Cristiani administration found increasing echoes in the rhetoric and behavior of the business associations. Their negative attitudes toward the Commission for Peace (Comisión de Paz — COPAZ), the publication of the Truth Commission's report on human rights abuses, the role of the Forum on Economic and Social Consensus (Foro de Concertación Económico y Social — known simply as the Foro), land transfers, and labor code reforms clearly showed that the business community was more interested in stability and the status quo than in issues of justice and reform. For example, in December 1992, the Truth Commission completed its work and compiled a list of over 100 individuals, many of them senior officers of the Salvadoran military, who were involved in the assassination of Archbishop Romero (1980), the rape and murder of four North American nuns (1980), and the killing of four Jesuit priests and their housekeeper and housekeeper's daughter on the campus of the Universidad Centroamericana (UCA) in 1989, as well as numerous other human tragedies. In an editorial published in *El Diaro de Hoy*, the leader of ANEP criticized the findings of the Truth Commission as "counterproductive," "destabilizing," and "unprovable."

With respect to economic and redistributive issues, the unwillingness of business associations to accommodate the changes called for in the peace accords are even clearer. In May of 1992, COPAZ created the tripartite Foro, which had eight representatives each from government, labor unions, and business associations (ANEP, ASI, the Chamber, and others). The limited mandate of the Foro was to formulate recommendations concerning a new labor code, programs of reconstruction in war-torn communities, and ways to ameliorate the impact of structural adjustment on the poorest sectors of society. The Foro had no mandate with respect to the most important socioeconomic issue facing the country: privatization, land transfers, and jobs. Business associations boycotted it because of land invasions by peasants, who were impatient with the interminable delays and red tape involved with the land-transfer program. ANEP, the Chamber, and ASI accused the FMLN of encouraging the land invasions and demanded that the squatters be evicted and the seizures halted before they would agree to join the Foro (Arriola and Mena 1992, 213-25).

CONCLUSION: BUSINESS ASSOCIATIONS AND POLITICAL CHANGE

El Salvador has provided a unique opportunity to examine the fortunes of business associations in the context of both a revolutionary threat and a democratic transition. In the face of these profound political challenges, business associations have successfully adapted to new political institutions and pressures. There are three major ways in which business associations have adjusted to political change.

First, the leading associations, ANEP and the Chamber, now have larger, much more diverse memberships than they did during the 1960s and 1970s. ANEP's membership in the late 1970s numbered about 25 sectoral associations; today the number of members is close to 40. Purely agrarian interests, represented by the coffee, ranching, and sugar associations and firms, are still important but no longer predominate. The leadership of ANEP and the multi-sectoral Chamber of Commerce reflect this — most of the leaders' business interests are in retail, finance, real estate, construction, or manufacturing. The political power of El Salvador's traditional oligarchy, whose wealth was based on the control over land and labor and the financing and export of coffee, beef, and sugar, has been superseded. The most important associational members of ANEP are now a diverse group: ABECAFE, exporters of nontraditional exports, the reconstituted bankers association, the real estate association, the construction enterprises association, and the insurance and financial services associations, in addition to the more traditional Chamber and ASI. This shift has been explained in terms of changes in the Salvadoran economy itself, the destructive impact of the 12-year civil war, the economic intervention of the United States, and the creation of FUSADES in 1982.

A second change is that in the absence of a common threat to their fundamental interests and in the context of increasingly diverse interests, business is far from unified politically. Although some observers tend to conflate the interests of ARENA, ANEP, and business in general, sectoral differences, personal animosities, and institutional power struggles among business associations and business leaders continue. In the context of a more "normal" political and social environment, differences among business groups are likely to become more pronounced. One divisive issue is the structural adjustment process that has been deepening during the 1990s. Structural adjustment continues to erode the economic base of the traditional agrarian elites. They and the industrial bourgeoisie stand to lose from certain aspects of structural adjustment; agrarian elites will find a unified exchange rate tends to hurt their exports, while members of ASI complain about lowering tariffs on manufactured imports. Although some exporters look forward to enlarging their markets through regional integration and possible accession to NAFTA, others will lose to the greater competition from foreign competitors. Given these emerging differences and the absence of a threat from below, it is hard to imagine ANEP and the Chamber being able to act as the unitary "voice" of the private sector as they did in the crisis atmosphere of the 1980s. Whether opposition groups or the popular sectors will be able to exploit these divisions to their political advantage remains unclear.

A third change is that business associations have become more "professionalized." Part of this professionalism is related to the normalization of the business climate throughout the region. Associations spend more time serving the professional interests of their constituencies rather than engaging in political confrontation over policy differences. Business associations provide technical information and training to business firms, recognize the importance of community outreach, and are making inroads in improving education (particularly at the secondary level). Seminars designed to make Salvadoran entrepreneurs more competitive and develop marketing and management skills are now common. Technical assistance and training provided by FUSADES have helped many business associations establish the expertise necessary to serve their constituents more effectively.

The evidence suggests that in El Salvador, as elsewhere, the rise of business groups less tied to land ownership and the traditional sectors of the agrarian economy was instrumental in creating more fertile soil for the germination of democracy. One reason for this change is the reduced dependence of nonagrarian elites on the state to defend their property or enforce repressive labor conditions. On the one hand, they do not have large tracts of unused land that they must protect from land invasions or squatters; on the other, they do not require a large low-wage, seasonal labor pool, the maintenance of which historically has demanded extensive state-sanctioned coercion. The close link between rural security forces and land-owners does not have any ready parallel among the urban-based industrial groups that now control the major business associations. Indeed, the readiness with which these associations supported reductions and restructuring of the military during the peace negotiations suggests that business has come to regard the military more as a liability than as an asset. The increasing mobility of transnational capital in today's global economy means that individual governments in dependent national econo-mies are losing their importance as the locus of economic decisionmaking.

The new generation of leaders now in control of El Salvador's business associations has acquired an institutional stake in maintaining democratic practices. The electoral success of ARENA suggests that business can compete successfully and defend its own interests in the political arena. Concurrently, the "professionalization" of business associations has made them more effective interlocutors for business interests, while the creation of policy institutes and think-tanks, such as FUSADES, has made business associations much more capable and credible as pressure groups that use information rather than just personal connec-tions to persuade policymakers. The United States was instrumental in encouraging this process, by funding FUSADES and identifying business associations and leaders who were more accepting of the need for economic reform and political pluralism.

Of course, one must be cautious regarding the democratic propensities of Salvadoran business associations. It must be remembered that business itself did not invite a transition to democracy; rather, it came after a long and costly civil war. Only when it became obvious that the insurgents could not be defeated militarily did the government and business groups seek an accommodation with the FMLN. At that point, the need for peace and stability — the return of a normal business climate — rather than democracy per se was a major reason for negotiating the end of the war. Moreover, the institutional reforms of the peace accords that have advanced El Salvador's democratization came only after years of tough negotiations. The implementation of several provisions, especially those that involved concessions from business, including land transfers and the labor code, met with stiff resistance from business associations. Among the elite, there is little enthusiasm for anything approaching substantive equality for El Salvador's citizens. And there is disturbing evidence that the historic utilization of security forces to ensure the economic interests of business may be assuming new forms: Urban business owners and the government have proved quite willing to use the police to break strikes and to rid their communities of the poor and disenfranchised, labeling them now as common criminals.

Notes

1. Some of the research for this chapter was conducted during a visit to El Salvador in August 1991, supported by a grant from the Mellon Foundation.

2. CEPAL (Comisión Económica para América Latina y el Caribe) was an economic think-tank in Chile operated by the United Nations.

3. For an analysis of the reforms, see Instituto de Investigaciones Económicas (1982, 507-539).

4. For a more extensive analysis of FUSADES and its place within the Salvadoran business community and role in policymaking, see Kenneth L. Johnson (1993), Chapters 5 and 6.

5. Interview with USAID private sector liaison officer, San Salvador, August 1991. This official confirmed that FUSADES was created in part to strengthen the "moderates" (that is, the soft-liners) among the Salvadoran business community and refocus their energy on promoting business rather than opposing the government. However, he admitted that this goal was secondary to that of reorienting the government in the direction of macro-economic orthodoxy in order to control inflation and debt, expand exports, and thereby lessen the country's dependence on U.S. bilateral aid.

6. An examination of FUSADES' roster of founders and officers reveals that most members during 1985-1990 represented the interests of industry, manufacturing, retail, commerce, and services. A comparison of this roster with a list of members of the traditional oligarchy (Eduardo Colindres [1977], table 67, n.p.; and James Dunkerley [1988], table 41, 345-346) turns up only three names in common: Ricardo Hill Argüello, a large coffee exporter, and Roberto Orellana and Roberto Murray Meza, both major landowners and coffee growers prior to the 1980s. Significantly, Hill's primary interests were in coffee exports and processing, rather than landowning or cultivation.

7. *Técnicos* are apolitical financial experts, most of whom have been steeped in orthodox (neoliberal) economic doctrine. Many of them received training abroad, particularly in Chile and the United States.

8. Interview with private sector liaison officer of USAID, San Salvador, August 1991.

9. Interview with Roberto Vilanova, ANEP Executive Director, San Salvador, August 1991.

10. Comparison of annual reports for 1989-1991 from ASI, ANEP, and the Chamber with those of FUSADES.

11. According to the FUSADES *1990 Annual Report*, FORTAS provided training to 40 executives from 18 different business associations that year.

12. Asociación Nacional de Empresa Privada (1985, 131-132) criticized both the content of the proposals as well as the means by which the government developed them — without consulting domestic interests and without debate.

13. See Cámara de Comercio e Industriales (1987, 532); Asociación Salvadoreña de Industriales (1985, 593); and Asociación Nacional de Empresa Privada (1987, 931).

14. Compare ARENA's platform (1988, 1121-24) with FUSADES 1985.

15. Among Cristiani's cabinet appointees affiliated with FUSADES were Central Bank director Roberto Orellana Milla (former director of the Chamber of Commerce), Economy Minister Arturo Zablah (former head of ASI), and minister of MIPLAN Mirna Lievano.

16. Interview with Roberto Ortiz, executive director of ASI, San Salvador, August 1991.

17. Interview with Juan Domenech, executive director, ANEP, San Salvador, August 1991.

References

Acevedo, Carlos. 1991. "El significado político de las elecciones de 10 de marzo 1991." *Estudios Centroamericanos* 45 (March-April): 152-166.

Alianza Republicana Nacionalista. 1988. "Hacia el rescate nacional." *Estudios Centroamericanos* 43 (November- December): 1121-1124.

Anderson, Thomas. 1971. *Matanza: El Salvador's Communist Revolt of 1932.* Lincoln, Neb.: University of Nebraska.

Arriola, Joaquín, and David Mena. 1992. "Alcances y límites de la concertación social en El Salvador." *Estudios Centroamericanos* 47 (March): 213-225.

Asociación Nacional de Empresa Privada. 1987. "Posición ante la aprobación de las leyes agrarias." *Estudios Centroamericanos* 42 (November/December): 931.

Asociación Nacional de Empresa Privada. 1985. "Pronunciamiento de ANEP frente a las medidas económicas anunciadas por el gobierno." *Estudios Centroamericanos* 41 (January-February): 131-132.

Asociación Salvadoreña de Industriales. 1985. "ASI y la Cámara sobre las nuevas medidas cambiarias." *Estudios Centroamericanos* 40 (July-August): 593.

Bulmer-Thomas, Víctor. 1987. *The Political Economy of Central America since 1920.* New York: Cambridge.

Cámara Salvadoreña de Industria y Comercio. 1987. "La Cámara sobre la verdad sobre la segunda fase de la reforma agraria." *Estudios Centroamericanos* 41 (November-December): 532.

Campbell, Jane. 1968. "The Chamber of Industry and Commerce of El Salvador: A Latin American Interest Group." Master's thesis, Tulane University, New Orleans.

Castro Morán, Mariano. 1987. *La función política del Ejército salvadoreño en el presente siglo.* San Salvador: Universidad Centroamericana José Simeón Cañas.

Colindres, Eduardo. 1977. *Fundamentos económicos de la burguesía salvadoreña.* San Salvador: Universidad Centroamericana Editores.

Coto, Celso R., Mildred Carcamo, and José Antonio Recinos. 1990. "La intervención del estado en la economía salvadoreña en el período 1970-80 y la privatización de la CORSAIN." Unpublished thesis, Universidad Centroamericana José Simeón Cañas, San Salvador.

"Crónica del mes: enero." 1987. *Estudios Centroamericanos* 42 (February): 122.

Cuenca, Breny. 1992. *El poder intangible: La AID y el estado salvadoreño en los años ochenta.* Managua: CRIES.

Dunkerly, James. 1988. *Power in the Isthmus.* London: Verso.

FUSADES. Various years. *Annual Report.* San Salvador: Department of Economic and Social Studies.

FUSADES. 1990. *¿Cómo está nuestra economía?* San Salvador: Department of Economic and Social Studies.

FUSADES. 1985. "Lineamientos de un nuevo modelo económico para El Salvador." *Boletín Económico y Social* 7 (November).

Gaspar, Gabriel. 1990. "Crisis y politización empresarial en Centroamerica." *Presencia* 2 (6): 99-109.

Gaspar, Gabriel. 1989. *El Salvador: El asenso de la nueva derecha*. San Salvador: CINAS.

Goitia, Alfonso. 1989. "El estado en momentos de crisis: la redefinación del papel del estado." *Realidad Económica y Social* 3 (May-June): 290-305.

Gordon, Sara. 1977. "La transformación agraria en El Salvador: Un conflicto interburgués." *Estudios Sociales Centroamericanos* 12 (September): 13-21.

Inforpress. 1988. "Los empresarios ante la crisis de Centroamérica." *Inforpress Centroamericana* (special issue).

Instituto de Investigaciones Económicas. 1982. "Evaluación de las reformas." *Estudios Centroamericanos* 37 (May-June): 507-539.

Johnson, Kenneth L. 1993. "Between Revolution and Democracy: Business Elites and the State in El Salvador in the 1980s." Ph.D. dissertation, Tulane University, New Orleans.

López Vallecillos, Italo. 1976. "Reflexiones sobre la violencia en El Salvador." *Estudios Centroamericanos* 31 (January-February): 9-30.

López, Carlos Roberto. 1984. *Industrialización y urbanización en El Salvador. 1969-79*. San Salvador: Universidad Centroamericana.

López, Roberto. 1986. "La nacionalización del comercio exterior en El Salvador: Mitos y realidades en torno al cafe." *Estudios Centroamericanos* 41 (May-June): 389-410.

Marín, José. 1989. "Existe un pensamiento de la Nueva Derecha en El Salvador?" *Realidad Económica y Social* 3: 16-33.

Montgomery, Tommie Sue. 1995. *Revolution in El Salvador: From Civil Strife to Civil Peace*. 2nd edition. Boulder, Colo.: Westview.

Paige, Jeffrey. 1993. "Coffee and Power in El Salvador." *Latin American Research Review* 28 (3): 7-40.

Pelupessy, William. 1991. "La economía política del ajuste estructural." *Realidad Económica y Social* 15 (May-June): 241- 269.

Ramírez Arango, Sergio. 1985. "The Political Role of Private Sector Associations in Central America." Ph.D. dissertation, Harvard University, Cambridge, Mass.

Rosa, Herman, and Alexander Segovia. 1989. "Financiamiento externo, deuda y transformación de la estructura productiva en el década de los ochenta." *Realidad Económica y Social* 3 (May-June): 2330276.

Rosa, Herman, and Roberto Suay. 1986. "El nuevo model económico norteamericanos para Centroamérica: El caso El Salvador." *Boletín de Ciencias Económicas y Sociales* 9: 7-21.

Spence, Jack, and George Vickers. 1992. *A Negotiated Revolution? A Two-Year Progress Report on the Salvadoran Peace Accords*. Washington, D.C.: Washington Office on Latin America.

Spence, Jack, George Vickers, and David Dye. 1995. *The Salvadoran Peace Process and Democratization: A Three-Year Progress Report and Recommendations*. Washington, D.C.: Washington Office on Latin America.

Stahler-Sholk, Richard. 1994. "El Salvador's Negotiated Transition: From Low-Intensity Conflict to Low-Intensity Democracy." *Journal of Interamerican Studies and World Affairs*. 36(4): 1-60.

White, Alastair. 1971. *El Salvador*. New York: Praeger.

Zamora, Rubén. 1976. "Seguro de vida o despojo? Análisis de la transformación agraria." *Estudios Centroamericanos* 31 (September-October): 511-534.

CHAPTER SIX

Revolution and the Hyperpoliticized Business Peak Association: Nicaragua and el Consejo Superior de la Empresa Privada

ROSE J. SPALDING

[W]e accept now, with clarity and pride, that the more the government gets involved in the production process, the more COSEP will get involved in politics.
COSEP President Enrique Bolaños (1987, 3)

B usiness associations and social movements are generally thought to represent two very different forms of civil society. Not only are these groupings normally drawn from different sectors of society (elite vs. mass), but they also are often thought to build on different organizational principles. Social analysts often assume that business associations embody bureaucratic rationality and engage in instrumental or planned pursuit of class interests. By contrast, they conceptualize social movements as spontaneous and protean expressions of identity politics.

Under certain circumstances, however, the distinctions between these two social forms will tend to blur, and business peak associations (BPAs) develop the intensity, defensive insularity, and charismatic leadership styles associated with mass-based movement politics. Among business associations, these "movement" traits typically appear in a context of political isolation and in response to deeply felt threats. Business associations founded in movement politics may rise quickly to political prominence and play a strategic role in challenging state adversaries. However, their origins cause them to suffer; their issue orientation is often narrow, which breeds inflexibility; and their adversarial style may not be appropriate for problem solving. The siege mentality that often undergirds movement politics complicates the task of negotiating both internal and external political openings. With limited adaptability, these business organizations may find it difficult to adjust to changing circumstances; their political fortunes may fall as sharply as they rose.

As Carlos Acuña argues in his chapter in this volume, "movement-like" business organizations "are generally not very efficient in contexts that require bargaining." These BPAs often pursue the appearance of homogeneity within the business class at the expense of real consensus, which may require painstaking construction; while pursuing abstract principles by issuing nonnegotiable demands, they may forgo achievable benefits. Associations of this type emphasize in-group solidarity and confrontational, line-in-the-sand politics. Inspired to defensive action by the threat of expropriations and the shut-down of communication with state elites, these organizations have difficulty maintaining momentum in less inclement times. Associational politics in Argentina periodically developed along these lines (Acuña in this volume). Mexico's Business Coordinating Council (Consejo Coordinador Empresarial — CCE) also followed this general pattern of sharp ascent and decline (Tirado in this volume).

Nicaragua's Superior Council of Private Enterprise (Consejo Superior de la Empresa Privada — COSEP) is probably Latin America's quintessential "movement-like" BPA. Forged out of a series of hard conflicts with the different regimes that governed Nicaragua in the 1970s and 1980s, this association developed a sharply ideological, hyperpoliticized style in the 1980s. Crusading leaders led the organization into daily battle with the regime, to the applause of faithful supporters. Business elites who were skeptical participated only peripherally; unwilling to challenge the leadership, they frequently resorted to self-censorship and political withdrawal.

When the threats and confrontations of the 1980s diminished in the 1990s' postrevolutionary context, COSEP's agglutinative powers weakened, and its centrality to political debate eroded. Nonetheless, COSEP made important contributions both to Nicaragua's democratic transition and to the process of neoliberal reform. This organization drew together and energized the elite's opposition to the Somoza dynasty, which held power from 1936 to 1979, and played a vital role in the overthrow of Nicaragua's traditional authoritarian politics. COSEP's participation in the anti-Somoza coalition allowed the opposition movement to emerge as a broad national front, not just a narrow, class-based revolutionary struggle. According to analysts like Wickham-Crowley (1992), who systematically compared 11 revolutionary movements from 1960 to the 1980s in Latin America, the cross-class character of the Nicaraguan movement to oust Anastasio Somoza was one of the key factors that explained its success.

The outcome of that struggle was not to the liking of COSEP's leaders once the Sandinista National Liberation Front (Frente Sandinista de Liberación Nacional — FSLN) consolidated control. The business class's behavior during the period of the revolution (1979-1990) reflects its complex views about the contending forces of democracy. As an advocate of delimited, procedural approaches to democracy and an opponent of more radical, redistributive versions, COSEP played an important role in redefining the concept of democracy that would prevail in Nicaragua.

Negative experience with the FSLN during the 1980s infused much of the business class with a fierce anti-state perspective and a strong rhetorical commitment to the free market. The liberalization process under the post-revolutionary government of Violeta Chamorro (1990-1996) was greeted with enthusiastic support by the business sector. Although COSEP was not part of the technocratic network that constructed the new economic order, the organization embraced the strong anti-state premises inherent in reform and cheered it on.

After neoliberal adjustments were implemented, however, COSEP leaders, particularly in the industrial and traditional agricultural sectors, were less sanguine. Nicaragua was the Central American laggard in undertaking reform. Building on antiquated and dilapidated infrastructure and pursuing reform in a tattered, postwar condition with no social consensus in favor of market transition, Nicaraguan elites found it difficult to compete in international markets. Faced with lagging economic performance, divided and uncertain, COSEP lost its edge as the premier advocate of neoliberal reform.

The baton for reform passed to new business associations that sprang out of specific growth areas in which liberalization did open opportunities. These emerging associations, which had a clearer and more sustained commitment to economic reform, preferred to remain independent of COSEP. Leaders of COSEP continued to support reform at key junctures but had difficulty negotiating consensus around the divisive issue of implementing the full package of neoliberal change. Mired in conflict, COSEP proved more comfortable fighting old battles with the FSLN than moving on to new ones.

COSEP's story can be divided into three phases: the founding years in the 1960s and 1970s, the consolidation phase in the 1980s, and the era of erosion in the 1990s.

THE POLITICAL DYNAMICS OF PEAK ASSOCIATION FORMATION: THE FOUNDING YEARS (1960S-1970S)

In Nicaragua, as in most of Latin America, business associations go back to the turn of the century (CADIN 1975; Walter 1993, 8-10; Spalding 1994, 43-48). Small organizations of producers in the coffee, cattle, and commercial sectors emerged early in the twentieth century; the subsequent development of the cotton and industrial sectors in the 1950s and 1960s sparked the development of new associations. Until the 1970s, however, most of these organizations failed to expand beyond their original regional or sectoral bases. Business associations generally only responded to the particularistic needs of producers in certain regions and were unable to develop a broader organizational reach or a clear project that would engage the entire business class. As a result, most of the associations were ephemeral; after a few episodic activities, they faded quickly with only a faint historical trace. Those that endured over several decades typically did so by virtue of special privileges granted to them by the state. Groups like the Managuan Chamber of Commerce (Cámara de Comercio de Managua), which were given, by law, representation in key government agencies, or like the Nicaraguan Cattle Ranchers Association (Asociación de Ganaderos de Nicaragua), which was founded and directed for many years by Nicaraguan President Luis Somoza, were among the few that persisted. Quasi-corporatist linkages with the state gave these business associations resources and durability but indentured and fragmented the business class. As Carlos Acuña and Kurt Weyland note in the chapters in this volume on Argentina and Brazil, respectively, these neocorporatist relations encouraged particularistic and clientelistic linkages that undermined the unity of the business class.

Associational dependence on the state had fragmented the private sector, and the pursuit of particularistic ends by individual interests strengthened Somoza's rule. But that dependence began to erode in the 1960s. An increasingly urban, financial, and industrial business class, with deepening trade, educational, and cultural connections to the international community, began to develop a separate political agenda that brought capital into conflict with the Somoza regime. Business elites from these sectors registered growing dissatisfaction with the corruption and arbitrariness of the decaying Somoza dynasty. Hostility to the dynasty's excesses sparked the first business-wide coordination effort in Nicaragua.

Organizationally, this effort involved a two-step process. First came the creation of the Nicaraguan Development Institute (Instituto Nicaragüense de Desarrollo — INDE), a new kind of business-civic association established in 1963. Second came the creation in 1972 of the Superior Council of Private Initiative (Consejo Superior de la Iniciativa Privada — COSIP, later COSEP), an umbrella organization that brought all of the major private sector associations together. Throughout the 1970s, INDE served as the prime catalyst for more comprehensive associational collaboration. It pushed forcefully to activate an encompassing BPA and served as a surrogate BPA during the period when COSIP waned.

INDE and the Construction of Civic Identity

INDE differed from previous business groups in its national (as opposed to regional or sectoral) reach and its civic aspirations. Unlike other producer associations, which focused on particularistic economic issues like taxes and credit or on the maintenance of local social hierarchies, INDE adopted a broader political and social mission. In keeping with the priorities of its principal funders, USAID and the Inter-American Foundation, it took on anti-communist and developmental tasks; its work in the 1960s included distributing anti-communist radio and television programs, creating university scholarship programs and vocational training centers, training workers in "non-political" unionism, and promoting rural cooperatives (INDE 1965; 1966; 1975). Supported by foreign donors,[1] INDE gained an unprecedented level of independence from the Somoza regime. Pursuing a broader, cross-class mission, INDE functioned as the missing agglutinative by bringing economic elites together across sectoral and regional lines.

The emergence of this new type of elite organization responded to the broad processes of capitalist development in Nicaragua during the 1950s and 1960s. Support from U.S. agencies bolstered this new-style organization, but the robust character of the association would not have been possible without the internal transformations underway within Nicaragua. The Nicaraguan economy had grown rapidly in the early 1960s, with annual growth topping 10 percent in the 1960-1965 period (Rosenthal 1982, 20). The creation of the Central American Common Market proved a catalyst to urban industrial growth.[2] This growth was supported by the development, in the 1950s, of a private banking system and bank-based economic groups (the Banco Nicaragüense — BANIC — group and Banco de América — BANAMER — group) and by the expanded developmental activities of the state-owned Banco Nacional de Nicaragua — BNN (Strachen 1976; Wheelock

Román 1980; Everingham 1996). This development fueled the expansion of a new kind of business elite that was better educated, more cosmopolitan, and more willing to challenge the political stranglehold of the Somoza family. It was this urban professional elite that made up INDE's core constituency.[3]

INDE possessed a higher level of organizational sophistication than its predecessors had obtained. It recruited a professional staff, established a series of development projects,[4] and produced annual reports complete with financial accounts. Perhaps most important, INDE offices served as a gathering place where leaders of several private-sector organizations could discuss common concerns. Inevitably, these discussions turned toward politics.

The Nicaraguan business elite had long had an understanding with the Somoza regime: the dynasty would provide a setting in which the elite could prosper, and the business class would leave the task of governing to the Somoza family. By the early 1970s, however, this understanding was breaking down. Growing participation in the regional economy was increasing the need for predictability and access to technically competent services that the Somoza dynasty was not prepared to provide. At the same time, the Somoza regime's political skills were deteriorating. The buoyancy and adaptability that had characterized the first Somoza regime under Anastasio Somoza García (1937-1956) (Gould 1990; Walter 1993) and the developmentalism found in the second under Luis Somoza Debayle (1956-1963) had disintegrated in the hands of the third Somoza president, Anastasio Somoza Debayle (1967-1971; 1974-1979). Political avarice, always a problem, intensified, and corruption became more visible. Moving into new businesses (land development, construction supplies, housing, banking), the Somoza family jostled broader sectors of the elite and violated an unwritten assumption that economic gains would be widely shared. Business elites felt increasingly powerless when faced with growing economic competition from Somoza family businesses and the threat of arbitrary state intervention. As the informal boundaries that had delimited the sphere of public corruption widened and the sweep of the Somoza family's economic empire expanded, elite opposition sharpened.

The regime also failed to keep the peace. Instead of maintaining order, the dynasty triggered the creation of a revolutionary movement, led by the FSLN, that waxed and waned through the 1960s. Although the business elite was not threatened directly by the FSLN, which remained very small through this whole period,[5] it saw the guerrillas' existence as proof of the political incompetence of a decaying regime. As evidence of the regime's declining ability to maintain law and order mounted, important strands of the business elite began to coalesce in opposition to the dynasty.

COSIP/COSEP: Launching a BPA

In 1972, INDE's leadership moved to bring this array of sectoral leaders together under its tutelage with the creation of COSIP. This umbrella organization linked 12 established associations, including the most significant groups that had emerged in the previous 20 years. (See Appendix.)

COSIP's first major act was to organize a national conference with more than 2,000 participants in March 1974. This conference, arranged by COSIP President Marco Zeledón, brought together as panelists and moderators such prominent business leaders as BANAMER's Ernesto Fernández Holmann, GRACSA's general manager Alfonso Robelo, and Casa Dreyfus's Enrique Dreyfus; top economic officials like Central Bank presidents Francisco Lainéz and Roberto Incer; and outspoken academicians like Ernesto Cruz, rector of INCAE (INDE 1975). This session culminated in a panel discussion that criticized the regime's corruption and lack of professionalism and called for joint efforts to modernize the state (setting up a professional civil service, auditing government accounts, and engaging in developmental planning). In response to the regime's unvarnished corruption following a 1972 earthquake that leveled large portions of Managua, the business and professional elite in Nicaragua pushed for internal state reform. Given the power of personalism and patronage in the Somoza regime, this moderate reform agenda would have required profound changes in the Nicaraguan state.

This essentially political conflict between an expanding urban elite and an entrenched dictatorial regime was not intense enough to generate a durable, well-defined, and encompassing peak association. The regime rejected the conference recommendations, and COSIP, which had neither a legal charter nor its own facilities, soon withered away. Although the Somoza regime's performance raised troubling questions about the future and cut into profits of particular firms, the business elite did not perceive an urgent threat to its class interests. After a brief sortie into oppositional politics, the first incarnation of this encompassing peak association fizzled in the mid-1970s, overcome by its own institutional weakness and the Somoza regime's divisive negotiating strategy.

As the Nicaraguan case demonstrates, simply forming an encompassing peak association does not ensure either its durability or its power. Similar findings have been identified in other cases. Francisco Durand (1991) reports, for example, that Peru's first two encompassing business peak associations dissolved quickly as a result of internal policy disputes. The process through which the business elite consolidates politically in spite of its divergent priorities and a history of competition is often an uneven one that proceeds through several phases.

After its initial success, COSIP faded into the background, and INDE stepped forward again as the direct negotiator for the private sector. With an established institutional structure, a professional staff, and a budget that was relatively independent of the regime, INDE became the stalwart of private-sector opposition during the escalating conflicts of the 1970s. Public confrontation with the regime in 1974 only strengthened this organization. INDE's membership rose rapidly, climbing from 89 in 1974 to 523 in 1976 (INDE 1975; INDE 1977). INDE was, however, still a modest urban association with essentially a civic agenda, not specifically a business or economic one. It was not broad-based enough to be a credible representative of business as a whole.

A second effort at cross-elite, multisectoral organization occurred at the end of the 1970s, as the Somoza regime became increasingly repressive and the business elite became increasingly disgruntled. Catalyzed by the January 1978 assassination of Pedro Joaquín Chamorro, a prominent opposition leader and scion of one of

Nicaragua's leading families, the business class again began to coalesce against the regime.[6] INDE mobilized support across the business elite for three major general strikes in 1978 and 1979. These strikes, backed by 16 private-sector associations, helped to sift out and reorganize the business elite.

In spite of pressures and threats from the Somoza regime, private sector organizations grew rapidly during the final phase of the dictatorship and led, by the time of the overthrow, to the resuscitation of COSIP (now renamed COSEP). Several new organizations in addition to the large network of established business groups fed into this encompassing peak association. Most importantly, in a country in which agriculture represented 34 percent of the GDP in 1979 (CEPAL 1982, 13), agricultural producers' associations now coalesced with the opposition. Independent organizing among agricultural producers culminated in the creation of the Nicaraguan Agricultural and Livestock Producers Union (Unión de Productores Agropecuarios de Nicaragua — UPANIC) in March 1979 under the leadership of major producers like Marco Antonio Castillo Ortíz, Julio César Castillo Ortíz, Jorge Salazar, Ernesto Salazar, and Juan Tijerino (UPANIC 1979). Starting with three core sectors — cotton, livestock, and coffee — this association gradually united a growing segment of the country's large and medium-sized agricultural producers. By the end of 1979, UPANIC had expanded to include producers in the dairy, rice, sorghum, banana, and sugarcane sectors.

When, striking out in retaliation, the Somoza regime revoked the legal status of INDE and the Chamber of Commerce and closed their offices, anti-regime business leaders moved to work clandestinely and in exile, now under the more inclusive and authoritative guise of the reactivated COSEP. Leaders of COSEP finally rejected Somoza's divisive requests for dialogue. Assuming that they would be able to establish control over the ragtag guerrilla force, COSEP supported the FSLN's call for a third national strike. On June 6, 1979, COSEP issued a communiqué calling for the immediate resignation of Somoza and the creation of a new government of national unity (COSEP 1979a). Eleven days after the Government Council of Nacional Reconstruction (Junta de Gobierno de Reconstrucción Nacional — JGRN) was formed in Costa Rica, COSEP issued a statement formally recognizing it as the new government (COSEP 1979b). By this point, COSEP had reemerged as the definitive representative of business and an important political player.

In sum, several exogenous and endogenous factors contributed to the creation and eventual consolidation of Nicaragua's encompassing peak business association in the 1970s. First, the nature of the Nicaraguan business class was changing. Backed by the growth of an active private banking system in the 1950s and new forms of development assistance in the 1960s, a growing and ambitious professional class emerged in key urban areas. The Central American Common Market also created new opportunities for expansion in the 1960s, particularly in the industrial sector. With deepening international connections, through both trade ties and their own educational experiences in the United States, many of these professionals pushed to redefine the roles of economic elites in their society. Inevitably, part of this redefinition centered on the political system. INDE became the organizational net that captured this reform-oriented segment of the business elite.

Second, financial and organizational support from USAID and the Inter-American Foundation bolstered these efforts by providing business reformers with the resources they needed to project a civic mission and launch development initiatives. The assistance provided by USAID supported organizing that transcended narrow, sectoral concerns, as would occur in the Salvadoran and Peruvian cases many years later (Kenneth Johnson in this volume; Francisco Durand in this volume). In the Nicaraguan case, where the regime was very attentive to U.S. preferences, this backing also legitimized INDE activity by implying the blessing of the U.S. government and offering the association some protection from regime retaliation.

The third element, which the comparative framework of this volume suggests was essential, was a deepening perception of threat. INDE's efforts produced a full-fledged encompassing peak association only when the domestic political imbroglio worsened. Perhaps more than most, Nicaragua's encompassing BPA developed in response to political rather than economic or social crisis. The activation of COSIP was not triggered by a sharp economic downturn that rallied business activism across the board, as occurred in Chile during the 1980s, nor by populist policy shifts, as occurred in Mexico in the 1970s and early 1980s. It responded instead to a political crisis of the state. The gap between what the business elite needed from the regime (access, order, regularity, capacity to implement policy) and what resulted under the regime (erratic policy intervention, misappropriation of state resources, outbreak of guerrilla activism, increasing uncertainty) widened sharply through the 1970s. The re-election of Anastasio Somoza in 1974 for a long seven-year term sharpened the tensions between the economic elite and the regime and propelled the business class into unified action. The failure of dialogue to remove Somoza, even as the status quo became unsustainable, drew the business elite into direct opposition. Threats that galvanize elite unification, therefore, do not necessarily come from the left, unions, or populist governments; elite unification may also be triggered by regime decay and declining state capacity if these processes pose long-term threats to the social order.[7]

Perhaps because Nicaragua's encompassing BPA resulted primarily from political developments, it lacked the solidity that characterized some other Latin American encompassing BPAs in their formative years. COSIP tended to spark with political crises and fade as they passed. As Eduardo Silva argues in his contribution to this volume, crisis and threat are amorphous concepts; passing crises may not be intense enough to generate organizational consolidation. After its initial foray into the political arena, COSIP withdrew into inaction for several years and was replaced by the more resilient INDE, a proto-peak association. As the political crisis sharpened at the end of the 1970s, however, COSIP/COSEP reemerged to speak on behalf of the broader business sector. When repression was directed against even members of the elite and endless regime-elite dialogues proved futile, the business class was able to rally once more behind a broad, multisectoral encompassing BPA.

ASSOCIATIONAL CONSOLIDATION AND MOVEMENT POLITICS IN THE SANDINISTA ERA (1979-1990)

COSEP might have fizzled again except for the sustained challenges posed by the Sandinista Revolution. The tensions that emerged between business and the

Sandinistas tempered and tuned this association. During the Sandinista Revolution (1979-1990), COSEP emerged as a coherent entity with a firmer institutional structure and a defined sense of mission. A deepening perception within the COSEP elite that the revolution threatened the capitalist class as a whole helped to consolidate the association. In the process of defining itself during the 1980s, COSEP pursued a hyperpoliticized and increasingly strident neoliberal line, abandoning the amorphous developmentalism it had embraced in its early years.

In documents from COSIP's first national conference in 1974, the Somoza regime had been called upon to establish a professional planning capacity and to address socially significant problems of housing, education, and transportation (COSIP 1974). COSIP demanded public accountability and a state apparatus that could promote the public good, thus challenging Somoza's preoccupation with private gain and with using the state for personal enrichment.

This interest in redefining the state and fostering national development made it possible for some business leaders to connect with the demands of the FSLN. Partial convergence on goals, however, did not imply a serious alliance. COSIP, INDE, and the Nicaraguan Chamber of Commerce (Cámara de Industrias de Nicaragua — CADIN), the most reform-oriented of the business associations, were clearly distinct from and skeptical of the FSLN; they engaged in repeated, fruitless dialogues with Somoza in search of some compromise agreement that would oust the president while forestalling revolution. Only when their push for change through dialogue failed did leaders of these organizations cooperate with the guerrillas and their elite interlocutors to force Somoza from power.

COSEP's links to a pro-reform, anti-dictatorial movement lent the association a certain populist patina during the opening phase of the revolution. Immediately after the fall of Somoza, several prominent business association leaders took positions in the Sandinista government. Alfonso Robelo,[8] former president of INDE and COSIP, for example, was named to the five-person governing council, as was Violeta Barrios de Chamorro, widow of Pedro Joaquín Chamorro. Marco Antonio Castillo, the first president of UPANIC, left the association to become vice president of the Banco Nacional de Desarrollo, the major state bank. Business leaders assumed an array of top policy and administrative positions within the new government.[9]

Within a short time, however, this business-state relationship deteriorated. COSEP shifted to the right and became one of the two leading domestic political opponents of the Sandinista government (along with the Catholic Church hierarchy). These transitions created a new "COSEP consensus" that became increasingly pro-market and anti-revolution.

Close examination of business elite politics in Latin America shows that elite ideological stances are not uniform across time and space (Bartell and Payne 1995, 264-265). Ideological preferences emerge in a dynamic context, based in part on strategic calculations about particular conjunctures. This process gives business ideology a certain protean character, especially during periods of dramatic social change. Business associations are, of course, unlikely to endorse an anticapitalist agenda (even though individual members of the elite sometimes do), but a range of ideological perspectives may be acceptable to the associations under various conditions. In Latin America, this range extends from embracing moderate forms of populism, in which state participation in development and selective nationalizations are supported, to endorsing neoliberalism and demanding a reduced state apparatus with market deregulation.[10] COSIP/COSEP's shift from endorsing the former to insisting on the latter suggests that the process of ideology formation responds to dynamic changes in domestic and international conditions.

In general, business elites will be more inclined to accept a populist state and even some measure of redistribution if state activism does not challenge the domestic capitalist class as a whole and instead divides sectors against each other, holding the promise of prosperity for some. However, when private property or the process of accumulation itself seems to be at stake and economic decline is generalized, the elite commonly responds by banding together and shifting sharply to the right. When the Allende government nationalized important large and even medium-sized enterprises in Chile in the early 1970s, for example, the business elite forged intense intra-associational linkages and became fiercely hostile to the regime (Campero 1984, 58-73). According to Silva (in this volume), the Chilean business sector's commitment to the market economy in the 1980s was partially grounded in this experience of loss and fear in the early 1970s.

COSEP's rightward swing in the 1980s was likewise triggered by gradually spreading survival fears. The FSLN consolidated its control over the government by placing top FSLN leaders in charge of all key ministries and expanded state participation in the economy by expropriating the extensive resources of "somocistas" and establishing monopolies in banking, foreign trade, and mining. These actions raised the suspicions of remaining business leaders and made them increasingly skeptical.

Business leaders' deepening sense of threat was exacerbated by a change in the leadership of Nicaragua's encompassing BPA. The departure of the most pro-revolution business leaders from COSEP in 1979-1980 to take positions in the Sandinista government left the association with fewer leaders who regarded reform sympathetically. Those who rose to COSEP leadership in the second generation were generally regime outsiders who were quicker to criticize. A cycle set in: expropriation followed by confrontation, followed by further expropriation, followed then by harsher confrontation.

Pitched battles erupted quickly. Within a year of Somoza's ouster, COSEP Vice-President Jorge Salazar joined with counterrevolutionary forces that were preparing an invasion to topple the FSLN. Killed by state security forces in 1980, reportedly during a weapons delivery, Salazar gained martyr status in COSEP circles. His picture was prominently displayed in the offices of COSEP affiliates for years afterward as an act of public defiance of the regime. Alfonso Robelo and Violeta Chamorro both left the JGRN before completing a year in office. The entire 1981 COSEP leadership (including President Enrique Dreyfus and all five vice presidents) openly denounced the government for its "Marxist-Leninist" and "totalitarian" tendencies (COSEP 1981) and distributed copies of this letter to the international press. Their subsequent conviction for this offense and the four-month imprisonment of the three COSEP signatories who did not flee the country cemented COSEP's official hostility to the regime.

Successive waves of expropriations also played a role in shifting the business sector further to the right. A significant portion of COSEP leaders were targets of expropriation,[11] including then COSEP Vice President Ramiro Gurdián in 1983 and COSEP President Enrique Bolaños in 1985. Roughly 20 percent of the agricultural land in the country was confiscated from "somocistas" in 1979-1980; an additional 10 percent (1,518 properties) was expropriated for a variety of reasons between 1981 and 1989 (CIERA 1989, I, 23, and IX, 40). Even those whose property was not expropriated were affected by this process, since many feared their turn would come. As the number of expropriations and regulations increased, the business climate deteriorated, the economy declined, and open warfare with the regime broke out.

Interviews I conducted in 1990-1991 with leaders in COSEP's agricultural affiliate UPANIC illustrate the depths of this antagonism. Of the 64 current and former UPANIC leaders I interviewed, 58 expressed unambiguous opposition to the FSLN government (Spalding 1994, 140). To some, the regime was technically incompetent and economically misguided, with policies that stifled initiative and discouraged production. One official concluded, "Under the Sandinistas, we were foremen practically, not owners. We were told what to produce and whom to sell to. . . . The Sandinistas were experimenting and centralizing, and it didn't have good results. There is not a Nicaraguan producer who has not taken some capital out of the country."[12] For other elites, the Sandinistas were primarily venal destroyers who had shredded the moral fabric of society. One leader of a COSEP affiliate concluded, "The Sandinistas never deceived me. I knew they were communists and I'm horrified by communists. . . . When they came to power, for me the world ended. . . . The Sandinistas are thieves who taught people to steal. The peasants lost more than they gained under them; they got a little land, but they lost honor, respect, Christianity."[13]

Deepening hostility to the Sandinista regime made many COSEP leaders archly pro-market and anti-state. When asked to describe the economic model they most preferred for their country, the most common choice among UPANIC national leaders I interviewed was "pure market capitalism." (See Table 1.) Proponents of this position denounced state regulation, called for the elimination of state enterprises,[14] and expressed support for the freest possible market system. The legacy of government intervention and extensive expropriation built a strong rhetorical conversion to free-market capitalism within the business elite, as it had in Chile during the 1970s.

In the words of one leader of a COSEP affiliate, "Nicaragua has never had free enterprise. There were always clans of power. The Somoza clan had power, then the FSLN put in its friends and relatives. Now UNO [Unión Nacional Opositora — National Opostition Union] is putting in its. We should not simply go back to the past. We need full capitalism now."[15]

We should be careful, however, not to overstate this position or to misread its implications. Even in Nicaragua, where state-business conflicts were most bruising, elite economic preferences were not uniform. Some business elites, particularly those who took up leadership positions in the National Union of Agricultural Producers and Ranchers (Unión Nacional de Agricultores y Ganaderos — UNAG), the Sandinista-sponsored producer association, were, not surprisingly, more sympathetic to the regime's mixed economic model. Twelve of the 17 UNAG leaders that I interviewed expressed support for the Sandinista government; although four others expressed mixed views, only one expressed opposition (Spalding 1994, 143).

Table 1.
Preferred Economic Model by BPA Leadership Level 1990-1991
UPANIC (percent)

	National leaders	Regional/ Sectoral leaders
	(n=26)	(N=38)
Pure market	50	29
Moderate capitalism	31	53
Mixed	15	16
Socialist	—	—
None	4	2
Total	100	100

Source: Author's interviews.

Even among COSEP leaders, economic views were not identical. Whereas 50 percent of UPANIC leaders at the national level affirmed a commitment to "pure market capitalism," 31 percent of national UPANIC leaders preferred "moderate capitalism," accepting regulation of the market and some state participation in the economy.[16] One national COSEP leader concluded:

> I prefer on principle that property be private, but you cannot fix in stone what will be state owned and what will be private. Generally the state should not build houses, but after a natural disaster, the state perhaps should do so. Some enterprises should be state owned using the principle of subsidiarity, meaning the product should be a state responsibility if the private sector is not able to produce it.[17]

This pattern was more pronounced at the subnational (regional and sectoral) levels. Just as Acuña's chapter in this volume identifies differences in the policy preferences and bargaining strategies of "4th level" and "2nd and 3rd level" business associations in Argentina, so my study of the Nicaraguan business elite identifies significant variations in the economic views of those occupying leadership positions at different levels. Whereas half of UPANIC's national level leaders endorsed "pure market capitalism," only 29 percent of leaders of regions or sectors took that position. The majority (53 percent) of UPANIC's regional/sectoral leaders preferred "moderate capitalism." Furthermore, regional/sectoral leaders were more likely than national ones to have worked with the Sandinista government on concrete projects. Indeed, several regional and several sectoral UPANIC leaders actually came to support the Sandinista regime, even running as FSLN candidates in the 1990 election.[18]

To some degree, differences in political behavior among COSEP leaders reflected a tactical decision to recruit strong, ideological opponents of the regime into the national leadership, where they would repeatedly confront the FSLN on political grounds, and to leave the sectoral and the regional leadership in the hands of moderates who would continue to negotiate with the regime. COSEP national leaders would routinely denounce FSLN transgressions and reject any attempt at dialogue. These leaders became highly politicized, even hyperpoliticized, continually challenging the legitimacy of the regime and doing so even when this had sharp economic costs. Leaders of sectoral associations like the Nicaraguan Association of Irrigated Rice Growers (Asociación Nicaragüense de Arroceros de Riego — ANAR) and leaders of regional organizations like the León Cotton Growers Association (Asociación de Algodoneros de León — ADAL), on the other hand, would continue to meet with government personnel to press for improved prices or easier access to productive inputs. This stance reflected the more pragmatic negotiating style and less extreme agenda of those outside the national limelight.

Like other movement-style encompassing BPAs, COSEP was not adept at acknowledging or representing its internal diversity. The organization was stamped by the "purer" and "more principled" positions taken by top national leaders, who endorsed confrontational politics and a radical shift toward economic reform. The perspectives of moderates and those of second-tier leaders were relegated to the margins, and real consensus on ideals and objectives was not seriously pursued.

Movement-style politics gave COSEP considerable visibility as a domestic opposition force. It propelled a whole generation of business leaders into direct engagement with the nation's tangled political life, and it gave particular force to the credo of market economics with which COSEP came to be associated.

COSEP Membership and Organization

The 12 business groups that joined to form COSIP included associations in sectors that were vital to the national economy, like CADIN and the Nicaraguan Association of Banking Institutions (Asociación de Instituciones Bancarias de Nicaragua), and others that were peripheral, like the Association of Automobile Distributors (Asociación de Distribuidores de Vehículos Automotores). According to early COSEP members, this wide variation in size and significance of affiliates made the organizational structure unwieldy and contributed to the organization's problems.[19]

When COSEP was revived in 1979, it used a new organizational scheme in which all associations were regrouped into seven national chambers (six after the banking chamber was eliminated following the July 1979 bank nationalization). These national chambers included INDE, which continued to play the leadership role, with seven regional branches; the Confederation of Nicaraguan Chambers of Commerce (Confederación de Cámaras de Comercio de Nicaragua), with 27 regional and sectoral affiliates; the Nicaraguan Chamber of Construction (Cámara Nicaragüense de la Construcción); CADIN; the Confederation of Professional Associations (Confederación de Asociaciones Profesionales — CONAPRO), with

12 affiliates; and UPANIC, with its eight national producer associations (which in turn had several dozen regional affiliates).

COSEP's membership tended to be weighted toward medium-sized and large producers as in other encompassing business peak associations in Latin America.[20] Unlike such encompassing BPAs as Mexico's CCE, however, COSEP did not include the nation's largest, wealthiest capitalists. The Pellas family, arguably Nicaragua's wealthiest, for example, did not participate directly in this association.[21] Elites of that magnitude preferred a more peripheral involvement; general managers hired to run their enterprises might participate, and executives from the country's larger enterprises might make financial contributions to the association. The few Nicaraguan elites who presided over large complexes of assets and directed leading economic groups did not, however, need to join such organizations, since their access to the political leadership was direct and, even under the FSLN, generally assured.[22] They could, in any case, enjoy "free rider" benefits without incurring the costs (government hostility, time, reciprocal obligations, collective policy constraints) of membership.

Nor did COSEP include many of Nicaragua's small businesses. COSEP seriously underrepresented small producers and enterprises, as did encompassing BPAs elsewhere in Latin America. COSEP leaders did make an effort, shortly after the FSLN's victory, to incorporate selected small producers into some regional associations; in the midst of revolution, this step was thought necessary in order to counter the organization's image as narrowly elitist and to prevent public denunciation. In the end, however, this recruitment drive was abandoned. In part, this reversal was due to the scarcity of leaders who were capable of crossing the class divide in their organizational work; in part, it was due to the dangers of organizational division and in-fighting that cross-class alliances presented.

The experiences of coffee growers in Matagalpa and cotton growers in Chinandega suggest the nature of these problems. Few COSEP leaders had the vision or charisma needed to mobilize skeptical small producers into established associations of agro-export elites. COSEP Vice-President Jorge Salazar, however, did; his efforts to recruit small coffee producers into the Matagalpa coffee growers' association in 1980 were reportedly remarkably successful.[23] But his organizational efforts soon led him into competition with the FSLN and drew government suspicion. Salazar's subsequent move into the counterrevolution and death at the hands of security forces brought this base-level expansion to a halt.

The active recruitment of small and medium-sized cotton producers by the Association of Cotton Growers of Chinandega (Asociación de Algodoneros de Chinandega — ADACH) in the early 1980s further showed the dangers that this inclusionary policy could pose to established elites. The new producers recruited into this traditional association of cotton elites soon outnumbered the old. In 1984, the new members mobilized to take over the association leadership; in the struggle that followed, the organization split in two. The established ADACH then spent years contesting the distribution of its assets.[24] Given these developments, COSEP soon settled back into its role as a representative of medium-scale and large-scale capital and displayed little interest in further expansion. Both its membership base and the socioeconomic extraction of its leadership retained a sharp upper-class bias.[25]

In order to manage the internal tensions that were inevitable in turbulent times, COSEP adopted several measures to soften leadership struggles. From 1972 until 1986, INDE's president automatically became the president of COSIP/ COSEP, anchoring COSEP in the urban, professional elite. Initially, this arrangement circumvented fights among various chambers. This bond disadvantaged several other more numerically or economically important associations like UPANIC, however, and eventually produced rather than resolved conflicts. In 1986, this requirement was eliminated, and board members were allowed to choose the organization's president from among any of the six chamber presidents. The presidents of each of the remaining five chambers were automatically designated vice presidents, who, along with two "directors" appointed by each of the chambers, made up COSEP's governing board.

In theory, the power of the COSEP president was diluted by the norm that decisions be made by consensus of this governing body. Formal communiqués, for example, had to be signed by all of the vice presidents. In the 1980s, when the sectoral associations were united in their opposition to the Sandinista government, such unanimity was not difficult to obtain, and the president had considerable authority to speak on behalf of the association. The organization issued regular statements and press releases challenging both overall government legitimacy and specific policies.

During the early 1980s, COSEP and its affiliates received funding from the U.S. government through USAID, a factor that also contributed to the association's rightward shift. External funding for COSEP was complemented by internal contributions from participating chambers. Chambers paid a fee for each of the three seats they held on COSEP's board of directors, and drives were conducted periodically to support special projects.

After the relationship between the United States and Nicaragua disintegrated and the Reagan administration began financing the *contra* war against the Sandinista government, U.S. funding for the Nicaraguan private sector was banned by the Nicaraguan government, and overt funding came to a halt. USAID funding was replaced, on a much smaller scale, with funds from the Konrad Adenauer Foundation, an affiliate of Germany's conservative Christian Democratic Party (CARANA Corporation 1991, 19-20). In addition to providing funds for INDE and CONAPRO, this foundation also financed COSEP's research arm, the Private Enterprise Institute of Economic and Social Research (Instituto de Investigaciones Económicas y Sociales de la Empresa Privada — INIESEP). Through INIESEP, COSEP attempted to construct an economic think tank that could anchor COSEP's economic vision and expose economic problems that the government preferred to conceal.[26]

With this organizational apparatus and financial support, COSEP survived in the 1980s. Despite U.S. backing, despite its inherent status as an encompassing peak association, and despite the high profile it maintained at home and abroad, COSEP had few institutional resources. It relied on a skeletal staff in rented facilities, had limited technical capacity, and drew its inspiration heavily from a small core of leaders who were willing to make extraordinary sacrifices on behalf of their political vision.

Postrevolution Challenges: Democracy and Neoliberalism in the 1990s

The deradicalization of the Sandinista Revolution in the late 1980s and the electoral defeat of the FSLN in 1990 opened new possibilities for the business elite. Ironically, however, just as the consolidation of the Sandinista Revolution had fed the consolidation of COSEP, the collapse of the FSLN government contributed to COSEP's political decline. COSEP reached its zenith as an archrival of the FSLN government in the 1980s. With the defeat of the FSLN, COSEP's agglutinative capacity declined. This outcome is in some ways paradoxical. Indeed, from the standpoint of COSEP leaders, the 1990s brought four positive developments that should have enhanced their organization's power and prestige.

First, economic reforms adopted by the postrevolutionary governments offered many investment and expansion opportunities for the business class. Under the government of Violeta Chamorro, private banks were allowed to reopen, and they soon dominated the financial system; foreign trade was largely turned over to the private sector; and most state enterprises were quickly privatized. In a few short years, the Nicaraguan economy underwent a dramatic metamorphosis in which the domestic business class was relocated at the center of the economic model.

Second, increasing pluralism in the political system as well as official validation of the business class in the 1990s offered business greater freedom to organize without fear of penalty. As Durand and Silva suggest in the opening chapter of this book, there is a certain affinity between the process of democratization and the development of encompassing BPAs. Increased tolerance for pluralism and stronger constraints on repression open more space for autonomous organizations of all types; BPAs have unprecedented opportunities to flourish with the deepening of procedural democracy. As the democratization process in Nicaragua moved into its postrevolutionary phase, many of the particular risks faced by business elites dissipated, and opportunities for open mobilization and media campaigns expanded.

Indeed, after the 1990 election, COSEP's membership reportedly increased (USAID 1994, 34). Membership no longer held the prospect of political penalty; in fact, it offered the prospect of access to resources. No longer fearful of expropriation and recognizing the power of COSEP's connections to the new government, some elites that had withdrawn from the organization or become inactive renewed their interest in COSEP membership.

Third, COSEP's financial situation brightened with the return of USAID after 1990. USAID extended two new grants to the organization: a $100,000 Center for International Private Enterprise (CIPE) award, which covered salaries of additional staff and external consultants, and a grant from the Special Initiatives Fund (SIF) that went largely to support TVCOSEP, a "micro-news" program that was aired twice daily on a privately owned television channel.[27] This support gave COSEP the opportunity to rethink its mission, and it launched several new initiatives in the early 1990s. Many prospective members came to see COSEP as a victor whose close association with the U.S. Embassy could bring rewards and opportunities in post-revolutionary Nicaragua.

Fourth, the postrevolutionary governments of the 1990s were friendly governments with which COSEP had substantial ties. COSEP leaders supported the UNO coalition that brought Violeta Chamorro to power in 1990, and the COSEP rank and file provided important logistical support (like organizing rallies and lending vehicles for transportation) for its campaign. True, COSEP's support was somewhat begrudging after its former President Enrique Bolaños lost his bid for a slot on the UNO ticket in August 1989. However, prominent COSEP leaders, like then-President Gilberto Cuadra, joined the Chamorro campaign as advisors. A number of business leaders later joined the Chamorro government; for example, cattle rancher Roberto Rondón became minister of agriculture and livestock. [28]

Arnoldo Alemán, who was elected president in 1996, had even closer ties to COSEP. Alemán rose to political prominence in 1989 as a leader in a COSEP affiliate (the Managuan coffee growers association) when his family's estate was expropriated during an ill-advised FSLN move against grumbling coffee producers. Aleman's alliance with COSEP was sealed when he chose Enrique Bolaños, a vivid symbol of COSEP's persecution, as his vice-presidential running mate.

In spite of these opportunities, COSEP did not flourish in the 1990s. Instead, it struggled with a number of challenges. These included the movement-style character of the association, deepening tensions over neoliberal economic reforms, and conflicts over competing concepts of democracy.

Sedimentation of Adversarial Politics

Organizations have stylistic propensities that are forged during defining periods and subsequently become difficult to change. Stylistic rigidities are particularly characteristic of movement-style organizations, which are often marked by emotional intensity and may develop top-down decisional structures. COSEP's consolidation during the hard early years of the Sandinista government had inclined it toward confrontational politics. That style, which had in some ways served the broad political interests of COSEP leaders during the 1980s, became an organizational trademark that they could not surrender, even during less adversarial times.

Even though official antipathy for COSEP ended with the Sandinista Revolution, the organization continued to have difficulty forging alliances. The Chamorro government, led by Minister of the Presidency Antonio Lacayo, attempted to build linkages to COSEP. Two rounds of *concertación* were called in 1990 and 1991 to push a broad dialogue among government, businesses, and workers on how to reconstruct the economy.[29]

Despite these efforts, COSEP remained confrontational, regarding the Chamorro government's push for national reconciliation as a form of conspiracy with the FSLN. The resignations of two COSEP leaders from the Chamorro government on the day it was inaugurated,[30] the refusal of COSEP representatives to sign either of the two *concertación* agreements, and COSEP's support for the new Association of Confiscated Property Holders (Asociación de Confiscados), which demanded the immediate return of all expropriated properties, reflected the growing friction between COSEP and the Chamorro government.

Throughout the 1979-1995 period, effective control over COSEP was centralized in the hands of a network of deeply politicized leaders, most of whom were at the helm during the period of struggle under the FSLN government.[31] Association leaders were chosen by a small group of insiders who elevated to power the most articulate defenders of the organization's preestablished position. Top leadership positions circulated among a handful of key leaders who rotated between COSEP's presidency and its Board of Directors. Those most drawn to COSEP, who tended to rise within the organization, were those who found its hostility to the FSLN most congenial.

In the 1990s, COSEP's traditional leaders were reinforced by a network of expatriates who returned to Nicaragua to reclaim their expropriated properties. The inability or unwillingness of the Chamorro government to dispose quickly of their claims, to halt ongoing land invasions, and to restore the traditional social relations in the workplace led many COSEP leaders to criticize the Chamorro government sharply[32] and to push for the continuing dismantlement of the Nicaraguan state.

COSEP's status as a defender of freedom and private initiative seemed less relevant in a postrevolutionary society. Its traditional anti-Sandinista and generally anti-government stance became increasingly antiquated. Presumably recognizing this problem, the COSEP president elected in 1995, Gerardo Salinas, moderated the tone of COSEP's public pronouncements. Organizational inertia, however, is difficult to reverse. By the mid-1990s, the signs of waning strength and influence were clear. The most dynamic new business associations chose not to affiliate with COSEP, U.S. financial support was largely withdrawn, and divisions emerged within COSEP over the economic direction of the country.

Loss of Agglutinative Power

The postrevolutionary period was a fertile time for private-sector organizing, and new chambers proliferated in strategic sectors. Independent organizations emerged among producers in nontraditional exports, in the reconstituted banking sector, among those interested in reestablishing commercial trade with the United States, and in new organizations for small businesses. Unlike cases explored elsewhere in this volume (the Dominican Republic in the 1970s, El Salvador in the 1980s and early 1990s), where the increase in the number of business associations served to strengthen the encompassing peak association, the development of new business associations in Nicaragua in the 1990s occurred almost entirely outside the COSEP framework. None of these new associations became affiliates of COSEP.

The first postrevolutionary association to emerge was the Nicaraguan Association of Producers and Exporters of Nontraditional Products (Asociación Nicaragüense de Productores y Exportadores de Productos No-Tradicionales — APENN). Hoping to have access to the export opportunities provided by the Caribbean Basin Initiative once relations with the United States normalized, APENN founders recruited heavily in 1990 to bring together a network of relatively sophisticated producers who would experiment with non-traditional exports. With financial support from USAID, APENN began offering technical services and information to its members, gradually reaching out, with USAID contracts, to develop a training program even for small producers and cooperatives. Unlike COSEP organizations, APENN was less focused on the political allegiances of its members; its affiliates even included producers who had been active in the Sandinista government.[33]

Following the reconstitution of a private banking sector, the Nicaraguan Association of Private Banks (Asociación de Bancos Privados de Nicaragua — ASOBANP) was founded in 1992. Like APENN, ASOBANP adopted an open admissions policy and included the general managers of all banks, even those who were publicly associated with officials in the Sandinista government.[34] By early 1997, ASOBANP had 12 bank affiliates, including every major financial institution in the country.[35]

The American Chamber of Commerce in Nicaragua (Cámara de Comercio Americana de Nicaragua — known by its English acronym, AMCHAM), which had been founded in 1975 but had fizzled during the 1980s, was revived with great fanfare in the 1990s. It quickly became one of the country's most visible private-sector organizations, hosting speakers and seminars, issuing a monthly newsletter, and participating actively in the policy review process. Incorporating prominent business leaders with a strong international trade orientation, this organization expanded rapidly to 150 members in 1995, surpassing the shrunken CADIN, which claimed only 140.[36]

Finally, after years of neglect by COSEP affiliates, small business owners also began to organize independent associations, including the National Chamber of Small and Medium Industry and Handicrafts (Cámara Nacional de la Pequeña y Mediana Industria y Artesanía — CONAPI) and the Nicaraguan Union of Small and Medium Enterprises (Unión Nicaragüense de Pequeña y Mediana Empresa — UNIPYME). These groups expanded rapidly and began searching for export opportunities (Vuskovic 1995).

Since all of these organizations chose to remain independent, COSEP's hegemonic position in the business sector began to erode. Unwilling to surrender their autonomy, and seeing few advantages in such affiliation, these associations competed with COSEP for international support and political access.[37] Although COSEP was spared the Dominican experience, in which independent associations merged in 1991 to form a second peak association, COSEP's inability to reel in these new business associations cut into its power as a peak organization.[38] Since these new associations were located in the most dynamic sectors of the emerging economy, their decision to remain outside COSEP was particularly damaging.

Loss of Financial Support

In 1994, USAID ended funding for most COSEP projects (although it did continue to support COSEP's agricultural affiliate, UPANIC). The dramatic reduction in all USAID funding for Nicaragua, which fell from US$267 million in 1991 to an estimated US$19 million in 1995,[39] coincided with a marked change in USAID funding priorities. In 1994-1995, USAID shifted its funding away from big business support toward small and medium-sized enterprises and basic social services (USAID 1995). CARANA Corporation, the consulting firm hired by USAID-

Nicaragua to assess the institutional needs of the Nicaraguan private sector, had recommended in 1991 that COSEP "increase and broaden its membership base, reaching out in particular to small business" (CARANA Corporation 1991, 2). In its final summary report on its Private Sector Support Project in March 1994, CARANA Corporation found that COSEP had failed to make this transformation (CARANA Corporation 1994). Although COSEP's agricultural affiliate UPANIC did, with USAID financial support, undertake a few projects that provided technical and administrative services to small producers,[40] in general COSEP's organizational reach among small businesses remained quite limited. Organizations like COSEP, which were perceived as highly politicized, institutionally underdeveloped, contributing little to economic reactivation, and in the domain of medium-to-large-sized businesses, were no longer the priority for USAID resources.

The end of USAID funding spelled an end to many of COSEP's special projects. By 1995, INIESEP, COSEP's research arm, had closed down, and TVCOSEP was taken off the air. The new Export and Investment Center (Centro de Exportaciones e Inversiones — CEI), an export-promotion center set up by the Chamorro administration, moved out of the COSEP office and relocated to a new facility.

COSEP faced a major organizational and financial challenge. Although technically obligated to pay monthly dues, most of COSEP's affiliates had ceased to do so.[41] Burdened by their own economic problems and the financial weakness of their members, four of COSEP's affiliates stopped making payments in 1993, and a fourth, CADIN, paid only a fraction of its dues. Of the six member chambers, only the Chamber of Commerce paid the full amount. The COSEP leadership attempted to compensate, with some success, by soliciting voluntary donations from the country's largest industrial firms,[42] but the inability or unwillingness of the chambers to sustain this encompassing BPA revealed underlying institutional problems.

Divisions over Market Reform

Given their negative experience with state involvement in the economy under both previous regimes, COSEP leaders were enthusiastic advocates of market reform during the period of transition. COSEP lent public support to reform at several crucial moments. The 1991 economic stabilization package introduced by Minister of the Presidency Antonio Lacayo won COSEP's public endorsement, for example, as did the 1996 tax reform proposal on the eve of a government meeting with international donors (COSEP 1991b; COSEP 1996). However, these strategic interventions cloaked internal divisions.

The actual experience of neoliberal transition proved more difficult than COSEP leaders expected. Producers quickly deprived of government subsidies and forced to face stiff competition in the international market often found themselves unable to meet the neoliberal challenge. The cotton sector, which had dominated the economy in the northwest portion of the country, simply collapsed, leaving idle land and soaring unemployment problems. Whole industrial sectors, like textiles and clothing, entered a sharp and sustained descent. The annual private investment level, which had, according to one calculation (Martínez Cuenca 1994, 15), fallen to 2.8 percent of GDP in 1979-1989, rose to only 6.5 percent in the 1990-1993 period, far below the 10.2 percent it had averaged in 1966-1978. The overall GDP growth rate, which had turned negative through much of the 1980s, stagnated in the 1990-1993 period (CEPAL 1995, 15). When growth resumed in 1994, it was modest and uneven; Nicaragua's GDP per capita remained one of the lowest in the hemisphere (CEPAL 1990, 25; CEPAL 1995, 15).

COSEP national leaders held the FSLN responsible for the negative trends in the 1990s, and they called for a faster and fuller return of expropriated properties, punitive action against FSLN leaders, and police action against strikers and land invaders. But some business leaders, particularly at the sectoral level, began raising questions about elements of the neoliberal model itself. The differential impacts of neoliberal transition tended to erode the "COSEP consensus." Although business elites in larger commercial establishments experienced a boom during this phase due to dramatically increased access to imported goods, producers in the industrial sector felt threatened by this onslaught of imports and urged caution (CADIN 1993). As credit problems mounted in 1995, indebted cattle ranchers mobilized demonstrations and blocked highways to pressure the government to deviate from IMF recommendations and pump more resources into the state bank. Even COSEP president Gilberto Cuadra questioned the rigidity of the model, concluding in 1995 that "the ESAF [Enhanced Structural Adjustment Facility] is not the solution to our problems" (G. Cuadra cree 1995; Spalding 1997, 257-259).

The marked variation in the consequences of transition for different economic sectors complicated the task of coordinating a common business response. Unable to forge a shared economic vision or a coherent set of policy recommendations, COSEP leaders tended to fall back on the discourse of the 1980s, hammering away at the FSLN for its assault on private property and at the Chamorro government for its failure to eradicate the vestiges of the revolution.

Perhaps COSEP would have played a more forceful role in mobilizing private-sector support for economic reform if the initial phase of reform had produced more positive results or if private-sector leaders had been able, as in the Chilean case, to propose modifications in the model effectively (Silva in this volume). In Nicaragua, however, market reform produced little growth, and many of those who did benefit from the changes were not integrated into the COSEP framework. Under these circumstances, COSEP did not spark sweeping elite endorsement for sustained marketization.

Nor were they able to push through a pragmatic adjustment to the model that might have allowed the government to deal more realistically with the limitations of market economics in the Nicaraguan case. Nicaragua's extraordinary foreign debt —US$11 billion in a US$1.8 billion economy in 1994— (World Bank 1996, 210, 220) and dependence on foreign financing reduced the leverage of all domestic actors in the formulation of economic policy. Unable to exert much influence on the economic plans proposed by international financial institutions, COSEP could not galvanize private-sector agreement around a set of pragmatic adjustments. Without a clear economic proposal or the capacity to influence policymaking seriously, COSEP was unable to unite the private sector around a common economic agenda.

Contestation about Democracy

COSEP contributed to democratization in Nicaragua by playing a vital role in Somoza's ouster. During the 1980s, COSEP forcefully defended the right to dissent, and, in the 1990s, it was a major advocate of using electoral mechanisms to achieve change. At the same time, the character of democracy as it had emerged in revolutionary Nicaragua was singularly challenging for the business sector. In a setting where a substantial segment of the population and major political actors viewed democracy as a force with which to mobilize the dispossessed and alter the distribution of resources, the implications of democracy for the business class were problematic.

The FSLN had not only won a revolution in 1979 but had also won an election in 1984, one in which it received a handy 67 percent of the vote. Although COSEP had denied the legitimacy of that election and prevented "its" candidate, Arturo Cruz, from officially registering to participate, many observers found the 1984 election to be an important step in the development of democracy and the FSLN to be clearly the party of preference of the vast majority (LASA 1984). In addition, Sandinista President Daniel Ortega received 41 percent of the vote in the 1990 election that he lost and a very similar 38 percent of the vote in 1996 (LASA 1990; Carter Center 1997). The FSLN, COSEP's nemesis, remained Nicaragua's largest and best organized political party into the 1990s. For Nicaraguan elites, therefore, democracy meant perpetual challenge by an adversarial force; it presented a much more complex set of issues than it generally did in Latin America.

When reflecting on the relationship between business elites and democracy in the 1990s, the central question is not, as it was in the 1970s and 1980s, whether Latin American business elites are "pro-democracy" or "pro-authoritarian"(O'Donnell and Schmitter 1986). Throughout the region, economic elites of the 1990s have played an important role in undermining the hold of authoritarian leaders and in supporting the process of political liberalization (Payne and Bartell 1995, 266-270). Although long-term historical analysis suggests that the bourgeoisie's role in the development of democracy is ambiguous (Rueschemeyer, Stephens, and Stephens 1992), at this historical juncture Latin American elites have widely supported democratization processes. The new issue for the 1990s concerns the types of democracy that business elites will endorse.

Evelyne Huber and John D. Stephens (forthcoming) describe the democratic forms consolidating in Latin America as "deficient democracies," characterized by limited capacity for participation of lower classes and by uneven protection of civil and political rights. Emerging out of authoritarian experiences that undercut the mobilization of popular sectors and in the context of neoliberal reforms that tend to weaken organized labor, these democratic arrangements pose few challenges to economic elites. The support of the business class for this type of democracy, therefore, comes at a very low cost. The willingness of Latin American elites to support democratic forms characterized by mass mobilization, in which social and economic rights are forcefully asserted and pressures for more equitable distribution are strong, remains open to question. The support of business elites for democracy, while real and crucial to its durability, may be limited to the constrained version in which elite interests are not deeply challenged.

Evidence from the Nicaraguan case supports this generalization and suggests some of the tensions that emerge when more radical versions of democracy are introduced. Democratic forms that challenged property rights, mobilized marginal sectors, and brought the country into conflict with the United States were quickly denounced by COSEP as "totalitarian"; those that affirmed the elite's property claims and moderated the marginal sector's social demands were accepted as legitimate. Radically expanded versions of democracy, which cut deeply into resources of this thin stratum of elites, mobilized COSEP into opposition. The elite acted not in pursuit of an authoritarian alternative, which was no longer an option in Nicaragua, but to build a coalition favoring a delimited or constrained version of democracy. As a peak association deeply involved in political debate and committed to a reduced role for the state, COSEP provided a forceful voice advocating limited social rights and regime resources. The Nicaraguan case suggests the limits of elite tolerance for distributive democracy.

CONCLUSIONS

Among Latin American encompassing BPAs, COSEP's most distinguishing trait was its intense politicization. Perhaps this was inevitable, given Nicaragua's decades-long political crisis. First emerging as part of the challenge to the Somoza dynasty and then consolidating as a key opponent of the FSLN government, this organization was born as a political agent. Movement-style traits, like mobilizational intensity, concentrated leadership, an emphasis on public unanimity, and a penchant for confrontation, were organization hallmarks through much of COSEP's history.

In the aftermath of the revolution, the center of political debate shifted into governmental institutions and political parties, and COSEP lost some of its political visibility. Both government and U.S. Embassy liaisons pushed COSEP to shift its focus toward more conventional business association activities like technological training, legislative analysis, and service-oriented activities. This transition, however, proved difficult. In the postrevolutionary period, COSEP found itself on the outskirts of most new associational development, struggling with financial difficulties and confronting deepening internal fragmentation.

A decade of sparring with the Sandinistas produced a tendency in COSEP to critique more than propose. When it articulated a set of objectives, the organization focused on highly generalized goals, like freedom, the sanctity of property, and anticommunism. This discourse contributed little to the concrete policy debate in the 1990s. COSEP became a less central player in Nicaraguan political life, despite its intensely political aspirations.

Nonetheless, COSEP remained undisputed as Nicaragua's encompassing business peak association. All of the other business organizations were much more narrowly targeted; only COSEP could claim to incorporate businesses across economic sectors and regional lines. Furthermore, many business elites viewed COSEP's political line with sympathy. As a result, COSEP was always given a seat at the table. It was routinely invited for consultations with the government, given representation on government boards and agencies, and asked to participate in international forums. But its hegemonic role was challenged by a surge of new business organizations that imposed fewer ideological criteria for membership, adopted a stronger emphasis on technical services, and employed more flexible negotiating strategies. Prompted by its declining fortunes and the urgings of pragmatism, COSEP began, by the mid-1990s, to struggle with a redefinition of its mission.

Notes

1. In the 1972-1978 period, INDE received an average of 60 percent of its funding from international donations (calculated from INDE, *Informe Anual*, various years).

2. Whereas the agricultural sector had an average annual growth rate of 11 percent in 1960-1965 but only 0.6 percent in 1965-1970, industrial sector growth was both more rapid and more sustained (15 percent in 1960-1965 and 8.9 percent in 1965-1970) (Weeks 1985, 64).

3. The organization began with 40 members in 1963 and grew to 76 members in 1965, mainly through personal recruiting by existing members. Active participants in INDE's committees in 1965 included such prominent business figures as Ernesto Fernández Holmann, Enrique Dreyfus, Felipe J. Mántica, Enrique Pereira, Julio Chamorro, and Luis Carrión Montoya (INDE 1965, 2 [appendix]). According to INDE's second *Informe General de Actividades* (1966, 5), 45 percent of its members were in commerce, 25 percent were in industry, and the remaining 30 percent were in financial institutions, services, and professions.

4. EDUCREDITO was set up to manage INDE's scholarship programs, and the Fondo Nicaragüense de Desarrollo (FUNDE) managed its cooperatives project. INDE also supported the development of a new business training institute, the Harvard University-affiliated Central American Institute of Business Administration (Instituto Centroamericano de Administración de Empresas — INCAE).

5. The FSLN was almost destroyed in the late 1960s; its membership in 1974 was only about 150 (Booth 1985, 139-143; Gilbert 1988, 5-11).

6. The business sector rallied to this cause despite Chamorro's nontraditional politics, which had tended to alienate some of the elite (Everingham 1996, 135-136, 145-147).

7. See also Payne (1994, 61-64) on the rising opposition of Brazilian industrial elites to the military government during the 1980s.

8. Robelo rose to prominence as the general manager of Grasas y Aceites, S.A. (GRACSA), a major cooking oil processing facility that had been launched with capital from U.S., Salvadoran, and Nicaraguan sources (Spalding 1994, 268).

9. Previous executive councilors of INDE and its affiliates included Dionisio Marenco, who later became Sandinista minister of planning and budgeting, and Pedro Antonio Blandón, who became director of the international reconstruction fund.

10. See Spalding (1994, 5-31) on the range of business reactions to various reform governments in Latin America between the 1930s and the 1980s. In this work I identified five factors that shaped the ideological positions of the business class during periods of social reform: the presence or absence of a traditional, hegemonic oligarchy; the level of organizational autonomy possessed by business associations; the nature of the threat posed by state actors; the political coherence of the regime in power; and the general viability of the new economic order. For the full argument, see Spalding (1994, 189-217).

11. Forty percent of the UPANIC leaders I interviewed in 1990-1991 had land expropriated during the Sandinista era, and many others described expropriations of relatives or neighbors.

12. Author's interview, Boaco, July 26, 1990.

13. Author's interview, Granada, October 10, 1990.

14. Respondents were asked specifically about three kinds of state enterprises: state farms, the state banking system, and state trade monopolies.

15. Author's interview, León, July 3, 1990.

16. A surprising 15 percent endorsed a "mixed economy" in which the state and private sectors would have roughly equal levels of responsibility.

17. Author's interview, Managua, September 6, 1990.

18. Perhaps the most prominent was the president of the national dairy association and a representative on the UPANIC Directorate, who ran for the National Assembly on the FSLN ticket in 1990. Several members of the UPANIC-affiliated León Cotton Growers Association (Asociación de Algodoneros de León — ADAL) also supported the revolution and became FSLN candidates. One FSLN candidate for municipal office in León had been an officer in ADAL and its representative in the UPANIC Directorate in 1988-1989, and two ADAL members were FSLN candidates for the National Assembly.

19. Author's interviews, Managua, August 19, 1986, and September 6, 1990.

20. It also was heavily weighted toward business elites residing in major cities and in the western portion of the country. Although INDE did include a chapter in Bluefields, most associations had no representation on the Atlantic Coast.

Determining COSEP's membership base is a challenge, especially for the period of the Sandinista Revolution. The antagonism that emerged between COSEP's national leadership and the Sandinista government made membership a source of political tension; members sometimes informally withdrew from these associations or joined multiple, competing associations. The harsh battles between COSEP leaders and Sandinista government officials, the general contraction of the large producer class due to expropriations and exile, and the expropriation of properties of highly visible COSEP leaders had a decidedly negative impact on COSEP's ability to recruit and retain members during the 1980s. On the other hand, COSEP's bold challenge to the Sandinista regime and its international connections to embassies and the media gave it a magnetic appeal to an increasingly disgruntled elite class.

COSEP leaders made little effort to collect or publicize membership data, perhaps fearing that the modest number of formal members would undermine their claims to represent the business class as a whole. This reluctance deepened after the formation of several pro-Sandinista producer associations, like the National Union of Agricultural Producers and Ranchers (Unión Nacional de Agricultores y Ganaderos — UNAG) and CONAPRO-Héroes y Mártires, which vied for the role of business representative and cut into COSEP's representational monopoly. COSEP and INDE statistics from 1984-1985, however, suggest that COSEP's membership hovered around 9,304, up from 3,784 in 1974. (See Appendix) The largest of these chambers was UPANIC, a particularly vituperative component of the organization, which claimed 6,397 members in 1985.

21. The Pellas family built an economic empire around the Ingenio San Antonio (ISA), Central America's largest sugar mill, expanding into rum production, cattle ranching, and various distributorships. In the 1950s, it founded the Banco de América and headed one of

Nicaragua's three major economic groups. See Strachen (1976); Gould (1990); Nicaragua Sugar Estates, Ltd. (1953); and Everingham (1996).

22. During the Sandinista period, the Pellas family was given a privileged position until 1988, when, following years of decapitalization and various political trespasses (*contra* funding was reportedly run through the Pellas family's offshore bank in Miami), the Ingenio San Antonio and its surrounding properties were expropriated. Even then, the family's lucrative rum monopoly and distributorships were unscathed, and a generous compensation agreement was negotiated. The government agreed to pay $637,000 for the land surrounding the mill and $12 million for the ISA itself, making payments of $1 million a year for 12 years. However, the FSLN government failed to meet the payment schedule, and the property was returned to the Pellas family by the Chamorro government (Author's interview, Nicaraguan Sugar Estates, Ltd., September 20, 1990).

23. Author's interview, Matagalpan Coffee Growers Association, Matagalpa, August 16, 1986; (Christian 1986, 202).

24. Author's interviews, Chinandega, May 28, 1990, and July 4, 1990.

25. COSEP presidents included Enrique Dreyfus of Casa Dreyfus, one of Nicaragua's larger retail outlets; Enrique Bolaños, part owner and manager of SIAMSA, one of Nicaragua's largest agro-industrial complexes; and Ramiro Gurdián, owner of one of Nicaragua's largest banana plantations and former administrator for Standard Fruit.

26. INIESEP published economic analyses in its periodic *Cuadernos Empresariales*. Basic economic data were difficult to obtain and, during the period of the *contra* war, often regarded as confidential. INIESEP had no capacity for independent data generation; its analyses depended on information obtained by paying civil servants, often in sensitive ministries, for copies of internal government reports. In 1988, the director of INIESEP, Mario Alegría, was convicted of engaging in this practice and sharing this information with U.S. Embassy personnel. His subsequent imprisonment undercut COSEP's research and publication efforts.

27. See CARANA Corporation (1991, 19); and two financial reports on COSEP by Paul Stone (1994a, 1994b).

28. Chamorro's son-in-law and campaign director, Antonio Lacayo, raised some eyebrows because of his prominent involvement in CORDENIC, a business-academic network that had advocated dialogue with the FSLN, but he too had durable links with COSEP. As general manager of GRACSA in the 1980s, he had been an active member of COSEP's industrial affiliate, CADIN.

29. The first round, in October 1990, allowed the government to introduce a series of neoliberal reforms, including cutbacks in government employment, reduction of subsidies, and the termination of the government monopoly control over trade and finances. The second round, running from May to August 1991, produced an agreement allowing workers in state enterprises to buy 25 percent of the stock in state industries undergoing privatization.

30. Their withdrawal was due to Chamorro's decision to allow Sandinista army chief Humberto Ortega, brother of outgoing President Daniel Ortega, to remain in his post as head of the army.

31. COSEP had only three presidents between 1982 and 1995 — Enrique Bolaños, Gilberto Cuadra, and Ramiro Gurdián.

32. UPANIC's hostility led it to publish a communiqué endorsing the June 1992 suspension of U.S. aid to Nicaragua that had been orchestrated by U.S. Senator Jesse Helms because of his displeasure about the pace of reform under the Chamorro government. (See UPANIC's "Comunicado" of June 11, 1992, published in *La Prensa*, June 21, 1992.) UPANIC took this step even though its own members were to be among primary beneficiaries of the funds, which included $50 million in medium-term and long-term credit for private producers in agriculture and industry. COSEP, on the other hand, did not publicly endorse the suspension of the aid. It did, however, publicly and privately denounce the government following a series of land invasions and transportation stoppages in April 1992. See COSEP's "Comunicado de prensa" of April 30, 1992, and its unpublished but distributed "Posición de COSEP ante Gobierno," May 4, 1992.

33. Author's interviews, APENN former president, Managua, June 24, 1995; APENN technical staff, June 26, 1995, and June 24, 1992.

34. Author's interview, former Asociación de Bancos Privados president, June 27, 1995. Legal status was obtained in 1994.

35. Affiliates were the Banco de Crédito Centroamericano, Banco de la Producción, Banco Mercantil, Banco de América Central, Banco de Finanzas, Banexpo, Interbank, Banco del Campo, Banco Caley Dagnall, Interfin, Banco del Café, and Delta Financiera.

36. Author's interview, AMCHAM vice president, June 28, 1995; author's interview, CADIN, June 30, 1995.

37. Note that the USAID-financed CEI included representatives from four private-sector associations (COSEP, APENN, AMCHAM, and ASOBANP), three of which were new and not affiliated with COSEP.

38. Some of these organizations, like APENN, did consider COSEP membership, but APENN leaders wanted to enter as a seventh chamber, equal in stature to any of the others. Because UPANIC insisted that APENN enter COSEP as an UPANIC affiliate with no special claim to its own seats on the Board of Directors, APENN opted for independence (author's interview, APENN, Managua, June 24, 1995).

39. USAID-Nicaragua, unpublished data, June 1995.

40. Under a USAID contract, the Jinotega Coffee Growers Association, a UPANIC affiliate, helped a network of small coffee producers pull together the documentation it needed to apply for bank credit in 1995. (Author's interviews as member of Latin American Working Group delegation with USAID-Nicaragua Mission Director George Carner, March 13, 1995; and observation of a meeting of Jinotega association President Eduardo Rizo and a group of small coffee producers, March 14, 1995. See also USAID/Nicaragua (1995).

41. Paul Stone's (1994a) report on COSEP's financial accounts indicates that, based on income for the last five months of 1993, SIF/CIPE funds accounted for 68 percent of COSEP's resources; voluntary firm donations represented 15 percent; rental income for space in COSEP's new headquarters amounted to 14 percent; and chamber dues payments represented only 2 percent.

42. Nineteen firms made donations to COSEP in 1993. The larger contributors included Nabisco Cristal, Embotelladora Milca, Didatsa Mil, GRACSA, and Compañía Licorera de Nicaragua (Stone 1994a).

References

Bartell, Ernest, and Leigh A. Payne, eds. 1995. *Business and Democracy in Latin America.* Pittsburgh: University of Pittsburgh Press.

Bolaños, Enrique. 1987. "Discurso pronunciado por el presidente del COSEP en ocasión del 'Día del Sector Privado.'" Managua: Teatro Cabrera. September 2. Unpublished document.

Booth, John A. 1985. *The End and the Beginning: The Nicaraguan Revolution.* 2nd ed. Boulder, Colo.: Westview Press.

Bulmer-Thomas, Victor. 1987. *The Political Economy of Central America since 1920.* Cambridge: Cambridge University Press.

CADIN (Cámara de Industrias de Nicaragua). 1993. "Estrategia para la reactivación productiva." Unpublished document.

CADIN. 1975. "Evolución histórica, organización y actividades de la Cámara de Industrias de Nicaragua." Paper presented at the round table on the Role of Employer Associations in Latin America. Río de Janeiro, Brazil, July 14-22.

Campero, Guillermo. 1984. *Los gremios empresariales en el período 1970-1983: comportamiento sociopolítico y orientaciones ideológicas.* Santiago: Instituto Latinoamericano de Estudios Transnacionales.

CARANA Corporation. 1991. "Nicaragua's Political Economy: The Role of the Private Sector." Report prepared for USAID/Nicaragua (July).

CARANA Corporation. 1994. "Technical Assistance to COSEP: Final Summary Report." Report prepared for USAID/Nicaragua (March).

Carter Center. 1997. *The Observation of the 1996 Nicaraguan Elections.* Atlanta: Latin American and Caribbean Program, Carter Center.

CEPAL (Comisión Económica para América Latina y el Caribe). 1982. *Notas para el estudio económico de América Latina 1981.* Mexico City: CEPAL.

CEPAL. 1990. *Notas para el estudio económico de América Latina y el Caribe 1989: Nicaragua.* Mexico City: CEPAL.

CEPAL. 1995. *Nicaragua: evolución económica durante 1994.* Mexico City: CEPAL.

CIERA (Centro de Investigaciones y Estudios de la Reforma Agraria). 1981. "Las clases sociales en el agro." Managua: CIERA. Unpublished manuscript.

CIERA. 1989. *La reforma agraria en Nicaragua 1979-1989.* Vols. 1-9. Managua: CIERA.

Christian, Shirley. 1986. *Nicaragua: Revolution in the Family.* New York: Vintage.

Colburn, Forrest D. 1986. *Post-Revolutionary Nicaragua: State, Class, and the Dilemmas of Agrarian Policy.* Berkeley, Calif.: University of California Press.

Coleman, William, and Wyn Grant. 1988. "The Organizational Cohesion and Political Access of Business: A Study of Comprehensive Associations." *European Journal of Political Research* 16: 467-487.

Collier, David, and Deborah L. Norden. 1992. "Strategic Choice Models of Political Change in Latin America." *Comparative Politics* 24:2 (January): 229-243.

COSEP (Consejo Superior de la Empresa Privada). 1979a. "Declaración del Consejo Superior de la Empresa Privada (COSEP)." June 6.

COSEP. 1979b. "Declaración del Consejo Superior de la Empresa Privada (COSEP)." June 27.

COSEP. 1981. Letter to Comandante Daniel Ortega Saavedra. October 19.

COSEP. 1987. Press release. April 29.

COSEP. 1990. "Pronunciamiento." October 24.

COSEP. 1991a. "Comunicado." January 23.

COSEP. 1991b. "Comunicado." March 5.

COSEP. 1992. "Comunicado de prensa." April 30.

COSEP. 1992. "Posición de COSEP ante gobierno." May 4.

COSEP. 1996. "Pronunciamiento del COSEP con respecto al 'Proyecto de Ley para el Fomento de la Estabilidad, las Inversiones y el Empleo.'" June 12.

COSEP. *Memorandum de la presidencia.* Various issues.

COSEP/INCAE/Ministerio de Economía y Desarrollo (MEDE). 1992. "Encuesta nacional a empresarios privados: algunos resultados preliminares." Unpublished document, May-June.

COSIP (Consejo Superior de la Iniciativa Privada). 1974. "Conclusiones sobre el tema: estrategia de desarrollo socio-económico para la década de los 70." Managua: Unpublished manuscript.

Cruz, Ernesto. 1974. "Estrategia de desarrollo para los años 70." Paper presented at the First Convention of COSIP, Managua, Nicaragua, March 1.

Cruz, Ernesto, and Kenneth L. Hoadley. 1975. *Necesidad de una política oficial sobre comercialización del algodón: el caso de Nicaragua.* Managua: INCAE.

Durand, Francisco. 1991. "Business Peak Associations in Latin America: The Case of Peru." Paper presented at the Conference on Business Elites and Democracy in Latin America, Kellogg Institute for International Studies, University of Notre Dame, Notre Dame, Indiana, May 3-5.

Durand, Francisco. 1994. *Business and Politics in Peru: The State and the National Bourgeoisie.* Boulder, Colo.: Westview.

Edmisten, Patricia Taylor. 1990. *Nicaragua Divided: La Prensa and the Chamorro Legacy.* Pensacola, Fla.: University of West Florida Press.

Evans, Trevor. 1987. "El algodón: un cultivo de debate." *Cuadernos de Pensamiento Propio* (April).

Evans, Trevor. 1995. "Ajuste estructural y sector público en Nicaragua." In *La transformación neoliberal del sector público*, ed. Trevor Evans. Managua: Latino Editores.

Everingham, Mark. 1996. *Revolution and the Multiclass Coalition in Nicaragua.* Pittsburgh: University of Pittsburgh Press.

Frente Amplio Opositor (FAO). 1978. "Programa Democrático del Gobierno Nacional." In *Nicaragua: reforma o revolución*, Vol. II. Instituto Histórico Centroamericano. n.p., December.

Frente Sandinista de Liberación Nacional (FSLN). 1990. "Análisis de la coyuntura y tareas de la revolución popular sandinista." In *Sandinistas: Key Documents/Documentos claves*, eds. Dennis Gilbert and David Block. Ithaca, N.Y.: Latin American Studies Program, Cornell University.

Fundación Internacional para el Desafío Económico Global (FIDEG). *El Observador Económico.* Various issues.

Gilbert, Dennis. 1985. "The Bourgeoisie." In *Nicaragua: The First Five Years*, ed. Thomas W. Walker. New York: Praeger.

Gilbert, Dennis. 1988. *Sandinistas: The Party and the Revolution*. London: Basil Blackwell.

Gould, Jeffrey L. 1990. *To Lead as Equals: Rural Protest and Political Consciousness in Chinandega, Nicaragua, 1912-1979*. Chapel Hill. N.C.: University of North Carolina Press.

Government of Nicaragua. 1992. "Nicaragua: Medium-Term Development Strategy 1992-1996." Document presented at the Consultative Group Meeting, Washington, D.C., March 26.

Huber, Evelyne, and John D. Stephens. Forthcoming. "The Bourgeoisie and Democracy: Historical and Contemporary Perspectives from Europe and Latin America." In *Contending Cultures of Human Rights and Democracy*, eds. Jeffrey Winters, Meredith Woo-Cummings, and Bruce Cummings.

INDE (Instituto Nicaragüense de Desarrollo). 1965. *Informe General de Actividades, Informe Económico*. Managua: INDE, Feb.

INDE. 1966. *Informe General de Actividades, Informe Financiero, Anexos 1965-66*. Managua: INDE.

INDE. 1975. "Resoluciones de la primera convención nacional del sector privado." In *Informe Anual de INDE y Sus Programas FUNDE y EDUCREDITO 1974*. Managua: INDE.

INDE. 1977. *Informe Anual de INDE y Sus Programas FUNDE y EDUCREDITO 1976*. Managua: INDE.

INDE. 1978. *Informe Anual 1977*. Managua: INDE.

INDE. 1979. *El sector privado en la insurrección 1979*. Managua: COSEP.

INDE. 1980. *Informe Anual 1979*. Managua: INDE.

INDE. 1985. *Informe Anual 1984*. Managua: INDE.

Instituto Histórico Centroamericano (IHCA). 1981. "The Case Regarding COSEP and CAUS Members." *Envío* no. 6 (November 15).

Instituto de Investigaciones Económicas y Sociales de la Empresa Privada (INIESEP). *Cuadernos Empresariales*. Various issues.

LASA (Latin American Studies Association). 1990. *Electoral Democracy Under International Pressure*. Report of the LASA Commission to Observe the 1990 Nicaraguan Election. Pittsburgh: LASA.

LASA. 1984. *The Electoral Process in Nicaragua: Domestic and International Influences*. Report of the LASA Delegation to Observe the Nicaraguan General Elections of November 4. Austin, Texas: LASA.

Luciak, Ilja A. 1995. *The Sandinista Legacy: Lessons from a Political Economy in Transition*. Gainesville, Fla.: University of Florida Press.

Martínez Cuenca, Alejandro. 1990. *Nicaragua: una década de retos*. Managua: Editorial Nueva Nicaragua.

Martínez Cuenca, Alejandro. 1994. "El comportamiento inversionista en Nicaragua." *Materiales de Estudio y Trabajo*, no. 13, Fundación Friedrich Ebert.

Ministerio de Desarrollo Agropecuario y Reforma Agraria (MIDINRA). 1989. "Marco estratégico del desarrollo agropecuario." In *La reforma agraria en Nicaragua 1979-1989*, vol. I. CIERA. Managua: Centro de Investigaciones y Estudios de la Reforma Agraria (CIERA).

Nicaragua Sugar Estates, Limited. 1953. *El Ingenio San Antonio 1890-1953.* Granada, Nicaragua: n.p.

O'Donnell, Guillermo, and Philippe Schmitter. 1986. *Transitions from Authoritarian Rule: Tentative Conclusions about Uncertain Democracies.* Baltimore: Johns Hopkins University Press.

Paige, Jeffrey M. 1989. "Revolution and the Agrarian Bourgeoisie in Nicaragua." In *Revolution in the World System,* ed. Terry Boswell. New York: Greenwood Press.

Payne, Leigh A. 1994. *Brazilian Industrialists and Democratic Change.* Baltimore: Johns Hopkins University Press.

La Prensa. 1995. "G. Cuadra cree que 1995 podría ser un mejor año," January 3.

Przeworski, Adam, and Michael Wallerstein. 1988. "Structural Dependence of the State on Capital." *American Political Science Review* 82:1 (March): 11-29.

Ramírez Arango, Julio Sergio. 1985. *The Political Role of the Private Sector Associations of Central America: The Cases of El Salvador, Nicaragua and Costa Rica.* Ph.D. Dissertation, Harvard University.

Ramírez Mercado, Sergio. 1982. "Los sobrevivientes del naufragio." In *Estado y clases sociales en Nicaragua,* Asociación Nicaragüense de Científicos Sociales. Managua: Centro de Investigaciones y Estudios de la Reforma Agraria.

República de Nicaragua. 1990. *Acuerdos de la concertación económica y social y la política exterior del Gobierno de Nicaragua.* Managua: Republic of Nicaragua.

Rosenthal, Gert. 1982. "Principales rasgos de la evolución de las economías centroamericanas desde la posguerra." In *Centroamérica: crisis y política internacional,* ed. Centro de Capacitación para el Desarrollo (CECADE) and Centro de Investigación y Docencia Económicas (CIDE). Mexico City: Siglo Veintiuno.

Rueschemeyer, Dietrich, Evelyne Huber Stephens, and John D. Stephens. 1992. *Capitalist Development and Democracy.* Chicago: University of Chicago Press.

Sholk, Richard. 1984. "The National Bourgeoisie in Post-Revolutionary Nicaragua." *Comparative Politics* 16: 3 (April): 253-276.

Spalding, Rose J. 1994. *Capitalists and Revolution in Nicaragua: Opposition and Accommodation, 1979-1993.* Chapel Hill, N.C.: University of North Carolina Press.

Spalding, Rose J. 1997. "The Economic Elite." In *Nicaragua without Illusions: Regime Transition and Structural Adjustment in the 1990s,* ed. Thomas W. Walker. Wilmington, Del.: Scholarly Resources Books.

Stone, Paul. 1994a. "Revisión financiera de COSEP." Unpublished consultant's report, February 24.

Stone, Paul. 1994b. "TVCOSEP." Unpublished consultant's report, February 23.

Strachen, Harry W. 1976. *Family and Other Business Groups in Economic Development: The Case of Nicaragua.* New York: Praeger.

Unión Nacional Opositora (UNO). 1989. "Programa de gobierno de la Unión Nacional Opositora." Managua: UNO. Unpublished manuscript, August 24.

UPANIC (Unión de Productores Agropecuarios de Nicaragua). 1979. Minutes of founding meeting. March 22.

UPANIC. 1985. "Acuerdo." July 2.

UPANIC. 1992. "Comunicado." June 11. (Published in *La Prensa* June 21, 1992.)

USAID (U.S. Agency for International Development)/Nicaragua. 1994. "Action Plan FY95-FY96." Unpublished report (March).

USAID/Nicaragua. 1995. "Nicaragua 2000: A Vision for the Year 2000." Unpublished report (March).

U.S. Department of State. 1988. *Nicaraguan Biographies: A Resource Book.* Special Report No. 74. Revised Edition. Washington, D.C.: Bureau of Public Affairs, Department of State.

Vilas, Carlos M. 1992. "Family Affairs: Class, Lineage and Politics in Contemporary Nicaragua." *Journal of Latin American Studies* 24: 2 (May): 309-341.

Vuskovic C., Pedro. 1995. "Las pequeñas empresas y las exportaciones no tradicionales." Paper presented at the seminar "Alternativas para la participación de las pequeñas empresas en las exportaciones no tradicionales." Managua, Hotel Mansión Teodolinda, June 22.

Walker, Thomas W., ed. 1985. *Nicaragua: The First Five Years.* New York: Praeger.

Walter, Knut. 1993. *The Regime of Anastasio Somoza, 1936-1956.* Chapel Hill, N.C.: University of North Carolina.

Weeks, John. 1985. *The Economies of Central America.* New York: Holmes & Meier.

Wheelock Román, Jaime. 1980. *Nicaragua: imperialismo y dictadura.* Havana: Editorial de Ciencias Sociales.

Wheelock Román, Jaime. 1985. *Entre la crisis y la agresión: la reforma agraria sandinista.* Managua: Editorial Nueva Nicaragua.

Wickham-Crowley, Timothy P. 1992. *Guerrillas and Revolution in Latin America.* Princeton, N.J.: Princeton University Press.

World Bank. 1996. *World Development Report.* Oxford: Oxford University Press.

Appendix
COSEP Affiliates and Membership

A. TIME OF FORMATION: 1974

Name of Association	Membership
1. Asociación de Criadores de Ganado Brahman de Nicaragua	140
2. Asociación de Distribuidores de Vehículos Automotores	18
3. Asociación de Ganaderos de Nicaragua	500
4. Asociación de Instituciones Bancarias de Nicaragua	7
5. Asociación de Productores de Arroz de Nicaragua	45
6. Cámara de Comercio	330
7. Cámara de Industrias de Nicaragua (CADIN)	338
8. Cámara Nicaragüense de la Construcción	76
9. Cámara Nicaragüense de la Industria Pesquera	15
10. Instituto Nicaragüense de Desarrollo	89
11. Sociedad Cooperativa Anónima de Algodoneros	226
12. Sociedad Cooperativa Anónima de Cafetero	2,000
Total Membership	3,784

Source: INDE (1975) and CADIN (1975)

B. DURING SANDINISTA ERA: 1985

Name of Association	
1. UPANIC*	6,397
FAGANIC (cattle)	3,578
FONDILAC (dairy)	1,236
UNCAFENIC (coffee)	820
CAAN (cotton)	372
ASCANIC (sugarcane)	180
ANPROSOR (sorghum)	136
ANAR (rice)	75
2. Confederación de Cámaras de Comercio de Nicaragua	1,986
3. INDE**	604
4. CADIN	263
5. Cámara de Construcción	54
Total Membership	9,304

*Does not include ANPROBA (bananas). The FSLN government took over banana production in 1980 and ANPROBA ceased to function.
**Based on membership data for five of INDE's most active regional affiliates.
Source: Unpublished COSEP data, 1985; INDE (1985).

CHAPTER SEVEN

Mexico: From the Political Call for Collective Action to a Proposal for Free Market Economic Reform

RICARDO TIRADO

INTRODUCTION

This chapter analyzes the relationship of organized business to the state in Mexico, and it examines the factors responsible for the emergence and trajectory of Mexico's encompassing business peak association, the Business Coordinating Council (Consejo Coordinador Empresarial — CCE). It also evaluates the CCE's political impact, including the Council's significance for the democratic vocation of the Mexican private sector. To provide a necessary backdrop to more current events, the chapter begins with an exposition of the rules that governed the relationship between business and the state from the end of the Mexican Revolution of 1910 to the end of the 1960s. The chapter then explores the factors that led to the creation of the CCE and describes the elements that shaped the identity and structure of the CCE. The Council's corporatist relationship with the state; its wide, heterogeneous, and asymmetric social base; and its mainly sectoral approach to affiliation all affected its representativeness. Having laid this foundation, the chapter analyzes the main factors that shaped the CCE's policies, strategies, and actions from 1975 through 1997. The conclusion draws out the comparative implications of the Mexican case by examining the impact of three conjunctures on the style of business's collective action, its relation to the state, and democracy.

BUSINESS-GOVERNMENT RELATIONS, 1910-1970

As a result of Mexico's development path, businesspeople did not become socially visible until the turn of the century. The 1910-1917 revolution and the 1934-1940 reformist movement under President Lázaro Cárdenas were major threats that spurred businesspeople to form associations through which to channel their collective action. Also, the authoritarian political system that emerged from these processes promoted corporatist structures and thus shaped business associations' organizational forms. Corporatist arrangements not only facilitated policy agreements between government and business but also allowed the state to exercise a measure of control over business associations. The main corporatist features were mandatory affiliation of business to trade chambers and the aggregation of those chambers into a confederation of chambers of commerce and confederation of chambers of industry (Shafer 1973; Tirado 1992).[1] In this period, the case of the Employers Confederation of the Mexican Republic (Confederación Patronal de la República Mexicana — Coparmex), founded in 1929, was an exception because it was a free affiliation association.

Between 1940 and 1970, the so-called "Mexican Miracle" stimulated the development of important industrial sectors. Business flourished, and a lot of mainly sectoral organizations developed and extended over the country. By the same token, assertive state intervention in the economy — which took place in the midst of uncertainty, discretionality, and corruption — was instrumental in creating a complex web of patronage and business connections among entrepreneurs, public servants, and politicians.

Although it was acknowledged that business actors had a role to play in the development of the country, open participation in politics was not considered legitimate for them. The revolution had placed entrepreneurs somewhat vaguely but effectively in the reactionary camp together with the Catholic Church, foreigners, and the National Action Party (Partido Acción Nacional — PAN). Although it had mandated the creation of business associations, the official party, the Institutional Revolutionary Party (Partido Revolucionario Institucional — PRI), refused to add a "business sector" to the party comparable to those it had created for the peasant, labor, and "popular" (middle class) sectors. Moreover, business chambers were excluded by statute from all political activity.

Despite the formal exclusion of business chambers from political activities, such as election campaigning and joining political parties, and despite the political controls of state corporatism, business associations, nevertheless, achieved considerable political influence in a broader sense. They ably defended their political and economic interests through other channels. The government always consulted with businesspeople before making important public policy decisions that affected their interests. In some cases, this practice became an implicit veto. A small circle of powerful financial groups became important in this respect. In concert with key government financial agencies that shared their orthodox view of the country's problems, these financiers helped shape most of the Mexican state's financial policy (Hamilton 1982; Maxfield 1990; Luna 1992a).

In cases where the business community's more general interests were at stake, sectoral peak associations tended to take the lead, working together efficiently when necessary.[2] The efficacy of the combined action of business associations occasionally was demonstrated when they toned down different government-sponsored policies. Those were, for example, the cases of an expropriation law of 1936 (Juárez 1984); a profit-sharing plan for workers of private companies in the early 1960s (Purcell 1975); and a fiscal reform in the early 1970s (Purcell and Purcell 1975; Maxfield 1990, 88-93). These successful actions contrast with those that failed on several other occasions, as when they uselessly opposed in 1950 the "Ley de atribuciones del Ejecutivo en materia económica," sponsored by President Miguel Alemán (Torres 1984, 47-132; Medin 1990, 117-118).

Another important feature of business-government relations was the formation of enduring private-sector political factions with origins dating back to the 1940s and earlier. Three political-ideological tendencies, with their attendant business organizations and leaders, emerged. These may be labeled "nationalist," "moderate," and "radical," according to the organizations' and leaders' positions vis-à-vis the government and its policies. Nationalists almost always supported the postulates of the revolution and the Mexican state that emerged from it — such as state intervention in the economy, public enterprise, land reform, political trade unionism, and a nationalist revolutionary ideology. They were highly influential from the 1940s through 1960s, particularly through the National Chamber of Manufacturing Industries (Cámara Nacional de la Industria de Transformación — Canacintra). Acting through the Confederation of Chambers of Industry (Confederación de Cámaras Industriales — Concamin) and the Mexican Bankers' Association (Asociación de Banqueros de México — ABM), the moderates generally accepted the government's policies, although not without criticism and frequent attempts to negotiate changes, which they won.[3] The radicals were always very conservative in matters like family, religion, and education; they rejected revolutionary postulates and often confronted the government. The radical faction's principal organization was the Coparmex. Antecedents of Coparmex can be found in the activities of the so-called "Grupo Monterrey," a small but strong group of Monterrey businessmen who had been politically active since the Porfiriato (1876-1910). Since the mid-1910s, when the revolutionary troops took over their companies and some of these businessmen fled to the United States for a while, and for decades after that, the Groupo Monterrey and the Coparmex, which they funded, played a significant radical role in business politics (Cerutti 1983 and 1992; Nuncio 1982; Saragoza 1988; Pozas 1993).[4] Despite their differences, these historical factions had a great deal in common: all three accepted the Mexican political regime's authoritarianism and its import-substituting economic development model.

ORIGIN OF THE CCE

Mexico faced serious problems at the beginning of President Luis Echeverría's term in 1970. One of them was the government's dwindling legitimacy, a product of the violent repression of the 1968 student movement. Another difficulty was that the import-substituting development model had begun to prove ineffective. The public sector seemed increasingly incapable of promoting economic growth, and the fruits of past growth were exceedingly poorly distributed, with vast sectors of the population remaining excluded from the benefits of economic development.

To counter these problems, Echeverría launched his "shared development" program. One of its goals was to restore the legitimacy of the government through "dialogue" and a "democratic opening." Another was to reinforce import-substituting industrialization — and in the process to strengthen the role of state-owned companies and revise the regulations governing the operation of foreign companies so that the country as a whole could increase its share in their profits. An additional goal was to promote increased wages and, consequently, expand domestic markets.

During the implementation of "shared development," the president and top-ranking government officials adopted rhetoric highly critical of private enterprise in general and foreign companies in particular. The government also lifted some restrictions imposed on political dissent, among them, bans on mass demonstrations by workers and peasants. It increased public spending, including investment in state-owned companies, and modified foreign investment rules. The government also authorized wage increases to compensate workers for inflation's effects on their purchasing power and boosted land distribution among peasants. These domestic policies were accompanied by a Third World-oriented foreign policy that advocated a "new economic international order" and established close ties with Chile's socialist government under President Salvador Allende.

Although these policies did not, in fact, constitute a drastic break with the past, businessmen overreacted, as if they generally faced a very real threat to their interests. They were uneasy in part because the government had taken to announcing impending policy measures without the customary prior consultation with the business sector. A case in point was fiscal reform. An escalation in the war of mutually disparaging remarks between businesspeople and public officials was a further contributing factor in the mounting tension between the private sector and the Echeverría administration.

Echeverría's six-year term ended in conflict, plagued by a drastic currency devaluation and insistent rumors of an impending coup d'état. Businesspeople complained vociferously about the loss of confidence provoked by "socialist bureaucrats" against whom they would be forced to take direct political action in order to save the day.[5] True to their word, they created an encompassing peak association through an alliance between their radical and moderate factions. Founded on May 7, 1975, the CCE aggregated virtually the entire Mexican business sector.

There are some similarities between the Mexican process and developments in other Latin American countries. In the context of the international and domestic economic crises of the 1970s and 1980s, business sectors in many countries were roused from their traditional apathy in the midst of popular mobilization and politicization. These processes mostly resulted from defensive actions undertaken to counteract the interventionist policies of governments such as Unidad Popular in Chile, the Christian Democrats in El Salvador and Guatemala, Velasquismo and Aprismo in Peru, and Sandinismo in Nicaragua.[6] Although the causes of economic deterioration among these nations differed, their governments all sought to renew growth through greater state involvement in the economy and to redistribute wealth toward the peasant, labor, and popular sectors. In some cases, these policies served to deepen economic destabilization. The business community developed an acute sense of mistrust and threat as well as a conviction that it was insufficiently represented politically (O'Donnell 1982). Virtually all the reformist experiences brought forth right-wing movements that in one way or another won.

These situations of political adversity and struggle generally strengthened organized business, leading at times to the founding of new associations. In some cases, these new organizations had hidden agendas, to form an encompassing peak organization capable of representing all the country's business sectors. As these new associations developed, they stimulated the active participation of business — both individually and collectively — in party politics.[7]

IDENTITY AND STRUCTURE OF THE CCE

The CCE was founded as an encompassing peak association, originally comprising six associations: the Confederation of National Chambers of Commerce (Confederación Nacional de Cámaras Nacionales de Comercio — Concanaco, founded in 1917), Concamin (founded in 1918), Coparmex (1929), ABM (1928), the Mexican Insurance Institutions' Association (Asociación Mexicana de Instituciones de Seguros — AMIS, 1946), and the Mexican Businessmen's Council (Consejo Mexicano de Hombres de Negocios — CMHN, 1962). Since the addition of the Mexican Securities Industry Association (Asociación Mexicana de Intermediarios Bursátiles — AMIB, founded in 1980) and the National Agricultural Council (Consejo Nacional Agropecuario — CNA, founded in 1984), the CCE has represented eight major business associations (See Table 1).[8]

Identity

Formed in the midst of acute political conflict, the CCE permanently unified the country's private sector under a single representative organization — an unprecedented event in Mexico. In part, the CCE accomplished this goal by successfully claiming to speak on behalf of all of Mexico's entrepreneurs. In drafting its solemn *Declaration of Principles* (CCE 1975a) and two other documents (CCE 1975b and CCE 1975c), CEE leaders exhorted businesspeople to recognize the CCE as *the* representative organization for all "entrepreneurs." They made a persuasive case for a more inclusive definition of the term "businessman." Under its new connotation, the term applied to all categories that in the past had labeled and segmented the private sector into different groups, such as "*patrón*" (employer), "industrialist," "merchant," "farmer," and others. The CCE also attracted followers by imbuing the term with a hitherto missing prestige and mystique in Mexico. Businessmen were dynamic individuals who coordinated the forces of capital and labor to produce goods and services; they were innovators, leaders, risk-takers, and organizers (CCE 1975a).

In addition to producing ideology, the CCE declared itself the political leader of business. Despite initial efforts by some founders to limit the CCE's scope of action, the Council claimed to speak for the entire private sector on such wide-ranging issues as the definition of the relationship among business, the state, and other social groups.[9] In this respect, the *Declaration of Principles* made the CCE appear not so much an innovator with an original project, as a defender of the general postulates that had hitherto regulated the relations between government and business. Although its guiding principles emphasized the natural right to private property, free enterprise, and the market, the document also endorsed the mixed economy, the state's right to intervention in certain circumstances, and development planning.

Table 1.
Structure of the Entrepreneurial Coordinating Council (CCE), as of 1993

Member organizations	CONCANACO	CONCAMIN	COPARMEX	ABM	AMIS	CMHN	CNA	AMIB
Base organizations	281 chambers	75 chambers 42 associations	57 centers				27 organizations	26
Constituency	899,250	125,500	1,700	18	59	37	250,000	
Percent*	70.442%	9.831%	0.133%	0.001%	0.005%	0.003%	19.583%	0.002%
Sector	Commerce	Industry	Employers	Finance	Insurance	Several	Agriculture	Finance

* Percentages indicate each organization's share of the membership in the CCE, in relation to the total 1,276,590 indirect affiliates.
ABM: Mexican Bankers' Association (Asociación de Banqueros de México)
AMIB: Mexican Securities Industry Association (Asociación Mexicana de Intermediarios Bursátiles)
AMIS: Mexican Insurance Institutions' Association (Asociación Mexicana de Instituciones de Seguros)
CCE: Business Coordinating Council (Consejo Coordinador Empresarial)
CMHN: Mexican Businessmen's Council (Consejo Mexicano de Hombres de Negocios)
CNA: National Agricultural Council (Consejo Nacional Agropecuario)
Concamin: Confederation of Chambers of Industry (Confederación de Cámaras Industriales)
Concanaco: National Confederation of Chambers of Commerce (Confederación Nacional de Cámaras de Comercio)
Coparmex: Employers Confederation of the Mexican Republic (Confederación Patronal de la República Mexicana)
Sources: Tirado and Luna 1995; Puga 1994b, 30 (Concamin); Rius 1994 (Concanaco); Coparmex 1992, 153-175 (Coparmex); Puga 1994b, 58 (CNA); Solórzano 1993 (AMIB); Fernández-Vega 1991 (CMHN); Interviews (ABM, AMIS).

The government's top officials, the leadership of the PRI, the major trade unions, and the peasant organizations all denounced the illegitimacy of the CCE's political stance and harshly criticized the association's founding principles. However, they never questioned the CCE's self-appointed role as the representative of business interests. The only opposition to the CCE's representational aims arose from within the business sector itself. The Canacintra — an industrial association with members including more than half of the country's industrialists, which had become a member of the moderate Concamin yet was still known as the champion of protectionism and the strongest bastion of the nationalist faction — rejected the CCE. The Canacintra argued that the CCE's platform was sharply opposed to its own nationalist stance and preference for state intervention in the economy.[10] This objection, however, was short-lived; in less than a year the Canacintra elected a new president who supported the CCE. This change sounded the death knell for the historical nationalist faction of the business sector, which then joined the moderates.

Structure[11]

The CCE's organizational structure has three defining features: it is basically sectoral; it has a broad, heterogeneous and asymmetrical base; and it is corporatist.

Sectoral logic. The fact that the CCE is organized essentially along sectoral lines partially explains its rapid and successful creation. Within the CCE, each economic sector is represented by a single peak association on the basis of a one-organization, one-vote rule. Thus, the entire industrial sector is represented by Concamin alone; the commercial and service sector, by Concanaco; the agricultural sector, by CNA; the insurance sector, by AMIS; the stock exchange sector, by AMIB; and the banking sector, by ABM. This organizational principle provides the mechanism by which the CCE, at least in principle, coordinates the actions of the entire private sector and can claim to speak on behalf of all its members.

Because the CCE mainly follows a sectoral logic of organization, other associative principles are relatively unimportant in the organization of the CCE. For example, company size is of little relevance, because medium- and small-scale entrepreneurs' associations are almost all excluded (Luna 1995). This holds true even for industry, although with the partial exception of the Canacintra (within the Concamin). Medium- and small-scale industrialists are indirectly and partially represented in the Canacintra only because of its catch-all nature. The Canacintra is chartered to represent industrialists in sub-sectors that for one reason or another do not have their own special business chambers. Moreover, among its members are very large businesses, including chemical and automotive companies that always have been denied official authorization to organize their own trade chambers.

The predominance of the sectoral logic of organization has had an unfortunate side effect. It has sharply reduced representation of small-scale business associations in the CCE. Of course, they are not completely excluded because they belong to the production chains of the sectoral associations, and, upon occasion, the organizations of small business play minor roles in business politics. Nevertheless, the prevalence of the sectoral logic is tantamount to the absence of real representation for the interests of these groups, which is not the case in many others.[12]

Less conspicuously, the CCE also downplays place or region as an organizing principle. Only three of its eight associations — CNA, Concanaco, and Coparmex — affiliate their members according to geographical location. The exclusion of medium and small entrepreneurs' associations and of regional organizations undercuts the CCE's claims to universal representation.[13]

Despite the predominance of sectoral logic in the CCE's organization, two key founding members, CMHN and Coparmex, were organized according to different criteria. The differences in their organizational logic and political posture discussed below are potential sources of tension among dominant business factions over control of the CCE, an organization that claims to speak for the entire private sector.

Since its founding in 1962, the CMHN has been an important member of the moderate faction, together with the ABM and the Concamin. The CMHN's members are 37 executives who control 70 of Mexico's most powerful conglomerates.[14] Although it maintains a low profile, the CMHN is quite influential at top government levels.[15] Given the undeniable economic importance of the companies owned and controlled by its members, the CMHN tends to assume that it represents virtually the entire business sector, and the government tends to acknowledge this. The CMHN's influence, however, is not widely touted.

In contrast, Coparmex, although also organized through free association rather than through mandatory affiliation, was founded and is controlled by business groups from northern Mexico. With a history that dates back to the 1920s, Coparmex heads the radical faction of business, the one that has always opposed the postulates of the Mexican Revolution. The Coparmex boasts a membership of about 1,700 businesspeople — representing mostly medium-sized and some large businesses — who are, in turn, from associations located in the main central and northern provincial cities.[16] Its associative principle rests on the category of employer, which tends to be synonymous with that of businessperson.

Broad, heterogeneous, and asymmetric base. The CCE is a giant. The members registered in its eight peak associations total more than 1,275,000 indirect affiliates (see Table 1), making it one of the largest business encompassing peak organizations in Latin America. In Mexico, no other business organization rivals it in size. This large organization is necessarily heterogeneous. It encompasses business concerns of all sizes, regions, and sectors. Its members include not only the leaders of Mexico's most important conglomerates but also small farmers and artisans through CNA, Canacintra, and other Concamin industrial chambers, and merchants from all over the country who have very little in common with the former.

The CCE's heterogeneity generates disparities both among its member associations and among diverse business interests they represent. Asymmetries of power are clearly present. Overall, the CCE's sectoral structure with the one-organization, one-vote rule favors the larger businesses as well as groups located mainly in the metropolitan area of Mexico City. Four of the members are small free associations that form the business sector elite: ABM, AMIS, and AMIB, in addition to CMHN. In contrast, Concamin and Concanaco each have many thousands of compulsory members. The CNA, with voluntary affiliation, has 250,000 members. Yet the four elite associations, with just 140, or 0.01 percent, of the CCE's 1,276,590 affiliates, are entitled to 50 percent of the votes within the decision-making organs of the Council. Of the four, the CMHN plays the lead role in representing the interests of large conglomerates. Its influence became fairly conspicuous between 1985 and 1990, when three of the CCE's presidents came from its ranks.

One should not conclude that the CCE is directly and mechanically dominated by the great conglomerates. They do, however, wield sufficient influence to veto candidates to the CCE presidency who are openly opposed by them. This is because the conglomerates have only one foot in the organization, so to speak. They keep one foot "out" (that is, take direct action outside the CCE structure) partly because they have enough power to safeguard their interests by themselves and seldom need to resort to the other business organizations for support. The conglomerates participate in the CCE in order to monitor the behavior of the other member organizations and use the Council when it suits their purposes. This business elite usually prefers to keep a low profile within the CCE, to the point that the CCE has often been headed by businesspeople not from the CMHN who have implemented policies different from those the great conglomerates would have preferred.

Corporatist. Another basic feature of the structure of interest representation for the Mexican private sector, with the CCE as its cornerstone, is its corporatist nature. Until 1996, all commercial and industrial businesses have had a legal obligation to affiliate with and pay dues to their respective trade chambers. Every trade chamber by law must affiliate with the corresponding sectoral peak association, the confederation of chambers of commerce (Concanaco) or the Confederation of Chambers of Industry (Concamin).[17] The chambers and their respective confederations are, according to law, "public autonomous institutions," "representatives of the general interests of commerce and industry in their jurisdictions," and "consulting organs of the state"; the creation of new chambers always requires official authorization.[18]

Compulsory affiliation, by providing the chambers and the confederations with a substantial membership and guaranteed financing,[19] has been one of the central pillars of the representation structure of the Mexican private sector.[20] The CCE's founding organizations used this mechanism to provide the Council with a vast social base, which, in turn, enabled it to declare itself the representative of all business sectors.

Although business representation has a corporatist base dating back to 1917, the creation of the CCE in 1975 signified a change in the structure of representation. Unlike affiliation with the chambers of commerce and industry and their respective confederations, affiliation with the CCE was voluntary. The Council resulted from a decision made outside the government (and even against it), and its legal status is a private non-profit association. In fact, the six business organizations that created the Council, and the two that joined afterward, acted based on individual decisions by their leaders, and legally there is nothing that can prevent the associations from withdrawing whenever they want.[21] Furthermore, the Council's record generally shows autonomy in relation to the government, on the one hand, and control of its base through corporatist mechanisms to benefit the business leadership, on the other.[22] This independence superimposed on a corporatist structure brings business sector representation by the CCE closer to societal than to state corporatism (see Chapter 1).

THE CCE IN ACTION

T his section describes the experiences that have molded the CCE's strategies and tactics from its inception in 1975 to 1997. The interpretations provided here are empirically supported by a quantitative analysis of the CCE's performance from 1975 to 1993. This analysis was carried out by reviewing, coding, and processing all the CCE's actions as reported in the Mexico City press. During these years, 1,946 actions were recorded and then classified according to content, subject, and support or rejection of government/state action (Tirado and Luna 1995). Figure 1 — Frequency of Actions, 1975-1993 — shows that the CCE was more active in 1975, 1982-1983, and 1986-1990, and less active in 1976-1982, 1984-1885, and 1990-1993.

Defensive Politicization: 1975[23]

This first stage in the CCE's history lasted only a few months after the Council's founding under the direction of Juan Sánchez Navarro, a radicalized leader from the moderate faction.[24]

The CCE's initial intervention defended the written and unwritten rules that had governed the relations between government and business in previous decades and opposed the growing state intervention promoted by President Echeverría.[25] Indeed, the Council insinuated that it would veto any PRI presidential candidate who sought to continue Echeverría's policy and flout the established rules. This implicit threat proved a useful strategy because the CCE emerged just six months before the PRI and the outgoing president, as was the custom, were to nominate the next presidential candidate of the PRI, who, following the pattern set since 1929, would invariably triumph. In July 1975, CCE President Sánchez Navarro confided to a friend, "The CCE has a very special role: to help Echeverría solve his problems. As you know, all we want is to stop him from making a mistake in his key decision, which is why we are prepared to act as a lightning rod in Mexican life."[26] In referring to "problems" and "key decision," Sánchez Navarro meant Echeverría's need to designate a successor.

The government responded to the Council's emergence by sharply questioning the legitimacy of businessmen's intervention in politics itself as well as some of the principles they had espoused. Once this harsh debate subsided in the spring of 1975,[27] the CCE virtually disappeared from the political scene.[28] In fact, the Council ran into trouble by the end of 1975. In addition to maintaining a low profile, it twice replaced leaders between November 1975 and February 1976. This instability probably reflected differences among the Council's founding factions, which from its inception had established limits on its scope.[29]

In the absence of the CCE, as the conflict with the government deepened during 1975 and 1976, the voice of business was increasingly monopolized by the most radical business faction and its primary organization, the belligerent Coparmex. By the end of Echeverría's administration in 1976, Comparmex had emerged as the most powerful organization in the Mexican private sector.

The private sector's debut on the political stage was linked to a rather diffuse public opinion campaign that consisted mainly of personal communication and rumors widely circulated among the middle- and upper-class social sectors (Loaeza 1977). Although the business sector lacked any visible leadership — and abstained from organizing mobilizations in the streets or formulating clear demands — the movement proved extremely effective in eroding the credibility of both the government and the president (Monsivais 1979). In 1976, massive capital flight put an end to the almost mythical stability of Mexican currency.

Depoliticization: 1976-1980

A depoliticized period began at the end of 1976 with the inauguration of President José López Portillo. In his address to organized business during his inaugural speech, López Portillo repeated his campaign pleas for a "truce" and distanced himself from the populist policies of his predecessor. The new president made business his privileged interlocutor and urged it to join the government in a "great alliance for production" (López Portillo 1977, 37 and 12). The major business organizations accepted the invitation, and the two sides duly signed a document cementing the deed. With this act, the government for the first time explicitly acknowledged the CCE's existence and the Council's claim to speak for the entire private sector. López Portillo's policy of moving closer to business was a salient feature of his six-year term. This rapprochement, dialogue, and basic agreement on policies — supported by abundant resources derived from the oil boom — toned down business mobilization, eased government-business relations, and stimulated a general depoliticization of the business sector. This is evidenced in Figure 1 by the small number of actions the CCE undertook during this period.

However, the lessening of tension did not signify an absence of discord. Certain radical business sectors insisted on more direct political action. For example, between 1977 and 1978, the CCE's president proposed organizing a private sector political party. However, the project failed to attract other members. They were captivated by López Portillo's policies and the high economic growth rates fueled by the oil boom. Mexico's entry into the General Agreement on Tariffs and Trade (GATT) was a further source of friction. Canacintra frankly opposed it, while the rest of the CCE's member organizations expressed various intermediate positions. Due to the disagreement among member organizations, the CCE abstained from the GATT debate. In 1980, the government decided not to join GATT (Story 1990, 173-202). The relative absence of conflict with the state contributed to the subsequent depoliticization of the CCE, which thereby joined the relative quiescence of the rest of organized business.

Political Counteroffensive: 1981-1984[30]

The fall of international oil prices in the middle of 1981 triggered the debt crisis in Mexico, which then spread through Latin America. The oil price collapse marked the beginning of a cycle of conflict and open confrontation between the government and the private sector that culminated in the nationalization of the private banking system on September 1, 1982, by President López Portillo. In the context of statist-populist government policies and high levels of socioeconomic conflict, the private sector again became politicized, and Mexican businesspeople launched a powerful political counteroffensive, which will be discussed later. They promoted and joined a new right-wing social movement similar to that of the 1970s and became active in party politics. A combative CCE, headed by former Coparmex leader Manuel J. Clouthier,[31] entered the fray. Clouthier's fiery rhetoric resonated among entrepreneurs and in Mexican society at large. As Figure 1 shows, these were the most active years of the CCE.

The CCE excoriated the banks' expropriation and called it a unilateral and illegal step toward "socialism" taken by the president of a corrupt and inefficient government.[32] The CCE called on citizens to end presidential authoritarianism by validating democratic and representative institutions, the division of public powers, and federalism. It exhorted citizens to use interest group associations to create a force capable of counterbalancing an oppressive brand of presidentialism. On economic issues, the CCE demanded free markets, the recognition of free enterprise as the engine of economic development, and a noninterventionist state. Although this discourse addressed citizens at large, it was slanted to forge unity within the business community.[33] The views of a unified private sector would carry greater weight in society and would let the CCE gain better representation in the political system in order to defend its world view. In short, although the CCE had some economic demands, its discourse centered on a surprising appeal to democracy and political action in the form of civil mobilization.

Such a departure implied a true redefinition of the historical radical faction mostly represented by Coparmex and Concanaco. Economic liberalization and democratic elements clearly had been added to their long-standing conservatism in other matters. As a result of this amalgamation, the new faction that emerged and replaced the old radical one may rightly be labeled "liberal-conservative."

Despite its combativeness, however, the CCE could not reverse the expropriation measures. This was partly because moderate industrialists believed the nationalization of the private banking sector was a fait-accompli that could, when all was said and done, benefit them. In addition, the left-wing faction of the PRI and the left in general enthusiastically supported the expropriation. Finally, the bankers themselves did not wish to add fuel to the fire and preferred to negotiate for good compensation. This setback notwithstanding, the powerful private sector movement that helped create the CCE had changed the ideological parameters of the political struggle in Mexico and would influence the banking reprivatization implemented a decade later.

Moreover, the new rhetoric fell on fertile ground of a different sort. It became the credo behind a new private sector political movement that appealed to other social groups in addition to business. This political movement was the product of a deep disaffection toward the government on the part of huge sectors of the population. A few months after the expropriation, the country witnessed the unheard-of launching of businessmen as mayoral candidates on behalf of PAN in a number of municipalities of Chihuahua state (Aziz 1994, 60). To everyone's even greater surprise, the government and the PRI acknowledged the victory of some of these opponents in the municipal elections. These successful candidates were northern businessmen with close links to local business associations, particularly to the Coparmex centers and to many Concanaco chambers.

Meanwhile, President Miguel de la Madrid's government, which took office in late 1982, anxious to make amends with the private sector elite, implemented a number of policies. It returned non-financial companies that had belonged to the banks to shareholders; it amply compensated bankers whose banks had been expropriated, giving back one-third of the shares in nationalized banks to the private sector; it launched a generous rescue plan for the most heavily indebted private firms, which primarily benefited the largest companies; and it fostered the creation of a new "parallel banking system," providing preferential conditions to enable private securities brokers to become leading financial actors, and began to privatize several public companies. These measures began to earn the de la Madrid administration the good will of the most powerful entrepreneurs.

By 1985, however, some important medium-sized private sector leaders who distrusted the government and were very interested in politics left their business associations and openly joined political parties to play a major role. This was because the business associations by their nature were not suitable forums for the business leaders' new fight. Thus, businesspeople and the PAN set their sights on gubernatorial races in selected states, openly defying the PRI's monopoly of governorships. The most conspicuous case was Clouthier, who had been president of the CCE when the banks were nationalized. He became the PAN's candidate for governor in his state and later the PAN's candidate in the controversial presidential elections of 1988. The mid-1980s' gubernatorial elections in the northern states of Sinaloa, Chihuahua, Sonora, and Nuevo León differed sharply from the Chihuahua municipal elections of 1982. Afraid of the scope of the movement, the government and PRI resorted to open electoral fraud to deny what seemed to be PAN's victories. The most shocking of these fraudulent elections was Chihuahua's gubernatorial election of 1986 (Aziz 1994). They also opened up the PRI to pro-business candidates who could neutralize the influence that Panista businessmen had achieved over large segments of the electorate.

The Neoliberal Proposal: 1986-1989 [34]

In the mid-1980s, the lingering debt crisis, inflation, dwindling oil prices, and the trade deficit, among other factors, fueled mounting economic instability during the de la Madrid administration. In the face of these intractable problems, the government shifted its approach to the political economy and sought business support for its actions. This change reinforced a new moderate faction of the CCE, a faction that embraced the principles of economic liberalism without significantly altering their traditional pragmatic behavior toward the government and the PRI. The CMHN, AMIS, and AMIB — the associations of large-scale industrial and financial capital — lay at the core of this "liberal-pragmatic" faction. Other moderates, speaking primarily through the Canacintra, opposed the opening of the economy, albeit less forcefully as time went by. Beginning in 1985, the liberal-pragmatic faction of the CCE, with the CMHN at its head, elected in succession three former CMHN presidents as CCE presidents.

The CCE's hegemonic liberal-pragmatic faction concurred with the de la Madrid technocrats (Centeno and Maxfield 1992),[35] the foreign creditors, and the government of the United States on the need to embrace neoliberal policies. In their view, regaining economic stability and growth depended on curbing government spending, privatizing public enterprises, deregulating markets, lifting controls on foreign capital, and reorienting investment toward the export of manufactured goods. Matching deeds to intention, the government began to open the economy to trade at the end of 1985 and, after joining GATT in 1986, immediately lifted the tariff barriers protecting Mexico's products beyond the terms agreed upon in GATT.

The alliance between the pragmatic liberals and government technocrats was cemented in 1987 when the government and the CCE signed the first of a series of anti-inflationary pacts.[36] Later, when Carlos Salinas de Gortari was already president, the government began to implement extremely important measures as requested by the elite, which will be discussed later in this chapter.

These events suggest that the liberal-pragmatic faction of business was asserting its dominance on economic policy issues within the CCE. This predominance, however, did not extend to electoral politics in 1988. In this arena, members of the liberal-conservative faction acted independently by launching Clouthier as the PAN's presidential candidate. Meanwhile, leaders of the liberal pragmatists, led by CCE president Agustín F. Legorreta, campaigned for the PRI's presidential candidate, Salinas. The real surprise of that election, however, was the emergence of Neocardenismo, a movement centered around Cuauhtémoc Cárdenas, the son of the renowned former president Lázaro Cárdenas (1934-1940). Highly influential with the popular classes, Cuauhtémoc Cárdenas vindicated the Mexican Revolution, questioned the new development model, and challenged the legitimacy of Salinas' victory — arguing, with reasonable grounds, that he had been the victim of widespread fraud (González 1989; Calderón and Cazés 1991).

The fact that Cárdenas won more votes than Clouthier did influence business's future political action. Since a PRI-PAN bipartisan administration was no longer feasible, entrepreneurs related to business associations began to pull out of electoral and party politics, particularly in regions where Neocardenismo had become firmly entrenched: Michoacán, Guerrero, the Federal District, and certain adjacent states. Fearing that the dissenting left would be able to win the elections democratically, the business associations used less vigorous democratic rhetoric, distanced themselves from political parties, and reduced their involvement in electoral politics greatly from the period of 1982-1988. This attitude showed a retreat from support for full political democracy to limited forms of political liberalization.

However, businesspeople as individuals did not abandon politics. In the north, where Neocardenismo and the Partido de la Revolución Democrática (PRD), which Cárdenas had formed after the 1988 elections, had failed to take root, the situation remained unchanged. In the rest of the country, once Neocardenismo's original popularity began to fade, PRI and PAN candidates with business backgrounds proliferated, although they now appeared to identify themselves more as citizens than as businesspeople and leaders of professional groups.

The electoral struggle continued over the next few years, and in 1990, for the first time in their long history, the government and the PRI were forced to admit the victory of an opposition candidate in a gubernatorial race. The winner was a Panista businessman. Since 1990, seven Panistas from the entrepreneurial sector have been elected governors: Ernesto Ruffo in Baja California, Francisco Barrio in Chihuahua,[37] Carlos Medina and Vicente Fox in Guanajuato, Alberto Cárdenas in Jalisco, Ignacio Loyola in Querétaro, and Fernando Canales in Nuevo León. Several others have been elected to federal, state, and municipal positions. The PRI has also presented some candidates with business backgrounds for governor as well as many others for minor posts subject to election. Recently, the PRD has done the same, albeit to a lesser extent.[38]

The Salinas Administration and the CCE's Loss of Legitimacy[39]

The Salinas government (1988-1994) was characterized by its powerful support of the neoliberal project.

It is worth noting that in the official adoption of an ideology identified as "social liberalism," "liberal" meant reduction of state involvement in the economy, while "social" meant the ostensible support of the poorest sectors of the population. However, this new ideology focused less on these officially adopted principles than on the notion of "modernization." Although the state never precisely defined its modernization policy, it obviously entailed the state's withdrawal from many of the activities in which it had traditionally been involved (often as an owner); the full acceptance of the fact that the world was undergoing a period of economic globalization that reached beyond national borders; acknowledgment of free market forces as the most effective mechanism for allocating resources, and, as a corollary to all this, the acceptance of private enterprise as the engine of the country's growth. In keeping with this, for the first time in history, a Mexican president publicly proclaimed that his government openly supported the largest conglomerates and companies in the country (Salinas 1993, 51). This statement was obviously a far cry from the ideology of the Mexican Revolution, which had underpinned the PRI and its government for many decades.

Foremost among the concrete measures implemented by the Salinas government was the privatization of public companies. Salinas enthusiastically continued the privatization of companies and public organizations begun by the de la Madrid government (Schneider 1990). Thus, the 12 years of these two administrations witnessed a spectacular change: 939 public entities (companies, organizations, and trusts) were privatized or closed ("disincorporated" in official jargon). The number of public entities dropped from a high of 1,155 reached by the end of President López Portillo's administration in 1982, to the 216 remaining public entities in 1994 when President Salinas left power.[40]

Among the privatized companies were many of the so-called "jewels of the crown": Teléfonos de México, the two largest airline companies, the Cananea mining company, the Altos Hornos and Siderúrgica Lázaro Cárdenas Las Truchas iron and steel companies, a group of many sugar mills, and the banks expropriated by the López Portillo administration.[41] The sales of a state television system with two national channels and some regional channels are also worth mentioning because of their impact on public opinion. The public sector's role in the national economy was significantly reduced.[42]

The transfer of this great mass of public property to the private sector has been compared to the huge expropriations under the Ley Lerdo of 1856 and other property rights reforms during the nineteenth century. During that period, vast property holdings immobilized by the "dead hands" of the clergy and the communal farmlands of indigenous peoples were publicly auctioned off by the government. At any rate, the large scale privatization under de la Madrid and Salinas permitted the consolidation of a new generation of businesspeople. Although these business-people had little in common with previous members of the Mexican business elite, they came to occupy a privileged position within it as a result of their vast, recently acquired power. This small group linked to the stock exchange was virtually unknown in the 1970s, but following the nationalization of banking in 1982, with the government's support of the financial activities conducted in their investment houses, they accumulated huge fortunes during the 1980s. With these fortunes, they purchased some of the most important banks and industrial and service companies in the country (Fernández 1993; Garrido 1993).[43]

Salinas' government negotiated its foreign debt and overtly promoted both direct and indirect foreign investment. To this end, he modified the foreign investment laws, toning down the most restrictive limits on access to the Mexican market and allowing 100-percent foreign capital investment in 80 percent of a total of 750 economic activities (Concheiro 1996, 127). In this favorable environment, foreign direct investment increased from $26.5 billion in 1989 to $60.6 billion in 1995.[44] Indirect foreign investment also grew rapidly, from $300 million in 1989 to $28.9 billion in 1993 (Banco de México 1996, 170).

The Salinas administration also repeatedly addressed deregulation of the economy. The main form of deregulation was undoubtedly trade opening, which eliminated import permits and reduced tariffs. This continued the trade opening actively promoted since the de la Madrid administration (Lustig 1992, 117-120). The North American Free Trade Agreement (NAFTA), negotiated during the Salinas administration, would, within 15 years, reduce import taxes to zero.

The Salinas government also modified many laws that restricted private companies' actions or established other official controls. One principal measure was to end agrarian distribution and move toward privatization of *ejido* lands. The Salinas government modified Article 27 of the 1917 Constitution, which reflected the revolutionary demand that the land in the vast *haciendas* be distributed among the landless peasants and the *ejido* (peasant communal farmlands) reinstated, prohibiting their sale or lease. The January 1992 reform ended land distribution policies implemented over several decades, and that created conditions under which approximately 3.5 million peasants might sell their plots of land, which together accounted for more than half of all Mexican territory.[45]

Although Salinas was unable to modify labor legislation itself, in practice, he encouraged more flexible labor relations that favored company-level negotiations and discouraged so-called "law-contracts" and collective negotiation by the industrial sector. The "National Accord to Enhance Productivity and Quality" (ANEPC) — signed by the government and the principal worker, peasant, and business representatives on May 25, 1992 — was a step in this direction.[46]

Salinas also modified Article 3 of the Constitution, which encapsulated another ideological principle of the Mexican Revolution: the prohibition of religious education in both public and private schools at the elementary level. The revised text allowed private schools to offer religious education.[47] Also, new editions of compulsory, free textbooks modified the negative view of the private sector, the Catholic Church, and other actors traditionally labeled "reactionary forces." Public elementary education was also partially decentralized through reforms by which the federal government transferred much of the responsibility and resources allocated to education in the 31 states and the Federal District (Loyo 1997).

The Salinas administration also changed Article 130, thereby altering the restrictive relationship between the Catholic Church and the state effective from the time of Benito Juárez.[48] The amended article acknowledged the church's existence and facilitated the establishment of diplomatic relations between Mexico and Vatican City State (García Ugarte 1993).

The legal status of the central bank, the Banco de México, was modified to make it more independent of the federal government and, therefore, capable at least in principle, of establishing policies without regard to decisions made by the central administration.[49]

The implementation of this set of measures, often before businesspeople demanded them, and the relative economic growth achieved during the Salinas administration consolidated faith in the upper segments of the private sector, established a strong alliance between the government and the business sector elite, and exalted President Salinas' image among the elite and among broad sectors of the public. This lasted until the final year of his administration, when unsolved problems escaped the government's control.

However, consolidation of the alliance between the elite and the government was not without problems. Despite their support of policies designed to achieve a more open economy, the CCE and the largest business organizations signed various anti-inflationary pacts that established price controls and constrained commitments to extend free trade. These policy contradictions were linked to the political tensions between conservative liberals and pragmatic liberals. Indeed, some businesspeople, particularly those who owned small and medium-scale businesses, regarded these pacts as impositions by their leaders.

The conflict highlighted the CCE's weaknesses: the heterogeneity of its social base; the disparities in its representativeness; and the struggle among CMHN, Coparmex, and CCE proper to lead the Mexican private sector. The liberal-conservatives challenged CCE's "pro-government" policy, the immoderate advocacy of the CCE and its president in striking bargains with the administration, and the Council's willingness to assume commitments that went beyond its coordinating role. Many businesspeople within the CCE, especially those with small, medium-sized, and provincial businesses, considered the liberal pragmatists' actions discriminatory unilateral policy impositions. Although the dissenting organizations did not express these complaints clearly or openly, they were able to enact an amendment to the Council's bylaws.[50] That change in 1991 allowed them to elect one of their leaders, a former Concanaco president, to the Council's board. The bylaw change, while minor, clearly mollified the disgruntled faction of largely small and medium-scale — and mainly provincial — businesspeople. Amid the conflict, the Council's activity declined (see Figure 1).

The CCE's internal conflict reduced its legitimacy. As a result, the Council had to camouflage its participation in the all-important NAFTA negotiations, even though these negotiations were absolutely crucial for the business sector. Clearly, NAFTA would define the basic framework for free-market economic restructuring, thus crowning the unilateral reforms already undertaken by presidents de la Madrid and Salinas. Furthermore, NAFTA was viewed as an insurance policy against any return to the protectionist and populist policies of former decades.

To conduct the NAFTA negotiations, CCE leaders, together with other business associations specializing in foreign trade, created a new encompassing peak organization, the Foreign Trade Business Organizations Coordinating Office (Coordinadora Empresarial de Organismos de Comercio Exterior — Coece). The Coece emerged in 1990, precisely when the government announced the beginning of the NAFTA negotiations. Under the leadership of Juan Gallardo Thurlow, a businessman from the elite capitalist groups, Coece assumed the representation of the private sector in the NAFTA negotiations and became the Mexican government's main interlocutor with the private sector.

Figure 1.
CCE Actions, 1975-1993

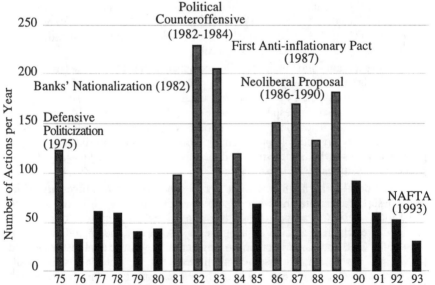

Source: Tirado and Luna, 1995.

The Coece adopted a broadly based sectoral structure that included up to 200 subsectors and, from the start, consulted systematically with its members to achieve "the universality, unity and true representativeness"[51] of the entire Mexican private sector. This meant that the negotiations were open to all business sectors. Thousands of meetings took place, but as negotiations advanced, small-scale businesspeople proved unable to cope, and the more powerful ones were left in a privileged position to negotiate. This naturally irritated the owners of small and medium-sized businesses, who once again felt excluded (Luna 1992b; Puga 1993). When NAFTA was signed in 1993, it became obvious that broad segments of the small and medium-sized business sector regarded the agreement with great trepidation despite the support it received from the CCE (Puga 1994a).

During these years, the Salinas government was notoriously wary of implementing the electoral reforms demanded by the opposition. The PRD, the Neocardenistas' party, under intense pressure from the government — and portrayed as violent, radical, and intransigent — gradually lost ground. Meanwhile, the PRI gradually recovered from its 1988 losses, winning the federal legislative elections in 1991[52] and winning the legislative and presidential elections on August 21, 1994.[53] The PAN's fortunes also improved, with the party winning one governorship in 1991 and one in 1992. However, PAN also forged controversial deals with the government and the PRI and was subsequently reproached by voters. In this changing scenario, businesspeople found opportunities and felt encouraged to participate in politics.

The day NAFTA came into effect, January 1, 1994, the Zapatista rebellion organized by the Indians in Chiapas began. The assassination of the PRI presidential candidate and Secretary-General, Luis Donaldo Colosio, in March 1994 — and above all the start of the economic debacle after Ernesto Zedillo began his presidency — rapidly eroded the apparent achievements of the Salinas government.

What had been held up as modernization and touted as Mexico's entry into the First World proved to be a disaster.[54] These events immediately reopened a debate on Salinas' economic policy, which had failed to avert yet another crisis and failed to alleviate the extreme poverty of much of the population — and showed the pressing need to speed up the democratic transition that Salinas had consistently postponed on the grounds that economic reform should take precedence. Salinas' image was destroyed along with the credibility of the government, the PRI, and to a certain extent the PAN, which had reached significant agreements with Salinas and supported some reforms he proposed.[55]

With this damage and the new moderation of the PRD, which could claim to have been the only party to have kept its distance from the disgraced Salinas, the PRI, on July 6, 1997, for the first time lost its absolute majority in the Chamber of Deputies. The PRD became the second national political force in that Chamber, although PAN had won the important governorships of Nuevo León and Querétero. Cárdenas, still the PRD's main leader, obtained the governorship of the most important entity in the country, the Federal District. At this point, political businesspeople were present in all the parties, although more so in the PAN and the PRI than in the PRD.

CONCLUSIONS

This section develops three orders of conclusions concerning the CCE's origins, its strategies for action, and implications for the attitudes of the CCE and business in general toward democracy.

The Creation of the CCE

The creation of the CCE was a milestone in a process that culminated in the emergence of an openly political role for business in Mexico. The main forces responsible for the creation of the CCE were perceived threats and the fear that the government might violate the traditional rules of the system. Consequently, the CCE's actions focused on defending the rules of the political game and on disqualifying those in a position to modify them.

The new organization was independent of the government. And although elite elements were undoubtedly instrumental in the CCE's creation, the Council's founding charter was based on the old corporatist structure, which provided it a broad, established social base. With more than 1,275,000 indirect affiliates, the CCE is an unusual example in Latin America of a large encompassing peak organization based on compulsory affiliation. It is also remarkable that the business elite was able to use this structure to exercise considerable influence within the new organization.

The Action Strategies Used and Their Consequences

The history of the CCE includes three stages of intense activity linked to three types of political leadership and three action strategies. The Council was founded in the defensive politicization of 1975. After a depoliticized period, 1976-1980, came the political counteroffensive of 1981-1984. The neoliberal proposal of 1985-1989 followed. After 1990, the organization lost legitimacy and adopted a lower profile.

During the CCE's initial intense activity in 1975, the moderate business faction employed a strategy of uniting the business sector in a powerful common front to defend the prevailing principles and rules of the political game. Their onslaught, which included elements of class action, condemned and helped curb the growing statism of the president and the government.

A depoliticized period began as López Portillo took office in 1976 and moved government closer to business. The second phase of political activity began as business and government came into conflict after the 1981 oil price crisis. Political activity intensified with the bank expropriations of 1982. The CCE reacted with a huge political counteroffensive that challenged Mexican authoritarianism in the name of democracy and won sympathy from broad sectors of the population. This strategy was an example of class action by liberal-conservatives that was supported by a wide-ranging social movement.

The nature of this confrontation drew the CCE and its allies into the arena of direct political action. However, they came up against the limits imposed by the structure of the business associations, which no longer proved useful to them in their fight for power. The leaders then abandoned the business associations and shifted their allegiance to the political parties instead. They stood for election to posts taking advantage of their identity as businesspeople with links to private sector associations.

The third active phase began in 1985 under the leadership of the liberal pragmatists and focused on a proposal to implement a neoliberal development model. The elite business groups that headed the CCE reached a political understanding of great importance with the government technocrats that were the new political elite; agreement over the liberalization of the economy lay at the core of this understanding.

However, implementation of these policies led to disagreements and a loss of the Council's legitimacy among dissenting business sectors — primarily the small, medium-scale, and provincial businesses, that were trapped in the corporatist structure of Mexico's system of interest representation. Consequently, the CCE was forced to promote a new entity to aggregate the entire private sector to negotiate NAFTA. In the end, however, the elite business groups were the main business protagonists in the treaty.

These phases of private sector activity can be analyzed through three characteristics of the historical situations in which they were taken. These features are whether government interventions are private or state-oriented; whether the private sector supports the government's policies or opposes them; and whether the actions of government and business strengthen or weaken the encompassing peak organization.

Serious threats of government intervention tend to lead to unity in the business sector, a unity forged out of pressure from the business associations' social bases. This pressure may create or strengthen highly representative and legitimized peak associations. Their legitimacy and representativeness may then enable them to launch class actions and social mobilization — and even to enter party politics. At times, the intensity of their political and electoral actions will exceed the limits of the business associations' organizing principles, as it did in the mid-1980s, when CCE leaders pursued action through political parties, including the opposition PAN, as individual citizens.

Conversely, with the easing of political tension between the state and the business sector, associations with strong political presence and broad aims will decline and disintegrate, and encompassing peak associations will lapse into inactivity, with their leaders maintaining a low profile. At the same time, specialized business associations will become more active, behaving much like pressure groups and seeking to push the narrow private interests of the associations. Relative lack of conflict with the government from 1977 through 1980 dampened the CCE's political ardor.

The CCE's active pursuit of the liberal economic project between 1985 and 1989 also used "pressure group" tactics. However, when pressure group tactics implemented by the business elite dominated actions of the encompassing peak organization, this may have generated increasing tensions and divisive effects. Broad sections of the business sector felt excluded from the liberal economic project, as the Council used its corporatist mechanisms to exercise greater control over its member associations, thereby diminishing its representativeness.

The depoliticization of the CCE was followed by CCE actions that were closely involved with government economic policy and did not accommodate the entire private business sector. That led to differences, tensions, and lost legitimacy. This huge and heterogeneous encompassing business peak organization, rooted mainly in corporatist associations and practice, is thus threatened. The CCE runs the risk of breaking apart if compulsory affiliation to Concamin and Concanaco is eliminated.

The current system of intermediation of interests makes the CCE's representation structure less transparent and less representative. Despite its encompassing scope, it denies representation to many groups while concealing the limited representativeness of groups that now virtually monopolize all the available forums.

Such an opaque structure of business representation stifles interest in intermediation and, in turn, the entire political system. A representation neither diverse nor genuine puts the CCE out of step with a society now more complex and heterogeneous. The CCE does not contribute to the kind of institutional web required for recognition, management, and resolution of complex conflicts.

Business and Democracy

Historically, business and democracy have been distant relations in Mexico; the country has no tradition of democratic businesspeople. At crucial moments, such as the Tlatelolco student massacre in 1968, the private sector invariably opted for authoritarian solutions. This, however, changed when the expropriation of private banking caused a large spectrum of entrepreneurs to feel that they lacked the political space and representation they deserved — and goaded them into obtaining it.

They mobilized through the CCE and other organizations, appealing to citizens with a new form of discourse, urging them to make representative, democratic, and republican political institutions truly effective. This rhetoric proved so effective that businesspeople entered the political arena, joining overtly first the PAN, then the PRI, and finally the PRD. These mobilizations were undoubtedly a key factor in Mexico's slow, tortuous transition to democracy.

Although the emergence of Neocardenismo and the PRD in the controversial presidential election of 1988 forced political businesspeople to retreat and distance themselves from their democratic discourse and private sector associations, they soon returned to the political arena, encouraged during Salinas's administration by the erosion and subsequent moderation of the PRD, by the rise of the PAN, and by the PRI's recovery. These attitudes reflected the business elite's preference for limited forms of political liberalization instead of full political democracy.

The results of the July 6, 1997, elections, which showed a further decline of the PRI, the relative stagnation of the PAN, and the resurgence of a moderate PRD, have opened up the possibility of democratic transition. Political businesspeople are now entrenched, and their actions are beyond the control of the government, the parties, and the business associations themselves.

Notes

1. The mandatory affiliation to the chambers was introduced for the first time in 1936 by the Ley de Cámaras Comerciales e Industriales during President Lázaro Cárdenas' term. In 1941, the new Ley de Cámaras de Comercio y de las de Industria maintained this obligation (Congreso de los Estados Unidos Mexicanos 1936, 1941).

2. Guzmán, one of their leaders, explained, "It has been typical of Mexican business peak organizations that the more serious problems affecting their members are jointly studied by the directors of the main institutions representing private initiative. If a situation of this kind arises, the presidents of the [sectoral organizations] enter into immediate consultation and, if needed, their respective boards of directors and groups of specialists working for them enter into action. Thus, coherent decisions are made that regulate the actions of the business class. On this basis, joint statements or steps are taken with the participation of representatives of industry, commerce, businesspeople as employers, and banking. At other times — and this is the general rule — each organization acts only within its own functional area but knows it counts with the support of all the others" (Guzmán Valdivia 1960, 318).

3. They played an important role in the expropriation law, the profit-sharing plan for workers, and the fiscal reform.

4. For a summary of the origin of these business factions, see Tirado 1990.

5. For the business sector's reaction and analysis of its politicization, see Arriola 1981; Basáñez 1981; Zermeño 1982; Tirado and Luna 1986; and Millán 1988.

6. See Campero 1984; Durand 1994; and Gaspar 1988. For Brazil, see Dreifuss 1998. For Bolivia, see Conaghan 1991.

7. Despite very obvious differences, there were certain parallels in the United States. In the 1970s, large U.S. corporations felt that their power and legitimacy were threatened. The oil embargo, the Watergate scandal, the Vietnam war, the growing awareness of the problems of pollution, and a generalized skepticism about the responsibility of corporations — as well as other events — generated a broad-based social coalition. "A loose coalition of middle-class based consumer and environmental, feminist and civil rights organizations, assisted on occasion by organized labor, aided by a sympathetic media and supported by much of the intelligentsia, were able to influence both the terms of public debate and the outcomes of government policy in a direction antithetical to the interest of business" (Vogel 1983, 20, quoted by Coleman 1988, 13); also see Wilson 1985, 31-33. Between 1962 and 1973, 27 federal bills were passed on the environment, energy, security, health and consumer protection (Bertozzi 1990, 3-4). In response to this government activism and social movement, a new business entity — the Business Roundtable — was created; it achieved great prestige and influence within a very short time (McQuaid 1980; Bertozzi 1990, 22).

8. The ABM disappeared with the nationalization of the banking industry and reappeared and soon joined again with the CCE when the banks privatized.

9. The representation conferred on the CCE by its founders had certain restrictions, as shown by the rather trivial mission assigned to the entity (coordination), the short term of

office for its leaders (six months), and the restricted powers the leaders were granted. This confirms that the original intention of the founders was to create a "lightweight" organization that only slightly represented the business sector. They were, in fact, afraid that a strong, autonomous association might lead the business sector into conflicts that would worsen relations between business and government, which were already strained in 1975.

10. See "Nuestra tesis tiene 30 años de vigencia," in *Transformación*, May 1975.

11. This section closely follows Luna and Tirado 1992.

12. Italy has two business confederations — a Confederation of Small Businesses (Confederazione de la Picole Imprese — Confapi), comprising 40,000 small as well as medium-sized industries and three large associations encompassing over 800,000 craftsmen, and the Confederation of Italian Industry (Confederazione dell'Industria Italiana — Confindustria), representing large industry (Gröte 1992, 51, 153, 167). Likewise, France has a National Council of French Employers (Conseil National du Patronat Français — CNPF) and the General Confederation of Small and Medium-sized Businesses (Conféderation Génerale des Petites et Moyennes Entreprises — CGPME) (Magniadas 1991, 78-82). The United States also has two important industrial associations in which size is an organizational criterion: the National Association of Manufacturers (NAM), which used to represent only large industry and has approximately 13,500 affiliated members (Bertozzi 1990, 20-21), and the National Federation of Independent Businesses (NFIB), which has 470,000 members. In the NFIB, small businesses are a majority; 80 percent of its members have no more than 20 employees, while 66 percent have fewer than 10 (Sison 1990, 73-75). Japan has two trade and two employers' associations, one of each for large businesses and one of each for small and medium-sized businesses (Levine 1984, 324-326).

13. On the importance of regional organizational criteria, see Schmitter and Lanzalaco 1989 and Coleman and Jacek 1989.

14. In a newspaper report, Fernández-Vega (1991) estimated that they owned assets worth 100 billion new pesos and employed 450,000 workers.

15. Alan Riding (a journalist for the *New York Times* who covered Mexico for more than 12 years) reflected a widely held view when he said, speaking from the CMHN, "The Council has no statute, no office, no secretariat, no budget; it seeks to avoid any media reference to its very existence, and its sessions are held in the privacy of its members' homes, but its collective influence is immense" (Riding 1985, 109).

16. A source from Comparmex recognizes it 30,000 members (Bravo Mena 1987, 92).

17. See articles 5 and 23 of the "Ley de Cámaras de Comercio y de Industria," in Congreso de los Estados Unidos Mexicanos 1941.

18. See articles 1, 2, and 4, section IV; 9, section III; and 23 of the "Ley de Cámaras de Comercio y de Industria," in Congreso de los Estados Unidos Mexicanos 1941.

19. At least formally, it has been established that the dues may be collected in much the same way that public revenues are collected. This mechanism prevents free riders.

20. On January 1, 1997, the new "Ley de Cámaras Empresariales y Sus Confederaciones" came into effect. The new law did not stipulate mandatory affiliation to the chambers, although it did make compulsory inscription in a national firm's register (the Sistema de Información Empresarial Mexicano — SIEM) and subsequent payment of dues to the chambers (Congreso de los Estados Unidos Mexicanos 1996). Because the authorities gave business a de facto grace period to register, it has not been possible to judge the effects of the

new law. The response to date has not been very encouraging, since by mid-1997, only approximately 300,000 companies (from 1,024,750 formerly affiliated with all of the Concanaco and Concamin chambers) had registered with the SIEM, and there is no information on how many of those firms were affiliated with the chambers. See the SIEM web site at <http://www.secofi-siem.gob.mx/intranet.asp>.

21. The founding associations' affiliation to the CCE appears to have been decided from the top by their leaders at that time. There is no evidence that the large associations have ever provided an opportunity for their respective constituencies to express their views on the subject.

22. An empirical study covering all the Council's actions from 1975 to 1993 shows that the CCE has generally opposed the government (Tirado and Luna 1995).

23. For this period and the next, see Tello 1979; Arriola 1981; Saldívar 1981; Martínez Nava 1984; Luna, Millán, and Tirado 1985; Tirado and Luna 1986; Millán 1988; and Arriola 1988.

24. A well-known ideologue and former president of several business organizations.

25. The CCE's *Declaración de principios* (CCE 1975a) confirms the defensive thesis.

26. Sánchez Navarro's letter to Hugo B. Margain, July 1975. Margain was Mexico's ambassador to Great Britain and secretary of finance during the early years of Echeverría's administration. Quoted by Ortiz (1997, 12), who is currently studying Sánchez Navarro's archives.

27. See as examples, Buendía 1975 and Castillo 1975.

28. See Carton de Grammont 1992, 236-251.

29. As was previously noted, CCE founders set clear limits on the actions of the organization's leaders.

30. For this period, see Tello 1984; Luna, Millán, and Tirado 1985; Tirado and Luna 1986; Luna, Tirado and Valdés 1987; Maxfield and Anzaldúa 1987; Arriola 1988; Hernández 1988; Millán 1988; Camp 1990; Luna 1992a; and Heredia 1990 and 1992.

31. An agroindustrial businessman whose lands were on the verge of being expropriated by the Echeverría administration in 1976.

32. See Clouthier's declaration in *Excélsior*, September 3, 1982.

33. This new discourse appeared especially in the meetings called "México en la Libertad," which were held by the leaders of the CCE, Coparmex, and Cocanaco with businessmen, professionals, students, housewives, and other middle-class people in different cities primarily in the north during the next three months following the banks' nationalization. See some of the complete speeches by business leaders in Concanaco's magazine, *Decisión*, numbers 44, 45, and 46 (October, November, and December) of 1982.

34. For this period, see Camp 1990; Heredia 1990 and 1992; Luna and Tirado 1993; Tirado and Luna 1995; and Valdés 1997.

35. A famous remark by CCE President Agustín F. Legorreta, leader of the liberal-pragmatic faction and former president of the CMHN, was that "the most important economic decisions" of the nation "were made by the president of a presidentialist country with a cozy little group of 300 persons" (Ortiz 1988).

36. For these pacts, see Roxborough 1991 and Jarque and Téllez 1993.

37. On the Barrio election in 1992, see Mizrachi 1994.

38. For the Panista entrepreneurs and their political action, see Loaeza 1992 and Arriola 1994.

39. For this period, see Heredia 1995; Tirado and Luna 1995; Concheiro 1996; and Valdés 1997.

40. Data from Secretaría de Hacienda y Crédito Público and Secretaría de la Contraloría General de la Federación 1994.

41. On the privatization of banking, see Elizondo 1992. A total of 60 banks were expropriated in 1982, but, owing to closures and mergers, the total number had fallen to 18 by 1991.

42. This flow of huge masses of state property into private hands has had many consequences: the emergence of a new generation of entrepreneurs; the reduction of state expenditures to support public enterprises in economic trouble; the suppression of many high-level job opportunities for politicians and public officials; the sharp reduction of old state-company employees; the reconstruction of labor relations with certain old unions related very closely to the PRI; the receipt of huge sums of money into the government treasury; and so forth.

43. Some of them, such as Carlos Slim, joined the lists of international billionaires (Rogers and McCampbell 1993; Seneker 1993).

44. Figures for 1989 are from the U.S. International Trade Commission (Lustig 1992, 125), and those for 1990-1995 are from the Banco de México (Banco de México 1996, 173).

45. See Bovin 1996. For the constitutional reforms on agrarian matters and the new "Ley Agraria," see Comisión Permanente del Congreso General de los Estados Unidos Mexicanos 1992 and Congreso de los Estados Unidos Mexicanos 1992, respectively.

46. See the text in *Acuerdo Nacional para la Elevación de la Productividad y la Calidad 1992*.

47. For the constitutional reforms on education, see Comisión Permanente del Congreso General de los Estados Unidos Mexicanos 1992.

48. For the constitutional reforms on the relationship with the Catholic Church, see Comisión Permanente del Congreso General de los Estados Unidos Mexicanos 1992.

49. For the constitutional reforms on the central bank, see Comisión Permanente del Congreso General de los Estados Unidos Mexicanos 1993.

50. For this CCE conflict, see Luna and Tirado 1992.

51. Verbal participation of Guillermo Güemez (director of Coece) and Rodolfo Cruz Miramontes in the forum, "El TLC en la construcción de México para el libre comercio," organized by the Red de Acción frente al Libre Comercio en México, November 13, 1992, and quoted by Puga 1993, 63.

52. For these elections, see Gómez Tagle 1992.

53. For these elections, see Pascual 1995 and Pérez, Alvarado, and Sánchez 1995.

54. Annoyance against Salinas' administration grew during 1995. The main grievances can be summarized as follow: its responsibility for the new economic crisis unleashed in December 1994; its reluctance to fully implement the democratic reform demanded by the

country; the failure of its policies to reduce the abject poverty of broad sectors of the population; its alleged participation in the assassination of PRI presidential candidate Donaldo Colosio and concealment of Salinas' brother's suspected role in the assassination of the PRI's secretary-general; the boom in drug-trafficking during this period — together with the widespread involvement of the police, sectors of the armed forces and federal and state governments; the vast increase in crime and lack of safety in the country's main cities; the high levels of corruption — implicating members of the president's family and expressed in the privatization of state companies, particularly banks and highways, and in the lack of scrupulousness in the sale of banks and highway concessions, subsequently rescued by the government for exorbitant sums. For evaluations of the Salinas administration, see Meyer 1995 and Krauze 1997, 417-446.

55. For balances on the Salinas' administration, see Meyer 1995 and Krauze 1997.

References

Arriola, Carlos. 1981. *Los empresarios y el estado*. Mexico City: Consejo Nacional de Fomento Educativo, September 1980, No. 3.

Arriola, Carlos. 1988. *Los empresarios y el estado 1970-1982*. Mexico City: UNAM and Miguel Angel Porrúa.

Arriola, Carlos. 1994. *Ensayos sobre el PAN*. Mexico City: Miguel Angel Porrúa.

Aziz Nassif, Alberto. 1994. *Chihuahua. Historia de una alternativa*. Mexico City: La Jornada Ediciones and Ciesas.

Banco de México. 1996. *Informe anual 1995*. Mexico City: Banco de México.

Basáñez, Miguel. 1981. *La lucha por la hegemonía en México 1968-1980*. Mexico City: Siglo XXI.

Bertozzi, Dan. 1990. *Business, Government and Public Policy*. Englewood Cliffs, N.J.: Prentice Hall.

Bovin, Philippe, ed. 1996. *El campo mexicano: una modernización forzada*. Mexico City: Centro Francés de Estudios Mexicanos y Centroamericanos and Institut Français de Recherche Scientifique pour le Developpement et la Coopération.

Bravo Mena, Luis. 1987. "Coparmex and Mexican Politics." In *Government and Private Sector in Contemporary Mexico*, eds. Sylvia Maxfield and Ricardo Anzaldúa. San Diego, Calif.: Center for U.S. Mexican Studies, University of California.

Buendía, Manuel. 1975. "Grito patronal." *El Día*, May 11.

Calderón Alzati, Enrique, and Daniel Cazes. 1991. *Prontuario de resultados: elecciones federales de 1988*. Mexico City: Fundación Arturo Rosenblueth.

Camp, Roderic Ai. 1990. *Los empresarios y la política en México. Una visión contemporánea*. Mexico City: Fondo de Cultura Económica. Spanish translation of Camp, Roderic A. 1989. *Entrepreneurs and Politics in Twentieth-Century Mexico*. New York: Oxford University Press.

Campero, Guillermo. 1984. *Los gremios empresariales en el periodo 1970-1983: comportamiento sociopolítico y orientaciones ideológicas*. Santiago: ILET.

Carton de Grammont, Hubert. 1990. *Los empresarios agrícolas y el Estado: Sinaloa 1893-1984*. Mexico City: Insituto de Investigaciones Sociales, UNAM.

Castillo, Heberto. 1975. "La Declaración de Principios del CCE: ¿Discrepancia concertada?" *Excélsior*, May 15.

Centeno, Miguel Angel, and Sylvia Maxfield. 1992. "The Marriage of Finance and Order: Changes in the Mexican Political Elite." *Journal of Latin American Studies* 24:1 (February): 57- 85.

Cerutti, Mario. 1992. *Burguesía, capitales e industria en el norte de México. Monterrey y su ámbito regional*. Mexico City: Alianza Editorial and Universidad Autónoma de Nuevo León.

Coleman, William D. 1988. *Business and Politics: A Study on Collective Action*. Kingston, Ontario: Mcgill-Queen's University Press.

Coleman, William D., and Henry J. Jacek. 1989. "Capitalists, collective action and regionalism: An introduction." In *Regionalism, Business Interests and Public Policy*, eds. William D. Coleman and Henry J. Jacek. London: Sage Publications.

Comisión Permanente del Congreso General de los Estados Unidos Mexicanos. 1992. "Decreto por el que se reforman los artículos 3, 5, 24, 27, 130 y se adiciona el artículo decimoséptimo transitorio de la Constitución Política de los Estados Unidos Mexicanos." In *Diario Oficial de la Federación*, January 21.

Comisión Permanente del Congreso General de los Estados Unidos Mexicanos. 1992. "Decreto por el que se reforma el artículo 27 de la Constitución Política de los Estados Unidos Mexicanos." In *Diario Oficial de la Federación*, January 6.

Comisión Permanente del Congreso General de los Estados Unidos Mexicanos. 1993. "Decreto por el que se reforman los artículos 28, 73 y 123 de la Constitución Política de los Estados Unidos Mexicanos." In *Diario Oficial de la Federación*, August 20.

Conaghan, Catherine M. 1991. "Hot Money and Hegemony: Andean Capitalists in the 1980s." Paper presented at the Latin American Studies Association XVI International

Concheiro Bórquez, Elvira. 1996. *El gran acuerdo. Gobierno y empresarios en la modernización salinista.* Mexico City: Editorial Era and UNAM.

Confederación Patronal de la República Mexicana (Coparmex). 1992. *Directorio de socios.* Mexico City: Coparmex.

Congreso de los Estados Unidos Mexicanos. 1936. "Ley de cámaras comerciales e industriales." In *Diario Oficial de la Federación,* August 27.

Congreso de los Estados Unidos Mexicanos. 1941. "Ley de cámaras comerciales e industriales." In *Diario Oficial de la Federación,* August 26.

Congreso de los Estados Unidos Mexicanos. 1992. "Ley de cámaras comerciales e industriales." In *Diario Oficial de la Federación,* February 26.

Congreso de los Estados Unidos Mexicanos. 1996. "Ley de cámaras comerciales e industriales." In *Diario Oficial de la Federación,* December 20.

Consejo Coordinador Empresarial. 1975a. "Declaración de principios." *Excélsior*, México, May 8.

Consejo Coordinador Empresarial. 1975b. "Declaración sobre problemas nacionales." *Excélsior*, México, May 8.

Consejo Coordinador Empresarial. 1975c. "Anteproyecto para crear una imagen adecuada y fidedigna del sector empresarial en México." *Excélsior*, México, May 21.

Dreifuss, René. 1989. *O jogo da direita*. Petrópolis: Vozes.

Durand, Francisco. 1994. *Business and Politics in Peru*. Boulder, Colo.: Westview Press.

Elizondo, Carlos. 1992. "The Making of a New Alliance: The Privatization of the Banks in Mexico." Paper presented at the Latin American Studies Association, XVII International Congress, Los Angeles, September 23-27.

Fernández Aldecua, María José. 1993. *El gremio bursátil y los nuevos empresarios financieros*. Mexico City: Facultad de Ciencias Políticas y Sociales and Instituto de Investigaciones Sociales, UNAM.

Fernández-Vega, Carlos. 1991. "La élite del empresariado mexicano." *Perfil de La Jornada*, April 1 and 2.

García Ugarte, Marta Eugenia. 1993. "El Estado y la iglesia católica: balance y perspectivas." *Revista Mexicana de Sociología*, 55 (2): 225-242.

Garrido, Celso. 1993. *Los grupos privados nacionales en México. Evolución entre 1988 y 1993*. Mexico City: Universidad Autónoma Metropolitana-Azcapotzalco. Unpublished paper, October.

Gaspar Tapia, Gabriel. 1988. "Crisis y politización empresarial en Centro América." Seminario Grupo Empresarios y Estado de Clacso, Buenos Aires, November.

Gómez Tagle, Silvia. 1992. "Balance de las elecciones federales de 1991 en México." *Revista Mexicana de Sociología* 54 (1): 253-288.

González Graf, Jaime, ed. 1989. *Las elecciones de 1988 y la crisis del sistema político.* Mexico City: IMEP and Diana.

Gröte, Jürgen R. 1992. "Small Firms in the European Community: Modes of Production, Governance and Territorial Interest Representation in Italy and Germany." In *Organized Interests and the European Community*, eds. Justin Greenwood, Jürgen R. Gröte, and Karsten Ronit. London: Sage Publications.

Guzmán Valdivia, Isaac. 1960. "El movimiento patronal." *México: cincuenta años de revolución.* Mexico City: Fondo de Cultura Económica.

Hamilton, Nora. 1982. *The Limits of State Autonomy: Post-Revolutionary Mexico.* Princeton, N.J.: Princeton University Press.

Heredia, Blanca. 1990. "Ideas vs Interests. The Mexican Business Community in the 1980s." Conference Paper No. 26. New York: Columbia University.

Heredia, Blanca. 1992. "Profits, Politics, and Size: The Political Transformation of Mexican Business." In *The Right and Democracy in Latin America*, eds. Douglas A. Chalmers, Maria do Carmo Campello de Souza, and Atilio A. Borón. New York: Praeger.

Heredia, Blanca. 1995. "Mexican Business and the State: The Political Economy of a Muddled Transition." In *Business and Democracy in Latin America,* eds. Ernest Bartell and Leigh A. Payne. Pittsburgh: University of Pittsburgh Press.

Hernández, Rogelio. 1988. *Empresarios, banca y estado. El conflicto durante el gobierno de José López Portillo (1976-1982).* Mexico City: UNAM and Miguel Ángel Porrúa.

Jarque, Carlos M., and Luis Tellez K. 1993. *El combate a la inflación.* Mexico City: Grijalbo.

Juárez, Leticia. 1984. "El proyecto económico cardenista y la clase empresarial (1934-1938)." In *Clases dominantes y Estado en México,* eds. Salvador H. Cordero and Ricardo Tirado. Mexico City: Instituto de Investigaciones Sociales, UNAM.

Krauze, Enrique. 1997. *La presidencia imperial.* Mexico City: Tusquets.

Levine, Salomon B. 1984. "Employers Associations in Japan." In *Employers Associations and Industrial Relations,* eds. John P. Windmuller and Alan Gladstone. Oxford: Oxford University Press.

Loaeza, Soledad. 1977. "La política del rumor: México, noviembre-diciembre de 1976." *Foro Internacional* 17 (4).

Loaeza, Soledad. 1992. "The Role of the Right in Political Change in Mexico, 1982-1988." In *The Right and Democracy in Latin America,* eds. Douglas A. Chalmers, Maria do Carmo Campello de Souza, and Atilio A. Borón. New York: Praeger.

López Portillo, José. 1977. *Discursos pronunciados por el licenciado José López Portillo. Primer aniversario 1976-1977.* Mexico City: Talleres Gráficos de la Nación.

Loyo, Aurora, ed. 1997. *Actores sociales y educación: los sentidos del cambio.* Mexico City: Instituto de Investigaciones Sociales, UNAM.

Luna, Matilde. 1992a. *Los empresarios y el cambio político.* Mexico City: Editorial Era.

Luna, Matilde. 1992b. "Las asociaciones empresariales y la apertura externa." XVII International Congress of the Latin American Studies Association, Los Angeles, September 24-27.

Luna, Matilde. 1995. "La acción organizada del sector privado. Los empresarios pequeños." In *Micro y pequeña empresa en México*, eds. Thomas Calvo and Bernardo Méndez. Mexico City: Centro de Estudios Mexicanos y Centroamericanos.

Luna, Matilde, René Millán, and Ricardo Tirado. 1985. "Una nueva voluntad política." *Revista Mexicana de Sociología* 47 (4): 215-260.

Luna, Matilde, Ricardo Tirado, and Francisco Valdés. 1987. "Businessmen and Politics in Mexico, 1982-1986." In *Government and Private Sector in Contemporary Mexico*, eds. Sylvia Maxfield and Ricardo Anzaldúa. San Diego, Calif.: Center for U.S.-Mexican Studies, University of California.

Luna, Matilde, and Ricardo Tirado. 1992. *El Consejo Coordinador Empresarial. Una radiografía.* Mexico City: Instituto de Investigaciones Sociales and Facultad de Ciencias Políticas y Sociales, UNAM.

Luna, Matilde, and Ricardo Tirado. 1993. "Los empresarios en el escenario del cambio. Trayectorias y tendencias de sus estrategias de acción colectiva." *Revista Mexicana de Sociología*, 55 (20): 243-271.

Lustig, Nora. 1992. *Mexico. The Remaking of an Economy.* Washington, D.C.: The Brookings Institution.

Magniadas, Jean. 1991. *Le patronat.* Paris: Messidor, Editions Sociales.

Martínez Nava, Juan Manuel. 1984. *Conflicto estado-empresarios en los gobiernos de Cárdenas, López Mateos y Echeverría.* Mexico City: Editorial Nueva Imagen.

Maxfield, Sylvia, and Anzaldúa, Ricardo, eds. 1987. *Government and Private Sector in Contemporary Mexico.* San Diego, Calif.: Center for U.S.-Mexican Studies, University of California.

Maxfield, Sylvia. 1990: *Governing Capital. International Finance and Mexican Politics.* Ithaca and London: Cornell University Press.

McQuaid, Kim. 1980. "Big Business and Public Policy in the Contemporary United States." *Quarterly Review of Economics and Business* 20 (2).

Medin, Tzvi. 1990. *El sexenio alemanista.* Mexico City: Era.

Meyer, Lorenzo. 1995. *Liberalismo autoritario: las contradicciones del sistema político mexicano.* Mexico City: Océano.

Millán, René. 1988. *Los empresarios ante el estado y la sociedad.* Mexico City: Siglo XXI.

Mizrachi, Yamile. 1994. "Rebels without a Cause? The Politics of Entrepreneurs in Chihuahua." *Journal of Latin American Studies* 26: 137-158.

Monsivais, Carlos. 1979. "La ofensiva ideológica de la derecha." In *México hoy.* Mexico City: Siglo XXI Editores.

"Nuestra tesis tiene 30 años de vigencia." 1975. In *Transformación* 35:138 (May): 29-34.

Nuncio, Abraham. 1982. *El Grupo Monterrey.* Mexico City: Nueva Imagen.

O'Donnell, Guillermo. 1982. *El estado burocrático autoritario: triunfos, derrotas y crisis.* Buenos Aires: Belgrano.

Ortiz Rivera, Alicia. 1988. "Un grupito muy cómodo negoció el pacto." In *Unomásuno*, May 19.

Ortiz Rivera, Alicia. 1997. "Vínculos CMHN-CCE e influencia de ambas instituciones en el sistema político mexicano." Unpublished master's thesis. Mexico City: Instituto de Investigaciones Dr. José María Luis Mora.

Pascual Moncayo, Pablo. 1995. *Las elecciones de 1994.* Mexico City: Cal y Arena.

Pérez Fernández, Germán, Arturo Alvarado, and Arturo Sánchez G., eds. 1995. *La voz de los votos: un análisis crítico de las elecciones de 1994.* Mexico City: Miguel Angel Porrúa and Flacso.

Pozas, María de los Angeles. *Industrial Restructuring in Mexico.* San Diego, Calif.: Center for U.S.-Mexican Studies, University of California.

Puga, Cristina. 1993. "Las organizaciones empresariales mexicanas de comercio exterior." In *Organizaciones empresariales y Tratado de Libre Comercio,* ed. Cristina Puga. Mexico City: Facultad de Ciencias Políticas y Sociales and Instituto de Investigaciones Sociales, UNAM.

Puga, Cristina. 1994a. "Las organizaciones empresariales en la negociación del Tratado de Libre Comercio." In *Los empresarios ante la globalización,* ed. Ricardo Tirado. Mexico City: Instituto de Investigaciones Legislativas and Instituto de Investigaciones Sociales, UNAM.

Puga, Cristina, ed. 1994b. *Organizaciones empresariales mexicanas. Banco de datos.* Mexico City: Facultad de Ciencias Políticas y Sociales and Instituto de Investigaciones Sociales, UNAM.

Purcell, Susan Kaufman. 1975. *The Mexican Profit Sharing Decision: Politics in an Authoritarian Regime.* Berkeley, Calif.: University of California Press.

Purcell, Susan Kaufman, and John Purcell. 1975. "El estado y la empresa privada." *Nueva Política* 1 (2): 229-250.

Riding, Alan. 1985. *Distant Neighbors. A Portrait of the Mexicans.* New York: Alfred A. Knopf.

Rius Abbud, Fernando. 1994. "Un diagnóstico positivo." *Análisis El Financiero,* February 11.

Rogers, Alison, and Marlene McCampbell. 1993. "The Billionaires List." In *Fortune* No. 127 (June 28): 23-52.

Roxborough, Ian. 1991. "La inflación y los pactos sociales en Brasil y México." *Foro Internacional* 32 (2).

Saragoza, Alex. 1988. *The Monterrey Elite and the Mexican State, 1880-1940.* Austin, Texas: University of Texas Press.

Saldívar, Américo. 1981. *Ideología y política del estado mexicano.* Mexico City: Siglo XXI.

Salinas de Gortari, Carlos. 1993. *V Informe de Gobierno.* Mexico City: Presidencia de la República.

Schmitter, Philippe C., and Luca Lanzalaco. 1989. "Regions and the Organization of Business Interests." In *Regionalism, Business Interests and Public Policy,* eds. William D. Coleman and Henry J. Jacek. London: Sage Publications.

Schneider, Ben Ross. 1990. "The Politics of Privatization in Brazil and Mexico: Variations on a Statist Theme." In *The Political Economy of Public Sector Reform and Privatization,* eds. Ezra N. Suleiman and John Waterbury. Boulder, Colo.: Westview Press.

Secretaría de Hacienda y Crédito Público and Secretaría de la Contraloría General de la Federación. 1994. *Desincorporación de entidades paraestatales. Información básica de los procesos del 1 de diciembre de 1988 al 31 de diciembre de 1993.* Mexico City: SHCP, Secogef, and Fondo de Cultura Económica.

Secretaría del Trabajo y Previsión Social. 1992. *Acuerdo nacional para la elevación de la productividad y la calidad.* Mexico City: Secretaría del Trabajo y Previsión Social.

Seneker, Harold, ed. 1993. "The World's Wealthiest People." In *Forbes,* 152 (July 5): 66-111.

Shafer, Robert J. 1973. *Mexican Business Organizations. History and Analysis.* Syracuse, N.Y.: Syracuse University Press.

Sisson, Keith. 1990. *Los empresarios y la negociación colectiva. Un estudio internacional comparado.* Madrid: Ministerio del Trabajo y Seguridad Social.

Solórzano, María del Carmen. 1993. *La Asociación Mexicana de Casas de Bolsa y la reestructuración del sistema financiero mexicano (1980-1992).* Mexico City: Facultad de Ciencias Políticas y Sociales and Instituto de Investigaciones Sociales, UNAM.

Story, Dale. 1990. *Industria, estado y política en México. Los empresarios y el poder.* Mexico City: Grijalbo and Conaculta.

Tello, Carlos. 1979. *La política económica en México, 1970-1976.* Mexico City: Siglo XXI.

Tello, Carlos. 1984. *La nacionalización de la banca.* Mexico City: Siglo XXI.

Tirado, Ricardo. 1990. "La alianza con los empresarios." In *Entre la estabilidad y la guerra. El México de los 40,* ed. Rafael Loyola. Mexico City: Grijalbo and Conaculta.

Tirado, Ricardo. 1992. "El corporativismo empresarial mexicano." In *Relaciones corporativas en un período de transición,* eds. Matilde Luna and Ricardo Pozas. Mexico City: Instituto de Investigaciones Sociales, UNAM.

Tirado, Ricardo, and Matilde Luna. 1986. "La politización de los empresarios." In *Grupos económicos y organizaciones empresariales en México,* ed. Julio Labastida. Mexico City: Alianza Editorial and UNAM.

Tirado, Ricardo, and Matilde Luna. 1995. "El Consejo Coordinador Empresarial de México. De la unidad contra el reformismo a la unidad para el TLC (1975-1993)." *Revista Mexicana de Sociología,* 57 (4): 27-60.

Valdés Ugalde, Francisco. 1997. *Autonomía y legitimidad. Los empresarios, la política y el estado en México.* Mexico City: Siglo XXI and UNAM.

Vellinga, Menno. 1979. *Industrialización, burguesía y clase obrera en México.* Mexico City: Siglo XXI Editores.

Vogel, David. 1983. "The Power of Business in America: A Reappraisal." *British Journal of Political Science* 13 (1): 20.

Wilson, Graham K. 1985. *Business and Politics. A Comparative Introduction.* Chatham, N.J.: Chatham House Publishers.

Zermeño, Sergio. 1982. "De Echeverría a De la Madrid: las clases altas y el Estado mexicano en la lucha por la hegemonía." Woodrow Wilson Center for Scholars, Washington, D.C. Unpublished paper.

CHAPTER EIGHT

Organized Business, Neoliberal Economic Restructuring, and Redemocratization in Chile

EDUARDO SILVA

INTRODUCTION

A ccording to most early theories, Latin American business associations were weak, fragmented, and dependent on the state (Cardoso 1971; Cardoso and Faletto 1978; Schmitter 1971). The verdict of more recent work is divided. Stephan Haggard and Robert Kaufman (1995, 341-342) maintain that organized business in Latin America, by and large, remains frail and fragmented — at least sufficiently so to render dreams of building societal corporatism unrealistic. In contrast, other analysts conclude that although business associations in most Latin American countries may not be developed enough for neocorporatism, they have been getting stronger, developing more unity, and enjoying more independence from the state (Bartell and Payne 1995, 267-270; Malloy and Conaghan 1994, 207-209).

Despite their differences, analysts concur that organized business has developed more in Chile than almost anywhere else in Latin America in terms of political muscle, institutionalization, cohesion, and independence (Haggard and Kaufman 1995, 342; Bartell and Payne 1995, 263-264; Nelson 1994, 177, 181; Pastor and Wise 1996, 7, 16). Some analysts imply that Chile may be a model for other countries to emulate. What factors contributed to this outcome? What impact has organized business had on economic policymaking in Chile, especially with regard to the consolidation of free-market reforms? How has organized business responded to the challenge of democracy in Chile?

As the introduction and other chapters argue, the development of organized business in Chile parallels its development in Nicaragua, El Salvador, the Dominican Republic, Peru, and Argentina. Many Chilean business associations, including the encompassing association, emerged in response to the political success of organized labor, middle classes, and governments bent on economic reform or redistributive policies. However, the greatest spurt toward the modern development of organized business — the one admired by contemporary observers — occurred during the military government (1973-1989). In that setting, the threat was an economic crisis (1981-1983) so severe that it menaced the survival of the private sector as much as the excesses of populism had. The economic crisis razed the financial system (ironically leaving most of it in the hands of the government) and brought down the most important conglomerates; amidst countless bankruptcies, many of the nation's leading firms went into receivership. During this debacle, government technocrats refused to revise economic policies that had contributed to the crisis, and they pointedly excluded business from the policy process.

These circumstances drove business leaders to revive their associations to exert political pressure on the government and to use the encompassing association as a forum to forge a policy consensus. Business leaders endorsed market economics but with a more pragmatic, less orthodox cast than what they had seen implemented by 1979. The resulting policy consensus played a profound role in reequilibrating neoliberalism in Chile. Due to the political conjuncture after the crisis, the military government adopted many of the encompassing association's suggestions for economic recovery. In the process, the military government initiated a style of consultation with business in policy formulation that persists to this day.

The pattern of Chilean business regime loyalties during the economic crisis and its aftermath also supports the theoretical expectations raised in the introductory chapter. By negotiating policy changes with the business coalition, the military government assured upper-class support for continued authoritarianism. The political opposition struck a bargain with business groups when it realized that it could not wean them from the regime. In exchange for a stable transition to democracy within the terms of the authoritarian 1980 Constitution, the opposition promised not to change the economic model. The maintenance of those commitments — and of close consultation with business on many policy issues — has resulted in economic and political stability for Chile. The concluding section of this chapter discusses some broader theoretical implications of the Chilean case.

BUSINESS ASSOCIATION DEVELOPMENT AND PATTERNS OF INFLUENCE

A brief review of the relationship between business associations and the Chilean state helps to place the authoritarian period in perspective. It suggests that whether business elites are proactive or defensive, whether they are engines or obstacles to economic change, whether they are fragmented or cohesive, and whether they are technically sophisticated or not, all depend on larger domestic and international political and economic trends. This section examines the relationship between those contextual elements and the business associations' development, autonomy, strength, cohesiveness, and influence in policymaking from the middle of the nineteenth century to the early 1970s.

Chilean business associations originated in an effort to advance policy initiatives in the context of the elitist, protected democracies of the nineteenth and early twentieth centuries, the night watchman state, and worldwide liberalism.[1] That period spawned four important business peak associations in Chile: the National Agrarian Society (Sociedad Nacional de Agricultura — SNA) in the 1830s, the National Chamber of Commerce (Cámara Central de Comercio (CCC), which later became the Cámara Nacional de Comercio — CNC) in the 1850s, and the National

Mining Society (Sociedad Nacional de Minería — SONAMI) and the Society for Industrial Development (Sociedad de Fomento Fabril — SFF) in the 1880s.

In the context of the primary product export model and the night watchman state, these associations represented the interests of large-scale landowners, merchants, financiers, mine owners and industrialists (Cusack 1972; Arriagada 1970). Although the associations' relationship with the state was not institutionalized and although they were more like social and political clubs than modern, technically sophisticated organizations, they had active policy agendas and significantly influenced policy outcomes (Wright 1982; Véliz 1963). That they achieved their results despite their inchoateness is evident in the large number of presidents and economic ministers who came from their ranks.

This situation changed between the 1930s and the 1960s. The Great Depression and the development of a Chilean labor movement that was politically strong relative to most other Latin American countries had brought a shift in economic development strategy, a change in the state's role in the economy, and a leftward drift in electoral politics (Drake 1978). Beginning in the late 1930s, Chile adopted an import-substitution industrialization (ISI) strategy that moved the country away from laissez-faire and emphasized an increased role of the state in economic planning, regulation, and investment (Ellsworth 1945; Stallings 1978).

How did these changes affect the business associations' relationship with the state? The business associations were weakened. To the extent that the state developed its entrepreneurial and regulatory capacity at the expense of market-driven economic models, the associations became more defensive than proactive. Political elites forged deals with different economic sectors, which kept them from presenting a united front. Government's responses to the interests of middle and lower classes weakened the business associations politically (Drake 1978; Loveman 1979; Muñoz and Arriagada 1977).

The increasing defensiveness and fragmentation of business political action was relative, however. Business associations also felt the need to present a more united front in the face of an increasingly powerful state and more organized lower classes. The threat from below seemed especially acute in the 1930s. At first, business thought it had successfully weathered the storm; between 1931 and 1932, both a labor-sympathizing military government and a Socialist Republic proved short-lived. However, the second administration of President Arturo Alessandri (1932-1938) offered little relief. The private sector witnessed intense leftist agitation and the reconstruction of the labor movement in 1934, when the two major labor unions united in a confederation closely allied to the Socialist Party. The confederation's platform called for radical economic reform based on collective ownership of the means of production and exchange. Meanwhile, peasant discontent erupted in the countryside (Cusack 1972, 68).

The consolidation and confederation of labor unions, their alliances with revolutionary political parties, and rural unrest menaced all business sectors and landowners. This situation provided the needed "fright" to unite. To concentrate the political power of capitalists, in 1935, the business sectors and landowners formed an encompassing association: the Confederation of Production and Commerce (Confederación de la Producción y Comercio — CPC).[2] The CPC quickly entered the political fray in the late 1930s, backing international financier Gustavo Ross's presidential candidacy. This was a direct response to the formation of the Popular Front, in which organized labor had played an important role (Cusack 1972, 68). Nevertheless, as had occurred in early efforts to forge encompassing associations in Peru, Argentina, and the Dominican Republic, once the general threat diminished, so did the significance of the umbrella organization. Only the perception of renewed general threats in the second half of the 1960s revived the CPC.

The Popular Front was not the nemesis businessmen and landowners had feared. Business elites were given many seats on the boards of major state institutions, such as the Central Bank, the State Bank, and the Development Corporation (Corporación de Fomento — CORFO), the planning agency and holding company for parastatal enterprises (Menges 1966, 351; Cavarozzi 1975, 111-135). Business elites also enjoyed a close relationship with the centrist Radical Party, which dominated the Popular Front, and ministers were drawn from the business elites (Cusack 1972, 69; Cavarozzi 1975, 187). This pattern was institutionalized and persisted largely unbroken until the 1960s.

Because business elites gained access to the policy-making process and formed close ties to the dominant Radical Party, business concerns over the threat from below largely disappeared. However, as general threats to socioeconomic elites waned, intersectoral tensions rose, reducing the CPC's political significance (Cusack 1972, 69). The SFF supported trade protection; the CNC opposed protectionist measures, as did export-oriented mine owners; and the SNA resented industrial policy (Mamalakis 1966). Each of the sectoral peak associations used its channels of access to the policy-making process to advance its narrow interests.

These sectoral clashes, however, did not dissolve the encompassing business association, as occurred in the Dominican Republic, Peru, and Argentina (as described in this volume) and as Kenneth Johnson predicts (also in this volume) may be occurring in El Salvador. The CPC's resilience was probably due to its organizational structure and diversification of functions. CPC membership was initially limited to the four national-level sectoral peak associations that represented large-scale business and landowners — the SFF, the SNA, the CCC, and the SONAMI. Membership later expanded to include the Chilean Construction Chamber (Cámara Chilena de la Construcción — CChC) in the 1960s and the financial sector association (Asociación de Bancos e Instituciones Financieras — ABIF) in the 1980s. Equally significant, as Mancur Olson (1965) argues, key participants were few, mainly the presidents and vice presidents of the sectoral organizations. This focused representation differentiated Chile's encompassing business association from other cases in this volume where encompassing associations declined or even collapsed. For example, in the Dominican Republic, regional cleavages exacerbated intersectoral conflict, and the association collapsed. In Mexico, many more organizations participated in the encompassing association than in Chile, and unlike Chile, it also included regional organizations and the organizations of medium and small sector business. This organizational plenty and diversity were a source of debilitating divisiveness in the Mexican encompassing association. In Peru, extreme heterogeneity in organizing criteria swelled numbers and contributed to irrevocable divisions that sank several attempts to form an encompassing business association before 1984.

The allocation of functions among the presidency, the executive committee, and the general assembly of Chile's CPC also helped the association to survive under stresses that destroyed encompassing business associations in other nations. The office of the presidency enjoyed great flexibility. Constant consultation with peak associations was not necessary, although on major policy issues the CPC's presidency was beholden to an executive committee presided over by the presidents and vice presidents of the sectoral associations. The general assembly — a somewhat expanded version of the executive committee — met once a year, just to elect the next president. Thus, in periods of crisis, the relevant decision-making body — the executive committee — was small enough to build consensus for political action (Cusack 1972, 67). Peru's latest attempt to consolidate an encompassing association, more successful than its previous efforts, is (as analyzed by Francisco Durand in this volume) functionally similar.

Equally important, significant symbolic political functions of the CPC's presidency gave the association a reason to exist even when there was no crisis to induce consensus among member associations. The president of the CPC represented business in a wide range of public events, as well as before the president of Chile, before foreign dignitaries, and at prestigious events such as the signing of international treaties (Cusack 1972, 67). Among the cases in this volume, encompassing associations that declined under the stress of intersectoral conflict did not have significant symbolic political functions.

The reformist social and economic policies of the Christian Democratic government of President Eduardo Frei (1964-1970) revived the dormant CPC. The Frei administration "Chileanized" the copper industry, which had been dominated by foreign concerns, thereby substantially expanding the entrepreneurial state. The Frei administration also organized the unorganized poor, increased redistributive policies, and promoted a gradual shift to a more export-oriented economy. It also insulated policymakers from social groups and opposition political parties on the right and left more than previous governments had.

As occurred in many of the cases analyzed in this volume, organized business in Chile developed unity as the government increasingly competed with private enterprise, organized unorganized subordinate social groups, supported redistributional policies, and excluded business from policymaking. Business leaders from diverse economic sectors used the CPC as a forum to develop a common anti-statist ideology and discourse (Cusack 1972, 22-38). The crowning moment of this effort was a massive convention the CPC sponsored for business-people in 1967. In the months leading up to the convention, the executive committee of the CPC carefully put together a few small, tight working groups to craft a discourse and policy platform expressing the common needs and interests of the private sector. These working groups constructed a collective identity based on the concept of "entrepreneur." Their policy platform emphasized general issues, such as reducing state enterprise and regulation, making labor laws more flexible, and reducing arbitrariness in government decisionmaking (Cusack 1972, 22-38).

Organized business efforts to achieve greater unity probably contributed to the rightward shift in policy halfway through the Frei government's term. The discourse and platform developed through the CPC showed the Frei administration that it would face significant opposition from business in the media and from allied conservative political parties in the legislature. As a result, the government had to choose carefully which programs to pursue; setting priorities involved logrolling with organized business and conservative political parties. For example, the SFF flatly told the minister of economy to drop efforts to open the economy to international competition. The SFF indicated that unless the minister complied, it would mobilize conservative political parties to block the Frei administration's efforts to nationalize (with compensation) foreign copper companies.[3]

The private sector's fortunes worsened during President Salvador Allende's socialist government (1970-1973), when the business associations were shut out of the policy-making process. This was also a period in which large-scale industrialists and landowners faced widespread nationalization and expropriation of their property and in which medium-scale and small business felt victimized by the establishment of alternative distribution systems, the Juntas de Abastecimiento Popular (JAPs). This set of events galvanized the business community to action by 1972. Spearheaded by the SFF and the SNA, the CPC drew most other business sectors — including small-scale business — into vehement opposition to Allende's government (Gil, Lagos, and Landsberger 1979; O'Brien 1976; de Vylder 1976). Only the SONAMI, the mine owner's association, abstained.[4] Business mobilization played an important role in provoking the military coup.

This movement had two tracks, one public and one clandestine. The latter involved leaders of key conglomerates and of the SFF. They met on Mondays to plot strategy against the Allende government; hence they called themselves the Monday Club (O'Brien 1983, 34-35). By 1973 they had used the media to whip up substantial opposition to the government, funneled money from outside sources to the movement, forged links to the military, and brought together a team of technocrats to devise an economic program for a post-coup period.

The movement's more public efforts focused on mobilizing business against Allende's government. The initial move was to enlist owners of medium-scale and small businesses to the cause. This venture culminated successfully in December 1971; at a convention titled the Encuentro del Area Privada, the SFF and the CPC launched the Frente Nacional del Area Privada (FRENAP), which issued a call to arms against Allende's government (Stallings 1976, 139). By mid-June 1972, the SFF, the SNA, and the CNC had all developed a more combative stance and strengthened ties to conservative political parties who opposed the government in Congress. From then on, business associations helped organize massive lock-outs and transportation strikes, as well as a clear list of demands, the *Pliego de Chile*. This document, which focused heavily on the sanctity of private property rights, also called for greater participation in policymaking by organized business (Campero 1984, 71-72).

BUSINESS ASSOCIATIONS AND NEOLIBERAL RESTRUCTURING IN AUTHORITARIAN CHILE, 1973-1988

In the liberal phase of world economic and political development, business associations were active in Chile, and the private sector was the engine of economic growth. The failure of economic liberalism that resulted in the Great Depression, the growing importance of the state and planning, deepening democracy, and the rise of political movements that distrusted free markets and capitalists all put business peak associations on the defensive. However, the more the associations were marginalized and menaced in their vital interests of property and profits, the more they united and developed a common free-market discourse.

What was the fate of business peak associations under the "new authoritarianism" of military regimes in economically advanced South American countries in the 1960s and 1970s? Did the regimes' return to free-market economics, or at least renewed emphasis on capitalist development, bring a reassertion of business association activism at a level comparable to its activism in the nineteenth century? The short answer is no. According to most of the literature on the new authoritarianism of the 1960s and 1970s in Latin America, such regimes deliberately kept business associations weak, dependent on the state, and marginalized from economic policymaking (Malloy 1977).[5] More recent works corroborate those conclusions (Malloy and Conaghan 1994; Bartell and Payne 1995). How, then, to account for the current observation of increased proactiveness and unity among business associations?

Some argue that redemocratization awakened business elites from their slumber and opened political space for greater activism on their part (Malloy and Conaghan 1994; Bartell and Payne 1995). While this is undoubtably part of the answer, the Chilean case shows that economic and political crisis under military rule can produce similar reactions (Kaufman 1986). This development reinforces the classical observation that situations that threaten the vital interests of capital under any regime type may lead to more proactive policy stances and to more demands for inclusion in the policy-making process. Moreover, how government negotiates with business during crisis may be what defines the regime loyalties of capitalists.

To develop these observations, this section examines how changes in Chilean political institutions, as well as domestic and international economic shocks, affected business associations' cohesiveness, their relationship to the state, and their effect on authoritarian Chile's economic policy outcomes. For the purpose of exposition, this discussion centers on three distinct economic policy periods that roughly coincide with what Manuel Antonio Garretón has called the four phases of authoritarian regimes — reactive, foundational, crisis, and terminal (Garretón 1989). Although some of Garretón's phases (in particular the second one) include social and political models of transformation, the argument here concentrates on economic adjustment because it is more properly the sphere of business associations.

The Reactive Phase and Gradual Economic Restructuring, 1973-1975

In Garretón's analysis (1989), authoritarian regimes usually begin with a reactive period, one in which most actions are responses to the crisis that precipitated democratic breakdown. The period is an unsettled time in which projects and factions contend for dominance. In Chile, the reactive phase lasted approximately one year and a half, from October 1973 to April 1975. It was characterized by the dismantling of democratic political institutions and the massive repression of labor, leftist, and reformist groups, as well as by gradual adjustment to severe economic imbalances (O'Brien 1983). Economic adjustment policies featured a gradual approach to deflation, cautious tariff reduction in the context of Latin American integration, and financial sector reform and privatization, especially of assets seized by Allende's government (Foxley 1983; Edwards and Cox-Edwards 1987).

During this period, Chilean business peak associations, including the CPC, became much more proactive in defining an economic policy agenda, formulating economic policy, and influencing policy implementation. This proactive role originated with the peak associations' part in the broad coup coalition against Allende before and immediately after the coup in September 1973. It must be stressed that because business associations were part of a larger coup coalition, they were only one of several actors involved.

Business associations' participation in defining an agenda for free-market economic reform and in formulating and implementing it began in March 1973, a few months before the overthrow of Allende in September. It was then that military conspirators approached the Monday Club with a request to design an economic program for post-Allende Chile. A blueprint for economic recovery — *The Brick* (*El Ladrillo*) — was developed in the SFF's research department by economists from the SFF, leading business conglomerates, and the Christian Democratic Party (O'Brien 1983, 39-40; Fontaine 1988, 36-38; Cavallo, Salazar, Sepúlveda 1988, 63-70). The document proposed reestablishing a market economy, reducing state participation in the economy, and stimulating trade (Centro de Estudios Públicos 1992).

The SFF's involvement in the formulation of *The Brick* had three sources. First, the SFF president was a founding member of the Monday Club. Second, prominent businesspeople involved in the Monday Club were the directors of leading Chilean firms with membership in the SFF (E. Silva 1996, 71). Third, the SFF was the only business association sufficiently professionalized to possess a well-developed research department (Cusack 1972, 36-48).

After the coup, organized business did not play a very direct role in formulating policies prescribed by *The Brick*. Nevertheless, the CPC was not irrelevant to the process. The CPC played a key supportive part by ratifying the agenda for economic reform, by forming a strong lobby for gradual economic change both in the halls of power and in the media and by participating in some aspects of policy formulation. Sectoral peak associations also took part in formulating some policies, notably those on privatization and the opening of the economy to trade.

Just as the CPC organized its first convention in 1967 to forge a common discourse and economic program, it rallied business association support for a gradual approach to free-market economic restructuring after the coup in 1973. A month after the coup, CPC President Jorge Fontaine declared, "We are in the process of preparing plans that will be made public soon; we are clear on the requirements for national recovery" (El Campesino 1973a). Those preparations culminated in the second convention of the CPC in December of 1973. The second convention publicized a policy consensus among sectoral peak associations in favor of a gradual approach to the economic reforms outlined in *The Brick*. Not coincidentally, a high-level government economic planning meeting was held during the convention in the same building, the Diego Portales. On the last day of the convention, CPC leaders and the military government's economic team conferred behind closed doors. Following the meeting, the CPC declared itself in full agreement with the government's main policy objectives: a gradual approach to privatization, price deregulation, agile capital markets, devaluation, and tariff reform.[6]

However, not all was harmony among the peak business associations during this period. A conflict over tariff policy between the SFF and the other sectoral organizations illustrates that the CPC also developed a policy dispute settlement role among business associations. The collapse of democracy, the centralization of power in the economic policy-making team, and the pressing task of economic reconstruction signaled a change in the usual avenues sectoral organizations had used to defend their narrower interests. When sectoral peak organizations disagreed with general policy measures, they found that lobbying policymakers no longer worked. Action on general policies required presenting a common front, and the CPC was the vehicle for such activity. Nevertheless, individual sectoral peak associations could still successfully influence the formulation and implementation of sectoral policies over which there were no major disagreements in the executive committee of the CPC.

The SFF's endorsement of gradual trade barrier reduction illustrates the CPC's consensus-building role in the early days of the military government. At first, the SFF, and especially some of its subsectors, preferred retaining high tariffs over even very mild reductions in protection against imports. However, in the context of a military government repressive toward labor, industrialists could not appeal to traditional allies for support against trade opening. (Under democracy, labor groups and their political party allies in the legislature also supported high tariffs.) As a result, heavily protectionist subsectors of the SFF found themselves bereft of customary sources of indirect help, while the rest of the powerful peak associations — the SNA, the CNC, the CChC and the SONAMI — backed gradual tariff reduction.[7] As the lone dissenter in the CPC's executive committee, the SFF was forced to agree to gradual tariff reduction, which then became the CPC's official policy stance.[8] The SFF understood that it would need the full weight of business unity — expressed through the CPC — to negotiate degrees of trade opening with the military government's economic authorities. Moreover, SFF leaders also probably realized that in the interest of establishing political order after the collapse of democracy, a display of unity was prudent tactically.

Initially, the CPC successfully carried out its role as mediator between the government and dissenting sectoral peak organizations. For example, the CPC supplied the private sector's representative to the Advisory Committee for Tariff Policy (Comité Asesor de Política Arancelaria — CAPA), an agency of the Ministry of Finance created in 1974 to formulate tariff reduction policy.[9] In at least one case, the CPC effectively mediated a dispute between the CAPA and the SFF. When the CAPA wanted to reduce tariff levels for the electronics industry deeper and more rapidly than what the industry argued it could bear (Asociación de Industrias Electrónicas 1974; SFF 1974a), the CPC representative was able to get both sides to compromise by splitting the difference (Banco de Chile 1974b).

Sectoral peak associations also enjoyed wide access to policymakers in sectoral ministries at the latter stages of policy formulation and implementation, especially when both sides basically agreed to the policy.[10] For example, in November 1973, the SNA reported that it had met numerous times with the minister of agriculture to discuss deregulation policy for land markets, price freedom for agricultural products, price supports for crops, and liberalization of agricultural imports and exports (El Campesino 1973b). By the same token, the SFF frequently met with the minister of economy on privatization policy for nationalized firms.[11] Similarly the CNC convened with government officials on tax policy (Cámara Nacional de Comercio 1975).[12]

The Foundational Phase and Radical Neoliberal Economic Restructuring, 1975-1982

As the previous section explained, organized business was part of a larger coalition in favor of gradual free-market economic adjustment — one that included the directors of powerful leading firms, medium-scale and small enterprises, and the middle classes, and their political party allies, especially the Christian Democratic Party. Membership in that coalition, not to mention the leading role organized business had played in forging it, granted business associations greater influence over policymaking than they had had in the past decade. However, changes in the authoritarian coalition — especially in the military — coupled with hyperinflation weakened the associations' influence. As General Augusto Pinochet personalized power by consolidating one-man rule, he began to freeze out various elements of the coalition, beginning with medium-scale and small business and the Christian Democrats (Valenzuela 1991, 28-29 and 40-47). Then, in April 1975, Pinochet launched the foundational phase of the military regime and imposed the radical neoliberal economic model. To their dismay, business peak associations soon found they had little if any influence over economic policymaking (Campero 1984, 126-27 and 148-49).

Pinochet's advisors believed that economic change would lead to social transformation and recast Chile on libertarian economic and social principles. In this schema, an unshackled private sector would become the engine of economic growth. To achieve these ends, the radical neoliberal economic model emphasized drastic deflation to curb inflation, rapid and profound cuts in tariffs to encourage world trade, financial liberalization, and the swift privatization of state-owned companies. These privatizations included companies acquired by Unidad Popular as well as public enterprises established before 1970. The policies were radical both in extent and in speed of implementation compared with those in Argentina and Uruguay (Ramos 1986). For the most part, achieving those sweeping goals required the repression of organized groups to force individuals to conform to market logic.

During this period most Chilean business peak associations were not so much repressed or corporatized as simply ignored. The new state actors argued that these organizations got in the way of change because they favored narrow parochial interests over general, aggregate welfare. The economic policy agenda was to reinstate the private sector as the engine of growth. Yet organized business had become accustomed to its fetters — regulation, defending privileges granted by a highly distorted economy, and seeking particularistic favors from politicians in a position to grant them because of the state's role in the economy. The new neoliberal policymakers believed that the only way to break the conditions that condemned Chile to backwardness was to insulate themselves from the pressures of business elites that were, down deep, terrified of freedom (P. Silva 1991; Central Bank 1974a).[13] Neoliberalism was more radical in Chile than in Argentina and Uruguay in the degree to which the authorities ignored economic sectors that had difficulty adjusting (Handelman and Sanders 1981; Smith 1989).

This lack of influence over policy did not include a ban from the halls of power. Government officials routinely received leaders from the CPC and from the sectoral peak associations, although the officials habitually ignored the associations' policy recommendations during those meetings.[14] When policymakers refused to meet them, leaders from organized business sent memos and position papers, and they attempted to secure follow-up appointments. Again, these measures fell on deaf ears.

Most of organized business passively accepted this rejection. The SNA, particularly its southern members, proved to be the exception. These dairy and cattle producers could not convert their lands to producing export-competitive commodities — mainly fruits — as central valley producers were doing. Cereal producers, especially wheat growers, were also hard hit. These landowners mobilized in the South in protest of the government's radical free-market economics. They also prodded the SNA to adopt a more confrontational approach to relations with the military regime than other sectoral peak associations had taken. These efforts, which culminated in 1978, proved unsuccessful and provoked some repression against the regional organizations (Campero 1984, 172-77). These results caused internal conflicts in the SNA as well as the resignation of the SNA's president. The new leadership followed a more conciliatory and collaborative strategy, ignoring the plight of traditional crop landowners (Campero 1984, 200-209).

The military also adopted one state corporatist measure. According to Orlando Sáenz, a former SFF president, the military junta decreed that business associations were no longer free to elect their leaders. This froze the 1973 leadership that had supported the coup in office, and their replacements had to be approved by the junta.[15] This corporatist measure, however, did not deter business associations from attempting to defend their interests in the manner described above. The rule was lifted in 1981, and business associations could once again freely and regularly elect their leaders.

Since the military government excluded business peak associations from economic policymaking, what sources did it draw on to support radical neoliberal economic policies? Most analysts argue that neoliberal policies in Chile were the work of the military and the Chicago Boys, so called because the leading figures had studied neoclassical economics at the University of Chicago under Milton Friedman. In fact, the available evidence suggests that the military regime relied not only on this core of highly ideological economists but also on 1) a handful of powerful and rapidly expanding conglomerates that had the economic wherewithal to adjust to sharp economic change, 2) the support of the international financial community, and 3) heavy repression — all important factors in the formulation and implementation of the neoliberal policies (E. Silva 1993). Moreover, although business peak associations gained little influence over policy, external factors caused them to support the radical neoliberal model fervently, especially after 1978.[16] Ample international liquidity spurred rapid economic growth, largely in the trading and service sectors. Easy and plentiful hard currency credit allowed businesspeople to expand, speculate, or borrow to survive in an atmosphere of plenty. In short, from 1979 to 1981, business peak associations embraced neoliberal rhetoric during a short-lived economic boom with a speculative bubble for its foundation.

After what appeared to be successful economic stabilization, the military regime embarked on the political and social transformations of the foundational phase. Politically, it laid the foundations of an authoritarian or "protected" democracy (Loveman 1991 and 1994). The 1980 Constitution institutionalized the limited pluralism that characterizes authoritarian regimes (Linz 1964). During this same period, 1979-1982, the military regime also decreed sweeping social "modernizations" in pensions, health, education, and the labor code. Libertarian principles modeled on Friedrich von Hayek's philosophy guided all of these reforms. Taken together, these measures in the 1980 Constitution set up political institutions that guaranteed conservative forces the power to entrench the economic and social policies enacted during the radical neoliberal period. Large-scale capitalists were effectively given preponderant market, or private, power in a system in which noneconomic forms of organization were atomized (McConnell 1966; Lindblom 1977).

Crisis and Reequilibration: Business Associations and the Policy Consensus for Pragmatic Neoliberalism, 1982-1988

Between 1982 and 1988, the military regime's foundational aspirations encountered a severe test. Economic depression threatened the free-market economic model, and mass mobilization threatened the political model. Economic collapse and exclusion from the policy process were general threats to the private sector that prompted Chile's business peak associations to abandon their complacent stance and take a strong, proactive role in setting an agenda for economic policymaking. Availing themselves of the CPC's capacity to mediate intersectoral conflict, the sectoral peak associations hammered out an enduring policy consensus. This process culminated in July 1983 with the unveiling of a detailed economic recovery program.

Following that milestone, organized business gained significant influence in economic policymaking as the government began to implement many of its proposals.

These events raise two questions. How did economic crisis contribute to consensus building in organized business that resulted in the drafting of an alternative economic policy package? What conditions brought organized business back into the policy-making process?

External shocks precipitated a qualitative change in the business associations' behavior. The international liquidity crisis of the early 1980s hit the Chilean economy and business sectors hard. Gross domestic product plunged 14 percent, unemployment skyrocketed to approximately a third of the workforce, the financial system collapsed, and many firms were headed for bankruptcy or severe hardship.

The economic crisis, including its international dimensions, clearly signaled that the conditions that had allowed Chilean large-scale capital to survive orthodox free-market economics no longer existed. Beginning in 1982, organized business revived from its slumber over several stages. Initially, at the beginning of 1982, the reaction was timid and scattered; sectoral peak associations peppered ministers with isolated demands for relief.

What turned individual action and partial policy demands into concerted action around an integrated alternative economic policy package? Two factors seem to be the most salient: deepening, seemingly bottomless economic depression and the military government's relatively unswerving commitment to deflation in implementing the radical neoliberal economic model. As the economic crisis deepened during the second half of 1982, business associations still found government indifferent to their policy suggestions; the associations banded together.

A second stage in the political revival of organized business began in the second half of 1982 with the election of a more combative leadership to the CPC and the SFF. This signaled that organized business was willing to employ the CPC's intersectoral bargaining framework to overcome differences. The strategy was for the CPC to advance demands for reflationary policies from which all business sectors could benefit, while sectoral peak associations continued to press for sectoral-specific relief. By using the CPC, business leaders also hoped to show the government that the general interests of business, not just narrow, selfish concerns, were at stake.

In 1982, the economic authorities of the military government rebuffed organized business on nearly every front, offering only a few token changes. This launched the third stage in the political reactivation of organized business. During the first half of 1983, leaders of the sectoral peak associations labored in the CPC's executive committee to prepare a formal economic recovery program, an alternative to the government's laissez-faire orthodoxy.

Without abandoning their commitment to an open market economy, organized business began to hammer out reflationary and sectoral policies. It used the CPC to show the government that business stood united, that business policy demands could not be dismissed as the grumblings of narrow, selfish interests. The CPC concentrated on general policy issues. It argued that the higher inflation that would result from expansive monetary policy designed to stimulate economic recovery was desirable as well as necessary. In lobbying for policies that promoted exports while protecting domestic market producers, the CPC demonstrated that the entire private sector supported such measures. Meanwhile, sectoral peak associations continued to demand sector-specific policies for agriculture, commerce, construction, and finance (E. Silva 1996, 155-66). However, when they approached policymakers, they were accompanied by CPC leaders who had requested the meeting. The CPC leaders made their case for general issues first and went on to stress that sector-specific measures were also required. At that point, sectoral peak association leaders made their pitch.

The government responded to these demands with an emergency plan for economic relief in March 1983. Business leaders judged the plan much too tepid (Campero 1984, 277-278), and organized business swung into action in earnest. In a series of meetings and at least one retreat at the country estate of the CPC president, the leaders of the peak associations developed a consensus on acceptable limits for reflationary measures — such as levels of debt renegotiation, acceptable inflation rates, interest rates, and fiscal deficits. Thus, concrete figures were put to the more general demands of the recent past. Individual peak associations also proposed policies for sectoral recovery, which were then debated to gauge how acceptable they were to other sectors.[17] In the case of serious dispute, the CPC leaders told the peak associations that the CPC would not include the position in final policy documents or lobby for it when negotiating with government officials. Sectoral peak associations would have to lobby on their own. Again, the relatively small number of participants and the uniform national-level character of interest representation facilitated consensus building.

The SFF put the CPC's mechanism for dispute settlement to the test in a renewed conflict over levels of protection for industry. The SFF wanted the CPC to include a demand for differentiated tariffs in its proposals (SFF 1982). All other sectors preferred flat rate tariffs, although at slightly higher rates than the 10 percent in effect at the time. The SFF insisted differential tariffs were vital to the sector's recovery; the other sectoral associations were equally adamant in their opposition.[18] Given this lineup, the president of the CPC delivered an ultimatum: either the SFF dropped its demands or it would be banned from drafting the economic recovery program.[19] Faced with the prospect of being left out in the cold under circumstances where the only hope for policy change lay in united action, the SFF desisted.

In July 1983, the CPC publicly launched a formal program for economic recovery with the widespread distribution of a document titled *Recuperación económica: análisis y proposiciones* (CPC 1983).[20] In it, the CPC proposed that the government reschedule 100 percent of private sector debt at lower than market interest rates (5 percent above inflation); that it bring market interest rates more closely in line with international interest rates; and that it maintain a 4 percent deficit in fiscal spending and tolerate a 30 percent annual inflation rate. The document also petitioned the government for a commitment to high real foreign exchange rates and for public works and housing programs — as well as for export incentives in the form of drawbacks and for tax reform to stimulate investment and raise stock prices (CPC 1983).

How did the military government respond to the united business community's aggressive lobbying on behalf of its economic recovery program between early 1983 and mid-1983? It essentially ignored them until sometime between September 1983 and April 1984. This suggests that the conditions that forced business cohesion — an economic crisis that threatened vital interests and a government reluctant to give up the reigning economic orthodoxy — are not necessarily sufficient to increase business associations' role in economic policymaking.

What induced the military government to negotiate economic policy with business? The military government took its foundational mission seriously, and the massive monthly protest movements that erupted in May 1983 put the project for political transformation embodied in the 1980 Constitution in jeopardy. Initially, the main problem was not so much the demonstrations against Pinochet; they could be repressed. The difficulty was that right-wing political parties and even some business groups threatened to join the main center-left political coalition.[21] The regime realized that it had to recapture the loyalty of its core social and political support groups if it wanted to survive. As part of the strategy to accomplish that goal, it began to adopt policy measures that the pragmatic coalition advocated.

Between October 1983 and early 1985, the military government adopted many of the CPC's policy prescriptions for economic recovery. For example, the fiscal deficit was just under 4 percent in 1983 and rose to nearly 5 percent in 1984. Real short-term interest rates (30-90 days) declined from an average of 35 percent in 1982 to 16 percent in 1983 and 11 percent in 1984 (SFF 1985). The government also instituted a high real foreign exchange rate policy (Arellano 1988). Moreover, the authorities decreed a tax reform in January 1984 that in many respects came very close to the petitions of the CPC and individual peak associations. To stimulate investment, it reduced personal income taxes — and decreased some corporate taxes, eliminated others, and gave tax credits on retained profits (Marfán 1984). Inflation, however, often remained closer to the government's preferences than to those of the private sector: 23 percent for 1983 and 1984 (Arellano 1988, 76). The government made further concessions. Notably, in May 1984, it instituted a new plan for internal debt rescheduling that was more consistent with CPC demands (Arellano and Marfán 1986, 86; Arellano 1984, 10-12).

Equally significant was the military government's initiation of sectoral policies very much in line with demands made in *Recuperación económica*. In August 1984, the Ministry of Urban Affairs and Public Housing began a triennial housing and public works program. Meanwhile, industry got a promise from the government that it would develop a drawback policy. The debate over drawback policy focused on the devolution of significant value-added taxes to exporting firms and the reimbursement of customs tariffs on the imported components of export manufacturers.[22] In March 1983, the SFF had exulted when tariffs rose from 10 percent to 20 percent across-the-board. Then, in August 1983, officials slapped a 15 percent tariff surcharge on a long list of products.[23]

The government also implemented additional sectoral policies proposed by individual peak associations on the basis of the position papers they had drafted for *Recuperación económica*. This was only after the CPC had transformed the sectoral policies into an integrated three-year program — the triennial programs. The effort was led by Modesto Collados, president of the construction chamber, who headed a working commission the CPC sponsored for that purpose between 1983 and 1984 (*El Campesino* 1984c; SFF 1984b; Cámara Nacional de Comercio 1984). Policy concessions followed the creation of the triennial programs. For example, several of the SNA's key demands were met when many traditional agricultural products received reference prices (ceilings and floors), tax surcharges on imports, and low interest rates.[24] Commerce obtained special loans for working capital that had been demanded by the CNC (Cámara Nacional de Comercio 1983a). And the financial sector may have secured as much as $7 billion in various forms of aid between 1982 and 1985 (Rozas and Marín 1989; Arellano 1984).

By the end of 1984, the military government had implemented most of the CPC's general policy prescriptions for economic recovery and many of the sectoral peak associations' more specific demands. As a result, after 1984, organized business largely concentrated on preserving those achievements. Real wages remained low, interest rates continued to decline, and high exchange rates prevailed.

This meant that for the period between 1985 and 1988 (the remaining years of the military government), only two major issues remained pending for organized business. Industry (the SFF) wanted laws to promote nontraditional exports, and all business sectors — spearheaded by the CPC — supported the privatization of state-owned or state-controlled assets. The government obliged on both counts (SFF 1984a; Ministerio de Economía, Fomento y Reconstrucción and ASEXMA 1988).

A significant shift in business-state relations accompanied all of these policy changes, a demonstration that the military government had adopted another one of organized business's demand: better and more institutionalized access to the policy-making process.[25] Policies were not just demanded by the private sector and then accepted or implemented by the government (or imposed by government as had been the case in the past). Instead, policies were negotiated collaboratively between government and organized business. In this way, the dictatorship recaptured the undivided loyalty of business elites. Moreover, this arrangement significantly improved the professionalization of business organizations because they had to develop their research departments.

Increased access to and influence over the policy-making process rested primarily on a shift in the background of key economic ministers. In stark contrast to the earlier technocratic Chicago Boys, beginning in early 1984, most economic ministers were leaders of organized business, many of whom had helped draft *Recuperación económica*. For example, Collados, who headed the Ministry of Economy from 1984 to 1985, had been president of the Construction Chamber when he was appointed; Juan Délano, who headed the ministry from 1985 to 1987, was president of the Chamber of Commerce when he was appointed. Both Collados and Délano had been actively involved in formulating the CPC's economic recovery program. Implementation of the Triennial Plan, for which Collados had headed the CPC working group, was a condition of his accepting the government post.[26] The ministries in agriculture and mining were also headed by the former presidents or vice presidents of their sectors' associations, the SNA and the SONAMI. By the same token, ministers not from organized business were much more open to negotiation than their predecessors were. This was the case at the Ministry of

Finance, which stood at the apex of the ministerial hierarchy; Finance Minister Hernán Büchi (1985-1989) was the most prominent example.

These ministers closely collaborated with the CPC and sectoral peak associations to formulate and implement economic recovery policies based on the prescriptions of *Recuperación económica*. Also, the ministers proposed sectoral policies from the Triennial Plan and other policies advanced by the sectoral. In this system, the CPC leadership met frequently with ministers (and with President Pinochet) over such general policy issues as interest rates, and monetary policy.[27] The CPC leadership lobbied mi... sectoral policies that had received consensus among the peak assoc... ssociation leaders and technical departments then lobbied their sec... s, meeting not only with ministers but also with technical staff of the ministries' production boards. Another sign of new proactiveness in policy formulation was that the sectoral peak associations frequently arrived with draft legislation in hand to begin negotiations with government officials.

The policy-making process described above even received a measure of institutionalization under Minister of Economy Juan Délano (July 1985-July 1987). To handle the negotiation of sectoral policy, Délano created two national commissions, one for external and one for internal commerce. Subcommissions handled specific sectoral policy proposals.

The system of collaboration that emerged after 1983 stimulated an important change in many of the sectoral peak associations. They had to negotiate with the government on technical criteria rather than rely on personal favors, clientelism, or political threats. As a result, they had to develop their research departments. The formulation of policy on drawbacks, on housing and construction, and on price floors for agriculture and mining illustrates this change. In each of these instances, leaders of the sectoral association met with the sector's minister to secure approval of the policy. After that, the ministry's and the association's technical staffs worked out the details.

The policy process for legislation to promote nontraditional exports offers a good example of the collaboration between state and organized business, in which both the CPC and the sectoral peak associations took a more proactive role. The associations focused on drawback legislation (*reintegros*) during 1985 and 1986. Both the CPC and the SFF participated in the policy process. The CPC's role was mainly to keep drawback legislation on the policy agenda. To this end, the CPC had lobbied the minister of economy in 1984 to convince him of the need for drawback legislation. CPC participation at this stage persuaded government officials that the SFF's interest in drawbacks was more than a narrow, sectoral concern — that it had the backing of the entire private sector and was thus a legitimate claim.[28] Without the CPC's presence to show consensus, the minister might have dropped the issue from the policy agenda.

The SFF took over in the policy formulation stage. By then the National Commissions had been created, along with a Subcommission for Drawback Legislation in the National Commission for External Commerce. First, the commission chair and top bureaucrats met with SFF leaders to discuss broad issues; the SFF had already prepared draft legislation for these meetings (SFF 1984c). Second, after the parameters of the policy were negotiated, the technical departments of the Subcommission and the SFF hammered out the details.[29] This was also the process for the Ministry of Economy and of ministries responsible for sectoral policy on housing projects for construction, price floors for agriculture and mining, and commercial tax reform.[30]

It must be stressed that this system of interaction between the military government and the private sector was one of collaboration. Neither side "dominated" the other. Policy did not reflect the maximum positions of either party; it was usually a compromise between the two. Thus, the interpretations of business influence in economic policymaking during the period should focus more on the significance of negotiated partial gains, especially in light of the past, rather than conclude that their effect was negligible because the government did not immediately adopt an entire program and even rejected some demands.[31] For business to be judged influential only if a government quickly surrenders unconditionally to its demands seems an unrealistic yardstick.

Organized Business and Chile's Transition to Democracy, 1983-1988

As other cases in this volume illustrate, the Chilean case confirms contemporary arguments that businesspeople have no "natural" affinity for either democracy or military government. In large part, their regime loyalties depend on economic stability and the protection of vital interests (property rights and profits), both of which are key ingredients for maintaining a good business climate. The support businesspeople show for dictatorship or democracy also hinges on their access to the policy-making process, especially in hard times. In practically every other case (the Dominican Republic, Argentina, El Salvador, Brazil, Peru, and Nicaragua), lack of access to policymaking during either political or economic crisis, or during both, induced organized business to support democratization. Business associations were frequently joined by business leaders from prominent firms, as in Brazil (Cardoso 1986; Payne 1994). Business leaders' calls for democratization were often explicitly based on the belief that democracy would facilitate the political participation of business in policymaking.

In the other cases, organized business was the principal public vehicle that capital used to voice its support for democratization. Business participation in the process of political change legitimized the struggles of political parties, middle-class professional groups, students, and organized labor. Calls for democracy from organized business also implied that many of the deep conflicts of the private sector with subordinate social groups and their political allies that had contributed to the breakdown of democracy could be overcome. Democracy in Latin America was perhaps ready for free-market economics unfettered by strong redistributionist currents.

The Chilean case demonstrates that when the reverse holds true — when dictatorships meaningfully include business, and especially organized business, in the policy-making process — dictatorships can recapture the undivided loyalties of business. The Chilean case also supports hypotheses that the regime loyalties of businesspeople are strengthened further when their prescriptions find their way into policy — and that these loyalties are further strengthened when economic stability, and later growth, are restored. In Chile during the last years of Pinochet's rule, this meant strong support for the dictatorship.

The Mexican case further corroborates the utility of these variables — degree of access to the policy-making process, as well as some favorable policy outcomes — to explain the regime loyalties of businesspeople. Ricardo Tirado (in this volume) shows that when significant segments of Mexican business were excluded from the policy process and when faced with hostile policies, they supported political liberalization, if not democratization. This happened under President Echeverría and President López Portillo. Once the presidency began to include business in policymaking and reversed the populist stances under de la Madrid and Salinas, business backing for political liberalization was more equivocal.

Organized business support for continued authoritarianism in Chile was highly public and nearly unanimous. According to the 1980 Constitution, the military government had to hold a plebiscite no later than 1988 to determine whether Pinochet should continue as president of the nation. If the "yes" votes won, Pinochet would remain, and congressional elections would be held. If the "no" votes won, general elections for the presidency and for Congress would follow. Within organized business, the SFF was the first to back authoritarianism publicly. Protecting the pragmatic free-market economic model business and government had constructed beginning in 1984 was clearly the SFF's major objective. Throughout 1986, the SFF forcefully argued that major alterations to this model that had brought sustained economic recovery since 1984 would spell disaster.[32] The SFF was especially adamant with regard to the sanctity of private property rights.

The rest of organized business joined the SFF to support Pinochet between 1987 and October 1988, the date of the plebiscite. The SNA (landowners) and the CNC (commerce) were the most vocal in declaring their allegiance to Pinochet (*El Campesino* 1987a and 1987b; Cámara Nacional de Comercio 1988). In 1987, these associations helped organize the *comités cívicos*, a broad citizen campaign for Pinochet's presidency (Campero 1991, 146-49). Finally, the CPC publicly announced its backing for Pinochet at the beginning of 1988 (*El Campesino* 1988a and 1988b). Pinochet lost the plebiscite, and general elections were scheduled for December 1989. Organized business then strongly supported the presidential candidate of a coalition of conservative political parties. The candidate was former finance minister Hernán Büchi. He was considered the architect of Chile's economic recovery, whose success, in no small measure, was believed to rest on his willingness to include organized business in the policy process. He, too, lost the election.

Chilean business leaders accepted these electoral defeats by a center-left coalition of political parties — the Concertation of Parties for Democracy (Concertación de Partidos por la Democracia) — with equanimity. To be sure, the Concertación's victory in the presidential election introduced a higher degree of uncertainty for business. But it by no means implied significant changes in the economic model or the system of interaction between business and the state. The Concertación had repeatedly declared its commitment to the free-market economic model and its willingness to work with business. Moreover, a number of authoritarian enclaves in the 1980 Constitution provided conservatives near iron-clad veto powers against serious transgressions to that model. Thus, the strong allegiance of business to Pinochet in the plebiscite was probably because his rule offered the most *certainty* for continuing the economic policies of the late 1980s — including the system of collaboration between government and business and the lack of emphasis on redistribution. Those policies had spurred an unbroken record of rapid economic growth based on increased savings and investment in production. Büchi's candidacy was only a close second best, but given the Concertación's orientation and the protection of the Constitution, rejection of democracy was not warranted. It simply did not present serious threats to business.

Why was the victorious center-left coalition not a greater threat to business? The unity of business support for Pinochet and for the successful pragmatic neoliberal economic model, which organized business had helped forge and implement, moderated opposition to the dictatorship in two ways. First, between 1983 and 1984, that business support robbed the early opposition movement, led by the Democratic Alliance (Alianza Democrática — AD), of major capitalist and landowning allies, and it strengthened the military government's core social base. This gave the regime the fortitude to resist opposition demands for a more rapid transition to full political democracy. Pinochet and his supporters could bide their time and insist on a political transition within the institutional confines of the 1980 Constitution: a plebiscite in 1989 with Pinochet virtually assured of his candidacy; full elections in 1990 or 1997, depending on the outcome of the plebiscite; electoral laws designed without opposition participation (with all the consequent opportunity for gerrymandering); and application of the pragmatic neoliberal model without concern for social equity.

Second, the nearly unanimous allegiance of business to Pinochet and to the pragmatic free-market economic model between 1986 and 1988 induced the opposition to shy away from its earlier, more confrontational tactics and to moderate further its economic program.[33] The Concertación explicitly emphasized that it accepted the pragmatic neoliberal economic model, insisting that market logic would drive its approach to distributional issues. The Concertación further demonstrated its commitment to moderation by stressing social and political reconciliation in a deeply divided and traumatized polity, rather than pushing revenge for the abuses of 16 years of arbitrary rule (Latin American Studies Association 1989). In other words, the democratic opposition yielded its goal of broad economic reform in exchange for advancing political democratization. At the core of the implicit pact between the Concertación and the business coalition stood the decision of the reformist political parties — representing the middle class and some labor sectors — to commit themselves explicitly to pragmatic neoliberalism. In return, businesspeople, landowners, and conservative political parties accepted limited political change.

These concessions helped assure a smooth political transition as stipulated by the 1980 Constitution. By agreeing that pragmatic neoliberalism was no longer under debate, the opposition minimized the risk that the transition process might be reversed.[34] In 1988, this allowed the opposition to press for a clean election, to assure recognition for its victory and to set the stage for negotiated constitutional change with conservative political parties after the plebiscite.

Of course, an important intervening variable in this whole process was the taming or "renovation" of most of the radical left. From the early 1980s to 1988, growing numbers on the left, particularly in the Socialist Party, became much more social democratic (in a contemporary European sense). They joined Alianza Democrática, committed themselves to its platform, and pledged to abide by the terms of Chile's conservative transition from above.

This fact gave Chile's businesspeople more confidence that no matter who won the plebiscite, the economic model would not be dismantled. With no significant threat from below on the horizon, collaboration between business and the erstwhile opposition in a future government was possible. Harshly worded business declarations about the chaos of a "leftist" Concertación administration's legacy were belied by record levels of investment and a stable foreign exchange rate.[35]

ORGANIZED BUSINESS IN CHILE'S NEW DEMOCRACY

The Concertación kept its promise to retain the general macroeconomic policy guidelines of pragmatic neoliberalism. Moreover, establishing a climate of mutual trust between the new administration and the business community was one of its highest priorities. To that end, the Concertación began close consultation with organized business in moderate economic policy and social reform. The practice was dubbed "consensus politics." The maintenance of this style of collaboration between business and the state in Chile has indeed contributed to sustained rapid economic growth and political stability.[36] However, what is less clear is whether questions of social equity and deepening democratization receive their due under consensus politics (E. Silva 1996).

Beginning with the administration of Patricio Aylwin, and continuing into that of Eduardo Frei, there can be little doubt that the policy consensus hammered out by the CPC in 1983 has held together. In policy debates, the CPC — and key sectoral peak associations, such as the SFF and the SNA — insist on maintaining the flexible, pragmatic free-market economic model developed between 1984 and 1989. The CPC and the sectoral peak associations are quick to denounce deviations from the status quo of 1988 (Confederación de la Producción y Comercio 1991).

Two factors reinforce the unity of organized business. First, its policy prescriptions had enjoyed considerable success, as measured by high investment rates and rapid economic growth between 1986 and 1989. Second, business leaders were convinced that in democracy their associations must play a highly visible watchdog role in defense of the economic policies of that era. Thus, it was incumbent on the CPC to express unity of purpose where any policy of general interest was concerned. Of course, on specific sectoral policies, each peak association was free to follow its own path.

Organized business has been relatively successful in defending the interests of Chilean businesspeople and landowners under democracy. Two factors explain its increasing influence in policymaking.

One factor is the leverage that organized business gains through the mechanisms of consensus politics. The extensive system of consultation between business peak associations and key economic ministries ensures that the business point of view is represented in proposed bills and decrees. Organized business has used the mechanisms extensively whenever Concertación administrations have sought to change economic and social policies established during the military government. As usual, general policy issues were the purview of the CPC, and sectoral matters were handled by the respective peak association. CPC presidents and top leaders of several sectoral peak associations (the SFF, the SNA, and the CNC) all agreed that they enjoyed excellent access to policymakers in the executive branch. Moreover, they concurred that the interaction was more than symbolic. Business leaders found that government officials were reasonable and that they often incorporated the views of organized business in their decisions, although, of course, business associations did not always get 100 percent of what they wanted.[37]

The other factor that explains organized business's influence in policymaking is the 1980 Constitution's authoritarian enclaves. The charter abounds with features designed to protect conservative interests from reformists. Since it is still the law of the land, the structure of current political institutions is not fully democratic, which leaves reformist Christian and Social Democrats at a disadvantage. To begin with, the staunchly conservative military has significant autonomy from civilian control. As a result, civilian governments must continuously gauge the armed forces' reaction to public policies. Moreover, conservatives have a majority in the Senate because nine of its seats are appointed. The first appointments were made by Pinochet himself. By the same token, the selection rules for future "designated" senators heavily favor conservative appointees (Loveman 1991). Since the Senate has veto power over all legislation, control of the Senate by conservatives forces Concertación administrations to compromise. As a result, bills are often substantially watered down or simply placed on terminal hold.

Two key policy issues during the Aylwin administration (1990-1994) — labor code reform and tax reform — provide good examples of how the politics of collaboration and the Constitution's authoritarian enclaves together strengthened the effectiveness of organized business's participation in the policy process. With respect to labor code reform, the Aylwin administration favored tying wage policy raises to productivity gains (Larraín 1991). In theory, this approach satisfied organized business's demands for wage restraint to control inflation — without wholly abandoning the government's pledge to address long-postponed labor grievances. Achieving that goal required legislation to strengthen unions, a key labor movement demand.

The government proposed a bill that reformed three key aspects of the old labor code. First, the administration's proposals sought to make it more difficult and expensive to fire workers. Under the old code, employers could let workers go without showing cause and could hire replacements for strikers. Second, the Aylwin-backed bill permitted unions to negotiate contracts by economic sector rather than on a company-by-company basis. Unions could thus negotiate health benefits and job security clauses more easily. Third, the draft legislation mandated that non-union employees would have to pay union dues if they benefited from contracts negotiated by unions. This stopped short of the key Central Única de Trabajadores' demand of mandatory union enrollment (*Business Latin America* 1990c).

The CPC and such conservative political parties as Renovación Nacional consistently opposed all of these labor measures. First, the CPC and some sectoral peak associations voiced their objections directly in negotiations with the Ministry of Labor (the lead agency) and other relevant ministries, such as the Secretaría General de la Presidencia.[38] These negotiations proceeded point and counterpoint on the basis of technical studies prepared by the research departments of the government agencies and the business organizations. Second, the appointed seats in the Senate gave conservative forces a majority, which forced the administration to negotiate the labor reform bill point by point with Renovación Nacional.[39] As a result of the twin features of consensus politics and authoritarian institutions in Chilean democracy, the legislation bogged down (*Business Latin America* 1990b). Reforms that addressed the bare minimum of labor's agenda were gutted, and with them went labor's capacity to capture and retain wage increases on the basis of increased productivity.

The authoritarian enclaves and the consensus policy-making style also protected business interests in tax reform. The Concertación's concern over social inequality in Chile committed Alywin's administration to improving education and health services, providing loans and technical assistance to start small businesses, expanding nutritional programs for infants and pregnant women, and introducing consumption programs for the indigent (Larraín 1991).

Delivering on these campaign promises required higher levels of government spending, so the Aylwin government introduced legislation to increase taxes on business. Although the tax reform bill passed, its limits (between 10 percent to 15 percent of earnings) were lower than what the administration initially proposed. These lower levels were more acceptable to organized business because they were "pacted" between the CPC (under Manuel Feliú), the principal conservative political party (Renovación Nacional) that controlled the Senate, and the government (Boylan 1996). Clauses that tied tax revenue from these sources to specific social policies also made the bill more acceptable to the CPC.[40] However, the CPC could not block a provision that abolished levies on estimated income for the agriculture, mining, and transportation sectors and replaced them with taxes on actual earnings. The government gained additional revenue by raising the regressive value-added tax from 16 percent to 18 percent — and managed to transfer resources cut from the military's budget into those new social and economic programs.

These policy debates have been revisited during the second Concertación administration of Eduardo Frei, Jr. (1994 to present), with much the same results. The tax increase, which had a sunset clause, was extended (Weyland 1997, 43-44). Only the SFF openly opposed the increase. The other members of the CPC were once again relatively indifferent; the tax did not really affect their operating capacities. The Frei administration has also introduced a new labor code reform bill in an effort to mollify organized labor, a member of the Concertación's electoral coalition. This bill reintroduced some measures defeated under the Aylwin administration. As before, business peak associations, with the SFF as their most vociferous representative, have rallied against them, especially where industry-wide and sector-wide collective bargaining were concerned. Organized business also closed ranks to oppose the abolition of employers' rights to hire permanent replacements during strikes. The bill remains stalled in congressional committees, where it has already been watered down substantially.

In an overt move to maintain a sense of collaboration with organized business, the Frei administration twice convoked a National Production Forum, in 1994 and 1996, and later institutionalized the collaboration by forming a permanent commission. The principal interlocutors were the Ministry of Economy and the CPC and its member organizations, although in the second forum, organized labor also participated in a subordinate role. The forum themes included technology, taxation, exchange rates, regional economic integration, labor, and education among other issues. Under the auspices of the Ministry of Economy and the CPC, the National Production Forum has established long-term working commissions of government and business specialists to fine-tune policy changes with a view toward enabling business to perform more efficiently.[41] As in the two organizing forums, the operating mechanism is one in which the leaders of the CPC and the sectoral associations meet with government officials to define an agenda for action, after which the research departments of the sectoral peak associations and the relevant government agency hammer out the details of the policy based on technical criteria.

Not all has been smooth during the Frei administration. Early expectations on the part of organized business to develop an extremely close and agreeable relationship with the government were strained in 1995, when, contrary to promises made in the first year of the Frei administration, the Central Bank began to revalue the dollar. Under the stronger peso, most of organized business — with the exception of the financial sector (now recuperated from its collapse in the mid-1980s), importers, and the construction sector — has clamored for a weaker exchange rate. Whether the policy consensus of organized business unravels over revaluation remains to be seen.

However, close and amicable collaboration between the government and organized business in the negotiations over regional integration has stilled undercurrents of tension over the stronger peso. The Chancellory has made every effort to include delegations of business leaders in the policy-making process, and the CPC and its member organizations have praised the administration for that. In short, in neither the Aylwin nor the Frei administration has the consensual policy-making style — established to fine-tune policy reform in the interests of greater productivity and efficiency — resulted in a united, organized business community's obtaining all it wants. Nevertheless, by all accounts, the general relationship between organized business and government is positive, with each side gaining trust and confidence in the other, although not without occasionally testing the limits of each other's patience and endurance.[42]

CONCLUSIONS

Chile's history, especially from 1982 to the present, suggests that severe economic crisis followed by democratization in the context of economic success can transform organized business from an obstacle to economic development into a force for economic development. Economic crisis in the context of a closed authoritarian regime with highly centralized power forged a lasting policy consensus among the leaders of organized business. That consensus started an enduring system of collaboration between organized business and the government. Redemocratization and economic growth have, despite the emergence of some intersectoral tensions, reinforced the unity of organized business in the interest of defending past gains against the claims of other social groups.

In newly democratic Chile, consensus policymaking has granted organized business significant influence in policy formulation and implementation. It helps that both government officials and business leaders are committed to building a market economy, and that both have the technical capacity to participate in policy design. In this system, the CPC — the encompassing association of business — was key to fruitful interaction with the government. On issues that affected the entire business community, the CPC was a filter that permitted disagreement within organized business only on the most central points of the policy agenda. The CPC's filtering kept the organization's dispute resolution mechanism from getting overloaded and thus facilitated consensus building within organized business. On sector-specific issues, individual peak associations were free to negotiate with government policymakers.

Successive Concertación governments have refined several features in the system of interaction between business and the state. Without a doubt, the executive sets the policy agenda for incremental changes. But after that, organized business participates proactively in policy formulation. Ministers and other top bureaucrats and key consultants meet with representatives of organized business, including the CPC when general issues are at stake, and negotiate broad areas of agreement. Following that, policy formulation is turned over to the technical commissions of the relevant government agencies and the sectoral associations most affected by proposed policy. Negotiations between policymakers and individual business leaders are then carried out on the basis of the studies developed by the technical commissions. According to business leaders, exchanging information on the basis of technical criteria greatly facilitates negotiation.[43]

This system of consensus politics has built confidence within the Chilean business community that the Concertación intends to keep its promise to adhere to the main tenets of free-market economics. The system also demonstrates that businesspeople do not have to be ministers of state to achieve fruitful private-sector participation in the policy-making process. Flexibility and a commitment to market economics seem to be the key.

The system of interaction between business and the state also brings Chile very close to having a system of neocorporatist interest intermediation, as pointed out by Haggard and Kaufman (1995, 342). The organizational development is partially there. On the one hand, Chile has a consolidated encompassing business association and strong sectoral peak associations. These have well-equipped and competently staffed research departments. They also participate regularly in policy deliberations at ministries and government agencies, as well as in the more formalized aspects of policy formulation discussed above. On the other hand, the labor component of the tripartite negotiations characteristic of neocorporatism is seriously underrepresented. Although labor union delegates participate in most forums, they are occasionally excluded. More serious is the problem that organized labor is clearly politically subordinate to organized business. This stems from its numerical weakness, from the lack of strong support for labor in the dominant parties of the Concertación, and from the ability of conservatives to thwart labor's interests decisively in the Senate. As a result, organized labor does not have effective representation.

This truncated, quasi-neocorporatist interest intermediation raises further issues. What is the significance of organized business unity and economic policy proactiveness for the problem of democratic consolidation. What are their implications for the question of democracy and for whom?

Historically, business elites often have been considered obstacles to democratic stability. Intersectoral conflict has contributed to economic stagnation, and redistributive struggles in the midst of economic crises have incited capitalists to knock on the doors of the barracks (O'Donnell 1973). Given that interpretation of the past, optimistic observers view business unity around successful neoliberal socioeconomic policies as a hopeful sign for the consolidation of democracy, other things remaining equal. The absence of significant, debilitating dissension within the ranks of the private sector facilitates the implementation of growth-enhancing free-market economic reforms. The political weakness of social groups seeking to reform orthodox, free-market economic restructuring further enhances the prospects for consolidating democracy and neoliberal economics.

This perspective assumes that political and economic consolidation hinge on libertarian definitions of individual freedom and market efficiency and on avoiding serious consideration of the social impact of market power. Analysts with these assumptions worry that significant dissension over economic policy in the private sector might jeopardize the consolidation of fragile democracies and economic reform projects. Dissension might offer subordinate social groups seeking policy alternatives powerful business allies — perhaps enough support to push through significant reforms to neoliberal orthodoxy. These analysts fear a renewal of the "scourge of populism," with its unhappy association with economic and political instability, or, at the very least, delays and vacillation in implementing free-market reforms. They could arguably point to the fates of the Dominican Republic and Brazil (analyzed in this volume) as partial confirmation of their concerns.

Underlying this interpretation is the old — and correct — hypothesis that business elites support democracy if they are not threatened in their property and profits. But the interpretation pays little attention to the problem of the threshold at which a "threat" becomes an issue for mobilization, when mobilization is followed by destabilization and when destabilization ends in calls for coups. Consequently, analysts who view business unity and opposition weakness as cornerstones of democratic and economic consolidation view all reform with suspicion.

This is unfortunate, for the democracies that business elites support often require reforms to become full democracies; they have many "authoritarian en- claves" that protect their privileged relationship to the state — or at least keep opponents at bay. This was made very clear in Chile, where the leaders of organized business have consistently and adamantly opposed amendments to the restrictive Constitution of 1980. This opposition amounts to an admission that their democratic vocation remains confined to support for a protected or tutelary democracy. These conditions make it very difficult for subordinate social groups to press for needed political and economic reform that might make capitalists uneasy.[44]

Herein lies the irony of Chile's enviable successes. Close collaboration between the private and public sectors appears to be an important intervening variable for the achievement of economic and political stability. For business elites, such a relationship provides more security than do unwritten (or even constitu- tional) guarantees about property rights. Government policymakers, in turn, have an opportunity to observe more closely how entrepreneurs will react to proposed policy. The system is protected by the authoritarian enclaves of Chilean democracy. These place business and its political party allies in a superior, privileged position in the policy-making process with respect to other social groups. The organizational weakness of subordinate social groups further debilitates them and raises substan- tial barriers to their pursuit of reforms *in the context of market economies*. Organized business understands this and rallies to maintain the pillars of Chile's protected democracy. For the moment, such are the underpinnings of stability in Chile.

In conclusion, for many observers the Chilean case inspires optimism over that country's prospects for economic and political stability. In the context of a conservative regime transition from above, collaboration between a united and proactive national bourgeoisie and the state is seen as especially noteworthy for its contribution to stability. However, the social problems of capitalism in developing economies persist. And they are serious. Despite the optimistic spin, much research remains to be done on the issue of social equity — how the fruits of economic growth are distributed. If liberalism is to prevail, what are its consequences for the quality of life of vast underprivileged social sectors? How do we define social equity at the dawning of a new century? What are the currently contending definitions of social equity in the context of market economies, and which social groups support them? If economic and political stability depend on collaboration between government and business elites united behind pragmatic neoliberal economic policy packages, the "political will" required to address the social question seriously may not materialize.[45] Finding the political conditions under which national capitalists cease to feel threatened by a more just society in developing market economies is as worthy an intellectual task as uncovering the conditions for political and macro- economic stability.

Notes

1. Chile's democratic origins date to the 1830s.

2. The CPC later admitted the Chilean Construction Chamber in the 1960s and the Association of Banks and Financial Institutions in the 1980s. For an illuminating account of the debates over acceptance of the CChC, see Cusack (1972, 70-74).

3. Author interview with Sergio Molina, minister of finance during the administration of Eduardo Frei M., Santiago, Chile, May 1989.

4. The SONAMI's president was an Allende sympathizer, according to Manlio Fantini, a long-time SONAMI director. Author interview, Santiago, Chile, April 1989.

5. For an early challenge to such arguments, see Guillermo O'Donnell (1977).

6. For accounts of the Second Convention of the CPC, see the December 1973 issues of *Ercilla* and *El Mercurio,* as well as *El Campesino* (1973c). Additional data are from author interviews with Manuel Valdés, Santiago, Chile, March 1989. Mr. Valdés was vice president of the SNA from the early 1970s to late 1973 and was elected vice president of the CPC just before the December 1973 convention, which he was in charge of organizing.

7. Policy positions were mainly derived from business association publications. For the SNA, see *El Campesino* (1973b and 1974); for the CNC, see CNC (1975). For the SONAMI, I relied on an author interview with Manlio Fantini, one of the SONAMI leaders of the period, Santiago, Chile, April 1989; for the CChC's policy position, I relied on an author interview with Pablo Araya, the CChC's director of studies, in Santiago, Chile, April 1989.

8. For the minority position in the SFF, I relied on author interviews with Gustavo Ramdohr (former director of the metal sector association, ASIMET), Santiago, Chile, August 1988, and with Orlando Sáenz (president of the SFF at the time), Santiago, Chile, August 1988. For the majority position of the SFF, see Sáenz's speech in *Informativo SFF* (1974b).

9. Author interview with Juan Ignacio Varas, the CPC's representative to the CAPA, Santiago, Chile, November 1988.

10. Author interviews with Orlando Sáenz (former president of the SFF), Santiago, Chile, September 1988, and Manuel Valdés (former vice president of the SNA and the CPC), Santiago, Chile, March 1989.

11. Author interview with Orlando Sáenz (former president of the SFF), Santiago, Chile, August 1988.

12. During this period the Cámara Nacional de Comercio was called the Cámara Central de Comercio.

13. Up to 1977, a few business associations — notably sectors within the SNA and the SFF — opposed some radical neoliberal policies. The SNA, more so than the SFF, took a public conflictual stance; however, the government ignored them. See Campero (1984) and Banco Central (1974a).

14. Author interviews with Manuel Valdés (vice president of the SNA and the CPC), Santiago, Chile, March 1989, and Humberto Prieto (secretary general of the CNC), Santiago, Chile, October 1988.

15. Author interview with Orlando Sáenz (former SFF president), Santiago, Chile, August 1988.

16. For business association rhetoric regarding support for the radical neoliberal model between 1979 and 1980, see *El Campesino,* the SFF's *Informativo SFF,* and the CNC's *Memoria Anual* (1982).

17. The CPC maintained an incomplete file on these proceedings — officially marked as pertaining to the subsequent policy document titled *Recuperación económica: análisis y proposiciones* (CPC 1983). Documents with sectoral demands and position papers on general economic policy were found in the CPC file. Several of these documents were also published in other sources; see, for example, SONAMI (1982, 1983); CNC (1983b); CChC (*Estrategia* 1983a and 1983b); SNA (1983).

18. The SNA strongly opposed differentiated tariffs, so much so that it went on record against them in an untitled and undated position paper it presented at CPC deliberations over economic recovery policy in June 1983. This document reiterated the SNA's stance at a CPC executive council meeting in November 1982 (CPC 1982) and in speeches by SNA president Germán Riesco (*El Campesino* 1982c). SONAMI had gone on record against differentiated tariffs in November 1982 (*Estrategia* 1982). The CNC made its position clear in its annual report (CNC 1983a). The construction chamber was ambivalent at best. So was the financial chamber, as expressed in a cryptic letter by its president to the CPC dated November 12, 1982. After the financial crash of January 20, which precipitated a change in the financial chamber's leadership, the CChC supported differentiated tariffs (*El Mercurio* 1983). But by then, the sector had been devastated by the country's financial crisis (and had been partially blamed for it in ways that implicated its outgoing president, Javier Vial) so that the CChC was not a useful ally for the SFF.

19. Author interview with Jorge Fontaine (CPC president during this period), Santiago Chile, April 1989.

20. The document was distributed to Pinochet, the members of the junta, all economic ministers, and the press.

21. During this period, Pinochet began a process of highly controlled political liberalization that involved his interior minister, right-wing political parties, and the major opposition movement Alianza Democrática. A month or two before these negotiations began — at the time the CPC distributed its economic recovery plan to Chile's economic ministers — the SFF cautioned that although the private sector did not wish to break with the government, it might be forced into opposition (*Qué Pasa* 1983). In the same spirit, Jorge Fontaine, president of the CPC, declared that as a rule, business only sought confrontation with governments when its survival was at stake. The authorities should realize, continued Fontaine, that adherence to orthodox deflation would lead to ruin (*Revista Hoy* 1983).

22. Drawbacks improve the international competitiveness of an export product by reimbursing to exporting firms domestic taxes that raise the cost of the product.

23. The surcharges had not been part of the CPC consensus; as a result, most sectoral peak associations protested them vigorously and were not sorry to see the minister of finance replaced shortly thereafter.

24. *El Campesino* (1982a; 1982b; 1983; 1984a; 1984b; 1985).

25. First, the government appointed leaders from organized business to high offices. Second, the Ministry of Economy, under Juan Délano in 1985, established National Commissions that brought together the private and public sectors. This was especially effective in the drawback legislation procedure. Third, when Modesto Collados was minister of economy, he created the Economic and Social Council (CES), which brought together government, business, and, nominally, labor. In addition, access to ministers and undersecretaries was much easier and more fluid than in the past.

26. Author interview with Pablo Araya (director of studies for CChC), in Santiago, Chile, May 1989.

27. Author interview with Jorge Fontaine (CPC president during the period), Santiago, Chile, April 1989.

28. Confederación de la Producción y Comercio, minutes of executive meeting No. 619, July 16, 1984, and No. 633, November 19, 1984. The CPC followed this effort with a letter to Finance Minister Luis Escobar, No. 630, December 19, 1984. The letter stressed that economic recovery policy should include incentives for manufacturers.

29. Minutes of the meetings of the Subcommission for Drawback Legislation, National Commission for External Commerce, 1985 and 1986.

30. Author interviews, all conducted in Santiago, Chile, with Gustavo Ramdohr (president of the Nontraditional Exporters of Manufactures Association), August 1988; Manuel Valdés (president of the SNA), March 1989; Efraín Friedman (member of SFF elected council), November 1988; and Carlos Recabarren (director of the CNC research department), January 1989.

31. For more negative assessments, see Campero (1991).

32. These views were repeatedly stressed in the SFF's industry journal *Revista Industria* (SFF 1986a, 1986b, 1986c) and in such other outlets as Memoria Anual (SFF 1984b) and *Qué Pasa* (1986).

33. In other words, the AD moderated its initial advocacy of significant social and economic reform in exchange for political democratization. Although the AD had committed itself to prudent balance of payments and fiscal management as well as an open economy from the very beginning, it had also advocated a stronger state role in the economy in earlier stages of the transition. Since it felt that state enterprise was legitimate, the AD emphasized that Chile should have a mixed economy. Distributional issues — the social debt — were also a prominent aspect of the discourse from 1983 to 1985. As the plebiscite drew nearer and business stood firm behind pragmatic neoliberalism and Pinochet, the AD retreated from the mixed economy idea to one in which the state would use arms-length industrial policy, emphasizing fiscal policy and taxation. Distributional issues were discussed within the limits of the pragmatic neoliberal model.

34. The opposition's strategic choice was consistent with the prescriptions advocated by O'Donnell and Schmitter (1986).

35. In August 1988, I asked a representative of the SFF about business distrust of the Concertación. He replied, "We have to write that for campaign reasons. Nobody really believes it."

36. In terms of political stability, no major political actors are engaging in confrontational tactics or adopting anti-system rhetoric. By the same token, Chile enjoys sustained

GDP growth, an average of almost 7 percent over the last seven years, and at about 25 percent per year, its investment rates are higher than has been historically true for Chile (Valenzuela 1997).

37. These data are from author interviews conducted in June 1992 and July 1992 in Santiago, Chile, with Antonio Guzmán, president of the CPC; Manuel Feliú, president of the Banco Concepción and past president of the CPC; Pedro Lizana, member of the executive committee of the SFF; Raúl García, secretary general of the SNA; and Alfonso Mujica, vice president of the CNC.

38. Author interview with Joseph Ramos, Labor Ministry consultant for the Labor Code Reform, Santiago, Chile, July 1992. The Secretaría General de la Presidencia, headed by Edgardo Boeninger during the Aylwin administration and Genaro Arriagada during the Frei administration, acts as a troubleshooting institution, with oversight of other ministries. Its main task is to smooth out conflicts of interest between ministries as well as between government agencies and the private sector.

39. Interview with Luis Maira (president of the Izquierda Cristiana Party), in *Qué Pasa* (1990b).

40. Author interview with Manuel Marfán, a key Ministry of Finance negotiator with the private sector, June 1992.

41. Author interview with Oscar Muñoz, coordinator for the Ministry of Economy of the Second National Production Forum, in Santiago, July 1996.

42. Author interviews with business leaders — among them the current and past president of the CPC — and advisors to the government in Santiago, June 1992 and July 1992.

43. Author interview with Pedro Lizana (president of the SFF), Santiago, Chile, June 1992.

44. Bartell and Payne (1995, 277) have also pointed to this possibility, as have Haggard and Kaufman (1995, 262-263).

45. Sergio Molina, minister of planning and development, blamed the government's difficulties in the area of social equity on this issue; seminar on the United Nations Development Programme's Informe de Desarrollo Humano, 1992, Ex Congreso Nacional, July 16, 1992. For a critique of the concept of political will, see Goldsworthy (1988).

References

Arellano, José Pablo. 1988. "Crisis y recuperación económica en Chile en los años 80." *Estudios Cieplan* 24 (June): 63-84.

Arellano, José Pablo. 1984. "La difícil salida al problema del endeudamiento interno." *Estudios Cieplan* 13 (June): 5-25.

Arellano, José Pablo, and Manuel Marfán. 1986. "Ahorro, inversión y relaciones financieras en la actual crisis financiera chilena." *Estudios Cieplan* 20 (December): 61-93.

Arriagada, Genaro. 1970. *La oligarquía patronal chilena.* Santiago: Ediciones Nueva Sociedad.

Asociación de Industrias Electrónicas. 1974. Memorandum to Minister of Finance Jorge Cauas and Minister of Economy Fernando Léniz, July 11.

Banco Central. 1974a. *Minutas del Comité Asesor de Política Arancelaria.* Santiago: CPC.

Banco Central. 1974b. *Comité Asesor de Política Arancelaria.* Minutes of the meeting of November 22.

Bartell, Ernest, and Leigh Payne. 1995. "Bringing Business Back In: Business-State Relations and Democratic Stability in Latin America." In *Business and Democracy in Latin America*, eds. Ernest Bartell and Leigh Payne. Pittsburgh, Pa.: University of Pittsburgh Press.

Boylan, Delia M. 1996. "Taxation and Transition: The Politics of the 1990 Chilean Tax Reform." *Latin American Research Review* 31 (1): 7-31.

Business Latin America. 1990a. "Business Outlook, June." (June 4): 172-174.

Business Latin America. 1990b. "Chile's Labor Code Reforms." (July 23): 230.

Business Latin America. 1990c. "Unions Threaten Strikes as Chile's New Labor Code Gets Bogged Down in Senate." (September 3): 279.

Business Latin America. 1990d. "Business Outlook: Chile." (December 3): 392-393.

Cámara Nacional de Comercio. 1975. *Memoria Anual, 1974-1975.* Santiago: CNC.

Cámara Nacional de Comercio. 1982. *Memoria Anual 1981-1982.* Santiago: CNC.

Cámara Nacional de Comercio. 1983a. *Memoria Anual, 1982-1983.* Santiago: CNC.

Cámara Nacional de Comercio. 1983b. Memorandum to Jorge Fontaine, President of the Confederación de la Producción y Comercio regarding conclusions of the CNC's general council meetings, March 23-24. Santiago, March 28.

Cámara Nacional de Comercio. 1984. Memorandum to Minister of Finance Carlos Cáceres, No. 52/84. Santiago, March 30.

Cámara Nacional de Comercio. 1988. *Informe Económico, Anual 1988.* Santiago: CNC.

Campero, Guillermo. 1991. "Entreprenuers Under the Military Regime." In *The Struggle for Democracy in Chile, 1982-1990*, eds. Paul Drake and Iván Jaksić. Lincoln, Neb.: University of Nebraska Press.

Campero, Guillermo. 1984. *Los gremios empresariales en el período 1970-1983: comportamiento sociopolítico y orientaciones ideológicas.* Santiago: ILET.

El Campesino. 1973a. "Entidades agrícolas cooperan con autoridades: producción y comercio. No. 10 (October): 9.

El Campesino. 1973b. "Fijación de nueva política agropecuaria." No. 11 (November): 11.

El Campesino. 1973c. "Segunda convención de producción y comercio." No. 12 (December): 3.

El Campesino. 1974. "Memoria de actividad, 1972-73." No. 1-2 (January-February): 26-28.

El Campesino. 1982a. "Urgente solución a graves problemas del agro." No. 10 (October): 9-10.

El Campesino. 1982b. "Sobretasa arancelaria a productos lácteos." No. 11 (November): 7.

El Campesino. 1982c. "Germán Riesco, presidente de la Sociedad Nacional de Agricultura, opina sobre aranceles diferenciales." No. 11 (November): 6.

El Campesino. 1983. "Anunció ministro Prado nuevos créditos para paliar los problemas del agro." No. 1-2 (January-February): 3.

El Campesino. 1984a. "Banda de oleaginosas." No. 8 (August): 10.

El Campesino. 1984b. "Banda de precio para el trigo." No. 12 (December): 12.

El Campesino. 1984c. "Programa trienal." No. 12 (December): 14.

El Campesino. 1985. "Crecimiento de actividad agrícola en 1984." No. 1-2 (January-February): 6.

El Campesino. 1987a. "Acuerdo de Jahuel." No. 6 (June): 10-15.

El Campesino. 1987b. "Inaguración FISA '87: discurso del presidente de la SNA, José Moreno." No. 11 (November): 29-31.

El Campesino. 1988a. "Respaldo a proceso institucional." No. 1-2 (January-February): 7.

El Campesino. 1988b. "Visión de presente y futuro." No. 5 (May): 9.

Cardoso, Fernando Henrique. 1986. "Entrepreneurs and the Transition to Democracy in Brazil." In *Transitions from Authoritarian Rule: Comparative Perspectives*, eds. Guillermo O'Donnell, Philippe C. Schmitter, and Laurence Whitehead. Baltimore: The Johns Hopkins University Press.

Cardoso, Fernando Henrique. 1971. *Las ideologías de la burguesía industrial en sociedades dependientes: Argentina y Brasil*. México: Siglo 21.

Cardoso, Fernando Henrique, and Enzo Faletto. 1978. *Dependency and Development in Latin America*. Berkeley, Calif.: University of California Press.

Cavallo, Ascanio, Manuel Salazar, and Oscar Sepúlveda. 1988. *La historia oculta del régimen militar*. Santiago: Editorial La Epoca.

Cavarozzi, Marcelo. 1975. "The Government and the Industrial Bourgeoisie in Chile, 1938-1964." Ph.D. Dissertation, University of California, Berkeley.

Centro de Estudios Públicos. 1992. *El Ladrillo: bases de la política económica del gobierno militar chileno*. Santiago: Centro de Estudios Públicos.

CPC (Confederación de la Producción y del Comercio). 1982. Minutes of the Executive Committee Meeting No. 577, November 25.

CPC. 1983. *Recuperación económica: análisis y proposiciones*. Santiago, July 4.

CPC. 1991. "Conclusiones del consejo extraordinario de la Confederación de la Producción y Comercio," Santiago, September.

Cusack, David. 1972. "The Politics of Chilean Private Enterprise under Christian Democracy." Ph.D. dissertation, University of Denver.

Drake, Paul W. 1978. *Socialism and Populism in Chile, 1932-52*. Urbana, Ill.: University of Illinois Press.

Edwards, Sebastian, and Alejandra Cox-Edwards. 1987. *Monetarism and Liberalization: The Chilean Experiment*. Cambridge, Mass.: Ballinger Publishing Co.

Ellsworth, P.T. 1945. *Chile: An Economic Transition*. New York: The Macmillan Company.

Ercilla. 1973. December, various issues.

Estrategia. 1982. "Crisis económica y reactivación." August 16-22: 12.

Estrategia. 1983a. "Cámara de la Construcción: acción rápida y efectiva." February 21-27: 8.

Estrategia. 1983b. "Plan de vivienda: condiciones de estabilidad para el sector." October 3-9: 13.

Fontaine, Arturo. 1988. *Los economistas y el presidente Pinochet*, 2nd ed. Santiago: Editora Zig-Zag.

Foxley, Alejandro. 1983. *Latin American Experiments in Neoconservative Economics*. Berkeley, Calif.: University of California Press.

Garretón, Manuel Antonio. 1989. *The Chilean Political Process*. Boston: Unwin Hyman.

Gil, Federico, Ricardo Lagos, and Henry A. Landsberger, eds. 1979. *Chile at the Turning Point: Lessons of the Socialist Years*. Philadelphia: ISHI.

Goldsworthy, David. 1988. "Thinking Politically about Development." *Development and Change* 9 (3): 505-530.

Haggard, Stephan, and Robert Kaufman. 1995. *The Political Economy of Democratic Transitions*. Princeton, N.J.: Princeton University Press.

Handelman, Howard, and Thomas G. Sanders. 1981. *Military Government and the Movement Toward Democracy in Latin America*. Bloomington, Ind.: Indiana University Press.

Kaufman, Robert. 1986. "Liberalization and Democratization in South America: Perspectives from the 1970s." In *Transitions from Authoritarian Rule: Comparative Perspectives*, eds. Guillermo O'Donnell, Philippe C. Schmitter, and Laurence Whitehead. Baltimore: The Johns Hopkins University Press.

Larraín, Felipe. 1991. "The Economic Challenges of Democratic Development." In *The Struggle for Democracy in Chile, 1982-1990*, eds. Paul Drake and Iván Jaksić. Lincoln, Neb.: University of Nebraska Press.

Latin American Studies Association. 1989. "The Chilean Plebiscite: A First Step Toward Redemocratization." *LASA Forum* 19 (4): 18-36.

Lindblom, Charles. 1977. *Politics and Markets*. New York: Basic.

Linz, Juan. 1964. "An Authoritarian Regime: Spain." In *Cleavages, Ideologies and Party Systems*, eds. Erik Allardt and Yrjo Littunen. Helsinki: Academic Bookstore.

Loveman, Brian. 1979. *Chile: The Legacy of Hispanic Capitalism*. New York: Oxford University Press.

Loveman, Brian. 1991. "¿Misión Cumplida? Civil Military Relations and the Chilean Political Transition." *Journal of Interamerican Studies and World Affairs* 33 (3): 35-74.

Loveman, Brian. 1994. *The Constitution of Tyranny: Regimes of Exception in Spanish America*. Pittsburgh: University of Pittsburgh Press.

Malloy, James M., ed. 1977. *Authoritarianism and Corporatism in Latin America*. Pittsburgh: University of Pittsburgh Press.

Malloy, James M., and Catherine M. Conaghan. 1994. *Unsettling Statecraft: Democracy and Neoliberlism in the Central Andes*. Pittsburgh: University of Pittsburgh Press.

Mamalakis, Markos J. 1966. *La teoría de los choques entre sectores*. No. 83. Universidad de Chile: Instituto de Economía.

Marfán, Manuel. 1984. "Una evaluación de la nueva reforma tributaria." *Estudios Cieplan* 13 (June): 27-52.

McConnell, Grant. 1966. *Private Power and American Democracy*. New York: Vintage.

Menges, Constantine. 1966. "Public Policy and Organized Business in Chile: A Preliminary Analysis." *Journal of International Affairs* 20 (2): 343-365.

El Mercurio. 1973. December, various issues.

El Mercurio. 1983. "Jorge Yarur, presidente de la Asociación de Bancos e Instituciones Financieras, analiza el momento económico." February 25.

Ministerio de Economía, Fomento y Reconstrucción and ASEXMA. 1988. *Medidas de fomento a las exportaciones chilenas ponen el mundo a sus manos*. Santiago: Ediciones OPLANE.

Molina, Sergio. 1992. "United Nations Development Programme: Informe de Desarrollo Humano, 1992." Seminar held in Santiago, Ex Congreso Nacional, July 16.

Muñoz, Oscar, and Ana María Arriagada. 1977. "Orígenes políticos y económicos del estado empresarial en Chile." *Estudios Cieplan* 16.

Nelson, Joan. 1994. "Labor and Business in Dual Transitions." In *Intricate Links: Democratization and Market Reforms in Latin America and Eastern Europe*, ed. Joan Nelson. New Brunswick, N.J.: Transaction Publishers.

O'Brien, Philip, ed. 1976. *Allende's Chile*. New York: Praeger Publishers.

O'Brien, Philip. 1983. *The Pinochet Decade*. London: Latin American Bureau.

O'Donnell, Guillermo. 1973. *Modernization and Bureaucratic Authoritarianism*. Berkeley, Calif.: Institute of International Studies.

O'Donnell, Guillermo. 1977. "Corporatism and the Question of the State." In *Authoritarianism and Corporatism in Latin America*, ed. James M. Malloy. Pittsburgh: University of Pittsburgh Press.

O'Donnell, Guillermo, and Philippe Schmitter. 1986. *Transitions from Authoritarian Rule: Tentative Conclusions*. Baltimore: Johns Hopkins Univeristy Press.

Olson, Mancur, Jr. 1965. *The Logic of Collective Action*. Cambridge: Harvard University Press.

Pastor Jr., Manuel, and Carol Wise. 1996. *The Politics of Free Trade in the Western Hemisphere*. North South Agenda Paper 20 (August): 1-21.

Payne, Leigh. 1994. *Brazilian Industrialists and Democratic Change*. Baltimore: Johns Hopkins University Press.

Qué Pasa. 1983. "Las proposiciones empresariales." No. 639 (7 July): 12-14.

Qué Pasa. 1986. "Empresarios y política: ¿ al margen hasta cuando?" No. 785 (April 24): 10-11.

Qué Pasa. 1989. "Tributación: el terror de los empresarios." No. 955 (27 July): 32-33.

Qué Pasa. 1990a. "Empresarios: 'armados' para la democracia." No. 986 (1 March): 6-9.

Qué Pasa. 1990b. "El gobierno empieza a operar en una ruleta Rusa." No. 1021 (November 5): 4-7.

Ramos, Joseph. 1986. *Neoconservative Economics in the Southern Cone*. Baltimore: Johns Hopkins University Press.

Revista Hoy. 1983. "Empresarios: historia de un peligro secreto." No. 311 (6 July): 27-28.

Rozas, Patricio, and Gustavo Marín. 1989. *El mapa de la extrema riqueza: 10 años después.* Santiago: Ediciones Chile-América.

Schmitter, Philippe C. 1971. *Interest Conflict and Political Change in Brazil.* Stanford, Calif.: Stanford University Press.

Silva, Eduardo. 1993. "Capitalist Coalitions, the State, and Neoliberal Economic Restructuring." *World Politics* 45 (4): 526-59.

Silva, Eduardo. 1996. *The State and Capital in Chile: Business Elites, Technocrats, and Market Economics.* Boulder, Colo.: Westview Press.

Silva, Patricio. 1991. "Technocrats and Politics in Chile: From the Chicago Boys to the Cieplan Monks." *Journal of Latin American Studies* 23 (2): 385-410.

Smith, William C. 1989. *Authoritarianism and the Crisis of Argentine Political Economy.* Stanford, Calif.: Stanford University Press.

SFF (Sociedad de Fomento Fabril). 1974a. Memoranda to Undersecretary of the Ministry of Economy, Sergio de Castro. November 6-7.

SFF. 1974b. "Anexo al Informativo No. 71: Discurso del Sr. Orlando Sáenz, presidente de la Sociedad de Fomento Fabril, en la 90a junta ordinaria de sociedad." *Informativo SFF* 7 (February-March): 1-10.

SFF. 1982. "Informe final de la comisión SFF para estudiar una alternativa al sistema arancelario." October 20, unpublished manuscript.

SFF. 1984a. *Revista Industria* 87 (6).

SFF. 1984b. "Plan Trienal." *Sociedad de Fomento Fabril: Memoria, 1983-1984.* Santiago: SFF.

SFF. 1985. *Endeudamiento interno.* Santiago: SFF.

SFF. 1986a. "Acciones prioritarias 1986." *Revista Industria* 89 (1): 11.

SFF. 1986b. "Editorial: los programas políticos y el sector productivo." *Revista Industria* 89 (2): 51.

SFF. 1986c. "Derecho de propiedad: reforzamiento de la empresa privada y economía libre." *Revista Industria* 89 (2): 61-62.

SFF. 1986d. "Exposición del presidente de la Sociedad de Fomento Fabril en la 102 asamblea de socios." *Revista Industria* 89 (3): 117-122.

Sociedad Nacional de Agricultura. 1983. Memorandum regarding working sessions of the Confederación de la Producción y Comercio. Santiago, August 26.

SONAMI (Sociedad Nacional de Minería). 1982. "Letter to President Augusto Pinochet," Santiago, August 3.

SONAMI. 1983. "Observaciones y sugerencias sobre documento de la Confederación." Letter to Jorge Fontaine, president of the CPC, No. 501, November 7.

Stallings, Barbara. 1978. *Class Conflict and Development in Chile.* Stanford, Calif: Stanford University Press.

Valenzuela, Arturo. 1991. "The Military in Power: The Consolidation of One Man Rule in Chile." In *The Struggle for Democracy in Chile, 1982-1990*, eds. Paul Drake and Iván Jaksić. Lincoln, Neb.: University of Nebraska Press.

Valenzuela, Arturo. 1997. "The Chilean Miracle: Lessons of South America's Success Story." *Harvard International Review* 19 (4): 24-30.

Véliz, Claudio. 1963. "La mesa de tres patas." *Desarrollo Económico* 3 (1-2): 241-247.

Vylder, Stephan de. 1976. *Allende's Chile.* Cambridge, Mass.: Cambridge University Press.

Weyland, Kurt. 1997. "Growth with Equity in Chile's New Democracy." *Latin American Research Review* 32 (1): 37-67.

Wright, Thomas C. 1982. *Landowners and Reform in Chile: The SNA, 1919-1940.* Urbana, Ill.: University of Illinois Press.

CHAPTER NINE

Collective Action and the Empowerment of Peruvian Business

FRANCISCO DURAND

The Peruvian business class initially took shape as an archipelago of interest groups. From the early 1900s and for more than 70 years, no business sector or leader was able to coalesce the country's trade associations under the same roof on a permanent basis. Only for limited periods in times of crisis did the different business interests come together. This situation worsened in the 1970s, when interventionist government elites implemented policy without consulting business associations and leaders. In 1984, the pattern reversed when the heads of key trade associations founded the Confederation of Private Business Institutions (Confederación de Instituciones Empresariales Privadas — CONFIEP), a peak business organization that continues to operate in the late 1990s. The Peruvian case thus speaks of a remarkable degree of institutional transformation.

This chapter's analysis of CONFIEP's process of formation, organization, and development focuses on business as a collective actor over the long view. Collective action is understood herein as a political response to changing circumstances, when endogenous and exogenous factors combine to provoke business mobilization and organizational development. A peak business association is the result of unified forms of collective action. It can be defined as an encompassing organization that incorporates, mobilizes, and represents a wide array of trade associations. Business institutional development takes place when the encompassing association becomes accepted as a vehicle of collective representation by both business (firms, sectoral trade associations) and others (government, labor unions, political parties) and after a process of professionalization takes place.

This chapter identifies the factors that prevent or foster business organizational unity in order to explain under what circumstances businesses become collective actors (Martinelli 1994, 493) and how a peak association makes business a more effective political and policy player.[1] This study of collective action undertaken by the Peruvian business community is centered on critical junctures that occurred between 1930 and 1998 during and after the oligarchic period. A critical juncture manifests itself as a political crisis when a deep alteration of the correlation of forces takes place.[2] This alteration is provoked by changes in the balance of power between the elites and the masses and between the elites and government. One key argument about the logic of collective action is that critical junctures offer good conditions for business unity, but unity does not crystallize into permanent organizational forms unless conditions endogenous to the business class are present. Exogenous factors — economic crises and regime crises, social tensions that threaten elite interests, and breakdowns in business-government relations — only generate limited, temporary forms of unity. This chapter argues that endogenous factors, the degree of economic and social articulation among the different components of the business class, the nature of business leadership, and the role of trade associations within the political system also condition the development of more complex forms of business organization and their potential for unification.

Once the process of formation of a durable encompassing association is explained, this chapter shows how the troubled history of collective business action in Peru has forced business leaders to develop highly inclusive rules and procedures to deal effectively with internal divisions. Based on this institutional design, the encompassing association has been able to professionalize and has become capable of influencing the policy-making process more effectively. The enhanced role of CONFIEP, the encompassing association, is particularly evident in the late 1980s and 1990s, when it became a key participant in the policy and political debates of the period. It has helped to defeat antibusiness, populist decisions and to shape the implementation and adjustment of neoliberal policies. CONFIEP has also influenced the nature of the political debates by taking a stand in favor of conditional support for democracy, a position that has strengthened and, at the same time, limited the semi-authoritarian nature of the Alberto Fujimori administration. CONFIEP is well positioned to attempt enhancing business influence upon civil society in the current post-populist era.

OLIGARCHIC HEGEMONY

D uring the period of export development and incipient industrialization (1880s-1960s), Peru's economy relied on a strong, highly diversified export sector. The ruling class was led by the *agrarios*, a pro-export landed oligarchy, allied to traditional landowners, import-export merchants, mine owners, and foreign enclaves. This powerful coalition supported open-market policies and opposed protectionist measures benefiting manufacturing industries. A small, urban-industrial bourgeoisie located in Lima and Arequipa played a marginal role in economic development (Thorp and Bertram 1978, 24). Links among petroleum, mining, industrial, and agrarian interests were weak (Valderrama and Ludmann 1979, 49). Each sector, located in a different part of Peru's geographically rugged territory, made class coordination difficult.[3] The proud, aristocratic, landed oligarchy isolated itself in the Club Nacional, the center of social life in Lima. In the 1920s, only two industrialists were members (Laos 1929). In the late 1960s, according to a sample of industrialists, only 5 percent reported membership in this exclusive club (Wils 1979, 207). Compared to Chile, Argentina, or even Brazil, Peru's ruling class was characterized by extreme economic, regional, and social disarticulation (or disjointedness), a trait that impeded organizational unity and more legitimate, consensual forms of political influence by business interests.

The National Agrarian Society (Sociedad Nacional Agraria — SNA) was the reigning, uncontested business association. Other important associations were the National Mining and Petroleum Society (Sociedad Nacional de Minería y Petróleo — SNMP) and the Chamber of Commerce of Lima (Cámara de Comercio de Lima — CCL), representing mining and import-export businesses, respectively. A weak industrialists' association, the National Industries Society (Sociedad Nacional de Industrias — SNI), was also part of the associational landscape, as were chambers of commerce that existed in the main provincial cities.[4] All of these associations were founded in the 1880s and 1890s.

This first generation of trade associations had formed on a voluntary basis, which established a tradition of autonomy and non-governmental interference that prevented future attempts at implementing state corporatism. Each association defended its own interests independently. In the 1920s, the exporting oligarchy, given its economic clout, developed direct links with the state without the mediation of political parties. Thus, the elites expressed themselves through private mechanisms and via trade associations for the most part. In contrast, the most active political parties were mass organizations led by populists, the American Popular Revolutionary Alliance (Alianza Popular Revolucionaria — APRA), and socialists, the Peruvian Communist Party (Partido Comunista Peruano — PCP), who articulated the concerns of labor unions and peasant organizations in party structures (Sulmont 1977, 41 ff.). While the popular sectors formed highly politicized labor unions strongly linked to radical parties, business established independent trade associations to defend its economic interests but lacked a political party. In this context, progressive forces and a weak industrial bourgeoisie were trapped between two poles, a powerful agrarian oligarchy and radical popular forces, without much political space in between, space where those interested in struggling for industrial development and moderate political alternatives would operate.

The way this political system was established had profound consequences during political crises because it conditioned how business reacted to challenges posed by critical junctures and left a lasting negative legacy that limited the collective action and the organizational unity of the business community.

The Unión Social and the Great Depression

The business community's first attempt at generalized collective action occurred in 1930. Dictator Augusto B. Leguía, with close ties to the sugar industry and foreign capital, had been in power for 11 years when international prices and demand suddenly collapsed. Soon after, massive unemployment in sectors such as sugar, copper, textiles, and construction generated massive social unrest (Portocarrero 1981, 82-83). The crisis weakened dictatorial rule and opened the way for political action.

In August 1930, Peruvian Army Col. Luis M. Sánchez Cerro led a broadly supported coup that easily succeeded in ousting Leguía (Miró Quesada 1947, 69-117). Facing a new political situation, the elites tried to establish relations with the Sánchez Cerro government. Agrarios, mine owners, and investors of foreign capital were in favor of economic reforms to stabilize the economy. By late 1930, exporters believed the dynamism of cotton, oil, and gold exports could lead to an economic recovery if the government succeeded in maintaining a firm course of outward development (Thorp and Bertram 1978, 151, 156, and 164). The exporters' agenda was difficult to implement because of the unstable political situation. Sánchez Cerro headed a weak, provisional government challenged by rising popular demands and social movements in urban and rural areas. The military was deeply divided, and none of Peru's political parties could stabilize the situation. To the elites, Sánchez Cerro seemed the most viable alternative to the threats of revolution and participatory democracy. After the collapse of the Leguía administration, *apristas* (APRA followers), communists, and minor socialist organizations became the center of opposition forces (Planas 1994, 240).

Major threats against all elite segments came from two mass parties that viewed Sánchez Cerro as an ambitious dictator who was supported by the agrarios and unwilling to compete in democratic elections against the popular forces. The communists were the first to clash with the oligarchic alliance and Sánchez Cerro. On November 8, 1930, while organizing a congress of mine workers in central Peru, unions led by the PCP took over mining centers in Cerro de Pasco and La Oroya and marched to Lima to protest government labor policies. At Malpaso, the army stopped the march with brutal force, killing and wounding several workers. The labor confederation, the Peruvian General Workers Union (Central General de Trabajadores del Perú — CGTP), founded in 1929 by socialists, supported the miners and called for a general strike, a decision that forced the government to escalate repressive measures. Another source of elite fear was APRA, a fast-growing political party that took advantage of the vacuum left by the communists to mobilize labor unions after their leaders were imprisoned and deported. The reaction of the business community to the double threat of a weak government and the mobilization of *apristas* and communists was to coordinate and mobilize business interests in a united front (*Mundial,* October 17 and November 14, 1930). In the 1930s, the military and the economic elites saw a common threat in these two forces and labeled it *aprocomunismo,* implying that the two were equally dangerous. (The term was coined by the conservative newspaper, *El Comercio.*) Meetings were led by SNA's president, Pedro Beltrán, a cotton planter from Cañete. Eight trade associations participated — including CCL and SNI — together with professional associations of lawyers, doctors, and dentists (Basadre 1975, 44). Elite unity, however, was limited because SNMP and the Arequipa Chamber of Commerce were absent. Under Beltrán's leadership, the business movement attempted to transform itself into a political organization, the Social Union (Unión Social). APRA opposed the Social Union as an elitist, pro-dictatorial movement, and the two soon clashed. A Social Union rally, held on November 24, 1930, at Plaza San Martin, was violently disrupted by apristas (*Mundial,* November 28, 1930). From that moment on, the Social Union did not dare to take to the streets again. Elites continued to be united in the hectic months that followed but only until political order was reestablished. The political crisis was resolved when Sánchez Cerro, the military *caudillo* coopted by the elites, won the 1931 election against Víctor Raúl Haya de la Torre, APRA's candidate. Further consolidation occurred in 1932, when the government succeeded in crushing a popular uprising in Trujillo organized by APRA. Several thousand people were executed after the army regained control of the city (Sulmont 1977, 72). Sánchez Cerro's assassination by an aprista gunman in 1933 opened the door to a military government closely tied to the oligarchy.

In 1934, Beltrán and the agrarios attempted to form a pro-exporting party, the National Agrarian Party (Partido Nacional Agrario — PNA), to defend "the development of extractive industries: agriculture, cattle raising, and mining" (Beltrán 1994, 107). Beltrán's project failed to attract support, and the PNA soon vanished from the scene. Agrarios then retreated to the SNA to coordinate the defense of agrarian interests. The industrialists, left on their own, timidly advocated the development of Peru's domestic industry through the SNI (Caravedo 1976).

Business unity in the 1930s lasted only until the governability crisis ended. No durable peak association was established. Although the agrarios failed to create an elite party, no other forms of collective action were needed as oligarchic rule had been restored. Economic, political, and social disarticulation continued among the different business sectors.

CNCP and the Postwar Crisis

The second attempt at business unification occurred under similar circumstances in 1945 and 1948. In 1945, when growing cities saw the rapid development of the middle class and urban masses, Peru shifted in the direction of democracy, and mass parties again seized the opportunity for political action. José Luis Bustamante, elected president with popular support, soon antagonized all business sectors. As the war ended, a surge of imports and negative conditions for exports created a balance-of-payments bottleneck. The export sector, the main engine of economic growth, declined 21 percent between 1945 and 1948. Exchange and price controls constrained exports and the domestic market, and soon prices began to rise. Fiscal problems generated by the continued expansion of the government payroll and the legislated wage increases demanded by labor unions created a climate of economic uncertainty for business (Thorp and Bertram 1978, 188-189).

The newly formed democratic government had a weak foundation, and, as in 1930-1932, it became trapped in the politics of polarization. President Bustamante, an independent personality, was elected thanks to the support of established parties. APRA was the uncontested force inside and outside Congress. APRA's founder and leader, Haya de la Torre, wanted to define the course of government personally. Bustamante, however, resisted APRA's influence. For this reason, the early understanding between Bustamante and Haya lasted only a few months. As contradictory pressures from APRA and the economic elites mounted, the government's stability deteriorated rapidly. In 1946, aprista cabinet members resigned, and APRA began organizing mass demonstrations and supporting labor strikes. An even more serious crisis followed in January 1947, when Francisco Graña, director of La Prensa, a newspaper owned by Beltrán and closely linked to the SNA, was assassinated by an aprista gunman. Outraged by the crime, the business elites and the conservative press demanded immediate repression of APRA (Chirinos Soto 1989, 141). Bustamante initially hesitated to use force, but as the crisis worsened, he appointed members of the military to key cabinet positions and ordered the army to repress APRA and the union movement. In October 1948,

Interior Minister Gen. Manuel A. Odría seized power. The coup counted on open support from *La Prensa*, Beltrán, and the coalition of trade associations formed against Bustamante. Soon after, Beltrán was nominated head of the Central Reserve Bank, and economic policies were reversed in the direction of free trade and export interests.

Between 1945 and 1948, the level of social threat was not as intense as in 1930-1931, since parties and labor unions had less radical demands and revolutionary options were not considered, but the overall political scenario seemed quite threatening to the elites. Labor union activism was particularly intense. In 1944, the apristas formed their own labor confederation, the Peruvian Workers' Confederation (Confederación de Trabajadores del Perú — CTP), and an agrarian confederation in 1947, the Peruvian Peasant Confederation (Confederación Campesina del Perú — CCP), to extend their influence over the popular sectors (Sulmont 1977, 81-83). The CTP and the CCP led a series of strikes in all major labor centers and on modern *haciendas* (farms). Bustamante's immediate policy response was to recognize unions and satisfy labor demands, but the labor movement kept pressuring the government.

During the period from 1945 through 1948, the collapse of business-government relations and threats from labor unions and APRA triggered business unification and forced the elites to confront the government and even to conspire against it. On September 13, 1945, less than three months after Bustamante became president, eight business associations — SNA, CCL, SNI, and SNMP and four minor organizations — formed a peak association, the National Trade and Production Committee (Comité Nacional del Comercio y la Producción — CNCP). The CNCP was led by SNA President Julio De la Piedra (Portocarrero 1986, 108). The CNCP's first public communiqué, published in *La Prensa* (December 12, 1945), set an anti-government tone by accusing President Bustamante of conciliating with the "arbitrary, excessive demands of labor unions." When *La Prensa* director Francisco Graña was assassinated in 1947, business unity increased. In this context, Beltrán, the owner of the newspaper, emerged again as the key business leader. Calling an urgent meeting of CNCP's coordinating committee, Beltrán organized a business lockout and attempted to use the peak business association, CNCP, to form a political party, the National Alliance (Alianza Nacional). The party's goal was to stop APRA, which was seen as an ideologically intolerant, socially threatening political force, and to press the government to shift economic policies in favor of exporters.

This second attempt to create a conservative, pro-oligarchic political party failed, and the SNA continued to be the only organization to aggregate agrarian interests. As soon as the crisis ended, businesspeople from the emerging modern sectors —industrialists, developers, and merchants linked to the domestic market — retreated to their sectoral organizations with no further political commitment. They neither supported the National Alliance nor questioned the orientation of economic policies. The oligarchy, despite its failure to organize an agrarian party, continued to act on its own, given that relations with the government were now fully restored. The subordinate attitude of the emerging business sectors indicated that they recognized their minority status compared with Peru's economic elites. In the coming decades, business organizations representing the modern sectors rapidly developed, but their respect for oligarchic interests remained unchanged. Four new, urban-based trade associations — pharmaceuticals, banking, construction, and customs agencies — and one export trade association — fishing — formed between 1945 and 1968 (Durand 1994, 32-35). The ideological influence of these business interests grew as two new centrist parties, Popular Action (Acción Popular) and Christian Democrats (Democracia Cristiana), emerged and popularized the idea of modernization. However, these trends, which favored a process of industrialization led by the modern private sector, were stopped by a military coup that profoundly altered the nature of business-government relations in Peru.

THE NEW BOURGEOISIE

The 1968 military revolution, led by Gen. Juan Velasco Alvarado, which supplanted Fernando Belaúnde, irreversibly hurt the oligarchy by abolishing the SNA, expropriating *La Prensa*, and redistributing land to peasant organizations. As a result of this swift anti-elite offensive, Beltrán and all institutions that represented agrarian interests vanished from the political arena.[5] An interventionist state grew rapidly, thanks to expropriation of foreign enclaves, the creation of more than 100 state-owned enterprises, and the introduction of economic controls. Profit redistribution and co-management mechanisms were also introduced.

Following the coup, business associations representing modern business sectors quickly expressed their support for the new government, adapting themselves to the new scenario. Given the history of elite disarticulation, the agrarios were left alone, abandoned to their tragic destiny without any expression of solidarity from the private sector. Trade associations inevitably became the centers of business activism, as other avenues of collective action were closed by government decree. The military imposed a tight institutional control over the political process (Cotler 1994, 91). Access to the new government was difficult for business. One of the few institutions that formed business links with the government was the Peruvian Business Administration Institute (Instituto Peruano de Administración de Empresas — IPAE), founded in 1959 to foster the principles of scientific management. The IPAE was the organizer of the Annual Executives' Conference (Conferencia Anual de Ejecutivos — CADE). CADE provided a space for businesspeople from modern sectors, in theory, supporters of social change, to become acquainted with military leaders and policymakers in a friendly atmosphere.[6]

The positive relationship between the military and modern business elites changed as new tensions arose. In July 1970, the government instituted a number of unilateral policy initiatives, such as the Industrial Law that gave the state control over basic industries, the introduction of Labor Communities (co-management organisms), and the Labor Stability Law, all of which negatively affected the domestic private sector. Business elites believed that the government was moving toward socialism or a mixed system that would relegate the private sector to a subordinate role. Despite its concerns, business failed to react effectively. The SNI was the only trade association to question the 1970 reforms openly. In 1971,

Raymundo Duharte, a young and energetic individual, was elected SNI president. Highly critical of the government, Duharte was the first business leader to express elite fears in public, saying, "There is undoubtedly a plan designed to annihilate the private sector" (Sociedad de Industrias 1977, 530). Duharte soon discovered that the military had already established a pattern of business-government relations that left critics little room in which to maneuver. Not only did the government continue to use CADE as a forum for dialogue with the private sector, but it also created a number of advisory councils where pro-government businesspeople were invited to participate.

Alternative efforts to join together the isolated business sectors had little chance to succeed. In 1972 and 1973, SNI, now the leading business association, became a center of active conservative opposition to the government (Ferner 1982, 167-68). Tensions escalated in 1972, when Duharte openly rejected a governmental attempt to place Industrial Community leaders within trade associations' boards of directors. Duharte was supported by the conservative press, APRA, and the Christian Popular Party (Partido Popular Cristiano), a party that split off from the Christian Democrats. He also accused the government of dividing the business community by appointing hand-picked business leaders to government advisory councils, and he criticized IPAE and CADE participants for supporting the government. In November 1973, the government nationalized the fishing industry, confirming Duharte's and his followers' fears. The Front tried to bring together several trade associations and civilian opposition leaders, but its initiative met with little support. Most trade associations and business leaders remained aloof. As trade associations were the only established channel of political action at that time, opposition parties used the SNI to push Duharte onto a confrontational course. The government's response was harsh. Duharte was deported on charges of conspiracy, and the SNI was forced to drop the "N" from its name because the government no longer recognized it as a "national" institution.[7] As soon as the confrontation ended, most business leaders continued to have dialogues with the government and to attend CADE conferences. They were fully aware that the powerful military government pursued a policy designed to keep the different business sectors apart and to avoid unified business pressure. This strategy, known as the "slicing policy" (like "divide and conquer"), rewarded business collaboration with the government and punished its opposition to government policies. Interventionist policies taken by an insular executive could be implemented more easily when confrontation with organized business was avoided. In the past, if industrialists had been subordinated to oligarchic rule, in the 1970s, the state prevailed over a highly disarticulated new bourgeoisie, whose internal divisions helped the military rule from above.

This situation, which challenged all private interests because it limited their ability to shape policy decisions collectively, forced business to continue to seek ways to empower itself politically. In the late 1970s and early 1980s, the collapse of militarism and statism, rising social movements, together with the challenges of open economies and democracies elsewhere in the region, accelerated organizational activism in the business community despite internal divisions caused by recession and neoliberal economic policies.

The UEPP and the 1977 Crisis

Led by Gen. Francisco Morales Bermúdez, the leader of a coup that ousted Gen. Velasco in 1975, the military initiated a conservative policy shift. Morales Bermúdez was aware that the economic situation debilitated the role of the military and made it difficult to continue with state-led growth. This situation favored business interests, which saw an opportunity to force the government to abandon social reforms, reduce state controls, and initiate a privatization program (Pease 1979). In May 1977, as an expression of the changing correlation of forces in favor of business, Walter Piazza, head of the powerful construction conglomerate COSAPI, became minister and immediately implemented a harsh stabilization plan. Led by CGTP, labor unions representing all sectors and regions reacted against the "business-military dictatorship" and the "IMF-sponsored" economic plan, calling for a national strike. In July 19, 1977, more than 300,000 workers were mobilized across the nation (Durand 1982, 135). The military government reacted by repressing all social movements, removing the now unpopular minister Piazza, and suspending implementation of the stabilization plan.

The following months saw a political crisis that isolated the government. Morales Bermúdez broke off relations with international banks and multilateral organizations, received little support from the business sector, and was pressured by social movements to stop implementing the stabilization plan and to call for elections. After the national strike, approximately 2,000 union leaders were laid off, and more than 100 party activists were imprisoned in an attempt to please business demands and stop popular reactions (Pease 1979, 246). In late 1977, the government finally crafted a new coalition by making pacts with domestic economic and political elites, that is, the business sector and party leaders of the right and center. Elections were called, and relations with multilateral organizations were normalized.

The agreement with the business sector was based on the gradual abandonment of radical reforms and the inclusion of business leaders in the cabinet. To appease the political parties, the government promised to hold elections for a constitutional assembly in May 1978 and general elections in 1980. Once business elites and party support were secured, the military started to negotiate with the IMF and to face the challenges from the left.

Despite the more favorable redefinition of relations with the military, uncertainty was still high for business elites. Many business leaders distrusted the government's commitment to dismantle the reforms, change labor legislation, and speed up privatization. In addition, negotiations with the IMF led to economic policy changes that would negatively affect business sectors operating in the domestic market. Business as a whole also faced an unusually aggressive union movement. When workers who were leaders of their labor unions were laid off, this generated solidarity and hunger strikes in all economic sectors. The business class at this critical juncture was unified against labor and pressed the government for legislative changes. At the CADE conference in November 1977, Morales Bermúdez quickly announced changes in legislation on Labor Communities. He also announced the end of agrarian reform. Under these circumstances, collective business action crystallized for a while. After the CADE conference, in order to make sure that the government's promises were implemented and to continue pressing the government to open up cabinet positions to the private sector, several business leaders decided to join forces to create a peak association. The Peruvian Private Businessmen's Union (Unión de Empresarios Privados — UEPP) was formed by eight trade associations in December 1977, under the leadership of Juan Antonio Aguirre Roca, SNI president and renowned CADE speaker. Membership, however, was limited to trade associations linked to the domestic market — SNI, Exporters Association (Asociación de Exportadores), Pharmaceutical Laboratories Association (Asociación de Laboratorios Farmacéuticos), Peruvian Chamber of Construction (Cámara Peruana de la Construcción), Peruvian Automotive Industries Association (Asociación Peruana de la Industria Automotriz), and Committee for Agricultural and Cattle Development (Comité de Desarrollo del Agro y la Ganadería). Absent were key trade associations linked to the import-export economy, such as CCL, SNMP, and the powerful Bank Association (Asociación de Bancos) (Durand 1982, 140-141).

Though the UEPP project was short-lived, it became an important learning experience. It was difficult for industrialists to provide effective leadership to all business sectors. At this time, different policy alternatives that could determine changes in the economic model were at stake. In addition, business leaders had little experience in dealing with the complexities of collective business action. Two problems emerged: sectoral leaders disagreed on economic policy changes, and internal disputes over leadership erupted. Despite its problems, the UEPP obtained some results. It supported the government in early May 1978, when a mission composed of governmental and business leaders — including UEPP's president — traveled to Washington, D.C., to negotiate a financial agreement and an economic stabilization plan (Pease 1979, 281). As part of the process leading toward a pact, SNI President Gabriel Lanata was appointed minister of industry, becoming the first trade association leader to join the cabinet since 1968. The political crisis was also resolved. Despite the climate of labor unrest and political violence, elections for the constitutional assembly were held as scheduled in May 1978.

After the military government secured a position of power and the team of economists obtained international financial support, the business coalition dissolved. In July 1978, UEPP ceased to operate. Lanata resigned as minister of industry after open disagreements with the rest of the cabinet on how to privatize the cement industry. The UEPP supported Lanata's criticism of the government for raising interest rates and lowering trade tariffs, a stance that deepened business divisions between sectors. To make matters worse, the government induced internal disagreement among UEPP members. A policy decision favored the Exporters' Association (Asociación de Exportadores — ADEX) with a generous tax rebate on non-traditional exports — CERTEX — while lowering trade tariffs. The slicing policy thus continued to cause dissension among business interests while avoiding generalized business opposition to governmental initiatives taken unilaterally by the executive.

The 1983-1984 Crisis: CONFIEP Is Born

In the Peruvian case in the 1980s, both the transition to democracy and the weakening of state elites favored business associativism. (Associativism refers to the formation of more business associations, an activation of existing business associations, and an increased participation of business associations in the political process.) Through the Constitutional Assembly's election to draft a new constitution in 1978, the move toward democracy had begun, a process in which business elites and trade associations participated actively. The new Constitution came into effect in July 1980, two months after presidential and congressional elections had taken place. Former President Fernando Belaúnde Terry was elected. After the traumatic experience with the Velasco government, business leaders sensed that access to the state and the monitoring process of government policies were easier under democratic conditions. Democracy, or an intermediate, semi-authoritarian regime, seemed to be the preferred option for most business leaders.

Neoliberalism was more disturbing to business interests, but its divisive impact among economic sectors — industrialists and developers versus traditional exporters — did not actually block the formation of a peak association. Despite disagreements over trade policies, a broad consensus developed to support privatization, deregulation, and anti-labor union legislation. Other problems, such as political uncertainty and sociopolitical violence that threatened private property, created an urgent need for business coordination.

Business leaders who were involved in the UEPP experiment in 1977 knew the economic policy debate could split them into several competing factions and, as in the past, doom efforts to coalesce several trade associations under a single roof. Therefore, the focus of collective business action was to enhance business participation in the policy-making process on issues that cut across all sectors, such as labor legislation, privatization, taxes, and anti-terrorist legislation. Initially, the debate over trade tariffs was left to individual trade associations. A group of business leaders committed to enhancing business unity avoided manifesting any opinions on the subject, waiting for an opportunity to coalesce the different business sectors. It came in 1984.

The gravity of the 1983 economic recession was expressed in a negative GDP annual growth rate of 10 percent. Natural disasters, declining exports, and increased external competition with domestic industries combined to make the crisis particularly severe (Iguíñiz 1986, 315 ff.). The government was led by President Belaúnde Terry, who, despite 1980 campaign promises to reactivate the economy and create "a million jobs," kept introducing neoliberal policies in order to receive international financial support. A pattern of top-down policy changes taken by the executive soon generated tensions. The SNI and ADEX openly criticized the lowering of trade tariffs and the elimination of tax rebates for non-traditional exporters, a position viewed with sympathy inside Belaúnde Terry's party (*El Comercio*, February 26, 1983). As the recession deepened, Belaúnde Terry also faced stronger opposition from APRA and the left. In November 1983, at the CADE conference, two key business segments — bankers and mine owners — jumped on the "reactivation" bandwagon, seeking governmental relief for the recession and joining forces with industrialists. Aguirre Roca, at that time chair of CADE '83, expressed business anxieties, "This year the emergency situation forces us to propose alternatives of immediate application in order to avoid an economic collapse" (IPAE 1983, 11).

Other elements in the political scenario worried businesspeople and prompted meetings among several trade associations. The municipal elections of November 1983 showed increased public support for APRA and the left. In Lima, a Marxist was elected mayor, and APRA won a majority of municipalities across the nation. Terrorist attacks launched by the Shining Path (Sendero Luminoso) and the Tupac Amaru Revolutionary Movement (Movimiento Revolucionario Tupac Amaru) escalated from 219 in 1980 to 1,760 in 1984 (DESCO 1989, 32). During the 1985 elections, it seemed clear that apristas stood to win, a perception that worried businesspeople because the two forces represented the dangers of interventionism.

In 1984, the Belaúnde Terry administration attempted to overcome its isolation by appointing Sandro Mariátegui, in theory a pro-business supporter, as minister of economy. As a sign of the trend toward unification, a joint public communiqué of four trade associations, all linked to the domestic market, demanded reactivation policies and manifested support for Mariátegui (*El Comercio* June 20, 1984). Minister Mariátegui welcomed the support; however, under intense and contradictory domestic and international pressure, he abruptly decided to raise taxes on banking credit to 17 percent (*Caretas*, July 16, 1984).

Outraged by Mariátegui's decision, the heavily indebted business sectors openly condemned the measure and demanded negotiations. An urgent meeting took place in late July, but Mariátegui was unwilling to make concessions. After negotiations failed, business leaders abandoned the meeting and soon after demanded immediate changes. To their surprise, the sudden breakdown in relations with the government had an immediate effect: it forced Mariátegui to retreat and lower the tax rate on credit to 8 percent.

This was the turning point that triggered business unity and pushed business associations further in the direction of mobilization because collective action had achieved immediate, tangible results. Quickly, it became evident that unity was a precondition for effective pressure politics. Julio Piccini, who became CONFIEP's first president in 1984, was one of the leaders who forced Mariátegui to change the tax policy on credit. Recalling that immediately after the July victory, business leaders from several trade associations decided to form a confederation, Piccini said, "This victory, highly successful by the way, made us think about and appreciate the value of unity" (*Presencia*, November 1994, 11). The trend toward unification continued in early 1984. Forums for leaders of different trade associations were held to prepare a business proposal for a National Development Project to be presented at CADE '84. Business leaders were trying to find a middle-of-the-road policy course to avoid the cost of a unilateral turn toward structural adjustment programs that might be taken by the government. The CADE forum, according to Piccini, provided a much needed space for coordination, "The presidents of several trade associations became friends after participating in the forum. That is where we all decided to create a confederation."[8]

Economic linkages among business sectors also came into play in the 1980s. First, the privatization of some industries offered investment opportunities to capitalists from different sectors to form joint ventures. Second, several private banks (Latino, Interandino, and Comercio) were formed by a coalition of powerful investors. Third, trading on Lima's Stock Exchange, operating since 1976, favored inter-elite articulation, a trait manifested in interlocking directorates of leading firms.[9] Fourth, economic power groups — native conglomerates known as *grupos* — became consolidated during this period. Although economic differences between business sectors linked to the domestic market and exporters were still significant, the process of internal restructuring that was taking place gradually made those sectoral differences less acute. In the 1980s, the Peruvian business class clearly was becoming more homogeneous than in the past.

In November 1984, CONFIEP was formed after four months of deliberations among heads of several trade associations who participated in the CADE business forums. Piccini, as CADE's first president, emphasized the importance of business unity in his inaugural speech, "CONFIEP will always be careful to respect the jurisdiction of member trade associations. . . . CONFIEP is, thus, unity within diversity" (*Industria Peruana*, November 1985, 12). The goals of the confederation were very general, the rules were inclusive and oriented toward conflict resolution, and the leadership was focused on unification issues: the defense of the private sector's role in the national economy, a demand for consultation on initiatives, and a call for political unity to avoid "legal instability" (*El Comercio*, November 21, 1984). Seven key trade associations representing a diversity of economic sectors joined CONFIEP: SNI, SNMP, CCL, Peruvian Construction Chamber (Cámara Peruana de la Construcción), National Fishing Society (Sociedad Nacional de Pesquería), National Confederation of Chambers of Commerce (Confederación Nacional de Cámaras de Comercio), and the Radio and TV Association (Asociación de Radio y Televisión).[10] Two key associations — ADEX and the Bank Association — became members the following year, widening CONFIEP's representative role. Since the banks were controlled by the grupos, their incorporation as members was an indication that big business, usually a free rider and, therefore, an obstacle for generalized collective action, preferred to join the organization rather than stand alone.

The Battle of the Banks: CONFIEP Is Consolidated

In 1984, both exogenous and endogenous factors positively combined to increase business unity. The business community's ability to coordinate through an umbrella organization, however, was still to be challenged by the state. President-elect Alan García showed no interest in recognizing the new organization. García preferred to engage in dialogues with business leaders at CADE conferences.[11] To complement this strategy, he established a separate alliance with a handful of grupo leaders in order to promote investment. Instead of confronting the government and criticizing García's slicing policy, CONFIEP quietly continued to lobby for business unity, while it organized business congresses and public conferences to recruit more members and gain national visibility. Unification of business was still fragile and incomplete.

In 1985, the need for a peak association was not evident for all business sectors. Most preferred to follow a double-track strategy: the grupos and individual businesspeople could establish independent relations with the García administration, while simultaneously supporting CONFIEP. This approach was known as the "cheap shield" because only a handful of business leaders were burdened by organizational tasks but all segments could potentially benefit from CONFIEP's ability to defend the private sector as a whole.[12]

The tide turned in favor of CONFIEP's consolidation in July 1987, when García suddenly announced his decision to break off relations with big business and nationalize the banking system. A fiscal crisis was looming, and international currency reserves were decreasing dramatically. García's response was to present a project to nationalize the banks. He argued that the grupos were delaying investment projects and the banks — controlled by grupos — were involved in currency speculation and capital flight. As Ricardo Tirado demonstrates in his chapter on Mexico in this volume, nationalization attempts against banking interests can enhance business unity when trade associations feel strong enough to challenge state interventionism, a phenomenon that has emerged in Mexico and Peru since the 1970s. In the Peruvian case, to a greater extent than in Mexico, all trade associations supported those in danger of being expropriated. At this critical juncture, CONFIEP became the only organization that could collectively defend the interests of the banking sector, thanks to its public, inclusive nature. Now the grupos were the ones in need of CONFIEP as a shield against expropriation and as the private sector's collective voice to win public opinion support and compete in the propaganda war launched by García and APRA. Feeling a common statist threat, 10 other trade associations joined the confederation in late 1987, quickly enhancing its role as an umbrella organization.[13] The battle of the banks was CONFIEP's political baptism, making it a respected player.

External forces also helped CONFIEP's formation and consolidation. In the mid-1980s, as Rose Spalding and Kenneth Johnson corroborate in their chapters on Nicaragua and El Salvador in this volume, the U.S. Agency for International Development (USAID) began to channel funds to business associations in Peru and Central America in order to reinforce the political role of the private sector threatened by guerrillas. Thanks to USAID support, from the beginning, CONFIEP relied upon generous external financing. The grant — US$2 million annually, according to CONFIEP sources — paid for facilities, staff salaries, conferences, and the publication of conference proceedings and a monthly newspaper (*Presencia*).[14] This financial aid came at a moment when it was critical to sustain the initial efforts of institutional development.

INTERNAL ORGANIZATION

B ecause of Peru's record of deep internal divisions within the business sector, the goals of the peak organization were geared at defending general interests and fostering harmonious relations among all members. A united front was the only way to counteract the effects of the government's slicing policy, differences of economic interests, and disputes over leadership positions.

CONFIEP was conceived of as a *gremio de gremios*, an encompassing organization representing trade associations from a diversity of economic sectors.[15] CONFIEP's main goal, as stated in confederation bylaws, was to represent members on "issues of common interest." According to its manager, Eduardo de Voto, the confederation "must go beyond sectoral interests." It should deal with "macro issues" and leave individual trade associations to defend "micro issues" that are sectoral in nature and not important to other business sectors. CONFIEP may eventually defend specific interests on behalf of a particular sector, but only when a trade association is not powerful enough to force negotiations with the government. The confederation is also designed to mediate disputes among sectoral associations on issues involving competing interests in conflict.

The bylaws clearly indicate CONFIEP's highly inclusive organizational design. The organs that aggregate and represent interests, the general assembly, the directive council, and the executive council, are based on the premises that all voices must be heard and that all business sectors should rotate in leadership positions.[16] The general assembly is the main body where the trade associations have the same voting power — one member, one vote. Former CONFIEP presidents and members of the executive committee also participate in the assembly.

The executive committee is composed of a minimum of seven and a maximum of 15 directors, each director representing an economic sector. The executive committee appoints special committees to deal with issues of general concern, such as labor, taxes, political matters, planning, social security, and institutional image. These committees help to incorporate business leaders who do not hold positions in trade associations. Managers and chief executive officers of the most powerful grupos and firms participate in the committee system, enhancing CONFIEP's links with big business.

CONFIEP presidents hold office for one year and can be reelected for a second term. Selection of presidents is based strictly on the principle of rotation, giving each sector an opportunity to lead the confederation. A sector can hold the presidency a second time only after a three-year hiatus. Again, these rules reveal a concern for business unity as no sector or president can stay in power for more than two years.

The Presidents

Between 1984 and 1998, CONFIEP had nine presidents: Julio Piccini, a developer; Miguel Vega Alvear, an industrialist; Ricardo Vega Llona, a nontraditional exporter; Rafael Villegas, a merchant; Reynaldo Gubbins, a mine owner; Jorge Camet, a developer; Juan Antonio Aguirre, an industrialist; Arturo Woodman, a nontraditional exporter; Jorge Picasso, a banker; and Alfredo Sotomayor, a fishing exporter. The first five were elected for only one year because of members' initial deep distrust of centralized power.[17] The institutional need for a more stable leadership and increasing trust on the part of trade association members led CONFIEP to accept one reelection. Since 1989, each president has remained in power for only two years, and none has been reelected.

Given the high degree of public exposure of CONFIEP leaders during the battle of the banks against President García, most CONFIEP presidents became public figures, and several became involved in the political process. Miguel Vega Alvear and Ricardo Vega Llona were party leaders in Mario Vargas Llosa's Libertad movement, and both were elected senators in 1990. In 1992, Camet was appointed to the cabinet, where he remained more than five years. Woodman headed a governmental agency in 1992, the National Social Compensation Fund (Fondo Nacional de Compensación Social), before becoming CONFIEP's president. After his presidency, he rejoined the government as head of the Peruvian Sports Institute (Instituto Peruano del Deporte) in 1996.

Membership and Representation

As of 1997, CONFIEP was composed of 22 trade association members (see Table 1). The most important regional organization is the Confederation of Chambers of Commerce (Confederación de Cámaras de Comercio — CONFECAMARAS), which comprises 31 chambers of commerce from every major Peruvian city. CONFIEP's members and leaders are mostly representatives of large and medium-sized businesses. Because sectoral associations are Peru's main type of business associations, CONFIEP has members representing all major economic sectors, across a spectrum of primary, secondary, and tertiary economic activity. Membership in trade associations varies greatly. In the case of the smallest — banking and private pension funds — membership ranges from 10 to 13 firms, respectively. CONFECAMARAS claims to be the largest, with more than 10,000 members, followed by 2,500 in Lima's Chamber of Commerce. The average size of a CONFIEP member association, excluding CONFECAMARAS, is 1,500 firms.

Most large and medium-sized firms are included in the trade associations. The only group not represented properly is the booming small businesses. As a response to this representational weakness, CONFIEP made efforts to include small business associations as one more economic sector to be represented in the organization. In 1995, the confederation formally invited small business leaders to participate as regular members. CONFIEP's main interest in bringing them in was to avoid independent negotiations between small business organizations and the government. In late 1995, the Confederation of Small Businesses (Confederación Nacional de la Micro y Pequeña Empresa — CONAMYPE) was formed for the purpose of uniting several associations to join CONFIEP. The effort succeeded, and CONAMYPE was admitted as a new member that same year.

CONFIEP's business leaders are mostly from the oldest sectoral associations and big sectoral firms rather than the grupos. Most association leaders represent firms and sectors that need access to political power on a regular basis. Grupo leaders participate in CONFIEP's internal activities to a limited extent and are more prone to act as free riders and to engage in one-on-one negotiations with the government. They operate inside and outside CONFIEP's framework. The grupos do not need CONFIEP to have access to or influence over the government, although they support the confederation because it serves as a shield from erratic political decisions — such as nationalization of the banks — and as a public voice for the business class as a whole.

Table 1.
CONFIEP's Member Trade Associations

Trade Association	Date Founded	Date It Joined CONFIEP	Number of Members
Sociedad Nacional de Industrias, SNI	1896	1984	1,654
Asociación de Exportadores, ADEX	1974	1984	1,160
Sociedad Nacional de Minería y Petróleo, SNMP	1896	1984	753
Cámara de Comercio de Lima, CCL	1888	1984	2,500
Sociedad Nacional de Pesquería, SNP	1952	1984	120
Cámara Peruana de la Construcción, CAPECO	1954	1984	1,048
Asociación de Radio y Televisión, ARTV	circa 1965	1984	30
Asociación Peruana de Empresas de Seguros, APESEG	1904	1985	10
Confederación de Cámaras de Comercio, CONFECAMARAS	1970	1986	10,000
Asociación de Bancos, ASBANC	1967	1986	13
Cámara Nacional de Turismo, CANATUR	1970	1986	180
Asociación Peruana de Empresas Aéreas, APEA	1979	1986	16
Asociación Automotriz del Perú, AAP	1926	1987	220
Asociación de Ingenieros Constructores del Peru, AIC	1945	1987	36
Asociación Peruana de Empresas Compradoras de Seguros, APECROSE	1976	1987	n.a.
Asociación Peruana de Avicultura, APA	1938	1987	250
Asociación Nacional de Laboratorios Farmacéuticos del Perú, ALAFARPE	1953	1987	55
Asociación de Agentes de Aduana del Perú, AAAP	1950	1988	308
Sociedad Nacional de Exportadores, SNE	1989	1993	n.a.
Asociación de Empresarios Agrarios, AEA	1993	1993	n.a.
Asociación de Administradoras Privadas de Fondos de Pensiones, AAPFP	1993	1993	10
Confederación Nacional de la Micro y Pequeña Empresa, CONAMYPE	1995	1995	n.a.

n.a.= not available.
Sources: CONFIEP and other associations' records. Data on membership provided by CONFIEP in 1995. Elaboration: Francisco Durand.

Issues and Tactics

CONFIEP's history indicates that the business sector's collective institutional responses are geared primarily toward negotiations with the executive, the center of the political system. Relations with Congress, the courts, and civil society are secondary. A high degree of power centralization in the executive and the traditional presidential influence over Congress force players to focus on key power holders. To deal with the executive, the most capricious and insular of all public institutions, CONFIEP has sought to establish a permanent working relationship with the president, cabinet members, and key governmental regulatory agencies. A secondary, usually complementary objective, is to influence public opinion by disseminating the private sector's views on major policy and political issues and to bargain with other social groups, labor in particular. Lobbying in Congress is usually left to individual trade associations, unless a critical piece of legislation is being debated. The relative unimportance of Congress is also due to the fact that most neoliberal legislation has been approved by the executive through extraordinary legislative powers and under strong external influence.

CONFIEP's defense of general class interests is aimed at 1) preventing legislation that negatively affects property rights and limits the role of the private sector, 2) supporting legislation and implementation of laws that empower the role of the business community as employers and private property owners, and 3) moderating or changing legislation and policy implementation that define the orientation of the economy. These goals are achieved primarily through agreements with an incoming administration — usually in a closed meeting between the president-elect and a CONFIEP delegation — followed by intense public and private lobbying. An agreement broadly defines the degree and modalities of access to the decision-making process. From then on, signals of stable relations occur if the Peruvian president agrees to deliver the closing speech at the CADE conference and CONFIEP congresses. President García, for example, who continued to implement the slicing policy, attended all CADE conferences but never any CONFIEP congresses. President Fujimori, more respectful of business autonomy than his predecessor, has always given the closing speech at both events. Fujimori's presence at CONFIEP's fourth congress in January 1991 was critical in reassuring a large group of business leaders from different sectors and regions that the new administration maintained open lines of communication with business and planned to defend private interests (Castillo 1991, 8-11).

CONFIEP's tactics range from negative to positive. Negative tactics are usually employed publicly and vary from angry comments in the press — usually in interviews with business leaders — to more balanced public communiqués that criticize government decisions. A negative tactic is used when access to the government is difficult or relations are strained or broken. Only when relations are broken — as happened between 1987 and 1990 during the García administration — does CONFIEP resort to litigation, negative advertising, threats of lockouts, and even protest politics, such as street demonstrations and open support for antigovernment political rallies. Positive tactics are based on regular, private, and often unpublicized meetings at all levels of the decision-making process. If the meetings do not yield results, particularly if changes are promised by the state's elites but are not carried out — a common bureaucratic practice known as the *mecedora*, the "rocking chair" — CONFIEP resorts to a combination of public pressure and intensive lobbying. Until meetings are arranged and effective dialogue and negotiation take place, CONFIEP remains in the trenches, constantly criticizing or attacking the government. Under the Fujimori administration, CONFIEP has developed a more stable, positive, predictable pattern of relations, a process consolidated by business support for the 1992 presidential coup and Fujimori's reelection for five more years in 1995. In spite of the alliance, bureaucratic insulation continues to be a problem for business leaders, making access to government difficult.[18]

The limits of the business sector's influence in the 1990s are set mostly by the degree of bureaucratic insulation of politicians and experts and the pervasive role of multilateral organizations — the IMF, in particular — in shaping economic policy decisionmaking. Since 1976, all Peruvian governments have signed stabilization plans and structural adjustment agreements with the IMF in a highly secret, closed negotiating process. Unilateral, surprise policy decisions traditionally have triggered a pattern of reactive, defensive behavior on the part of business until policies are gradually adjusted by domestic pressure, that is, "nationalized." Prevention of antibusiness legislation was most successful in mid-1987, when CONFIEP mobilized the business sector as a whole and used protest politics to prevent the takeover of the banking system. Undoubtedly, this was the confederation's most outstanding policy victory. CONFIEP also has been effective in supporting legislation in areas such as the privatization of public firms and cooperatives and the reduction of labor rights — job security, benefits — particularly during the Fujimori administration.

In contrast with the García administration, relations between business and the Fujimori administration have been remarkably stable but not free of tension. In May 1990, CONFIEP's executive committee held a meeting with the incoming president and reached a number of agreements.[19] President Fujimori offered constant communication with trade associations and the incorporation of CONFIEP leaders into his cabinet, a practice that started in 1992, when Jorge Camet became minister of industry, and later, in 1993, minister of economy. Liliana Canale, from the National Exporters Society (Sociedad Nacional de Exportadores — SNE), replaced Camet as minister of industry. In 1992, Arturo Woodman, also from the SNE, was appointed director of the National Social Compensation Fund. Two other business leaders held cabinet positions in 1994-1995, Efraín Goldenberg and Alfonso Bustamante. Through informal meetings and the direct channels mentioned above, business leaders lobbied silently and effectively for legislation on behalf of their own interests. Some of the most important pro-business changes were introduced in 1991 as part of a legislative package that was issued by the executive through extraordinary powers. The legislative package was directed by Carlos Boloña, minister of economy, who counted on the technical expertise of several CONFIEP experts paid by USAID. Later on, when Camet replaced Boloña as minister of economy, contacts with the government took place through Camet and Canale whenever the ministers felt like listening to business demands.[20] Moderating and changing legislation as well as influencing economic policy on tax, trade, and monetary issues have proved difficult for the business peak organization. The influence of multilateral organizations and the insulation of regulatory agencies, particularly those in charge of monetary and tax policies, explain CONFIEP's modest accomplishments. In some of these policy areas — trade tariffs, for example — intrabusiness disagreements are common. In addition, business organizations initially did not develop the institutional expertise needed to propose coherent policy alternatives in a way that would match the recommendations of governmental and international experts. In regard to tax policies, CONFIEP consistently has manifested its discontent since a tax reform was initiated in 1991 (*Presencia*, November 1994, 5). Even through their most effective channel, Minister Camet, CONFIEP initially had difficulty lobbying effectively and often complained about the high degree of insulation of the tax administration. However, patience and constant pressure have finally yielded results.[21] For three years, CONFIEP demanded the elimination of a special 2-percent tax on assets, which was favored by the IMF and had been in force since 1992. After prolonged infighting, the government reached an agreement with business leaders to lower the rate to 1.5 percent in 1995 (*El Peruano*, July 7, 1995). In an interview, Arturo Tello, CONFIEP's manager, said that Camet initially was unwilling to listen to the business community's collective demands. Tello quoted Camet as saying, "It was the IMF that posed the most serious resistance." In 1994, when CONFIEP concluded that dialogue had not produced positive results, it threatened to denounce in the press the lack of understanding with the economic team. The government finally agreed to set up a meeting with business leaders and experts from different ministries and regulatory agencies. According to Tello, "In the end, we won some minor concessions, about one out of five of all changes requested. The relationship is not very fruitful but we continue to support the government."[22]

After intense public pressure and private lobbying, business was able to achieve other important results. In September 1996, the government made a major concession by approving a law to help businesses by means of a generous plan to restructure tax debts acquired since 1990. In April 1997, Camet again lowered the 2-percent tax on assets to 0.5 percent, thus meeting CONFIEP's demands (*Expreso*, April 25, 1997). In July, when Fujimori was in need of business support, another tax rate — FONAVI — was lowered by two percentage points (*Gestión*, August 26, 1997).

The business community's pressure for policy changes not only has increased in the second half of the 1990s but also has become more sophisticated, thanks to CONFIEP. Instead of reacting to policy designed by others, CONFIEP is now playing a different game. As Eduardo Silva argues in his study of the Chilean encompassing association in this volume, professionalization is a critical factor to empower business policy-making capabilities. CONFIEP, as the CPC, its Chilean counterpart, has become more capable of anticipating changes and proposing major legislative initiatives in a timely fashion, a sign of institutional maturity. Thanks to its organizational empowerment and professionalization, business is moving from being merely reactive to taking on a more fruitful, proactive stance. The creation of a pro-business think tank in 1994, the Political Economy Institute (Instituto de Política Económica — IPE), funded by CONFIEP leaders, major grupos, and multilateral organizations, has helped business make more specific, detailed, and comprehensive policy proposals (*Presencia*, March-April 1994, 8). IPE's formation represents a major leap forward both in terms of the business community's institutional development and its ability to participate more effectively in the policy debates of the 1990s. Together with IPE, CONFIEP has also manifested other signs of professionalization. In the late 1990s, CONFIEP founded the Productivity Institute to study microeconomic issues and the Entrepreneurial Club to foster social linkages and interaction with foreign investors. The Club also serves as CONFIEP's new headquarters (*Presencia*, September 1996, 10; and November 1996, 67). These three institutions propel CONFIEP in a new direction because they help business develop capabilities to link short- with long-term interests and to manage both micro- and macroeconomic issues.

Indeed, emphasis on long-term issues has always been a dilemma for CONFIEP leaders, who are usually trapped between specific demands and the need to foresee policy and economic developments. The original intent of its founders was to develop a "thinking institution," but CONFIEP initially moved in the direction of making short-term demands. As of 1998, 13 years after its founding, CONFIEP has unquestionably matured as an institution and is more capable of participating in policy debates in a more substantive, broader manner.[23]

The Debate on Democracy and Neoliberalism

As an umbrella organization, CONFIEP has held internal discussions concerning the extent of business support for neoliberal economic policies and democracy. The debate on neoliberal economic policies is understandable, given that Peru's policy orientation has been highly unstable and business has not easily supported the changes. Since 1977, industrialists, developers, and small business owners have resisted neoliberal policies and supported political actors who defend market protectionism, while exporters and import-export merchants have fought for liberalization. As the crisis deepened in the 1980s, the balance of forces within the business class finally shifted in favor of neoliberalism, a process that was visible inside trade associations. The "conversion" of most business sectors that support free market economics occurred in 1987, when President García attempted to reinforce the role of the state in the economy through nationalizations and price regulations. This critical juncture created an unbridgeable gap between the populist option and the business class. To business, statism was more dangerous than economic liberalism. Besides, the grupos, thanks to their control of the banking system, diversified investments, and improved management, accepted the challenge of increased competition. There was no other viable alternative. For most business sectors, big business in particular, it was better to accept the policy course and fight for better conditions while adjusting to the new model than to oppose it. From 1987 on, business leaders, through CONFIEP, have supported economic liberalization more consistently. CONFIEP has passed from silence to pragmatic endorsement. The last major debate on trade tariffs took place in 1990-1991, when the Fujimori government opted once more for economic liberalism. On this occasion, industrialists did not condemn the model but demanded a higher, more differentiated system of trade tariffs than the one proposed by the policy team (*Caretas*, November 11, 1991). The degree of market openness and the opportunities to adjust to changes have been the key issues rather than the new model itself. Through its public statements, CONFIEP has helped to express the new correlation of forces within the business community that favors a pragmatic, more national version of neoliberalism. To that end, CONFIEP has lobbied with varying degrees of effectiveness to force the government to take into account business demands in favor of a less painful transition. CONFIEP's stance indicates the extent of business accommodation to the new model.

The second issue, democracy, has been debated constantly since President García attempted to nationalize the banking system and his administration entered a period of fiscal chaos, corruption, and widespread terrorism. Pro-coup coalitions were formed in the late 1980s but never predominated inside CONFIEP, which served as a place to exchange ideas. Since consensus inside CONFIEP was never reached, the debate helped to prevent business support for a military takeover, a signal the generals received and understood. In the early 1990s, as the crisis and chaos deepened, CONFIEP supported Fujimori's April 1992 presidential coup as a way to assure conditions of governability without endorsing a full-fledged authoritarian alternative. According to Arturo Tello, CONFIEP's manager at that time:

> In 1992, with the coup, we gave Fujimori massive support and published in the press a communiqué backing the government. From then on, relations with Fujimori became closer, and we have participated in trade missions with the president. We are concerned about democracy, yes, but democracy with order. It is not a question of being undemocratic; there is first a problem of order to be solved.[24]

Business support for Fujimori has been conditional. A concentration of power in presidential hands was accepted as long as a quick restoration of constitutional order followed. This position of conditional support is inspired also by the need to avoid isolation from the international community, a precondition for growth in a globalized economy. Businesses need at best democracies and at a minimum semi-authoritarian regimes. CONFIEP did support the coup but also advocated the restoration of democratic procedures, confident that Fujimori enjoyed popular support and that his government could continue its pro-business orientation.

CONCLUSION

The longitudinal analysis of collective business action in Peru indicates that conditions for unity occur at critical junctures characterized by extreme uncertainty. These key moments combine four factors: a deep economic recession, a political crisis expressed in regime changes or sudden policy shifts, serious difficulties for business in gaining access to political power, and the emergence of labor mobilization and leftist activism that threaten private interests.

The combination of these four factors makes the collective defense of general economic interests more important for business than the defense of sectoral, individual interests. The likelihood of developing a more encompassing and permanent form of organized collective action at these critical junctures is also influenced by the degree of business economic articulation, the nature of business leadership, and the role of trade associations in the political system. Disarticulated elites, who manifest strong regional, social, and economic cleavages, are less prone to collective action than more homogeneous, economically articulated business elites. Traditional oligarchic leaders, who blindly defend sectoral interests, are less likely to build durable organizations than modern leaders who are more interested in empowering the business community to propel the institutional development of encompassing associations. Isolated trade associations trapped in sectoral competition and lacking linkages to political parties are more prone to suffer from state interventionism and bureaucratic policy discretion. Trade associations united under an encompassing association can redefine relations with government to enhance the role business plays in policy and political outcomes. An encompassing association not only serves as a vehicle to voice demands and to lobby more effectively, but it also has the potential to play the "legitimacy game," redefining the role of trade associations in the political system by projecting the business community toward civil society.

This transformation of business's collective capabilities is analyzed as Peruvian society passed from the oligarchic to the populist period and from the populist one to a neoliberal one, when a highly positive combination of factors, exogenous and endogenous, took place in the second half of the 1980s. Once CONFIEP was established, the process of institutional development finally took off.

The troubled history of Peruvian business peak associations, plagued for so long by internal divisions, shaped the nature of the large encompassing organization. CONFIEP emerged as a more inclusive association, specifically designed for conflict resolution and to represent a diversity of business interests. CONFIEP now represents a superior, proactive form of interest aggregation. As a key private-sector institution, it has politically empowered the business community. CONFIEP became an effective shield to protect businesspeople when private property was attacked by populist and socialist forces; a vehicle to voice demands in public on behalf of the business sector as a whole; and a more effective and professionalized channel of dialogue, consultation, and negotiation with policymakers and political leaders.

CONFIEP's stances on two key issues of the 1980s and 1990s, democracy and neoliberalism, indicate that business as a whole tends to provide conditional support on both counts. Support of democracy depends on the government's ability to provide order and stability. CONFIEP openly backed Fujimori's presidential coup in 1992 but also advocated a quicker restoration of democracy, acting as a moderating force that reduced the influence of more authoritarian factions within the government. Between authoritarianism and democracy, the Peruvian business community leaned more toward democracy or semi-democratic forms of government.

CONFIEP was born in the midst of the policy debates of the 1980s. Willing to craft consensus and keep the private sector united on general issues, it initially avoided taking a stand on trade liberalization and neoliberalism but supported privatization efforts and changes in labor legislation. After nationalization of the banks, when the links with populism were broken, CONFIEP shifted toward conditional support for neoliberalism. Business sectors have used the organizational umbrella to lobby the government more effectively and "nationalize" policy decisions taken by insular bureaucracies and international experts. The peak association has thus empowered the business community politically. It may also help the post-oligarchic bourgeoisie to move in new directions and gain the social respect the old oligarchy never obtained. A peak association has the potential to help business gain much needed social legitimacy. Its confederated form is well suited to transform not only relations with the state — it is the only institution that represents business class interests in public — but also relations with civil society. A political analyst, Sinesio López, argues that Peru's interest group system is fully grown "vertically." All social groups, business included, have their own representative organizations, but it remains to be seen if they can interact "horizontally," looking for common ground instead of confronting each other (López 1991, 161). A peak association can bridge several interest groups in civil society, in particular, labor, small business, and the informal sector. The incorporation of small business associations under CONFIEP's umbrella is an important, albeit limited, step in this process. Despite the past record of class conflict, negotiations with the CGTP, the labor confederation, have occurred several times in the 1990s. If this continues to be the case, the chances for democratic stability, based on competition and interaction among groups that can debate and find points of agreement, may be enhanced in the future. Thanks to CONFIEP, the business community is beginning to realize that political stability is based not only on stable relations with government but also on closer, more consensual relations with civil society.

Notes

1. For a comparative study of the role of organized business in developing countries, see Maxfield and Schneider (1997).

2. The concept of critical junctures used in this chapter is based on Collier and Collier (1991, 27-29).

3. For an analysis of the regional basis of the economy at the time of export-led development, see Drinot (1996).

4. The founding date of trade associations indicates this process of growing organizational diversity. See Table 1.

5. Beltrán's family hacienda, Motalván, was expropriated in 1969, together with *La Prensa*, the newspaper owned by several oligarchic families and Beltrán (Portocarrero 1986, 83). On the agrarian reform and dissolution of the SNA, see Valderrama (1979, 64-70). On Beltrán's reaction to the Velasco government, see his collection of newspaper articles published in Spain (1979).

6. The author interviewed Edgardo Palza, CADE organizer for 15 years, several times between 1976 and 1994. According to Palza, IPAE's idea was to transform CADE into a "small congress." Interview with Palza, Arequipa, November 1976.

7. For a detailed documentation of business-government relations during the Velasco administration, see Sociedad de Industrias (1977).

8. Interview with Julio Piccini. Lima, May 1986.

9. For an empirical study on interlocking directorates of firms operating in the stock exchange, see Soberón (1985).

10. According to Edgardo Palza, SNI and CCL constantly disagreed on how to form the new organization. Julio Piccini, a developer, was elected first president because "He was more neutral, accepted by all." Interview with Palza, Lima, September 1986.

11. According to Edgardo Palza, CONFIEP proposed to García a "social pact" among CONFIEP, labor, and the government. García declined the offer. He wanted to be the architect of the alliance. Interview with Palza. Lima, September 1986.

12. A few months before the nationalization attempt, Palza stated that business leaders wanted to "manage uncertainty through CONFIEP" rather than remain uncoordinated if a political crisis were to arise. Interview with Palza. Lima, September 1986.

13. Why was CONFIEP more effective than its Mexican counterpart in defending the banks? The answer lies in the type of political system. Peru's civil society, as this chapter argues, is stronger and more autonomous than Mexico's. State corporatism never developed, not even under the Velasco administration. In Mexico, the state yielded more power and exerted more influence over interest groups such as CANACINTRA and CONCANACO.

14. According to Arturo Tello, CONFIEP's manager from 1991 to 1994, 90 percent of the budget was covered with USAID funds. Interview with Tello. Lima, May 1995.

15. A *gremio* is an association or guild.

16. Non-controversial decisions are approved by simple majority. Decisions that are strongly opposed by members representing one sector cannot be approved until investigated by a multisectoral commission that reports findings to the directive council.

17. Actually, the first term provision was limited to six months! According to Edgardo Palza, "This was a controversial topic since the beginning." Interview with Palza. Lima, September 1986.

18. Conversation with Luis Abugattas, director of SNI's Institute of Social and Economic Studies. London, June 1997.

19. Interview with Arturo Tello. Lima, May 1995.

20. Interview with Arturo Tello and Eduardo de Voto. The latter replaced Tello as CONFIEP manager in 1995. Lima, May 1995.

21. As noted in the introductory chapter, business associations are not regarded as key policy players by several scholars. A more detailed analysis focused on encompassing business associations in the long run indicates business plays an important role in agenda setting, policy evaluation, and policy adjustment.

22. Interview with Arturo Tello. Lima, May 1995.

23. In 1995, Arturo Tello believed that CONFIEP could play two roles. Trade association leaders wanted CONFIEP to dedicate most of its time to specific legal matters and preferred to hire lawyers such as Tello and De Voto, litigation experts, as CONFIEP managers. Tello believes that CONFIEP should develop a national leadership ability that requires focusing on broader long-term issues. A positive sign of this process is the 2021 Committee headed by Manuel Sotomayor, one of the younger, more intellectually sophisticated business leaders. Interview with Tello. Lima, May 1995. In 1998, Sotomayor was elected president of CONFIEP.

24. Interview with Arturo Tello. Lima, May 1995.

References

Abugattas, Luis. 1997. Interviewed by Francisco Durand. London, June.

Basadre, Jorge. 1975. *Historia de la república del Perú.* Lima: Editorial Universitaria.

Beltrán, Pedro. 1979. *La verdadera realidad peruana.* Madrid.

Beltrán, Pedro. 1994. *Pensamiento y acción (selección de textos).* Lima: Instituto de Libre Mercado.

Caravedo, Baltazar. 1976. *Burguesía e industria en el Perú 1933-1945.* Lima: Instituto de Estudios Peruanos.

Caretas. 1984. July 16.

Caretas. 1991. November 11.

Castillo, Manuel. 1991. "Empresarios: período de gracia y equilibrios precarios." In *Quehacer,* No. 68: 8-11.

Chirinos Soto, Enrique. 1989. *Historia de la república*, Vol. 2. Lima: Editores Importadores.

Collier, David, and Ruth Berins Collier. 1991. *Shaping the Political Arena.* Princeton, N.J.: Princeton University Press.

El Comercio. 1983. February 26.

El Comercio. 1984. November 21.

Conaghan, Catherine M., and James M. Malloy. 1994. *Unsettling Statecraft.* Pittsburgh: University of Pittsburgh Press.

Cotler, Julio. 1978. *Clases, estado y nación en el Perú.* Lima: Instituto de Estudios Peruanos.

Cotler, Julio. 1994. *Política y sociedad en el Perú.* Lima: Instituto de Estudios Peruanos.

DESCO (Centro de Estudios y Promoción del Desarrollo). 1989. *Violencia Política en el Perú.* Lima: DESCO.

Drinot, Paulo. 1996. "Peru, 1899-1930: A Beggar Sitting on a Gold Mine?" Paper presented to the international workshop on Economic History of Latin America in the 20th Century, organized by Oxford University, St. Anthony's College, Lake Atitlán, Guatemala, December 8-11.

Durand, Francisco. 1982. *La década frustrada. Los industriales y el poder, 1970-1980.* Lima: DESCO.

Durand, Francisco. 1994. *Business and Politics in Peru.* Boulder, Colo.: Westview Press.

Durand, Francisco. 1997. *Incertidumbre y soledad. Reflexiones sobre los grandes empresarios de América Latina.* Lima: Fundación Friedrich Ebert.

Durand, Francisco, and Eduardo Silva, eds. 1998. *Organized Business, Economic Change, and Democracy in Latin America.* Coral Gables, Fla.: North-South Center Press at the University of Miami.

Expreso. 1997. April 25.

Ferner, Anthony. 1982. *La burguesía industrial en el desarrollo peruano.* Lima: ESAN.

Gestión. 1997. August 26.

Garrido, Celso, ed. 1988. *Empresarios y estado en América Latina.* Mexico City: CIDE-Fundación Ebert-UNAM.

Iguíñiz, Javier. 1986. "La crisis peruana actual: esquema para una interpretación." *Las crisis económicas en la historia del Perú,* ed. Heraclio Bonilla. Lima: Fundación Friedrich Ebert.

IPAE (Instituto Peruano de Administración de Empresas). 1983. *Anales de la XXI conferencia anual de ejecutivos.* Lima: IPAE.

Laos, Cipriano. 1929. *Lima, la ciudad de los reyes.* Lima: Editorial Perú.

López, Sinesio. 1991. *El dios mortal.* Lima: Instituto Socialismo y Democracia.

Martinelli, Alberto. 1994. "Entrepreneurship and Management." *The Handbook of Economic Sociology,* eds. Smelser, Neil, and Richard Swedberg. Princeton, N.J.: Princeton University Press.

Maxfield, Sylvia, and Ben Ross Schneider, eds. 1997. *Business and the State in Developing Countries.* New York: Cornell University Press.

Miró Quesada, Carlos. 1947. *Sánchez Cerro y su tiempo.* Buenos Aires: El Ateneo.

Mundial. 1930. October 17, November 14, November 28.

Palza, Edgardo. 1976. Interviewed by Francisco Durand, Arequipa, Peru, November 1976, and Lima, Peru, September 1986.

Pease, Henry. 1979. *Los caminos del poder.* Lima: DESCO.

El Peruano. 1995. July 7.

Piccini, Julio. 1986. Interviewed by Francisco Durand, Lima, May.

Planas, Pedro. 1994. *La república aristocrática.* Lima: Fundación Friedrich Ebert.

Portocarrero, Gonzalo, 1981. "Del monetarismo al keynesianismo: la política económica durante la crisis del 30." *Economía* (7): 81-98.

Portocarrero, Gonzalo. 1986. *De Bustamante a Odría.* Lima: Mosca Azul Editores.

Presencia. 1994. March-April and November.

Presencia. 1996. September and November.

Soberón, Luis. 1985. "Integración y diferenciación sociales en el sector empresarial." In *Socialismo y Participación* (32): 61-75.

Sociedad de Industrias. 1977. *La revolución y la industria.* Lima: Sociedad de Industrias.

Sulmont, Denis. 1977. *Historia del movimiento obrero peruano.* Lima: Editorial Tarea.

Tello, Arturo. 1995. Interviewed by Francisco Durand, Lima, May.

Thorp, Rosemary. 1991. *Economic Management and Economic Development in Peru and Colombia.* Pittsburgh: University of Pittsburgh Press.

Thorp, Rosemary, and Geoffrey Bertram. 1978. *Peru 1890-1977.* New York: Columbia University Press.

Valderrama, Mariano. 1979. *La oligarquía terrateniente: ayer y hoy.* Lima: Pontificia Universidad Católica del Perú.

Valderrama, Mariano, and Patricia Ludmann. 1976. *7 años de reforma agraria peruana.* Lima: Pontificia Universidad Católica del Perú.

de Voto, Eduardo. 1995. Interviewed by Francisco Durand, Lima, June 1995.

Wils, Fritz. 1979. *Los industriales, la industrialización y el estado nación en el Perú.* Lima: Pontificia Universidad Católica del Perú.

Windmuller, John P., and Alan Gladstone. 1984. *Employers Associations and Industrial Relations.* Cambridge, U.K.: Clarendon Press-Oxford.

Contributors

Carlos H. Acuña (Ph.D. candidate, University of Chicago, 1994) is associate professor at the Universidad de San Andrés, Argentina. He is editor of *La nueva matriz política argentina* (Nueva Visión 1995) and co-editor of *Latin American Political Economy in the Age of Neoliberal Reform* (North-South Center Press 1994). Dr. Acuña is working on a book project on the historical role of Argentine business elites in the political process (forthcoming 1999).

Francisco Durand (Ph.D., University of California, Berkeley, 1991) is associate professor of political science at the University of Texas, San Antonio. His works include *Incertidumbre y soledad: reflexiones sobre los grandes empresarios de América Latina* (Fundación Ebert 1997); *Business and Politics in Peru* (Westview Press 1994); and articles in *Oxford Development Studies, Nueva Sociedad, Revista Mexicana de Sociología,* and *Tiers Monde.* He is researching tax reforms in Latin America and changes in the Peruvian political system under President Fujimori.

Rosario Espinal (Ph.D., Washington University-St. Louis, 1985) is associate professor of sociology and director of the Latin American Studies Center at Temple University. She has published two editions of *Autoritarismo y Democracia en la Política Dominicana* (CAPEL 1987, and Editorial Argumentos, 1994) and articles in the *Journal of Latin American Studies, Bulletin of Latin American Research, Electoral Studies, Development and Change, Hemisphere, Latin American Perspectives,* and *Nueva Sociedad.* Dr. Espinal is researching changes in political parties and the organization of civil society in the Dominican Republic.

Kenneth L. Johnson (Ph.D., Tulane University, 1993) is assistant professor of government at Eastern Kentucky University. He has done research on the roles of Salvadoran and Central American economic elites and has published "Demise of Castro?" in *Intercambio.* Dr. Johnson is doing research on legal education in Latin America and consults for Price-Waterhouse on political and business climate risk analysis.

Eduardo Silva (Ph.D., University of California, San Diego, 1991) is associate professor of political science and fellow at the Center for International Studies at the University of Missouri-Saint Louis and an adjunct senior research associate of the North-South Center at the University of Miami. He is author of *The State and Capital in Chile* (Westview 1996) and co-editor of *Elections and Democratization in Latin America* (CILAS, San Diego 1986). His articles have appeared in *World Politics, Comparative Politics, Development and Change, Journal of Latin American Studies,* and the *Journal of Interamerican Studies and World Affairs.*

Rose J. Spalding (Ph.D., University of North Carolina at Chapel Hill, 1978) is professor of political science at DePaul University. She is author of *Capitalists and Revolution in Nicaragua: Opposition and Accommodation 1979-1993* (University of North Carolina Press 1994) and the editor of *The Political Economy of Revolutionary Nicaragua* (Allen & Unwin 1987).

Ricardo Tirado (Master, Universidad Nacional Autónoma de México, 1978) is a researcher at the Instituto de Investigaciones Sociales de la UNAM in Mexico City. He is the editor of *Los empresarios ante la globalización* (UNAM and Instituto de Investigaciones Legislativas 1994) and author of *Clases dominantes y estado* (UNAM 1984) and *Mexico: poder empresarial* (Terranova 1983). He has coordinated the Entrepreneurs and the State Section of the Latin American Social Sciences Council (CLACSO). Mr. Tirado studies trade associations and technological innovation in Mexico.

Kurt Weyland (Ph.D., Stanford University, 1991) is associate professor of political science at Vanderbilt University. He is the author of *Democracy Without Equity: Failures of Reform in Brazil* (University of Pittsburgh Press 1996) and many articles on social and economic policy in journals such as *Comparative Politics, International Studies Quarterly, Studies in Comparative International Development*, and *Comparative Political Studies* (forthcoming). He is conducting research for a book on the politics of market reform in Argentina, Brazil, Peru, and Venezuela.

Index

A

AAPIC (Argentine Production, Industry, and Trade Association — Asociación Argentina de la Producción, la Industria y el Comercio) 62

ABDIB (Brazilian Association for the Development of Basic Industries — Associação Brasileiro para o Desenvolvimento das Indústrias de Base) 77

ABECAFE (Association of Coffee Processors and Exporters — Asociación de Beneficiadores y Exportadores de Café) 124, 131, 132, 135, 136, 139

ABM (Mexican Bankers' Association — Asociación de Banqueros de México) 185, 187, 189, 190

Acción Coordinadora de las Instituciones Empresarias Libres. *See ACIEL*

Acción Popular. *See Popular Action*

ACIEL (Coordinating Action for Free Business Institutions — Acción Coordinadora de las Instituciones Empresarias Libres) 63, 64, 65, 66

ACIS (Association of Merchants and Industrialists of Santiago — Asociación de Comerciantes e Industriales de Santiago) 102, 103, 105, 110, 111

Action for Democracy Group. *See GAD*

AD (Democratic Alliance — Alianza Democrática) 236, 237

ADACH (Association of Cotton Growers of Chinandega — Asociación de Algodoneros de Chinandega) 160

ADIMRA (Association of Industrial Metalurgists — Asociación de Industriales Metalúrgicos) 65

ADOEXPO (Dominican Association of Exporters — Asociación Dominicana de Exportadores) 114

ADOZONAS (Dominican Association of Free Trade Zones — Asociación Dominicana de Zonas Francas) 114

advisory councils 260

AEIH (Association of Industrial Enter-prises of Herrera — Asociación de Empresas Industriales de Herrera) 110, 111

agrarian
  elites 3, 9, 11, 12, 16, 20, 25, 28, 30, 84, 124, 126, 127, 130, 131, 132, 139, 140, 219, 220, 222, 227, 235, 236, 238, 254, 255, 257, 258, 259, 276
  reform 10, 76, 106, 127, 135, 261

agrarios 254, 255, 256, 257, 259. *See also agrarian elites*

agriculture 102, 103, 106, 124, 153, 163, 239
  exports 124, 257
  policy 226, 230, 232, 233, 234
  sectoral 2, 4, 15, 21, 51, 59, 61, 230, 232, 233, 234
  subsidize 99

Aguirre Roca, Juan Antonio 262, 263, 267

AIRD (Industrialists' Association of the Dominican Republic — Asociación de Industriales de la República Dominicana) 103, 104, 105, 106, 110, 111

Alemán, Arnoldo 163

Alemán, Miguel 184

Alessandri, Arturo 219

Alianza Democrática. *See AD*

Alianza Popular Revolucionaria Americana. *See APRA*

Alianza Productiva. *See AP*

Alianza Republicana Nacionalista. *See ARENA*

Allende, Salvador 12, 33, 156, 186, 222, 224

Alliance for Progress 126

Altos Hornos 197

Alvear, Miguel Vega 267, 268

AMCHAM (American Chamber of Commerce in Nicaragua — Cámara de Comercio Americana de Nicaragua) 165

American Chamber of Commerce 109, 113

U

V

W

Y

Z